STUDIES IN THE EARLY HISTORY OF BRITAIN

General Editor: Nicholas Brooks

Wessex in the Early Middle Ages

Wessex in the Early Middle Ages

Barbara Yorke

Leicester University Press
London and New York

LEICESTER UNIVERSITY PRESS
An imprint of Cassell Publishers Limited
Wellington House, 125 Strand, London, WC2R 0BB
215 Park Avenue South, New York, NY 10003

First published 1995

British Library Cataloguing-in-Publication Data

A CIP catalogue record for this book is available from The British Library

ISBN 0 7185 1314 2 (Hardback)
    0 7185 1856 X (Paperback)

Library of Congress Cataloging-in-Publication Data

Yorke, Barbara, 1951–
    Wessex in the early Middle Ages / Barbara Yorke.
      p. cm. – (Studies in the early history of Britain)
    Includes bibliographical references and index.
    ISBN 0–7185–1314–2 (hc). – ISBN 0–7185–1856–X (pbk.)
    1. Wessex (England) – History 2. Anglo-Saxons – England – Wessex – History 3. Great Britain – History – Anglo-Saxon period, 449–1066.
    I. Title. II. Series.
DA152.Y673 1995
942′.01–dc20
                                  95–14446
                                    CIP

Typeset by Mayhew Typesetting, Rhayader, Powys
Printed and bound in Great Britain by SRP Ltd, Exeter

Contents

Foreword

The aim of the *Studies in the Early History of Britain* is to promote works of the highest scholarship which open up virgin fields of study or which surmount the barriers of traditional academic disciplines. As interest in the origins of our society and culture grows while scholarship becomes ever more specialized, interdisciplinary studies are needed not only by scholars but also by students and laymen. This series will therefore include research monographs, works of synthesis and also collaborative studies of important themes by several scholars whose training and expertise has lain in different fields. Our knowledge of the early Middle Ages will always be limited and fragmentary, but progress can be made if the work of the historian embraces that of the philologist, the archaeologist, the geographer, the numismatist, the art historian and the liturgist – to name only the most obvious. The need to cross and to remove academic frontiers also explains the extension of the geographical range from that of the previous *Studies in Early English History* to include the whole island of Britain. The change would have been welcomed by the editor of the earlier series, the late Professor H.P.R. Finberg, whose pioneering work helped to inspire, or to provoke, the interest of a new generation of early medievalists in the relations of Britons and Saxons. The approach of this series is therefore deliberately wide-ranging. Early medieval Britain can only be understood in the context of contemporary developments in Ireland and on the Continent.

Barbara Yorke contributes the fourth regional survey in a series which aims to provide brief, well-illustrated and up-to-date syntheses of the settlement and history of all the principal regions of early medieval Britain. Since Wessex was the source of the dynasty that unified the English kingdom in the tenth century, parts of its history are familiar both to students and to scholars, and Dr Yorke has had a particularly challenging task to disentangle national from regional history. But as with Pauline Stafford's companion volume on the East Midlands and Margaret Gelling's on the West Midlands, there prove to be enormous benefits in concentrating upon local themes and contexts. Dr Yorke's own research into the early history of the West Saxon kingdom and see have equipped her superbly to reassess the fundamental changes – ethnic, political, religious and social – that turned southern Roman Britain into late Anglo-Saxon Wessex. It is a privilege to welcome this stimulating analysis to the series.

N.P. Brooks
University of Birmingham
July 1994

List of Illustrations

Cover Cross-shaft from Codford St Peter (Wilts), showing a dancing man, perhaps David dancing before the Lord [photograph: British Museum]

Acknowledgements

A book of this type does not get written without the help of a large number of individuals and I would like to thank all those who have been so generous to me with their time and expertise. In particular I would like to thank the following for providing me with details of work which was unpublished or in press and for discussing many problems of interpretation with me: Steve Bassett, John Blair, Bruce Eagles, Harold Fox, Patrick Hase and David Hinton. Others have been extremely helpful in tracking down illustrative material and providing me with additional background information. I would like to thank especially John Allan, Mick Aston, Martin Biddle, John Crook, Barry Cunliffe, Chris Gerrard, Michael Hare, Tony King, Alan Morton, Ian Riddler, Edward Roberts, Warwick Rodwell and Leslie Webster. I owe particular thanks to Kay Ainsworth and David Allen of Hampshire County Museum Service for much hard work in the archives and for producing so many fine photographs for me. Peter Jacobs of the Audio-Visual Aids Department, King Alfred's College, kindly undertook a number of photographic assignments for me and I am also grateful to Paul Stonell for photographing the Romsey rood. I have a major debt of gratitude to Harry Buglass of Birmingham University who drew all the maps and line-drawings and so brilliantly transformed ghastly scribbles from me into something intelligible.

The book has been longer in its genesis than I had originally intended and has been squeezed into the interstices between other professional commitments, but I am grateful to King Alfred's College for providing me with a term of study leave which hastened its completion. Parts of it have been tried out before a wider public at lectures and seminars and I am grateful for opportunities provided by the Hampshire Field Club, Birmingham University Medieval History Seminar, Leicester University Department of Local History and the Department for Continuing Education, University of Oxford. Discussions at such conferences and seminars have been extremely valuable in extending ideas and alerting me to new sources of information. Throughout I have been guided by the series editor, Nicholas Brooks, who has waited patiently for the completion of the manuscript and provided me with much valued advice and support. Finally, I would like to record my deep gratitude to my husband Robert, who has provided much encouragement and accompanied me on visits to many sites, as well as using his expertise to track down elusive publications.

Introduction

The main focus of this volume is on the six historic shires of Devon, Somerset, Dorset, Wiltshire, Berkshire and Hampshire (including the Isle of Wight) during the period 400 to 1066. A poll of Anglo-Saxonists would probably reach some consensus that this area could be designated as 'Wessex', in the context of the early Middle Ages, and that it was the heartland of the West Saxon kingdom. However, although all of the region was dominated at some point before 900 by West Saxon kings, control of certain areas was intermittent and the whole of the six shires did not come securely into the hands of the West Saxon royal house until the ninth century, by which time they also controlled other areas of southern England. Some of the key sources covering the early history of Wessex, such as the *Anglo-Saxon Chronicle*, were produced in the ninth century and can give an impression that West Saxon dominance of the region was more straightforward and inevitable from an early date than was in fact the case. The six shires of Wessex were neither a natural region in terms of their physical geography nor one which was suggested by earlier political and administrative divisions.

Although between them the six shires are very variable in terms of their geology and resultant physical geography, the dominant landscape is chalk downland stretching from the Berkshire Downs in the north through Wiltshire to the coastal plains of Hampshire and eastern Dorset (fig. 1).[1] Rivers rising in the chalk divide the downlands and, in the south, make their way to the sea through the poorer, younger soils of the Hampshire Basin, while the northern downlands are bisected by tributaries of the Thames. Other parts of Wessex are in terms of their geology part of regions which extend beyond the boundaries of the six shires. In the east, within Hampshire, is the western extremity of the weald, while eastern Berkshire links with the sandy and clay soils of western Surrey. To the west of the chalklands lies the southern portion of the great Jurassic limestone ridge, which runs from the cliffs of Lyme Bay in Dorset up through Somerset to the Cotswolds and beyond. Western Somerset and Devon are dominated by older rocks which form a 'highland' region within Wessex; the carboniferous limestones of the Mendips and the Quantocks, separated by the low-lying Somerset

---

1. B. Cunliffe, *Wessex to AD 1000* (1993), 1–4, 326–8.

	Recent		SECONDARY	Jurassic		
TERTIARY	Oligocene and Eocene			Triassic		
SECONDARY	Chalk		PRIMARY	Permian		
	Gault and greensand			Millstone grit and culm measure		
	Wealden			Old red sandstone and Devonian		
				Granites and other intrusives		
				Archaen		a

0   50 miles

0   70 kilometres

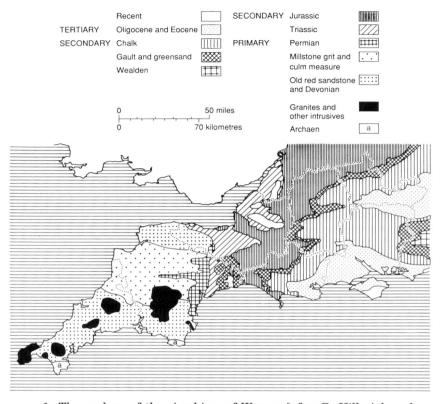

1. The geology of the six shires of Wessex [after D. Hill, *Atlas of Anglo-Saxon England* (1981), fig. 5]

levels, the Devonian rocks of Exmoor and the granite of Dartmoor. In geological terms Exmoor and much of Devon forms a distinct entity with Cornwall.[2] South-eastern Devon, however, is more closely allied with the mixed soils of neighbouring Dorset.

About half of the land in the six shires can be reckoned as good farming land even if little of it is of the highest quality.[3] The chalklands had been much favoured by prehistoric farmers, as the large number of surviving prehistoric monuments suggests, but on the upper slopes the soil is relatively light and by AD 400 was no longer ideal for crop production. The river valleys divide the chalklands into natural territories which contained within them a mixture of the resources necessary for mixed farming and were a natural focus of settlement. In the Iron Age many of these

2. E.A. Edmonds, M.C. Mckeown and M. Williams, *British Regional Geology. South-West England* (1975); M. Todd, *The South-West to AD 1000* (1987), 1–6.
3. D. Hill, *An Atlas of Anglo-Saxon England* (1981), 7.

downland blocks were dominated by a hill-fort.[4] Intermittent belts of clay supported more woodland in the Anglo-Saxon period than has survived until today, particularly where the chalklands gave way to younger rocks. Notable expanses of woodland occurred between the chalklands and the low-lying areas of the Hampshire basin, between the western area of the chalklands and the limestone Jurassic ridge (Selwood) and to the north of the chalklands in northern Wiltshire and eastern Berkshire.[5] Some of the most distinctive regions were those with poor agricultural land whose inhabitants were obliged to develop particularized modes of farming and ways of life, though it is unlikely that they ever supported large populations. These areas include the heathlands of Hampshire (the New Forest) and eastern Dorset, the Somerset levels and the moors of Devon and Somerset. However, some of the areas with poorer farming lands had the compensation of resources which were scarce elsewhere in Wessex. The resources available to the coastal communities need not be spelt out, though the importance of salt production should be mentioned. The Mendips and Dartmoor were exploited for respectively their lead (and silver) and tin deposits from the prehistoric period onwards.

By the late Iron Age Wessex was divided between tribal kingdoms which formed the bases of the Roman *civitates*.[6] Although the core tribal areas can be recognized from coin and pottery distributions, it is more difficult to reconstruct the exact extent of their boundaries and, indeed, such certainty can hardly be expected without written records delineating bounds. Figure 2 shows a suggested reconstruction of the Roman *civitates*. It can be seen that the whole of the territory of the Durotriges and Belgae was encompassed within the six shires of later Wessex, and most of that of the Atrebates. However, the western part of Somerset and Devon belonged with Cornwall to the territory of the Dumnonii, while the northern part of Somerset was probably in the territory of the Dobunni, whose *civitas* capital was at Cirencester. The extension of Belgic territory to the region of Bath is based principally on Ptolemy's statement that *Aquae Sulis* was in the territory of the Belgae, but as there are no other clear indications of this it may be that Ptolemy was mistaken.[7] It is also possible that the territory of the *civitas* of the Regni which was administered from Chichester extended a little way further west than the present boundary between Hampshire and Sussex, while that of the Atrebates extended beyond northern Hampshire into part of Sussex and Surrey. In the early fourth century, when Britain had been divided

4. Cunliffe, *Wessex to AD 1000*, 165–200.
5. O. Rackham, *Trees and Woodland in the British Landscape* (1976).
6. P. Salway, *Roman Britain* (1981), 40–61, 573–88; M. Todd, *Roman Britain 55 BC–AD 400* (1981), 44–59, 122–8; M. Millett, *The Romanization of Britain* (1990), 9–39, 65–9, 104–33.
7. Cunliffe, *Wessex to AD 1000*, 235.

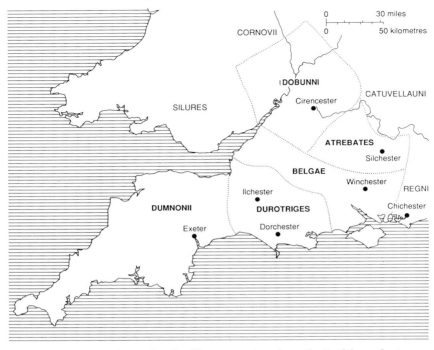

2. Roman *civitates* in the Wessex region: hypothetical boundaries [after M. Millett, *The Romanization of Britain* (1990), 67 and M. Todd, *Roman Britain 55 BC–AD 400* (1981), 125]

into four dioceses, all of the later territory of the six shires of Wessex (except the small part that may have belonged to the *civitas* of the Regni) lay in *Britannia Prima* which was administered from Cirencester. It will be observed that none of the reconstructed boundaries of the Roman *civitates* corresponds exactly with later shire boundaries, with the possible exception of part of the boundary between the Durotriges and the Belgae.

The territory of the Dumnonii has produced far fewer signs of Romanization than the other areas of Wessex (see fig. 3).[8] Its only town was the *civitas* capital at Exeter and the few villas which have been identified lay in the area between Exeter and the border with the Durotriges. Elsewhere native forms of settlement persisted and penetration of Roman material culture was slight, though forts and other military installations show that the Romans had been anxious to establish their authority within the province. At least one major Roman road extended westwards from Exeter, which the modern A30 follows for much of its route, and some of the numerous small

8. A. Fox, *South-West England* (2nd edn., 1973), 136–57; S. Pearce, *The Archaeology of South-West Britain* (1981), 132–64; Todd, *South-West to AD 1000*, 189–235.

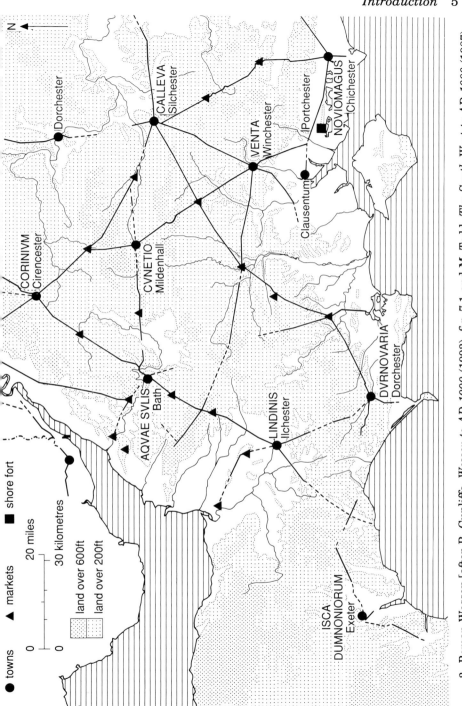

3. Roman Wessex [after B. Cunliffe, *Wessex to AD 1000* (1993), fig. 7.1 and M. Todd, *The South West to AD 1000* (1987), fig. 7.1]

ports of Devon may have been visited by Roman merchants; a port on Plymouth Sound to ship supplies of tin from Dartmoor is particularly likely. Exeter itself was the main port, with ships coming from north-west Gaul and, possibly, direct from the eastern Mediterranean, as suggested by finds of Greek coins from the city and elsewhere in the south-west.

The rest of Wessex is marked by far greater signs of change as a result of the Roman conquest with the construction of greater and lesser towns, villas for the aristocracy and widespread circulation of Roman goods (fig. 3).[9] A network of Roman roads connected the *civitas* capitals and lesser centres, and supplemented the existing trackways along the ridges of hills and river valleys. Several centres of pottery production were established, including Poole, Savernake (Wilts), Alice Holt (Hants) and in the New Forest, and new industries, such as the provision of building stone, were stimulated. Fieldwork suggests that Wessex was intensively farmed, with new areas opened up for crop production, probably to meet not only the demands of Roman authorities, but also a rising population which may have reached a peak in the fourth century not to be attained again for several centuries.[10] However, development was not completely uniform within Wessex. The greatest concentrations of villas lay in the vicinity of towns and these were not regularly distributed throughout the region. There was a dearth of towns in central Wessex and a corresponding lack of villas; one explanation has been that much of Wiltshire may have been administered as an imperial estate. In contrast there is an unusually dense distribution of villas in Somerset around Bath and Ilchester, many of which seem to date from the late third century or later. The area is one of good agricultural land, but it has been suggested that the villas may have been built by rich incomers from Gaul fleeing barbarian attacks during the third century.[11]

The eventual emergence of Wessex and its shires could not have been predicted from the administrative configurations of the late Roman period, nor, it will be argued, from the political alignments of *c.* 600. Wessex was created by the conquests of the royal house of the Gewisse, largely within the seventh and eighth centuries, and its subdivisions were structures they imposed upon the countryside, even if there were various factors outside their control which helped decide where boundaries were to run. A major task of the historian of Anglo-Saxon Wessex must be to trace the processes by which its various regions become part of one political entity. However, to do

---

9. S. Applebaum, 'Roman Britain', in *The Agrarian History of England and Wales AD 43–1042*, I.ii, ed. H.P.R. Finberg (1972), 3–277; Millett, *Romanization of Britain*; Cunliffe, *Wessex to AD 1000*, 201–65.
10. D. Benson and D. Miles, *The Upper Thames Valley: An Archaeological Survey of the River Gravels* (1974); Millett, *Romanization of Britain*, 181–6.
11. K. Branigan, 'Villa settlement in the West Country', in *The Roman West Country*, ed. K. Branigan and P.J. Fowler (1976), 120–41.

so is complicated by the fact that parts of what became. Wessex really need to be viewed in the context of regions outside the allotted six shires, especially for the fifth and sixth centuries. There are also problems with nomenclature. It was not until the ninth century that the shires took on the forms they possessed, give or take some minor adjustments, until the 1974 local government reforms. However, it is convenient to use the shires as reference points before then, especially in the absence of earlier regional names or ones that can be easily interpreted. When this is done a general area is being indicated rather than one rigidly contained within later shire boundaries. All references are to shires in their pre-1974 form, when the Christchurch area was part of Hampshire, the Avon formed the northern boundary of Somerset and the Thames the northern boundary of Berkshire.

From the ninth century the problems for the historian of Wessex change. Wessex becomes part of a larger unit, at first embracing all of the country south of the Thames, but then in the course of the tenth century extending to most of England as it would be defined today. It will be argued that Wessex retained a certain distinctiveness because of its administrative organization and the patronage of the royal house which, in certain respects, was concentrated in the region. The emphasis will be on how events affected Wessex itself, though sometimes these need to be viewed in a broader context. It is also the case that because Wessex is one of the regions of the country best provided with written records for the early Middle Ages its material has been much used to suggest a general picture for Anglo-Saxon England as a whole especially for various social and economic matters. Thus, when writing on a topic such as the position of women in Wessex, one is in danger of producing something which will sound all too familiar because much of it has been seen (not necessarily correctly) as being typical of all Anglo-Saxon regions. Unfortunately there is not the space to draw extensive contrasts with other areas – a task which will in any case become much easier once the series of regional histories of 'Britain in the Early Middle Ages' has been completed!

1 A Period of Transition: Wessex *c.* 400–*c.* 600

The period 400–600 was a momentous one in the history of Wessex for it saw the rapid decline and disintegration of the Roman way of life, the advent of Germanic settlers and the evolution of new polities with concomitant results for many facets of life within the area. However, one unfortunate characteristic of the time is that few written records were kept, although subsequently some of the regimes whose power originated in the period developed the desire to record what they thought – or wished to think – had occurred. The usual practice has been to approach the history of these two centuries through the scanty written material even if this has meant stretching the few contemporary sources beyond what they can bear and ignoring the shortcomings of those written at a later date. As the corpus of archaeological evidence has gradually expanded, it has become increasingly difficult to accept that the written sources can provide an adequate narrative of what occurred throughout the region. Recent archaeological analysis has begun to suggest new strategies through which the period can be studied and, as more excavations are written up and the theoretical framework is refined, so will the period cease to appear such a 'dark age'.

THE END OF ROMAN BRITAIN

For much of the fourth century AD Wessex appears as prosperous and outwardly Romanized. The higher ranks of society in particular seem to have enjoyed a time of considerable prosperity reflected in the erection or refurbishment of substantial villas.[1] When administrative or social reasons called them to town the aristocratic villa owners would have occupied the large town houses which have been discovered away from the main streets in many of the *civitas* capitals.[2] The aristocracy by the fourth century seems to have

---

1. A.S. Esmonde Cleary, *The Ending of Roman Britain* (1989), 105–10; M. Millett, *The Romanization of Britain* (1990), 186–201.
2. Esmonde Cleary, *Ending of Roman Britain*, 64–8.

preferred to spend its money on the aggrandizement of private residences rather than on civic responsibilities and public buildings were no longer kept up in the way that they once had been.[3] The public baths at Exeter had fallen into disuse by the late third century and at Silchester the basilica had been given over to metalworking.[4] But the pattern was not consistent throughout the region. Although Exeter may have housed a relatively small population and been dominated by private estates, Winchester seems to have been something of a fourth-century boom town with large town houses demolished to make way for industrial activities and less substantial buildings which presumably housed the workers.[5] Martin Biddle has interpreted these developments as support for the theory that the imperial *gynaeceum* at *Venta*, mentioned in the *Notitia Dignitatum*, was located at Winchester. Both Winchester and Dorchester (Dorset) are surrounded by substantial cemeteries dating to the fourth century which may not only reflect the size of their urban populations, but also their roles as central places for the surrounding countryside.[6] Small towns also flourished and may have been more significant than some of the *civitas* capitals as economic and trading centres.[7]

However, there are signs of a downturn in the prosperity of the most Romanized sectors of the community in the last quarter of the fourth century. Economic problems have often been seen as having been exacerbated by increasingly severe 'barbarian' raids, but recent studies have thrown doubt on whether apparent references to attacks by Franks and Saxons on the 'Saxon shore', which included eastern Wessex, have been correctly interpreted.[8] The possibility of raids by Irish on the western shores of Wessex remains and signs of destruction in a number of villas in the vicinity of the Bristol Channel in the fourth century have been attributed to them; some of the villas seem to have been abandoned

3. D.A. Brooks, 'A review of the evidence for continuity in British towns in the 5th and 6th centuries', *Oxford Journal of Archaeology, 5: 1* (1986), 79–84; Esmonde Cleary, *Ending of Roman Britain*, 71–2, 108–10.
4. P.G. Bidwell, *The Legionary Bath-House and Basilica and Forum at Exeter*, Exeter Archaeological Reports, *1* (1979), 122; M. Fulford, *Guide to the Silchester Excavations 1979–81: Amphitheatre and Forum Basilica* (1982).
5. M. Biddle, 'The study of Winchester: archaeology and history in a British town', *PBA, 69* (1983), 93–135, at 111–15.
6. D.E. Farwell and T.L. Molleson, *Excavations at Poundbury 1966–80. Volume II: The Cemeteries*, DNHAS monograph, *11* (1993); G.N. Clarke, *Pre-Roman and Roman Winchester, part II; The Roman Cemetery at Lankhills*, Winchester Studies, *3* (1979).
7. Millett, *Romanization of Britain*, 143–51; M. Millett and D. Graham, *Excavations on the Romano-British Small Town at Neatham, Hampshire, 1969–1979* (1986).
8. P. Salway, *Roman Britain* (1981), 374–444, for traditional interpretation; P. Bartholomew, 'Fourth-century Saxons', *Britannia, 15* (1984), 169–85, and J. Cotterill, 'Saxon raiding and the role of the late Roman coastal forts of Britain', *Britannia, 24* (1993), 227–40, for revisionist interpretations.

subsequently, but others were refurbished.[9] Potential threats, whether from external or internal sources, seem to have prompted a major overhaul of the defences of towns and forts in the region, perhaps after the arrival of Count Theodosius in 369. The defences of Ilchester, Bath and Winchester seem to have been improved by the addition of bastions, and the small town of *Cunetio* (Wilts) may have been provided with substantial stone walls for the first time.[10] The Roman settlement at Bitterne (probably to be identified with *Clausentum* of the Antonine Itinerary) was also fortified,[11] and joined Portchester and, probably, Carisbrooke as fortified ports in the Solent at the western end of the 'Saxon shore' network.[12] Detachments of *limitanei* (frontier troops) manned the forts and traces of such a garrison have been found at Portchester.[13]

There was evidently no intention of abandoning Britain as a Roman province in the late fourth century, but its fate was ultimately decided by destabilising events in the Roman Empire as a whole in the first decade of the fifth century. Some of the background to what occurred has been preserved in the works of continental writers. In 406 three imperial claimants were successively raised by the army in Britain, the last of whom, Constantine III, was killed at Arles in 411; the last remnants of Britain's field army had probably gone with him.[14] The Byzantine historian Zosimus, writing at the turn of the fifth and sixth centuries, records a revolt in Britain in 409 and the expulsion of imperial officials, and this seems to have been followed soon after by an official severance of Britain from the Roman Empire when Emperor Honorius informed the *civitates* that they must now manage their own affairs.[15] There has been much discussion about the reliability of these continental sources, their dating of events and even whether some references actually pertain to Britain at all,[16] but there seems little doubt that in or around 410 Britain ceased to be part of the Roman Empire, because the archaeological evidence – or rather the

9. K. Branigan, 'Villa settlement in the West Country', in *The Roman West Country*, ed. K. Branigan and P.J. Fowler (1976), 136–41.
10. B. Cunliffe, *Wessex to AD 1000* (1993), 268–73.
11. M.A. Cotton and P.W. Gathercole, *Excavations at Clausentum, Southampton 1951–54* (1958).
12. D.E. Johnson (ed.), *The Saxon Shore*, CBA res. rep., *18* (1977); S. Johnson, *The Roman Forts of the Saxon Shore* (1979); V.A. Maxfield (ed.), *The Saxon Shore. A Handbook* (1989); Cotterill, 'Saxon raiding'.
13. B. Cunliffe, *Excavations at Portchester Castle. Vol. I: Roman* (1975).
14. Orosius, *Libri Historiarum Adversum Paganos*, VII, 40, 4, ed. C. Zangmeister (Vienna, 1882); Zosimus, *Historia Nova*, VI, 2, 1, ed. L. Mendelssohn (Leipzig, 1887).
15. Zosimus, *Historia Nova*, VI, 5 and 10; M. Winterbottom (ed.), *Gildas. The Ruin of Britain and Other Documents* (1978), Ch. 18–21.
16. See for instance, E.A. Thompson, 'Britain AD 406–410', *Britannia, 8* (1977), 303–18, and 'Fifth-century facts?', *Britannia, 14* (1983), 272–4; P. Bartholomew, 'Fifth-century facts', *Britannia, 13* (1982), 261–70; I. Wood, 'The fall of the western empire and the end of Roman Britain', *Britannia, 18* (1987), 251–62.

lack of it – is unequivocal. Roman coin issues and objects manufactured in the Roman Empire outside Britain ceased to arrive after
the first decade of the fifth century, and the native pottery industry
seems to have collapsed soon after.[17]

There seems little doubt that the severance of Britain from Rome
led to some fundamental changes within the province as a whole
and we can see this most clearly from the archaeological record.
Although occupation of many towns in Wessex continued well into
the fifth century, signs of town life are rare in the latter part of the
century and in a number of cases the latest occupation levels were
covered by a layer of 'black' earth which may have been formed by
the collapse of the timber and wattle superstructures of Roman
buildings and their subsequent recolonization by plants.[18] It seems
to have become neither practicable nor desirable to keep up the
villa buildings and these were either adapted to a simpler way of
life (often identified in early excavations as 'squatter' occupation) or
were abandoned. A dramatic demonstration of the dereliction which
resulted was uncovered in excavations at Meonstoke (Hants), where
the gable-end of one of the elaborate fourth-century villa buildings
was found *in situ* where it had collapsed.[19] However, Roman
buildings and artefacts were not immediately replaced by a new
diagnostic material culture, so that for much of the fifth century the
archaeological record cannot easily reveal what was happening to
most of the Romano-British inhabitants of Wessex; Roman pottery
and other artefacts may have remained in use for some time and it
is no longer necessary to imagine an immediate downing of tools
and rushing to the hills in 410.

Nevertheless, the rapid decline of many of the outward signs of
Romanization is something which seems to require explanation and
it is presumably to be found in the knock-on effects of the severance
of Britain from the Empire. Simon Esmonde Cleary has recently
discussed the importance of the heavy demands made by the late
Roman tax system in dictating the pattern of life in the province.[20]
Small farmers had to farm intensively to produce enough surplus to
pay their taxes; towns thrived because they were the places in
which merchandise was exchanged for coin; certain sectors of the
nobility also seem to have done well perhaps because they were
responsible for collecting the taxes which presented various
opportunities for corruption and the purchase of the properties of
those who could not afford to pay. Once Britain was cast off from

---

17. M. Fulford, 'Pottery production and trade at the end of Roman Britain: the case
against continuity', in *The End of Roman Britain*, ed. P.J. Casey, BAR, *71*
(1979), 120–32; J. Kent, 'The end of Roman Britain: the literary and numismatic
evidence reviewed', in *End of Roman Britain*, ed. Casey, 15–27.
18. Brooks, 'Continuity in British towns', 86–9; Esmonde Cleary, *Ending of Roman
Britain*, 131–4.
19. A. King, 'Excavations at Meonstoke, Hampshire' (forthcoming).
20. Esmonde Cleary, *Ending of Roman Britain*, 73–5, 139–61.

the Roman Empire the pressures imposed from outside would have been removed and some internal changes would have been bound to occur; towns, for instance, must have lost much of their former *raison d'être*.

It must be stressed that the disappearance of Roman structures and artefacts and most outward signs of the Roman way of life occurred equally throughout Wessex and so the appearance of Germanic settlers in eastern Wessex should not be considered as the main cause of change there. Nevertheless, the subsequent settlement of Germanic peoples did mean that the material culture and history of parts of Wessex was to differ in the fifth and sixth centuries. A distribution map of Germanic forms of burial brings out very clearly the contrast between the eastern and western parts of Wessex (fig. 4). The three western shires of Devon, Dorset and Somerset are largely devoid of Germanic burials and most of those which have been found are late in the sequence and on the borders of Somerset or Dorset.[21] In eastern Wessex, on the other hand, – that is Berkshire, Hampshire, the Isle of Wight and Wiltshire – Germanic forms of burial are to be found throughout the region even if not uniformly distributed within it. Consequently the histories of western and eastern Wessex in the fifth and sixth centuries will need to be considered separately.

WESTERN WESSEX: THE TESTIMONY OF GILDAS

Virtually the only written source which provides any guide to what happened in the west of Wessex following the collapse of Roman authority is *De Excidio Britanniae* (*The Ruin of Britain*) by the British cleric Gildas. The work is not a history, but an extensive sermon whose first part reviews in a rather generalized fashion some of the events of the fifth century with the intention of conveying to a contemporary audience that the evils which had befallen their ancestors were a direct result of their shortcomings as Christians.[22] Gildas's audience were intended to take note and attend to their own sins lest comparable disasters befell them. No dates are provided, but there are various chronological indicators

---

21. A. Meaney, *A Gazetteer of Early Anglo-Saxon Burial Sites* (1964). For a useful review of Dorset evidence see C.J.S. Green, 'Early Anglo-Saxon burials at the "Trumpet Major" public house, Allington Avenue, Dorchester', *PDNHAS 106* (1984), 148–52; for Somerset, E. Horne, 'The Anglo-Saxon cemetery at Camerton, Somerset, parts I and II', *PSANHS, 74* (1928), 61–70, and *79* (1933), 39–63; and for a general review, B. Eagles, 'The archaeological evidence for settlement in the fifth to seventh centuries AD', in *Medieval Settlement in Wessex*, ed. M. Aston and C. Lewis (forthcoming). For a significant find of early Saxon material from Dorset, see B. Eagles and C. Mortimer, 'Early Anglo-Saxon artefacts from Hod Hill, Dorset', *Ant J*, 73 (1993), 132–40.
22. Gildas, *Ruin of Britain*, Ch. 2–26.

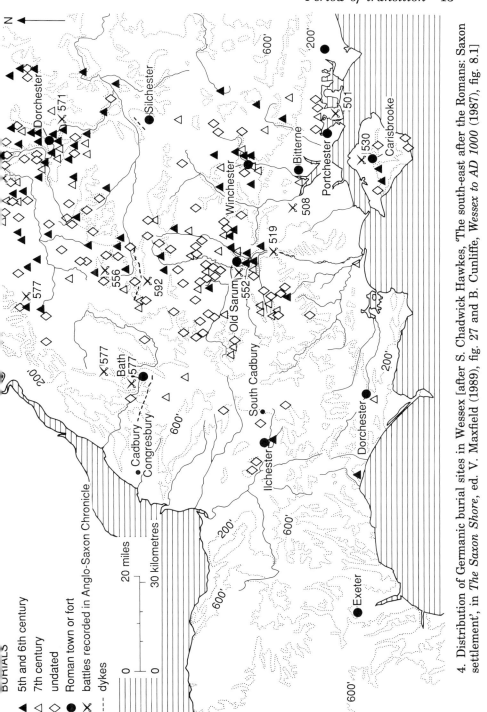

4. Distribution of Germanic burial sites in Wessex [after S. Chadwick Hawkes, 'The south-east after the Romans: Saxon settlement', in *The Saxon Shore*, ed. V. Maxfield (1989), fig. 27 and B. Cunliffe, *Wessex to AD 1000* (1987), fig. 8.1]

BURIALS

▲ 5th and 6th century
△ 7th century
◇ undated
● Roman town or fort
✗ battles recorded in Anglo-Saxon Chronicle
- - - - dykes

Dorchester
✗ 571
Silchester
Bitterne
Portchester
Carisbrooke
✗ 530
✗ 508
Winchester
✗ 519
✗ 501
✗ 577
✗ 556
✗ 592
Old Sarum
✗ 552
Bath
✗ 577
✗ 577
Cadbury
Congresbury
South Cadbury
Ilchester
Dorchester
Exeter

N ←

200'
600'
200'
600'
600'
200'
600'
600'

0   20 miles
0   30 kilometres

within the work. At one point Gildas reveals that he was born in the year of the battle of Mount Badon and is writing in his forty-fourth year.[23] The later *Annales Cambriae* ('Welsh annals') date Badon to 516, though the source of the computation is not known. The same work also gives the death of Maelgwn of Gwynedd, one of the contemporary kings whom Gildas mentions, under the year 547, which has been corrected to 549. Although these indicators are not ideal, they are responsible for the usual assumption that Gildas was writing towards the middle of the sixth century.[24] Recently some commentators have pointed to factors which might push back the date closer to 500, such as the high standard of Gildas's Latin, which was evidently the result of a traditional classical education which one might not expect to be still available in Britain in the sixth century.[25]

There is also some uncertainty about where Gildas lived and worked. The only contemporaries he addresses by name are five kings who ruled in western England and Wales.[26] Opinion is divided about whether their inclusion is an indication that Gildas was writing in the West Country. On the one hand, he was certainly well-informed on events in the west and refers to an incident involving Constantine of Dumnonia as having taken place *hoc anno*,[27] but, as various commentators have pointed out, Gildas's criticisms of the rulers are so vituperative that it is hard to imagine that he would have dared to write about them in that way if he were living in territory controlled by any of them.[28] Nicholas Higham has ingeniously suggested that Gildas may have been writing in the territory of the Durotriges, which could explain how he came to have detailed knowledge of Dumnonian affairs yet felt safe to criticize its rulers; certain geographical indicators could support this identification.[29] Attractive though this proposition is, it is hard to locate Gildas with any certainty as other parts of his work could be interpreted as showing a particular knowledge of the north-east of England.[30]

23. Gildas, *Ruin of Britain*, Ch. 26.
24. D.N. Dumville, 'The chronology of *De Excidio Britanniae*, Book 1', in *Gildas: New Approaches*, ed. M. Lapidge and D.N. Dumville (1984), 61–84.
25. M. Lapidge, 'Gildas's education and the Latin culture of sub-Roman Britain', in *Gildas: New Approaches*, ed. M. Lapidge and D.N. Dumville (1984), 27–50; M.W. Herren, 'Gildas and early British monasticism', in *Britain 400–600: Language and History*, ed. A. Bammesberger and A. Wollmann (Heidelberg, 1990), 65–83.
26. Gildas, *Ruin of Britain*, Ch. 28–36.
27. Gildas, *Ruin of Britain*, Ch. 28.
28. E.A. Thompson, 'Gildas and the history of Britain', *Britannia, 10* (1979), 203–26 (at p. 225), and Dumville, 'Chronology', 80.
29. N.J. Higham, 'Old light on the Dark Age landscape: the description of Britain in the *De Excidio Britanniae* of Gildas', *Journal of Historical Geography, 17* (1991), 363–72.
30. Thompson, 'Gildas', *passim*; Dumville, 'Chronology', 79–80; and P. Sims-Williams, 'Gildas and the Anglo-Saxons', *Cambridge Medieval Celtic Studies, 6* (1983), 1–30.

None of the fifth-century incidents to which Gildas alludes can be specifically related to western Wessex, including the British resistance to the Saxons organized by Ambrosius Aurelianus which culminated in the victory at *Mons Badonicus* (Mount Badon). Nevertheless the assumption has often been made that the battle did take place in Wessex, and Badbury Rings (Dorset) has been a favoured contender for the site.[31] The identification is possible on etymological grounds, though there are also several other candidates that would be just as suitable, both in Wessex and further afield.[32] One reading of Gildas's account could place Mount Badon outside Wessex, for the only specific group of Saxons he mentions seem to have been settled in the north-east of England to counteract the Picts, so that it could be argued that Ambrosius's resistance is more likely to have been centred in the north than in the south.[33] Later legends linking Ambrosius with Amesbury (Wilts) and Arthur, the all-purpose British hero of the sub-Roman period, with various locations in the west are just that – legend not history. The Amesbury/Ambrosius connection probably derives from the similarity of the first element in the names,[34] and, although various West Country legends may have been incorporated in the Arthurian cycle, Arthur is as much a mythical figure of the north as of Wessex.[35]

DUMNONIA

What Gildas has to tell us that is of undoubted value is that at the time he was writing kingdoms had developed within some of the former *civitates* of western Britain. The only ruler he specifically mentions from within Wessex is Constantine, 'tyrant whelp of the filthy lioness of Dumnonia'.[36] Constantine had earned Gildas's wrath for his many adulteries and for the murder in the very year that Gildas was writing of two royal princes, a crime which was all the more heinous because it had taken place in a church and Constantine held the office of abbot. It sounds from what Gildas says of Constantine and the other western rulers (or *tyranni* as he

31. J.N.L. Myres, *The English Settlements* (1986), 159–60.
32. M. Gelling, 'A chronology for English place-names', in *Anglo-Saxon Settlements*, ed. D. Hooke (1988), 59–76 (at pp. 60–1); T. and A. Burkitt, 'The frontier zone and the siege of Mount Badon: a review of the evidence for their location', *PSANHS, 134* (1990), 81–93.
33. Gildas, *Ruin of Britain*, Ch. 22–3; Thompson, 'Gildas', 215–18, and Dumville 'Chronology', 70–2. In Bede's *Ecclesiastical History*, I, 15, Gildas's words are taken to apply to the settlement of Kent by Hengist and Horsa.
34. J. Morris, *The Age of Arthur: A History of the British Isles from 350 to 650* (1973), 100; Myres, *English Settlements*, 160–1, 212–13.
35. R. Bromwich, 'The character of early Welsh tradition', in *Studies in Early British History*, ed. N.K. Chadwick (1954), 83–136 (especially 123–9).
36. Gildas, *Ruin of Britain*, Ch. 28–9.

chose to describe them) that they were typical early medieval rulers, whose authority was backed up by the military households they maintained. The kings provided protection and justice for the people they ruled, though to Gildas's mind it was more appropriate to speak of them using their military powers for extortion and persecution. The families of some of the rulers he castigates seem to have been in power for at least two or three generations and Constantine probably belonged to a comparable dynasty. He is, however, the only king of Dumnonia of whose name we can be certain before Geraint, who was a contemporary of King Ine of Wessex (688–726) and in correspondence with Aldhelm.[37] A supposed genealogy of Dumnonian kings is included within a collection of Welsh genealogies, but seems to belong to the world of fiction rather than historical fact.[38]

Gildas saw his world as one that was far removed from the days of the Roman Empire and speaks of the Romans and the British as different nations. He records that many outward signs of the Roman world such as the towns had long since disappeared, but a number of the kings he names, including Constantine, had Latin names. Gildas also wrote in Latin and presumably expected his audience to be able to understand him.[39] However, Latin was to him the language of the Church rather than the Roman Empire, for another of the assumptions he makes about his society is that it was Christian. Christianity was sufficiently embedded within society for it to have been corrupted by too close an association with the secular values of society, a problem exemplified by the degenerate Constantine becoming an abbot. Although there is evidence of Christianity being established in much of Wessex by the end of the fourth century, there are no positive indications of its practice at that time from Dumnonian territory (apart from in Exeter) and it is usually assumed it was introduced there in the course of the fifth century.[40]

The only other form of written evidence from early medieval Dumnonia is that of the inscribed memorial stones.[41] There are 16 category I stones from the part of Dumnonia within later Wessex (that is 15 from Devon and 1 from western Somerset) which either have positive indications of a date pre-*c.* 700 or no definite indications of being of a later date (fig. 5). Within England the only

37. *Anglo-Saxon Chronicle s.a.* 710; M. Lapidge and M. Herren (trans.), *Aldhelm: the Prose Works* (1979), 140–3, 155–60.
38. Jesus College MS 20; P.C. Bartrum (ed.), *Early Welsh Genealogical Tracts* (1966), 45; S. Pearce, 'The traditions of the royal king-list of Dumnonia', *The Transactions of the Honourable Society of Cymmrodorion* (1971), 128–39; R. Bromwich (ed.), *Trioedd Ynys Prydein. The Welsh Triads* (2nd edn., 1978), 314–16, 355–60.
39. Lapidge, 'Gildas's education', 27–50.
40. See Chapter 4, 153–4.
41. E. Okasha, *Corpus of Early Christian Inscribed Stones of South-West Britain* (1993) which supersedes earlier discussions.

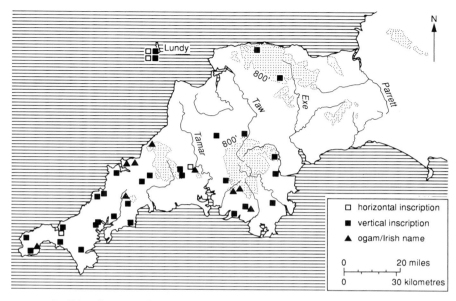

5. Distribution of memorial stones in Devon and Cornwall [after S. Pearce, *The Archaeology of South-West Britain* (1981), fig. 5.4]

other examples of these stones are from Cornwall (which has at least twice the number in Devon) and an isolated group of five from Wareham (Dorset) (see fig. 19).[42] Most of the Devon examples contain simply the name of the commemorated person, sometimes with the qualification that he is 'son of . . . X' (only one of the stones is to a woman). Most of the stones have been removed from their original places of erection, but a group of four at Lundy were found in a churchyard and many others may have been associated originally with burials. It might appear that these stones have little to tell us about early medieval Dumnonia, but in fact they help to confirm many facets of the picture provided by Gildas. Most of the stones include Latin and six specifically Latin names are used, but even the Celtic names have been declined usually as Latin nouns. The stones may ultimately derive from the Roman tradition of erection of stone memorials to the dead. Some of the stones include Christian symbolism, a chi-rho or inscribed cross within a circle, and, although it may be unwarranted to see all those commemorated as Christians, the stones provide some corroborative evidence for the spread of Christianity through Dumnonia after 400.

The stones can also take us beyond what Gildas can tell us. A stone from Sourton (near Lydford, Devon) appears to have included the word *principi* and may be an indication of the existence of lesser

---

42. For Wareham stones see Chapter 2, 69–72.

rulers beneath the level of the Dumnonian king.[43] An individual commemorated at Southill has the name 'Cumregnus', perhaps suggestive of, at the least, regnal aspirations.[44] There are close parallels for the Dumnonian stones in Wales, which is a possible source for them, though one should not rule out the possibility of common influences from the Roman world, contemporary Gaul and Ireland on two societies which, as Gildas seems to suggest, were very similar.[45] Of course, many Welsh saints' *Lives* preserve the tradition of missionaries travelling from Wales to convert Dumnonia, but the historical value of these *Lives*, most of which were written later in the Middle Ages, is being increasingly called into question.[46] The stones also contain some evidence that Devon, like Wales, was subject to influences from Ireland, if not to Irish settlement.[47] A stone from Fardel (in South Hams) and one from Buckland Monachorum (near Tavistock) include, in addition to inscriptions in Latin, use of the Irish script of ogham and Irish names; another stone from Buckland commemorates 'the son of Maccodechetus', also an Irish name.[48] The stone from Fardel uses the Irish *maqi*, 'son of . . .', instead of Latin *filii*, perhaps implying that it was erected by or for a speaker of Irish, rather than just indicating a more general Irish influence.

Another area with which Dumnonia is thought to have had significant contact is Brittany, which is believed to have received a substantial influx of emigrants from Dumnonia in the period 400 to 600. Breton and Cornish are very closely related and two of the three early Breton provinces were those of the *Cornovii* (*Cornouaille*) and *Dumnonii* (*Domnonée*).[49] Yet the exact dating and circumstances of migration are uncertain. It is probably wrong to equate any emigration to Brittany with Gildas's account of Britons fleeing abroad,[50] as he seems to have been referring to Britons who had already come into contact with Saxons and there is no evidence of Germanic penetration to the Dumnonian peninsula before the seventh century. However, various references in continental sources gathered together by Kenneth Jackson could be taken to suggest that some Dumnonians had settled in Brittany by the end of the

---

43. Okasha, *Corpus*, no. 55, 260–3.
44. Okasha, *Corpus*, no. 56, 264–7; A. Fox, *South-West England* (2nd end., 1973), 160.
45. J. Knight, 'The early Christian Latin inscriptions of Britain and Gaul: chronology and context', in *The Early Church in Wales and the West*, ed. N. Edwards and A. Lane, Oxbow monographs, *16* (1992), 45–50; Okasha, *Corpus*, 31–42.
46. See Chapter 4, 161–2.
47. W. Davies, *Wales in the Early Middle Ages* (1982), 87–90.
48. Okasha, *Corpus*, nos. 13, 103–8; 60, 278–81; 59, 274–7.
49. P. Gallious and M. Jones, *The Bretons* (1991), 128–47; M. Todd, *The South-West to AD 1000* (1987), 238–40.
50. Gildas, *Ruin of Britain*, Ch. 25.

fifth century.[51] Jackson concluded from his study of the Celtic languages that major colonization would also have occurred in the sixth century, but be largely completed by 600 when he believed the Cornish and Breton languages began to diverge.[52] If his analysis is correct it must have been circumstances within Dumnonia, or new opportunities in Brittany, that caused emigration rather than direct pressure from Germanic peoples. It may be that various Dumnonians, like other Celtic and Germanic contemporaries, saw an opportunity to carve out new territories for themselves overseas, within another Roman province suffering the after-effects of the breakdown of Roman control, while others may have wished to distance themselves from the Dumnonian royal house.

SOMERSET AND DORSET

There are no specific references to Durotrigean rulers, but we do have evidence for a reoccupation of hill-forts in Somerset which could be taken to indicate the existence of a controlling elite. Particularly notable is the refurbishment of the Iron Age multi-vallate hill-fort of South Cadbury whose inner circuit of some three-quarters of a mile (1.2 km) was provided with a timber-framed rampart with revetments of dry-stone construction probably in the late fifth century (fig. 6).[53] On the highest point of the interior, the wall-trenches and post-holes of a substantial aisled timber hall were recovered. The construction was primitive by Roman standards when timber buildings of any pretensions were constructed on stone sleeper walls, but the aisled plan and the adherence to classical proportions in the double square design suggest a Roman ancestry. The finds from the site were notably few and poor, but crucial for the dating of the reoccupation to the late fifth and sixth centuries were imported sherds of amphorae and African Red Slip Ware which only seem to have been found on inland sites like South Cadbury which were of high status. South Cadbury can be equated with other hill-fort sites in Wales and south-western Scotland which were refortified in the sub-Roman period and possessed timber halls and pottery imported from the late Roman world and which Leslie Alcock has argued should be seen as the residences of sub-Roman rulers.[54]

A comparable, though smaller, site is Cadbury Congresbury, close to the north Somerset coast, which was also in origin an Iron Age hill-fort, but had only part of its Iron Age perimeter refurbished in

51. K. Jackson, *Language and History in Early Britain* (1953), 13–15.
52. Jackson, *Language and History*, 11–30.
53. L. Alcock, 'Cadbury-Camelot: a fifteen-year perspective', *PBA, 68* (1982), 355–88.
54. L. Alcock, 'New perspectives on post-Roman forts', in *Economy, Society and Warfare Among the Britons and the Saxons* (1987), 153–67.

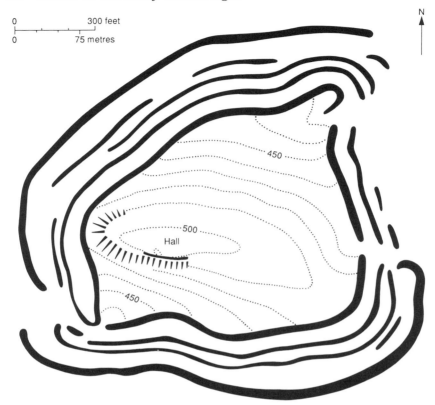

6. Plan of S. Cadbury hill-fort (Som); the inner bank of the Iron Age hill-fort was refortified in the sub-Roman period and the site of an excavated hall of the same period is indicated [after L. Alcock, *Economy, Society and Warfare among the Britons and the Saxons* (1987), fig. 13.2]

the sub-Roman period (fig. 7).[55] Cadbury Congresbury has produced more imported pottery than any other English site, apart from Tintagel in Cornwall, as well as evidence of fine metalworking and substantial feasting. Cannington hill-fort also seems to have been reoccupied in the post-Roman period and a substantial cemetery in use at the same time has been excavated in its vicinity. Reoccupation of hill-forts may have been more widespread in Somerset than in just these excavated examples.[56] Ian Burrow has demonstrated that 22 out of the 89 hill-forts in Somerset have produced Roman material which could indicate reuse in the late or post-

55. P. Rahtz *et al.*, *Cadbury Congresbury 1968–73. A Late/Post-Roman Hilltop Settlement in Somerset*, BAR, *223* (1992).
56. P. Rahtz, 'Celtic society in Somerset AD 400–700', *Bulletin of the Board of Celtic Studies, 30* (1982), 176–200.

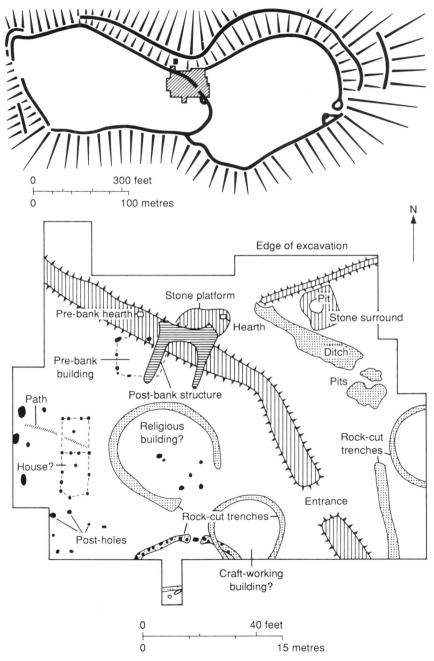

7. Plan of Cadbury Congresbury hill-fort (Som) with excavated sub-Roman features [after I. Burrow, 'Hillforts and Hilltops', in *The Archaeology of Somerset*, ed. M. Aston and I. Burrow (1982), fig. 9.12]

Roman periods.[57] Hill-forts were probably more than defensive sites and may have acted as focal points for a dependent region. Michael Costen has shown, for instance, that the large estate of Brent granted to Glastonbury Abbey in the late seventh century was probably centred on the hill-fort at Brent Knoll from which it took its name.[58] The people buried at Cannington may not all have been living in the hill-fort's interior, but may have been drawn from its subject district.

The substantial refurbishment of the defences at South Cadbury, which it has been estimated would have consumed 20,000 metres of timber, argues for the existence of an authority which could demand payments and services from the surrounding population.[59] An authority of this type may also have been responsible for the erection of the earthwork, West Wansdyke, which consists of a discontinuous north-facing bank and ditch running parallel and to the south of the River Avon from Maes Knoll to just south of Bath (fig. 8).[60] Dykes are notoriously difficult to date. West Wansdyke appears from its relationship with Roman features to be post-Roman, and the most likely contexts for it are either the period of refortification of hill-forts in the late fifth and sixth centuries or the competition between Wessex and Mercia in the seventh and eighth centuries.[61] The balance is tipped in favour of the earlier date by the inclusion of two hill-forts within the line of the dyke, Maes Knoll at its west end and Stantonbury about half-way along.[62] Its construction could have been a reaction to the extension of Saxon settlement into the Kennet Valley in (approximately) the late fifth century.[63] It should perhaps be seen as a recognized frontier rather than a strictly defensive work for it is not ideally placed to serve as the latter. If it is to be dated to the fifth and sixth centuries it has important implications for the development of Somerset, for it would appear to indicate that the area north of the river Brue which had been in the territory of either the Atrebates or the Dobunni had become associated with that of the northern Durotriges whose capital had been at Ilchester, only a few miles from the hill-fort of South Cadbury.[64]

Dorset, the territory of the southern Durotriges whose capital was at Dorchester, has so far produced little evidence for hill-fort

57. I.C.G. Burrow, 'Roman material from hillforts', in *The End of Roman Britain*, ed. P.J. Casey, BAR, *71* (1979), 212–29, and I.C.G. Burrow, *Hillfort and Hill-Top Settlement in the First to Eighth Centuries AD*, BAR, *91* (1981), 172–84; for Glastonbury Tor which has sometimes been viewed alongside the reoccupied hill-forts, but see Chapter 4, 163–4.
58. S 238/B 121; M. Costen, *The Origins of Somerset* (1992), 61–5.
59. Alcock, 'New perspectives', 153–67.
60. A. and C. Fox, 'Wansdyke reconsidered', *Arch J, 115* (1958), 1–48; N.J. Higham, 'Gildas, Roman walls and British dykes', *Cambridge Medieval Celtic Studies, 22* (1991), 1–14.
61. For the latter, see Ch. 2, 61–4.
62. Burrow, *Hillfort settlement*, 80–4.
63. See below, 30.
64. Costen, *Origins of Somerset*, 71–3.

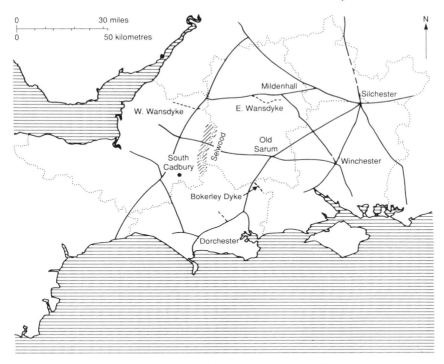

8. Selwood and the major dykes of sub-Roman Wessex in relation to Roman roads and major settlements and later shire boundaries (for further details of Bokerley dyke see fig. 23)

reoccupation, but then it has not had the advantage of a systematic survey like that carried out by Ian Burrow in Somerset. However, excavations have suggested that Bokerley Dyke on the easterly edge of Cranborne Chase was built in the post-Roman period when it would have controlled access to the Dorchester area along the Roman road of Akling Dyke and perhaps operated with other stretches of Dyke in its vicinity (fig. 8; see also fig. 23).[65] The line of Bokerley Dyke marked a very old frontier between eastern and western Wessex which may have stretched back to the Bronze Age.[66] It was also to have a long future as a frontier for to this day it is part of the boundary between Hampshire and Dorset. A substantial part of the land between Bokerley Dyke and West Wansdyke was occupied by the formidable natural obstacle of Selwood Forest, which seems to have run roughly between Gillingham (Dorset) and Chippenham (Wilts) (fig. 8).[67] Selwood, too, was to have a long

65. P.A. Rahtz, 'An excavation on Bokerley Dyke', *Arch J, 118* (1958), 65–99.
66. H.C. Bowen, *The Archaeology of Bokerley Dyke*, ed. B.N. Eagles (1990).
67. J.E. Jackson, 'Selwood Forest', *WAM, 23* (1887), 268–94; R. Grant, 'Royal forests: Selwood', in *VCH Wiltshire, IV*, ed. E. Crittall (1959), 414–17; M. McGarvie, *The Bounds of Selwood*, Frome Historical Research Group occasional papers, *1* (1978).

history as a significant boundary between east and west Wessex which will be referred to several times in later chapters, and the later county boundaries between Wiltshire and Somerset and north Dorset run through it. Selwood, West Wansdyke and Bokerley Dyke may have been more than natural and artificial boundaries to Saxon expansion. They may represent a negotiated frontier between Britons and Saxons which was to be of major importance for the subsequent development of the West Saxon shires.[68] Finds of Saxon artefacts in the west and Celtic objects in the east suggest relations between Saxon and British need not always have been hostile and that recognized frontiers need not have precluded interregional contacts.[69]

WESTERN WESSEX: REGIONAL AND FOREIGN LINKS

The different regions of western Wessex do not present a uniform picture from the surviving archaeological record. Inscribed memorial stones are found in Dumnonia, but not generally further east; reoccupied hill-forts are found in Somerset, but not apparently in Dorset or Devon, though both Dorset and Somerset have dykes. Although some of this may be due to different degrees of research, there may have been real differences in historical circumstance. Somerset and Dorset had a greater need than Devon to defend themselves against or reach an accommodation with their Saxon neighbours, while the memorial stones of Dumnonia and Wales may reflect the fact that Christianity may have taken a hold there at a later date than in Dorset or Somerset. But in other respects the future western shires may have shared similar experiences in the post-Roman period including the apparent reappearance of kingdoms (or analogous polities) within the former *civitates*. Although we do not know the circumstances in which such kingdoms were formed, it is possible to envisage that leaders of the aristocracy of the late Roman period could have taken over in the power vacuum following Roman withdrawal particularly if, like some of their counterparts in other areas of the late Roman Empire, they already kept bands of armed retainers to help enforce the collection of taxes.[70] It is tempting to see a direct transition from centres of Roman authority to ones more suited to the post-Roman world, from Ilchester to South Cadbury,[71] for instance, or from the heavily fortified late Roman villa of Gatcombe to Cadbury Congresbury, but such links can only be hypothetical.[72]

---

68. Costen, *Origins of Somerset*, 69–73.
69. See below and Ch. 7, 293–4.
70. Esmonde Cleary, *Ending of Roman Britain*, 9–10.
71. Alcock, 'Cadbury-Camelot', 211–12.
72. Rahtz, *Cadbury Congresbury*, 227–30.

The coasts of all three shires provided a means of access to and from Gaul and the Mediterranean, on the one hand, and the fellow Celtic Christian communities of Wales and Ireland, on the other. Common finds in these areas of Celtic Britain have led to claims of an 'Irish Sea culture province', demonstrated, for instance, by a common fashion in penannular brooches.[73] All have also produced fragments of fine wares and amphorae, that may once have contained wine or oil, which were imported from the Mediterranean. The material could have come via ports in Gaul, but Michael Fulford has argued for direct contact between Byzantium and western Britain in the fifth and sixth centuries.[74] The number of voyages should not be exaggerated; Charles Thomas's reductionist argument suggests the present finds might indicate no more than four.[75] Tin, according to the *Life of St John the Almsgiver*, and perhaps lead from the Mendips may have been among the commodities which drew foreign merchants to western Britain.[76] Findspots of small amounts of imported pottery along Devon and Somerset coasts (there are no finds at present from Dorset) may indicate landfalls and small trading communities like that excavated at Bantham (Devon),[77] but more substantial finds at high status sites like Cadbury Congresbury, South Cadbury or Tintagel (Cornwall) may indicate that secular powers had a considerable interest in foreign trade which may have helped to underpin their power (see fig. 75).[78] Individuals and ideas could have travelled by the same routes and there is no reason to see western Wessex as an outpost, isolated from other former provinces of the Roman Empire.

EASTERN WESSEX 400–600: BRITISH RULE AND THE SAXON *ADVENTUS*

There is no narrative account to tell us what happened in eastern Wessex in the immediate aftermath of 410. Some commentators have seen Gildas's *superbus tyrannus* (identified in later sources as

73. E.G. Bowen, *Saints, Seaways and Settlements in the Celtic Lands* (1969); E. Fowler, 'The origins and development of the penannular brooch in Europe', *Proceedings of the Prehistoric Society, 26* (1960), 149–77.
74. M.G. Fulford, 'Byzantium and Britain: a Mediterranean perspective on post-Roman Mediterranean imports in Western Britain and Ireland', *Med Arch, 33* (1989), 1–6.
75. C. Thomas, '*Gallici nautae de Galliarum provinciis* – a sixth/seventh century-trade with Gaul reconsidered', *Med Arch, 34* (1990), 1–26.
76. J.R. Maddicott, 'Trade, industry and the wealth of King Alfred', *Past and Present, 123* (1989), 3–51; for further discussion see Ch. 7, 294–6.
77. A. Fox, 'Some evidence for a Dark Age trading site at Bantham, near Thurlestone, South Devon, *Ant J, 35* (1955), 55–67; R.J. Silvester, 'An excavation on the post-Roman site at Bantham, South Devon', *PDAS, 39* (1981), 89–118; F.M. Griffith, 'Salvage observations at the Dark Age site at Bantham Ham, Thurlestone, in 1982', *PDAS, 44* (1986), 39–57.
78. C. Thomas, *Tintagel* (1993).

Vortigern), who made the fateful decision to invite Saxon federate troops to the island, as having control over much of Romanized Britain including Wessex, but that may be reading more into what he wrote than is warranted.[79] The picture provided by Gildas of federate troops initially working for a sub-Roman authority, but then, after their numbers had been reinforced from overseas, rebelling and seizing power, has also been very influential in the formulation of hypotheses about what might have occurred in eastern Wessex. Putting Gildas aside for the moment, one could observe that if British kingdoms or lesser polities emerged in western Wessex, one might *a priori* expect similar developments in the east, and one can find some similarities between the two halves of Wessex which might be the result of devolution of power to British leaders.

There has not been a systematic study of possible reoccupation of hill-forts in the post-Roman period in eastern Wessex, but some forts have produced evidence that could point in that direction,[80] and excavation of a hill-fort at Whitsbury Castle, near Fording-bridge (now Hants, but until 1895 in Wilts), produced positive evidence for the refurbishment of its defences.[81] There is also evidence for hill-forts becoming estate centres in the early Middle Ages and giving their names to large estates. Margaret Gelling has discussed the three examples of *Æscesbyrig* (Uffington Castle), Ashbury and Blewbury in Berkshire.[82] Amesbury, Malmesbury and Old Sarum (*Searoburh*) are probably similar examples from Wilt-shire,[83] and interest also attaches to Barbury Castle where (like Old Sarum) one of the battles recorded for the sixth century in the *Anglo-Saxon Chronicle* is said to have been fought.[84]

Eastern Wessex also has its dykes. The one which is most securely dated to the post-Roman period is East Wansdyke which runs for some fifteen miles from Morgan's Hill, near Devizes, across the Marlborough Downs to just west of Savernake and so separated the Kennet Valley from the rest of Wiltshire (see fig. 8).[85] East and West Wansdyke used to be considered as one monument, but there is no trace of a bank and ditch running between them, although

79. Gildas, *Ruin of Britain*, Ch. 22–4; J.N.L. Myres, *Anglo-Saxon Pottery and the Settlement of England* (1969); Morris, *Age of Arthur*, 55–86; S. Chadwick Hawkes, 'The south-east after the Romans: the Saxon settlement', in *The Saxon Shore. A Handbook*; ed. V.A. Maxfield (1989), 78–95.
80. P.J. Fowler, 'Hill-forts, AD 400–700', in *The Iron Age and its Hill-Forts*, ed. D. Hill and M. Jesson (1971), 203–13.
81. A. Ellison and P. Rahtz, 'Excavations at Whitsbury Castle Ditches, Hampshire, 1960', *PHFCAS, 43* (1987), 63–81.
82. M. Gelling, *The Place-Names of Berkshire, Part III*, EPNS, *51* (1976), 823–33.
83. J. Haslam, 'The towns of Wiltshire', in *Anglo-Saxon Towns in Southern England*, ed. J. Haslam (1984), 87–147.
84. *Anglo-Saxon Chronicle s.a.*, 556.
85. Fox and Fox, 'Wansdyke reconsidered'; H.S. Green, 'Wansdyke, excavations 1966 to 1970', *WAM, 66* (1971), 129–46; Eagles, 'Archaeological evidence for settlement'.

they are linked by the Roman road from Silchester to Bath. It is therefore possible that the two dykes and the road mark an agreed frontier that could have a context in later rivalry between Wessex and Mercia.[86] However, East Wansdyke has a much more considerable bank than its western counterpart (fig. 9), and that is a reason for thinking that they were not erected in the same campaign. The fact that the two dykes have the same name is not necessarily significant, as it seems to have been an Anglo-Saxon practice to name such earthworks after Woden, and other dykes, both in Wessex and elsewhere, carry Woden's *cognomen* Grim.[87] Amongst this group is the Grim's Bank to the north-west of Silchester, which runs south and parallel to the River Kennet and blocks the Roman road from Dorchester-on-Thames to Silchester, and whose most likely context is in the post-Roman period.[88] That some form of life did continue at Silchester is suggested by finds from the town dating to the period *c.* 400-600, including fragments of three Celtic brooches which would be otherwise more at home in western Wessex.[89] However, Silchester's famous ogham stone should probably not be used as evidence for post-Roman use of the town as a number of unusual features have suggested that it may not be genuine.[90] There are in addition other lengths of earthwork in eastern Wessex which could potentially date to the post-Roman period, including the Bedwyn Dyke (Wilts), the Devil's Ditch near Andover and the Froxfield entrenchments near Petersfield (Hants), but none of these can be dated at present.[91]

However, the possible defensive measure which has provoked most interest is the use of Germanic soldiers. Central to the discussion is a corpus of 'Germanic-style' military metalwork which was examined in an important article by Sonia Chadwick Hawkes and Gerald Dunning.[92] The earliest forms are thought to have been supplied to regular soldiers recruited from the Rhine frontier and brought to Britain by Theodosius. Later types may have been manufactured in Britain and they, it is argued, and presumably the

---

86. See Chapter 2, 61–4; there have also been arguments made in favour of viewing East Wansdyke in the context of rivalries within the West Saxon royal house – J.N.L. Myres, 'Wansdyke and the origins of Wessex', in *Essays in British History Presented to Sir Keith Feiling*, ed. H. Trevor-Roper (1964), 1–28; D. Kirby, 'Problems of early West Saxon history', *EHR, 80* (1965), 10–29.

87. M. Gelling, 'Place-names and Anglo-Saxon paganism', *University of Birmingham Historical Journal, 8* (1961-2), 7–25.

88. B.H.St.J. O'Neil, 'Grim's Bank, Padworth, Berkshire', *Antiquity, 17* (1943), 188–98.

89. B.H.St.J. O'Neil, 'The Silchester region in the 5th and 6th centuries AD', *Antiquity, 18* (1944), 113–22; G.C. Boon, 'The latest objects from Silchester, Hants', *Med Arch, 3* (1959), 79–88.

90. M. Fulford and B. Sellwood, 'The Silchester ogham stone: a reconsideration', *Antiquity, 54* (1980), 95–9.

91. Cunliffe, *Wessex to AD 1000*, 294–6.

92. S. Chadwick Hawkes and G.C. Dunning, 'Soldiers and settlers in Britain, fourth to fifth century', *Med Arch, 5* (1961), 1–71; Cunliffe, *Wessex to AD 1000*, 273.

9. Aerial photograph of East Wansdyke at All Cannings (Wilts)
[photograph: M. Aston]

troops who wore them, may have continued in use beyond 410. There have been various finds of such metalwork from Roman sites in Wessex and also from some Anglo-Saxon cemeteries. However, the question of the connection between the use of such Germanic troops and the Saxon settlement within Wessex is not entirely straightforward. Six graves (four adults and two children) in the late Roman cemetery at Lankhills, Winchester, have been interpreted as the burials of Saxons resident in the town in the late fourth century,[93] though that interpretation has had its critics.[94] One of the adult male burials was buried with belt-fittings of the type discussed above. There are a number of Anglo-Saxon cemeteries in the Itchen Valley, in the vicinity of Winchester, by the end of the fifth century, but whether a direct link can be traced between these and the putative Saxons of Lankhills is at present unclear.[95] Sonia Chadwick Hawkes has pointed to 'quite a number of late fourth and early fifth-century Roman belt-fittings' from her unpublished excavation at Worthy Park, King's Worthy (and some other cemeteries in northern Hampshire),[96] but none of these cemeteries seems to have produced brooches dating to the first half of the fifth century (see fig. 4).[97]

Another Roman site of potential interest in the search for continuity between late Roman garrisons and early Saxon settlement is the Saxon Shore fort of Portchester. Troops of indeterminate nationality with their families occupied the fort in the late fourth century. At some point in the fifth century distinctive signs of Germanic settlement are found, including a group of sunken-featured buildings and small post-built structures.[98] But the dating of this settlement is problematic. Much depends on a disc brooch which some authorities place early in the fifth century, but others date to the second half of the century. A very similar brooch is known from the site of the Roman settlement at Bitterne.[99]

In a rather different category is the evidence from the small Roman town of Dorchester-on-Thames (Oxon). Three early Germanic burials have been found near the town, a man and a

93. Clarke, *Lankhills*, 390–402.
94. R. Baldwin, 'Intrusive burial groups in the late Roman cemetery at Lankhills, Winchester–a reassessment of the evidence', *Oxford Journal of Archaeology, 4: 1* (1985), 93–104; Brooks, 'Continuity in British towns', 96–8.
95. The case for a significant continuity is put in M. Biddle, 'Hampshire and the origins of Wessex', in *Problems in Economic and Social Archaeology*, ed. G. de G. Sieveking *et al.* (1968), 323–41.
96. Hawkes, 'South-east after the Romans', 94.
97. H.W. Böhme, 'Das Ende der Römerherrschaft in Britannien und die angelsächsische Besiedlung Englands im 5. Jahrhundert', *Jahrbuch des Römisch-Germanischen Zentralmuseums, 33* (1986), 469–574.
98. B. Cunliffe, *Excavations at Portchester Castle, Volume II: Saxon* (1976); Cunliffe, *Wessex to AD 1000*, 285–6.
99. D. Hinton, 'Hampshire's Anglo-Saxon origins', *The Archaeology of Hampshire*, ed. S.J. Shennan and R.T. Schadla Hall, Hampshire Field Club monograph, *1* (1981), 56–65.

10. Fifth-century belt-set from Dorchester-on-Thames [photograph: Ashmolean Museum: all rights reserved]

woman at Dyke Hills and a woman at the Minchin recreation ground.[100] The man was buried with the most complete late Roman official belt-set so far discovered in England (fig. 10), and his grave probably contained weapons as well, though the circumstances of recovery in the nineteenth century mean that there is some uncertainty about its exact contents. The belt-set is probably of early fifth-century date thus making the Dorchester man a candidate for a Germanic soldier in the employ of a British rather than Roman authority. The two women were buried with similar belt-fittings and with Germanic brooches of early fifth-century date. In the vicinity of Dorchester a number of cremation and inhumation cemeteries seem to have been established on both banks of the upper Thames and its tributaries in the first half of the fifth century.[101] By the end of the fifth century settlement may have spread to the Vale of the White Horse and the Kennet Valley,[102] and it could have been this expansion which provoked the building of one or both of the Wansdykes.

The Dorchester area is at present the earliest known focus of Anglo-Saxon settlement in eastern Wessex and the only one to

100. T. Rowley, 'Early Saxon settlements in Dorchester on Thames', in *Anglo-Saxon Settlement and Landscape*, ed. T. Rowley (1974), 42–50; S. Chadwick Hawkes, 'The early Saxon Period', in *The Archaeology of the Oxford Region*, ed. G. Briggs, J. Cook and T. Rowley (1986), 64–108.

101. T.M. Dickinson, 'The Anglo-Saxon burial sites of the Upper Thames region and their bearing upon the history of Wessex' (D. Phil. thesis, Oxford University, 1979).

102. C. Scull, 'Excavations and survey at Watchfield, Oxfordshire, 1983–92', *Arch J*, *149* (1992), 124–281.

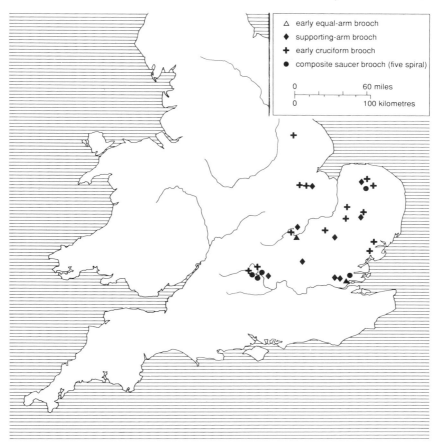

11. Distribution of early fifth-century Germanic women's brooches in England [after H.W. Böhme, 'Das ende der Römerherrschaft in Britannien und die angelsächische Besiedlung Englands im 5. Jahrhundert', *Jarbuch des Römisch-Germanischen Zentralmuseums 33* (1986), 469–574 and S. Chadwick Hawkes, 'The south-east after the Romans: Saxon settlement', in *The Saxon Shore*, ed. V. Maxfield (1989), fig. 28]

produce Germanic women's brooches which can be certainly dated to the first half of the fifth century (fig. 11). It must remain a matter for hypothesis whether we should see the upper Thames Valley settlers as fitting with the Gildas-model of hired soldiers who turned upon their British masters or simply as an invading force which penetrated the region via the River Thames and settled where they chose. But their settlement on both banks of the Thames was to have significant consequences for the history of the region. From this time until the ninth century the Thames ceased to be a frontier, as it seems to have been to the Roman *civitates* of the area, and instead the desideratum of contending powers was to control land on both of its banks.

Germanic settlements in other areas of eastern Wessex had been established by the end of the fifth century though it will be observed from fig. 4 that the distribution of cemeteries is not as intensive south of the Kennet and Thames valleys; central Wiltshire appears relatively well-endowed, but many of its 'undated burials' are individual burials inserted into prehistoric barrows. The distribution reveals the importance of river valleys for penetration and settlement, and this preference is also reflected in the choice of elements indicating habitation by water in the earliest strata of Saxon place-names.[103] River valleys were, of course, fertile areas which had been intensively farmed in the prehistoric and Roman periods and many Roman central places were situated on rivers. There are therefore various possible ways in which the contiguity of certain Roman and Anglo-Saxon settlements can be explained, and we are rarely in the position at present to be certain whether an apparent continuity of settlement is significant or not.

ANGLO-SAXON SOURCES FOR THE EARLY HISTORY OF WESSEX

Before any further assessment can be made of the political geography of eastern Wessex in the fifth and sixth centuries, the contribution of sources describing events in the period, but written in Anglo-Saxon kingdoms some centuries later, needs to be considered. Some readers may be surprised that such sources have not been introduced earlier, but it has become increasingly difficult to accept that the account of the West Saxon *adventus* provided by the late fifth and sixth-century annals in the *Anglo-Saxon Chronicle* can provide a chronological and narrative framework for events in the period.[104] Archaeological evidence does not equate with the *Chronicle*'s apparent picture of victories by the house of Cerdic opening up new areas of settlement. To give but one example, the Saxon material in eastern Wiltshire predates by over half a century Cynric's reported victory against the British at Old Sarum in 552.[105] The *Chronicle*'s account also fits uneasily with the information about

103. Gelling, 'English place-names', 69–76.
104. As attempted by, among others, G.J. Copley, *The Conquest of Wessex in the Sixth Century* (1954) and Myres, *Anglo-Saxon Pottery*.
105. Meaney, *Gazetteer of Anglo-Saxon Burial Sites* (1964), 268–9 (Harnham Hill), and 271 (Petersfinger); J. Musty and J.E.D. Stratton, 'A Saxon cemetery at Winterbourne Gunner, near Salisbury', *WAM, 59* (1964), 86–109; C.J. Gingell, 'The excavation of an early Anglo-Saxon cemetery at Collingbourne Ducis', *WAM, 70/71* (1978), 61–98; S. Davies, 'The excavation of an Anglo-Saxon cemetery (and some prehistoric pits) at Charlton Plantation, near Downton', *WAM, 79* (1985), 109–54; B. Eagles, 'Pagan Anglo-Saxon burials at West Overton', *WAM, 80* (1986), 103–20; G. Speake, *A Saxon Bed Burial on Sallowcliffe Down*, English Heritage arch. rep., *10* (1989).

the early West Saxon kingdom and settlement within the Solent area given in Bede's *Ecclesiastical History* (completed *c.* 731) which is the earliest narrative source for the region.[106]

But it is the content of its own annals which really damns much of the *Chronicle*'s account of fifth and sixth-century Wessex.[107] The *Chronicle* in the form in which we have it is a compilation of the later ninth century;[108] that is it was put together almost four centuries after the date it claims for the West Saxon *adventus*. This raises the problem of how events of the fifth and sixth centuries came to be written down. The Saxon settlers were not literate and so unlikely to have had any written account of their early history until after the first formal adoption of Christianity by a West Saxon king in 635. But what is more it is unlikely that they had the same concepts of history in the pre-Christian period as later.[109] There are several signs in the early West Saxon annals that traditions derived probably from oral story-telling have been forced into an annal format. The account of Cerdic and his son Cynric arriving off the coast of Wessex with five ships in 495 seems to belong to an established convention of Germanic foundation stories in which a pair of kinsman heroes appears with a small number of ships and after a few years' successful battling wins kingdoms for themselves and their successors.[110] Other features which are likely to have derived from an oral story-telling tradition are people invented from existing place-names. These include a mythical British king Natanleod who was supposedly defeated at *Natanleaga* (Netley: 'the wet wood'), Port who landed in 501 at Portsmouth (from Latin *portus*) and Wihtgar whose name derives ultimately from the Latin name of the Isle of Wight which he allegedly ruled.

It is very unlikely that any oral traditions of the West Saxon *adventus* would have contained any indication of dates and certainly could not have used the *anno domini* means of dating found in the *Chronicle*. Ever since the recognition of a duplication of events nineteen years apart in the *Chronicle* account of the late fifth and sixth centuries there have been suspicions about the accuracy of its early dates.[111] Any remaining trust in its chronology

---

106. B.A.E. Yorke, 'The Jutes of Hampshire and Wight and the origins of Wessex', in *The Origins of Anglo-Saxon Kingdoms*, ed. S. Bassett (1989), 84–96.
107. P. Sims-Williams, 'The settlement of England in Bede and the *Chronicle*', *ASE, 12* (1983), 1–41.
108. J. Bately, 'The compilation of the Anglo-Saxon Chronicle, 60 BC to AD 890: vocabulary as evidence', *PBA, 64* (1978), 93–129; S. Keynes, 'A tale of two kings: Alfred the Great and Æthelred the Unready', *TRHS, 36* (1986), 195–217, especially 196–8.
109. B.A.E. Yorke, 'Fact or fiction? The written evidence for the fifth and sixth centuries AD', *ASSAH, 6* (1993), 45–50.
110. H. Moisl, 'Anglo-Saxon royal genealogies and Germanic oral tradition', *Journal of Medieval History, 7* (1981), 215–48; Sims-Williams, 'Settlement of England'; N. Howe, *Migration and Mythmaking in Anglo-Saxon England* (Yale, 1989).
111. F.M. Stenton, *Anglo-Saxon England* (3rd edn., 1971), 22–3; K. Harrison, 'Early Wessex annals in the Anglo-Saxon Chronicle', *EHR, 86* (1971), 527–33.

has been overthrown by David Dumville's demonstration that the lengths of the reigns of sixth-century rulers in the *Chronicle* annals conflict with those given in another ninth-century West Saxon source, the West Saxon Regnal Table.[112] After the sixth century the two sources are in general agreement and seem to represent the same tradition, but it would appear that the reigns of the sixth-century West Saxon kings in the *Chronicle* have been artificially lengthened. The dates must be seen as among the least reliable parts of the early *Chronicle* annals. It is not safe to regard the *Chronicle* annals for events in Wessex in the fifth and sixth centuries as a reliable factual account of what occurred. That is not to say that they are a complete fiction, but as 'faction' any historical truth is very hard to untangle from its mythic undergrowth.

THE POLITICAL GEOGRAPHY OF EASTERN WESSEX IN THE SIXTH CENTURY: THE SAXONS OF THE THAMES VALLEY

The earliest king of the West Saxon dynasty to feature in Bede's *Ecclesiastical History* is Ceawlin who is described as the second of the great overlords who exercised power, probably in the form of the ability to exact tribute, over other southern kingdoms.[113] Bede also describes how Cynegils, the first of the dynasty to be converted to Christianity, founded a bishopric based on Dorchester-on-Thames in 635,[114] and, from parallels with other Anglo-Saxon kingdoms, one would expect that to mean that Dorchester was within the family's homelands. It also appears from what Bede says that the people whom Ceawlin and Cynegils claimed to rule were known as the Gewisse,[115] a name which may be derived from an Old English adjective meaning 'sure' or 'reliable'.[116] The term 'West Saxon' may only have come into regular use in the late seventh century when the Gewisse had taken over much new territory. A base in the upper Thames is compatible with the entries in the *Chronicle* for Ceawlin and other Gewissan princes active during his reign who between them are said to have captured Gloucester, Cirencester, Bath, Limbury, Aylesbury, Bensington and Eynsham,[117] though the reliability of these accounts is suspect and the dates are unlikely to

112.   D.N. Dumville, 'The West Saxon Genealogical Regnal List and the chronology of early Wessex', *Peritia, 4* (1985), 21–66.

113.   *HE,* II, 5; for overlords see B.A.E. Yorke, *Kings and Kingdoms of Early Anglo-Saxon England* (1990), 157–62.

114.   *HE,* III, 7.

115.   H.E. Walker, 'Bede and the Gewissae: the political evolution of the Heptarchy and its nomenclature', *Cambridge Historical Journal, 12* (1956), 174–86.

116.   R. Coates, 'On some controversy surrounding *Gewissae/Gewissei, Cerdic* and *Ceawlin*', *Nomina, 13* (1989/90), 1–11.

117.   *Anglo-Saxon Chronicle, s.a.* 571 and 577.

be correct. The *Chronicle* places Ceawlin's activities between 560 and 593, but David Dumville has shown that his reign was originally calculated at 7 or 17 years in length (different manuscripts of the West Saxon Regnal List support both readings) and he would calculate it as falling between either 581–8 or 571–88.[118] The *Chronicle* records Ceawlin's death a year after his expulsion following the 'great slaughter of Woden's Barrow', a Neolithic long barrow beside the Ridgeway, about a kilometre to the south of East Wansdyke.[119]

As the Thames Valley has produced the earliest and most intensive evidence for Germanic settlement within Wessex (fig. 11), it is not surprising that it was also at the heart of what seems to have been the most powerful of the region's kingdoms. It is impossible to define the exact area controlled by any of the early Gewissan kings and, indeed, it is likely to have fluctuated over time, but it would seem that their interests stretched well outside our region of eastern Wessex into Oxfordshire (i.e. north of the Thames) and perhaps as far as Gloucestershire. Nor are we in a position to say when an Anglo-Saxon kingdom was created in the upper Thames nor when Ceawlin's family first came to power. Tania Dickinson in her study of the cemeteries of the upper Thames noted a marked increase in the number of sword and other more complex weapon burials from the late fifth century.[120] By the late sixth and early seventh centuries there are archaeological finds which are compatible with a powerful kingdom with a wide range of contacts, including imported goods, especially from Kent and Francia, and use of coins, including a thrymsas 'runic' coinage probably minted in the Thames Valley in the early seventh century.[121] A possible 'princely grave' of the early seventh century was excavated at Cuddesdon (Oxon) in the nineteenth century and two swords, two blue-glass bowls, a bucket from Byzantium and remains of a piece of jewellery with garnets were recovered from the centre of a barrow.[122] They presumably accompanied a central burial, perhaps a cremation, though this was not found. A number of prone burials without grave-goods were arranged radially around the barrow; perhaps sacrifices made at the time of the barrow burial. There have also been a number of high status finds from Dorchester, including a gold *cloisonné* pyramidal stud and three gold coins. The place-name Cuddesdon means Cuthwine's hill, and it is tempting to associate it and other place-names in the Thames Valley and surrounding shires which have protothemes in *Cuth* or other elements used by the West Saxon royal house with members

---

118. Dumville, 'Genealogical Regnal List', 46, 50–6.
119. Gelling, 'Place-names and Anglo-Saxon paganism', 11–13.
120. Dickinson, 'The Anglo-Saxon burial sites of the Upper Thames region', 423–4.
121. For full details see Ch. 7, 296–9.
122. T.M. Dickinson, *Cuddesdon and Dorchester-on-Thames*, BAR, *1* (1974).

of the dynasty.[123] However, many names of this type may in fact have belonged to owners of the land in the later Saxon period, and it also seems to have been Anglo-Saxon practice to name prominent artificial features of the landscape after heroes or gods, as with Woden's barrow discussed above.[124]

THE JUTES OF WIGHT AND HAMPSHIRE

A kingdom was also founded on the Isle of Wight during the sub-Roman period. Bede describes how its last king Aruald and his two brothers were put to death by King Cædwalla when he conquered the island between 685 and 688.[125] The Isle of Wight's status as an independent political unit is also confirmed by its inclusion in the Tribal Hidage, a list of Anglo-Saxon provinces which was probably drawn up in the second half of the seventh century in connection with the collection of tribute by one of the great overlords.[126] The exact origins of the kingdom of Wight are obscure, but embedded in the *Chronicle* account are two legendary founders of the Wight dynasty, Stuf and Wihtgar, who are said to have taken control of the island in 534. Wihtgar is an eponymous founder whose name derives from the Latin name for the island (*Uecta / Uectis*) and *Wihtgara* is the term for the island's inhabitants in the Tribal Hidage.[127] Although the *Chronicle* claims that Stuf and Wihtgar were nephews of Cerdic, the Germanic settlers of the Isle of Wight were believed, as Bede tells us, to be Jutes not Saxons in origin, and Alfred's biographer Asser confirms that Stuf and Wihtgar were regarded as being of Jutish stock in ninth-century Wessex.[128]

The earliest burials identified from the island, which are probably late fifth or early sixth century in date, contain objects, especially types of brooch and pottery, which support the Jutish identification.[129] They also provide links with Kent which is claimed by Bede as another area of Jutish settlement. A connection between the royal houses of Kent and Wight is also implied by the inclusion of Uecta as a son of Woden in the genealogy of the kings of Kent, while Uictgisl and Uitta, who are given as the father and grandfather of Hengest, the legendary founder of the royal house of

123. Dickinson, *Cuddesdon*, 32–5.
124. M. Gelling, *Signposts to the Past. Place-Names and the History of England* (1978), 162–90.
125. *HE*, IV, 16.
126. W. Davies and H. Vierck, 'The contexts of Tribal Hidage: social aggregates and settlement patterns', *Frühmittelalterliche Studien*, 8 (1974), 223–93.
127. Yorke, 'Jutes', 88–9.
128. *HE*, I, 15; *Asser's Life of King Alfred*, ed. W.H. Stevenson (1904; repr. 1959), Ch. 2, p. 4.
129. C. Arnold, *The Anglo-Saxon Cemeteries of the Isle of Wight* (1982), 103–5.

Kent, also seem to have names derived from the same stem (Bede calls the inhabitants of the Isle of Wight *Uictuarii*).[130] These names need not mean that the kings of Kent and Wight shared common ancestors in reality, but they do suggest that at the time the genealogies were compiled there was a consciousness of a common origin of the two peoples and close links between the rulers of the two provinces. Not only have both produced fifth-century Jutish material, but in the sixth century there was a shared taste in Kent and the Isle of Wight for brooches whose decoration and form was ultimately influenced by types from southern Scandinavia, and some of the finest examples in the Isle of Wight seem to have been manufactured in Kent. Cemeteries from Kent and the Isle of Wight also contain certain prestige objects imported from abroad which are rare elsewhere in England, such as bronze Byzantine pails and bird brooches from Francia. The Isle of Wight and Kent are also linked by being the only areas in the south, apart from the Thames Valley, from which runic inscriptions dating to before 650 have been found.[131]

Though comparable, the richest Isle of Wight graves do not generally seem to have been as elaborately furnished as the richest graves in Kent, but there is one burial of a young woman from the Chessell Down cemetery, probably dating to the second half of the sixth century, which does take its place with the richest Kentish burials.[132] She is depicted, in a drawing made of her grave in the nineteenth century (fig. 12), wearing three great Kentish square-headed brooches on her breast in addition to the more usual brooches on either shoulder, one of which was a rare Frankish import. The rest of her jewellery consisted of a silver and a gold ring, an elaborate necklace of beads and on her forehead a headband of gold braid in Frankish fashion. Between her legs were a crystal ball and a perforated spoon and at her sides an iron weaving batten and another large iron artefact (possibly a key); all these objects are characteristic of the richest female burials in Kent and may have been selected to symbolize high status. At her feet were a bronze pail from Byzantium and two silver-rimmed wooden cups. The burial is exceptional among those from the island and seems to suggest more than the mere influence of Kentish fashions; possibly she was a high status Kentishwoman married into an island family.

Another 'Jutish' kingdom may have been established on the Hampshire mainland opposite the Isle of Wight. Bede says that the area was still known at the time he was writing (731) as *Iutarum natio*, 'the nation of the Jutes',[133] and place-names survive identi-fying various southern Hampshire locations as Jutish, including the

---

130. Sims-Williams, 'Settlement of England', 24–5.
131. Arnold, *Cemeteries of the Isle of Wight*, 104–9.
132. Arnold, *Cemeteries of the Isle of Wight*, 26–8; 51–60. Many of the objects are on display in the British Museum.
133. *HE*, I, 15.

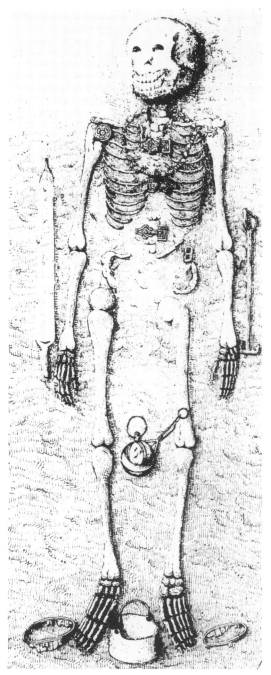

12. Rich female burial from Chessell Down cemetery (I of W) [C.R. Smith, *Collectanea Antiqua*, 7 vols. (1868), 6, plate 28]

New Forest (*Ytene*), Bishopstoke (*Ytingstoc*) on the River Itchen, a few miles south from Winchester, and a valley near East Meon (*Ytedene*).[134] These place-names were presumably formed by the Jutes' 'Saxon' neighbours, rather than the Jutes themselves, and so help delineate the western and northern boundaries of the Jutes in Hampshire. Some of the earliest pottery and metalwork from this territory are of types also found on the Isle of Wight.[135] However, the bulk of the sixth-century burials from the cemetery at Droxford (Hants) do not closely parallel those of the Isle of Wight and have just as much in common with those of the 'Saxon' areas of north Hampshire, southern Wiltshire and Sussex.[136]

Bede does not give a name to the Hampshire Jutish territory or state categorically that it was a kingdom, but the terminology he uses to describe the territory (*provincia*) and its people (*gens*) is the vocabulary he habitually applies to territories which were kingdoms.[137] Likely legendary founders of a royal house appear in the *Chronicle* annal for 501 recording the arrival of Port and his two sons Bieda and Mægla at Portsmouth. Port, like Wihtgar, is an eponymous founder whose name was probably taken from the Latin *portus*, 'a port', which seems to have been the name the Anglo-Saxons applied to Portsmouth Harbour as a whole and which was used with various qualifiers to indicate individual settlements in the area including Portsmouth, Portchester and Portsdown.[138]

REGIONES

We cannot say anything about the early political structures in Wiltshire south of Wansdyke nor in the area of Winchester and north Hampshire. We do not know when these regions came under the permanent control of the Gewissan kings, only that they had probably done so by the middle of the seventh century. We can though see something of administrative districts below the level of the kingdom which are called in charters and by Bede *regiones*. Although the main evidence for the *regiones* comes from records of or concerning the seventh century they are included here because they are likely to have originated before 600 and help to demonstrate the close links between parts of our region and other Anglo-Saxon kingdoms of the south-east in that period.

We know of one major subdivision of the southern Hampshire Jutes. Bede records how the overlord Wulfhere of Mercia in c. 660

134. Yorke, 'Jutes', 89–92.
135. Arnold, *Cemeteries of the Isle of Wight*, 102–6.
136. F. Aldsworth, 'Droxford Anglo-Saxon cemetery, Soberton, Hampshire', *PHFCAS, 35* (1979), 93–182.
137. J. Campbell, *Bede's Reges and Principes*, Jarrow lecture (1979), 1–2.
138. M. Gelling, 'Latin loan-words in Old English place-names', *ASE, 6* (1977), 1–14 (at 10–11).

transferred the Jutish province of the Meonware to the control of King Æthelwalh of the South Saxons.[139] The territory of the Meonware, 'the dwellers of the Meon', had probably been part of the canton of the *Regni* during the Roman period when the Portsmouth area is likely to have been administered from Chichester.[140] Wulfhere's transfer therefore briefly reunited the former territory of the *Regni*. We do not know how the Meonware came to be part of the Jutish province, but they provide a parallel between the southern Hampshire Jutish province and the kingdom of Kent where comparable subdivisions (lathes) are also found combining a topographical element with *ware* ('dwellers of . . .'), as shown on fig. 13.[141]

In seventh-century records we can trace units comparable to that of the Meonware in eastern Berkshire and north-east Hampshire and these too seem to have affinities with areas to their east. A charter of Frithuwald, subking of Surrey, granted in 672–4 to found a minster at Chertsey, defined the estate as sharing in part a common border with the adjoining province (*provincia*) of the *Sunninges* whose name is preserved today in Sonning in eastern Berkshire.[142] Adjoining the Sunningas to the west there seems to have been a comparable province of the Readingas who gave their name to Reading,[143] and to the south in north-east Hampshire, were the Basingas whose name survives in Basing and Basingstoke.[144] The early roles of Sonning, Reading and Basingstoke continued beyond the Anglo-Saxon period as they were the administrative centres for distinctive groupings of hundreds throughout the Middle Ages.[145] Another comparable group may have been the Horningas who gave their name to the hundred of Hormer (*Horningamere*) in which Abingdon was situated.[146] Similar groups with names whose second element was *-ingas* ('people of . . .') are to be found in other Saxon settlement areas of southern England including Surrey, Sussex and, north of the Thames, in Oxfordshire, Buckinghamshire, Hertfordshire and Middlesex.[147] Many of these districts are shown on fig. 13. Other possible *-ingas* groups in

139. *HE*, IV, 13.
140. B. Cunliffe, *The Regni* (1973), 126–49.
141. N. Brooks, 'The creation and early structure of the kingdom of Kent', in *The Origins of Anglo-Saxon Kingdoms*, ed. S. Bassett (1989), 55–74.
142. S 1165. J. Blair, 'Frithuwold's kingdom and the origins of Surrey', in *The Origins of Anglo-Saxon Kingdoms*, ed. S. Bassett (1989), 97–107.
143. Gelling, *Place-Names of Berkshire III*, 838–47.
144. D. Hinton, 'The place of Basing in mid-Saxon history', *PHFCAS, 42* (1986), 162–3.
145. H. Cam, 'Early groups of hundreds', in *Liberties and Communities in Medieval England* (1944), 91–106.
146. M. Gelling, *The Place-Names of Berkshire. Part II*, EPNS, 50 (1974), 431–2.
147. J. Blair, *Anglo-Saxon Oxfordshire* (1994), 35; Blair, 'Frithwold's kingdom'; K. Bailey, 'The Middle Saxons', in *The Origins of Anglo-Saxon Kingdoms*, ed. S. Bassett (1989), 84–96.

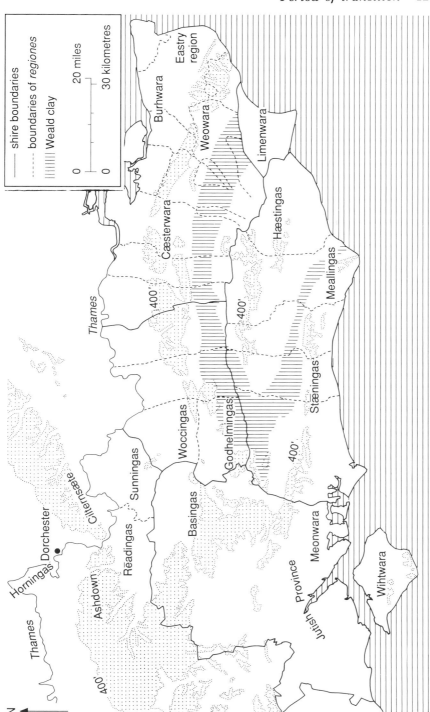

13. *Regiones* in southern England [after S. Bassett (ed.), *The Origins of Anglo-Saxon Kingdoms* (1989), figs. 4.2, 6.1 and 7.1]

Gewissan territory north of the Thames are the Feppingas/
Færpingas,[148] the Garingas who gave their name to Goring,[149] and
the Bensingas whose *tun* at Bensington/Benson seems to have been
an important royal vill and the administrative centre for a group of
hundreds later in the Middle Ages.[150] The most westerly *-ingas*
group to have been identified are the Stoppingas in Warwickshire
which in the seventh century was in the kingdom of the Hwicce.[151]
Groups of this type have not so far been recognized in Wiltshire or
north Hampshire, though some distinctive later administrative
groupings, such as that of the Wallops in Hampshire, may conceal
them.[152]

The first element of these *-ingas* names has often been
interpreted as an archaic personal name, though in most cases
there is no evidence for such a name having otherwise been used in
England.[153] Sometimes a topographical interpretation can be
offered as an alternative etymology; the Readingas, for instance,
may be either 'the people of Reada' or 'the people of the red one',[154]
and the Horningas are most likely to have taken their name from
'the horn of the land', that is the distinctive loop formed by the
River Thames at Abingdon.[155] Various explanations have been
offered for how these units might have been formed in the fifth and
sixth centuries. Many early commentators saw them as the territories of groups of settlers led by the individuals whose names were
compounded with *-ingas*, and Steven Bassett in a recent assessment
of the Stoppingas has commented 'they were a people who sound
like an extended family, perhaps with Stoppa as their founder or
the earliest remembered common ancestor'.[156] When we can study
the *-ingas* groups, and their Jutish counterparts compounded with
-ware, in the seventh century, they appear as administrative sub-
districts of kingdoms which might, like the Meonware, be transferred from one king to another in the aftermath of a battle and
were probably areas on which tribute was levied and collected.[157]
Their origins may be no more complex than as administrative
subdivisions, and the estates dependent on hill-forts discussed

---

148. *HE*, III, 21; Davies and Vierck, 'Tribal Hidage', 233, 277 and 283.
149. Gelling, *Place-Names of Berkshire III*, 815.
150. Cam, *Liberties and Communities*, 74, 76, 95, 99, 106 and 109.
151. S. Bassett, 'In search of the origins of Anglo-Saxon kingdoms', in *The Origins
     of Anglo-Saxon Kingdoms*, ed. S. Bassett (1989), 3–27, at 18–19.
152. For the Wallops see Cam, *Liberties and Communities*, 100. For an
     unconvincing attempt to reconstruct a *regio* in the vicinity of Winchester see
     E. Klingelhöfer, 'Anglo-Saxon manors of the Upper Itchen valley: their origin
     and evolution', *PHFCAS*, *46* (1991), 31–40.
153. Gelling, *Signposts to the Past*, 162–90.
154. M. Gelling, *The Place-Names of Berkshire, Part I*, EPNS, *49* (1973), 170.
155. Gelling, *Place-Names of Berkshire II*, 431–2.
156. Bassett, 'Origins of Anglo-Saxon kingdoms', 18 his n. 48 shows the name could
     also have a topographical origin.
157. J.E.A. Joliffe, *Pre-Feudal England: The Jutes* (1933); Brooks, 'Kingdom of
     Kent', 69–74; Blair, 'Origins of Surrey'.

earlier could provide an indication that such units may have been formed in the aftermath of the withdrawal from the Roman Empire and before Anglo-Saxon kingdoms came into being.

The administrative arrangements in southern and eastern Hampshire and the Thames Valley are pointers to these areas having close links with the Saxon and Jutish areas to their east in the sixth century, links which can be confirmed sometimes by other sources such as the connections between the royal houses of Wight and Kent or the dialect links which Margaret Gelling has discerned in the place-names of eastern Berkshire and the adjoining area of Surrey.[158] The later shire boundaries between Surrey and Berkshire/Hampshire may have had little significance in the sixth century. These areas of south-eastern England may have recognized a common overlord in the late sixth century. Bede's first three 'overlords' all came from the area – Ælle of the South Saxons, Ceawlin of the Gewisse and Æthelbert of Kent.[159] Ian Wood has suggested that the overlords in turn may have been paying tribute to Frankish kings as part of their North Sea 'empire' and that 'perhaps the early names in Bede's list are names remembered in Canterbury as kings acknowledged by the Merovingians and subsequently misinterpreted'.[160] Francia seems to have been the source of prestige items in southern England which are to be found in the richer graves and may have been among the gifts which made royal service attractive. However, some burials with Frankish goods may actually be the burials of Frankish settlers, merchants or adventurers.[161]

BRITONS AND ANGLO-SAXONS IN THE FIFTH AND SIXTH CENTURIES

There has been much debate recently about the scale of Germanic settlement in fifth and sixth-century Britain.[162] Population sizes are difficult to estimate and the numbers which can be calculated from the excavations of cemeteries are little help as on their own they would suggest a ridiculously small population when the number of years in which a cemetery is likely to have been in use is taken into account.[163] Few West Saxon cemeteries have been excavated in their entirety, but it seems that few exceeded a hundred burials

158. Gelling, *Place-Names of Berkshire III*, 840–1, 925–39.
159. *HE*, II, 5.
160. I. Wood, *The Merovingian North Sea* (Alingsås, 1983), quotation at 14.
161. For arguments for extensive Frankish settlement see V.I. Evison, *The Fifth-Century Invasions South of the Thames* (1965), and for a more moderate view Hawkes, 'The Early Saxon Period', 78–80.
162. C. Arnold, *Roman Britain to Saxon England* (1984); N.J. Higham, *Rome, Britain and the Anglo-Saxons* (1992).
163. Arnold, *Roman Britain to Saxon England*, 121–41.

even though they are likely to have been in use for 150–200 years.[164] However, it would seem that Germanic settlement in the region was on a sufficient scale to result in the introduction of new types of buildings, artefacts and burial practice. The material from cemeteries dominates the archaeological record. The Germanic settlers practised both inhumation and cremation, and mixed cemeteries are the norm in the Thames Valley and much of Hampshire, though in Wiltshire, where Germanic settlement seems to have occurred slightly later and probably from established centres in England, cremation is rare. In any cemetery a number of inhumations will be unfurnished or may contain only a knife, but in more substantial burials men were buried with one or more weapons and women wearing their standard *tract* attire of a dress fastened by a brooch on each shoulder and belted at the waist (fig. 14). Beads were regularly worn by women in the sixth century either at the waist or as a necklace strung between the two brooches. Additional grave-goods such as a pot or other container might be included as well. The pottery and metalwork which the earliest settlers brought with them has its closest Continental parallels in the area between the Elbe and Weser rivers,[165] thus confirming that the majority of incomers to the region were Saxon in origin as Bede reported[166] and the name 'West Saxon' implies. The evidence for Jutes in the Isle of Wight and possible Frankish settlers elsewhere has already been discussed.[167]

Although the cemeteries of our region have many broad similarities and by the sixth century certain forms of dress had become prevalent within it, it is also true to say that no two cemeteries are identical and that each community had patterns of burial ritual or dress peculiar to itself. For instance, although the cemeteries at Alton and Portway in northern Hampshire reflect a broadly similar Anglo-Saxon culture and both contained inhumations and cremations, there are some striking differences between them. Portway differs from Alton in the orientation of inhumations, the use of flint or plank-lined graves, the positioning of spears on the left-hand side of the skeleton and the apparent abandonment by Portway women in the later sixth century of the ubiquitous double brooch set to fasten gowns and a preference for girdle-hangers

164. For older excavations see Meaney, *Gazetteer*; for Wiltshire see n. 105; Berkshire and beyond, Dickinson, 'Anglo-Saxon burial sites' and Scull, 'Watchfield'; for Hampshire, V.I. Evison, *An Anglo-Saxon Cemetery at Alton, Hampshire*, Hampshire Field Club monograph, *4* (1988); A. Cook and M. Dacre, *Excavations at Portway Andover, 1973–1975*, OUCA monograph, *4* (1985); K.S. Jarvis, *Excavations in Christchurch 1969–1980*, DNHAS monograph, *5* (1983) and Aldsworth, 'Droxford'; for Isle of Wight, Arnold, *Cemeteries of Isle of Wight*.
165. Dickinson, 'Anglo-Saxon burial sites', 412–13; Evison, *Alton*, 44–5.
166. *HE*, I, 15.
167. See above, 43.

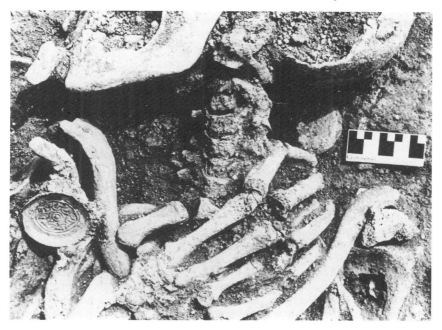

14. Female burial with pair of saucer brooches worn on the shoulder from Portway cemetery, Andover (Hants) (grave 35) [photograph: Hampshire County Museum Service]

instead.[168] Chris Arnold has observed of the Isle of Wight cemeteries that each one seems to have had its own characteristics and some grave-goods peculiar to itself.[169] Within a wider cultural framework individual communities evolved distinctive characteristics which are likely to reflect different experiences and cultural admixtures.

Fewer settlement sites which can be dated to the fifth or sixth centuries are known, but at Dorchester-on-Thames, Portchester, Chalton and Old Down Farm, Andover, examples of a distinctive Germanic structure, the sunken-featured building, have been excavated.[170] Such buildings could be used for accommodation, but also for a variety of agricultural and domestic functions including weaving, dairying and cooking.[171] However, although the Germanic element apparently dominates the archaeological record, when the distinctive Anglo-Saxon culture of the sixth century is carefully

---

168. Evison, *Alton*, and Cook and Dacre, *Portway*.
169. Arnold, *Cemeteries of Isle of Wight*, 102.
170. Rowley, 'Saxon settlements in Dorchester on Thames'; Cunliffe, *Excavations at Portchester Castle II*, 14–59; P. Addyman and D. Leigh, 'The Anglo-Saxon village at Chalton, Hampshire: second interim report', *Med Arch, 17* (1973), 1–25; S. Davies, 'Excavations at Old Down Farm, Andover, Part 1: Saxon', *PHFCAS, 36* (1980), 161–80, and see Ch. 6.
171. M. Welch, *Anglo-Saxon England* (1992).

examined it can be seen to have possible British as well as Germanic antecedents. The settlers brought with them their sunken-featured buildings, but apparently not the raised granaries and longhouses of the Germanic homelands.[172] The timber halls of sixth-century Saxon settlements such as Chalton and Cowdery's Down (Hants) have been interpreted as deriving their basic plan from timber buildings of the Roman and sub-Roman periods, though details of construction such as external buttresses and ridge-beams seem to be Germanic in origin (see figs. 21 and 68).[173] Burial practices can be traced back to developments in the Germanic homelands in the fourth century, but the cemeteries of Wessex also contain features such as the lining of burial pits with flint blocks, the wearing of rings and bracelets and the burial of token combs which are not typical of Saxon burials, but can be found in Roman cemeteries like Lankhills.[174]

Some cemeteries contain more specific evidence that they may have been used by people of both British and Saxon descent. A man from an apparently Germanic cemetery at Collingbourne Ducis (Wilts) was buried wearing a buckle of the late fifth or early sixth centuries, but also a late Roman gilded disc brooch worn at the shoulder in the Roman fashion.[175] At Frilford, near Abingdon (Berks), Anglo-Saxon burials were made from the early fifth to the late sixth century in a late Roman cemetery associated with a Romano-Celtic temple,[176] and the cemetery at Snell's Corner in southern Hampshire may be another example of a cemetery which began in the Roman period, but was subsequently used for interments in the Anglo-Saxon style.[177] In contrast, a cemetery at Queenford Farm, Dorchester-on-Thames, which seems to have come into use in the fourth century and, from the evidence of radiocarbon dates, remained in use until the sixth century, contained very little in the way of grave-goods and nothing overtly Germanic. The burials were characteristically unaccompanied, supine inhumations orientated west-east, a form of burial found in fourth-century Britain which in western Wessex continued into the fifth and sixth

---

172. G. Fehring, *The Archaeology of Medieval Germany*, trans, R. Samson (1991), 145–68.
173. S.T. James, A. Marshall and M. Millett, 'An early medieval building tradition', *Arch J, 141* (1985), 182–215; D. Hinton, *Archaeology, Economy and Society. England from the Fifth to the Fifteenth Century* (1990), 17–18.
174. Dickinson, 'Burial sites of the Upper Thames', 399–400; R.H. White, *Roman and Celtic Objects from Anglo-Saxon Graves*, BAR, *191* (1988), 152–66.
175. R. White, 'Scrap or substitute: Roman material in Anglo-Saxon graves', in *Anglo-Saxon Cemeteries: A reappraisal*, ed. E. Southworth (1990), 125–52.
176. R. Hingley, 'A Romano-British "religious complex" at Frilford', *Oxford Journal of Archaeology, 4* (1985), 201–14.
177. G.M. Knocker, 'Early burials and an Anglo-Saxon cemetery at Snell's Corner near Horndean, Hampshire', *PHFCAS, 19* (1955), 117–70; E.W. Black, 'Romano-British burial customs and religious beliefs in south-east England', *Arch J, 143* (1986), 201–39, at 219–20.

centuries, if not later.[178] These cemeteries have often been interpreted as Christian, though some have questioned whether this interpretation is appropriate for Queenford Farm,[179] but in any case it is likely to be the burial ground of the Roman and post-Roman inhabitants of Dorchester. It has been estimated that over 2,000 people were buried there which, if the cemetery was in use for 150 years, would mean it served a population of, on average, 340 people.

Cemeteries like Queenford Farm are difficult to date except through radio-carbon dating and comparable burial grounds elsewhere in eastern Wessex may have gone undetected. The lack of a distinctive sub-Roman material culture (also apparent in western Wessex) is one reason why the British of eastern Wessex have been so hard to detect. But another sign of their influence in the fifth and sixth centuries comes from place-name evidence. At first sight the place-names of eastern Wessex appear overwhelmingly Germanic, but one has to remember that not all names were created in the fifth and sixth centuries. Many place-names are first recorded in late Saxon charters or in Domesday Book and it appears that a new stratum of place-names was created from the eighth century onwards when large estates were split up and the new smaller estates were often called after their owners.[180] A study by Dr Barrie Cox of 224 place-names recorded between *c.* 670 and *c.* 730 showed that about a quarter of them had dropped out of use and had no modern equivalent.[181] Place-names likely to be of an early date in eastern Wessex suggest a degree of continuity with place-name practices of the Roman period. Some names of either British or Latin origin have survived virtually intact, such as the names of many rivers including the Avon, Thames, Ock, Kennet and Itchen (which may be pre-British), but also of some settlements such as Speen (Berks) which derives directly from Latin *Spinae*.[182] Other names may have a British or Latin element combined with an Old English one. Winchester, for instance, Old English *Uintan cæstir*, takes its first element from *Venta Belgarum*, the Roman name of the town, and its second from Old English *ceaster*.[183] Of course, *ceaster* itself is derived from Latin *castrum* ('fort') and was applied by Old English speakers to sites with Roman fortifications, though it may have entered the language before the migration

178. R.A. Chambers, 'The late and sub-Roman cemetery at Queenford Farm, Dorchester-on-Thames, Oxon', *Oxoniensia, 52* (1987), 35–69.
179. D.J. Watts, 'Infant burials and Romano-British Christianity', *Arch J, 146* (1989), 372–83, and see Ch. 4, 164–5.
180. See Ch. 6, 249–50.
181. B. Cox, 'The place-names of the earliest English records', *English Place-Name Society Journal, 8* (1976), 12–66.
182. Jackson, *Language and History*, 219–29; Gelling, *Place-Names of Berkshire III*, 800–4.
183. R. Coates, *The Place-Names of Hampshire* (1989), 176–7.

period. However, there are a number of instances from eastern Wessex where a place-name contains a Latin noun which accurately describes the nature of the place which may indicate contact between Old English and Latin speakers. Portchester combines both *ceaster* and Latin *portus* ('a harbour'), an element which appears in many place-names in the vicinity of Portsmouth Harbour, as well as being adopted as that of the supposed founder of Germanic settlement in the area.[184] Other Latin elements which appear in Old English place-names are *funta* ('a spring'), *campus* ('a field') and *vicus* ('street', 'quarter'). Of course, a very large number of place-names of the Roman period were lost, including that of *Calleva Atreabtaum* (Silchester), and *Tamese*, the original name of Dorchester-on-Thames, though the first element of its current name may be British.[185]

Gildas paints a terrible picture of the fate of the British at the hands of the Anglo-Saxons including rivers of blood, mass enslavement and destruction of towns and other settlements.[186] No doubt some of these things did occur, but, like Viking settlers later, it would not have been in the interests of Germanic leaders to eliminate the native population as they would have wanted to collect tribute and taxes from it. Some recent commentators have argued that the evidence suggests only small groups of German settlers whose influence was out of all proportion to their numbers because they became militarily and politically dominant.[187] It is very difficult to estimate the proportion of Anglo-Saxons to British in fifth and sixth-century Wessex, but it is unlikely that they were all warriors. There must have been humbler settlers as well who knew how to dig sunken-featured buildings, cremate their dead and make pottery by hand. The change of language in England, when contrasted with the continuity of Romance languages in other former provinces of the Roman Empire in western Europe, remains a powerful argument for settlement that was more substantial than just that of a few aristocrats and their warbands.

As we have seen, there is no longer any need to doubt the survival of a British population, and the culture described as 'Anglo-Saxon' can be seen to consist of British as well as Germanic elements. However, it is not so easy to understand the exact nature of British survival and different interpretations of the evidence are possible. Queenford Farm cemetery appears to show a British community following their own practices in spite of living in the area of Wessex with apparently the heaviest concentration of Germanic settlement. But the evidence from cemeteries further south could be taken to mean that by the sixth century British

---

184. Gelling, 'Latin loan-words'.
185. Gelling, *Place-Names of Berkshire III*, 801–2.
186. Gildas, *Ruin of Britain*, Ch. 25.
187. Higham, *Rome, Britain and Anglo-Saxons*, 209–36.

people had adopted the manner of dress and burial of the Germanic settlers, and one can readily appreciate that Germanic craftsmen might be patronized by Britons. But were the 'Anglo-Saxons' buried at Snell's Corner Germanic incomers or descendants of the Romano-British buried in the cemetery who had adopted new customs? Similar problems of interpretation are provided by Roman villa sites like that at Meonstoke (Hants). The Roman villa buildings collapsed or were pulled down in the late fourth century, but at some point in the fifth or sixth century post-holes for a building were dug over the villa remains and Germanic burials and other settlement evidence have been found nearby (fig. 15).[188] Interpretation could range from, on the one hand, seeing the site abandoned by its Romano-British inhabitants in the fourth century with the site lying derelict until reoccupied by Saxon settlers to, on the other, the site being utilized throughout the period by descendants of the Romano-British villa-owners who adapted to a simpler way of life and eventually acquired objects and customs, or perhaps even workers, of Germanic origin.

One of the most recent contributions to the debate on the status of the British is Heinrich Härke's study of warrior burials of the fifth and sixth centuries, which draws extensively on material from Wessex.[189] He has shown that the men buried with weapons were on average one to two inches taller than men buried without weapons, although they were apparently no better nourished and had the same incidence of hypoplasia, caused by undernourishment or illness in youth. As other studies appear to show that Saxon men were on average one and a half inches taller than Roman men, he offers the conclusion that 'the men buried with weapons in Anglo-Saxon cemeteries were predominantly or exclusively of Germanic stock, whereas the men buried without weapons included a sizeable Romano-British element'. The question of the interrelationship of British and Germanic settlers in early Wessex is by no means clear yet and will no doubt receive much further discussion in years to come. But any final assessment must take into account the possible Brittonic element in the Gewissan royal house. Cerdic, the supposed founder of the dynasty has an Anglicized version of the British name *Caraticos. Ceawlin's name may also be Celtic in origin, as was that of his descendant Cædwalla.[190] Other members of the royal house have names which combine British and Old English name-elements. The West Saxon dynasty was not the only one to claim ancestors with British names, but the use of Brittonic name-elements seems more pervasive than anywhere else. Possibly members of the dynasty were able to claim descent from a

---

188. King, 'Excavations at Meonstoke' (forthcoming).
189. H. Härke, 'The Anglo-Saxon weapon burial rite', *Past and Present, 126* (1990), 22–43. See also Arnold, *Roman Britain to Saxon England,* 128–41.
190. Coates, *Gewissae / Gewissei, Cerdic* and *Ceawlin'.*

15. Courtyard walls of the Roman villa at Meonstoke (Hants) cut by early Saxon pit or sunken-feature building, seen in quarter section during excavation [photograph: A. King]

prominent British family, for instance, by intermarriage. At the least, the names seem to acknowledge the significance of the British element in the population which they sought to rule.

Successful though the Gewissan house may have been by the end of the sixth century, it is unlikely that anyone would have prophesised that they would eventually emerge as rulers of the area encompassed by the later six shires of Wessex. That area had little political unity by 600 and was divided between a number of rulers of different origins – Saxon, Jutish and British – whose closest links often seem to have been with other provinces outside our region. When West Saxons of the ninth century looked back at this early period they gave the region more coherence than it actually seems to have possessed by projecting the activities of the legendary founders, Cerdic and Cynric, on to areas controlled by Jutes and other Saxons which were not securely held by Gewissan leaders until a later date. There seems to have been a clear geographical division between areas under British control and those dominated by rulers claiming a Germanic origin which was to leave its mark on West Saxon administration in succeeding centuries. Parts of the boundaries were delineated by substantial dykes which are impossible to date closely, but could be indicative of negotiated frontiers made at some point during the sub-Roman period. There are major differences in the archaeological finds from the British and Germanic areas though both are marked by the disappearance of characteristic features of Roman culture and the decay of many

Roman settlements. We cannot say how many Germans may have settled in eastern Wessex, but they came in sufficient numbers to cause major changes in material culture and language. Although cultural backgrounds were presumably very different, the circumstances of the period meant that those who rose to the top of the pile in both eastern and western Wessex were those who had some sort of military power behind them through which they could impose control over local populations in return for 'protection'. Because of such systems of power the experiences of inhabitants of eastern and western Wessex may not have been so different in the fifth and sixth centuries as one might at first expect.

2 The Creation of Wessex
c. 600–802

SOURCES

It was the military conquests of the Gewissan kings which brought
political unity and a common institutional framework to Wessex. It
is not possible to produce a complete narrative of the stages of
conquest, although the establishment of Anglo-Saxon religious
houses in the course of the seventh century meant that the
production of written records by Anglo-Saxons became possible for
the first time. It is usually assumed that the late ninth-century
compilation, the *Anglo-Saxon Chronicle*, incorporated annals that
were kept contemporaneously from some point in the seventh
century.[1] There is no indication in the language or construction of
the ninth-century text of the point at which this began,[2] but from
the middle of the seventh century annals become more circumstantial in the detail they record and include information such as
the gift of three thousand hides of land near Ashdown from King
Cenwalh to his kinsman Cuthred (648), or a great mortality of birds
(671) which would have been unlikely to have survived if not
written down soon after the events had occurred. The *Chronicle*
annals provide us with an important framework of events, in
particular a series of battles, but one should not assume that they
tell us everything of importance which occurred within the West
Saxon kingdom. The West Saxon ecclesiastic Aldhelm (d. 709) wrote
of the three great victories of King Centwine, but only one is
recorded in the *Chronicle*.[3]

One problem in trying to unscramble the information in the
Chronicle is that the location of many of the battles cannot be
satisfactorily determined. Fortunately few entries are as vague as
that for 682 which simply records 'Centwine put the Britons to

---

1. F.M. Stenton, 'The foundations of English history', in *Preparatory to Anglo-
   Saxon England*, ed. D.M. Stenton (1970), 116–26; K. Harrison, *The Framework
   of Anglo-Saxon History to AD 900* (1976), 132–41.
2. J. Bately, 'The compilation of the Anglo-Saxon Chronicle, 60 BC to AD 890:
   vocabulary as evidence', *PBA, 64* (1978), 93–129.
3. M. Lapidge and J. Rosier (trans.), *Aldhelm: The Poetic Works* (1985), 40–1, 47–9.

flight as far as the sea', but relatively few of the place-names which are provided can be matched with modern locations. That need not cast doubt on the validity of the entries as one would expect a significant percentage of early place-names to have been lost.[4] Early place-names are characteristically single words or simple compounds referring to topographical features and so frequently there is more than one possible identification for any location.[5] *Bradanforda* of the annal for 652 is only taken to be Bradford-on-Avon (Wilts) because that was the identification made by Æthelweard, who in the late tenth century translated the *Chronicle* from Old English into Latin.[6] Several candidates have been put forward for the site of the battle at *Peonnum* in 658 when Cenwalh put the Britons to flight as far as the River Parrett (Som). The name derives from the British word *pen*, 'a hill', a very common place-name element in the west country. W.G. Hoskins argued for Pinhoe or Pinn Beacon in Devon; Katherine Barker for Penn near Yeovil.[7] Both discussions are cogently argued, though there remains much to be said for the original nineteenth-century identification of Penselwood, a significant place near the meeting point of the boundaries of Wiltshire, Dorset and Somerset and site of a major battle with the Vikings in 1016 (in the record of which the name is given in the same form as the 658 annal).[8] But in the final analysis we cannot be certain which location was intended originally.

Hoskins was guided in his identification of locations by the belief that the *Chronicle* annals faithfully recorded the 'westward expansion of Wessex'. In fact, the places which can be identified with any certainty (excluding entries the *Chronicle* compiler has taken from Bede's *Ecclesiastical History*) are either in central Somerset or in the vicinity of the northern borders of Somerset, Wiltshire and Berkshire, an area for which control was contested between Mercia and Wessex throughout the seventh to ninth centuries (fig.16). Although the ninth-century compiler of the *Chronicle* was interested in putting together a 'national' history of the kingdom of Wessex, the original annals which were incorporated seem to reflect a more localized interest, presumably that of a religious house in Somerset or Wiltshire – Glastonbury or Malmesbury are the most obvious candidates.[9]

The *Chronicle* annals have to be supplemented by additional

4. B. Cox, 'The place-names of the earliest English records', *English Place-Name Society Journal, 8* (1976), 12–66; and see Ch. 1, 47–8.
5. M. Gelling, 'A chronology for English place-names', in *Anglo-Saxon Settlements*, ed. D. Hooke (1988), 59–76.
6. A. Campbell (ed.), *The Chronicle of Æthelweard* (1962), 19.
7. W.G. Hoskins, *The Westward Expansion of Wessex* (1970), 15–16; K. Barker, 'Pen, Ilchester and Yeovil: a study in the landscape history and archaeology of south-east Somerset', *PSANHS, 30* (1986), 11–45, especially 12–14 and 41; see also M. Todd, *The South-West to AD 1000* (1987), 272–3.
8. C. Plummer (ed.), *Two of the Saxon Chronicles Parallel* (2 vols. 1899), II, 28.
9. Harrison, *Framework of Anglo-Saxon History*, 134–5.

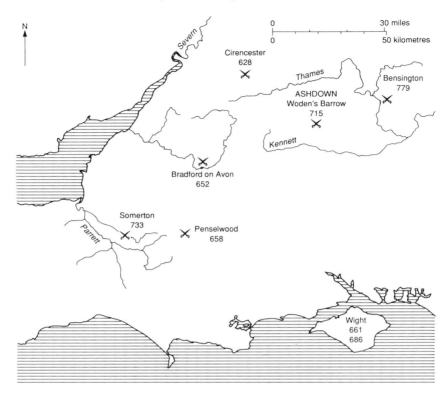

16. West Saxon battle sites which can be identified from *Anglo-Saxon Chronicle* annals for seventh and eighth centuries

sources of information to get as full a picture as possible of the growth of Wessex. Bede provides a full account (also utilized by the *Chronicle* compiler) of Cædwalla's conquest of the Isle of Wight in 686.[10] Bede's main informant for affairs in Wessex and Wight was Bishop Daniel of Winchester (appointed 705), who seems to have provided Bede with very precise details on the geography of the Solent area and how Cædwalla's conquest was achieved. Apart from Bede, our main source of information is the charters recording land grants to West Saxon religious communities;[11] the earliest of these at least provide a *terminus ante quem* for conquest of the area in which they are situated. Although all the West Saxon shires have some charters for the Middle Saxon period surviving, none of them

---

10. *HE*, IV, 15–16.
11. H.P.R. Finberg, *The Early Charters of Wessex* (1964); H. Edwards, *The Charters of the Early West Saxon Kingdom*, BAR, *198* (1988); M. O'Donovan (ed.), *Charters of Sherborne* (1988). See also Ch. 6, 244–6 for discussion of the introduction of charters into Wessex.

are original documents and we are mostly dependent upon versions copied into monastic cartularies in the post-Conquest period. In many instances the cartularies record only the grants for land still in the houses's possession at the time the compilation was made. Because of organizational changes within the Anglo-Saxon Church and the buying, selling and misappropriation of land at different periods (not to mention the complete disappearance of many religious communities and their archives both within the Anglo-Saxon period and later), only a small proportion of the charters originally granted out survive. Some idea of how much may have been lost can be derived from two thirteenth-century inventories of Glastonbury charters[12] and a list of royal benefactions to Sherborne.[13] These documents record many gifts of land which the houses do not seem to have possessed in 1086 and are not included in the surviving cartularies. Sherborne probably lost its pre-900 grants of land in Devon, Wiltshire and Somerset when new bishoprics were established for these shires by Edward the Elder in *c.* 909 (fig. 17).[14]

Having to study cartulary versions of the charters poses all sorts of problems for the modern historian.[15] The later scribes often miscopied and no doubt had problems in deciphering earlier handwriting; sometimes only parts of the earlier charters were reproduced and witness-lists in particular were likely to be cut short. Sometimes the scribes 'improved' upon the original versions, for instance by changing an earlier church dedication to one which was subsequently current or adding an *anno domini* date to a charter dated by other means. In other instances additional material was interpolated to help claim rights and privileges for the foundation not adequately spelt out in the original charter. Some charters are out-and-out forgeries and these are less of a problem to deal with than the substantially genuine charter which has received interpolations, as inappropriate language and formulae or historical errors usually betray them. Few, though, are as outrageous as the Glastonbury post-Conquest forgery of a charter of St Patrick which refers to his disciple Wellias and was concocted as part of a Glastonbury campaign to prove their exemption from visitations from the bishop of Bath and Wells.[16] In many instances what are

12. The list of contents of the *Liber Terrarum* and an inventory of charters made in 1247: T. Hearne (ed.), *Johannis Glastoniensis Chronica sive Historia de rebus Glastoniensibus* (2 vols, 1727), II, 370–9. See Edwards, *Charters of the Early West Saxon Kingdom*, 3–6, 62–77.
13. O'Donovan, *Charters of Sherborne*, xx and Appendix I, 81–2.
14. O'Donovan, *Charters of Sherborne*, l–lii.
15. For general discussion of such problems see F.M. Stenton, *The Latin Charters of the Anglo-Saxon Period* (1953); N. Brooks, 'Anglo-Saxon charters: the work of the last twenty years', *ASE*, 3 (1974), 211–31; P. Wormald, *Bede and the Conversion of England: The Charter Evidence* (Jarrow lecture 1984).
16. B 1; J. Scott (ed.), *The Early History of Glastonbury: An Edition, Translation and Study of William of Malmesbury's De Antiquitate Glastonie Ecclesie* (1981), 30–1 and 54–9.

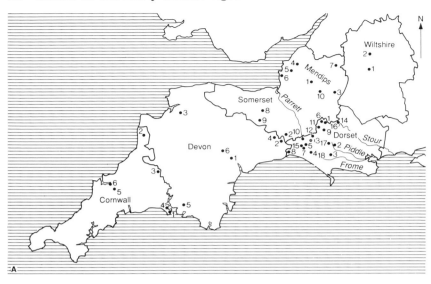

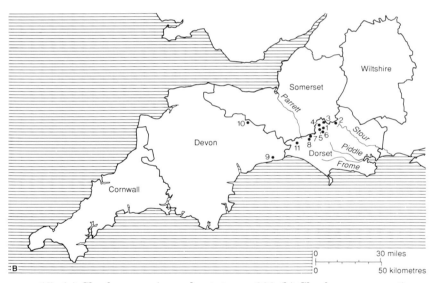

17. (a) Sherborne episcopal estates *c.* 900 (b) Sherborne monastic estates *c.* 1060 [after M.A. O'Donovan, *Charters of Sherborne* (1988), figs. 2 and 3]

termed forgeries were attempts to provide documentation for estates legitimately owned or claimed by the foundation but for which they lacked written title. At the time of monastic revival in the late tenth century Bishop Æthelwold made a concerted effort to recover lost estates for his foundations in Abingdon and Winchester and at this point many of their charters seem to have been 'rewritten' to enhance these claims.[17] Such an effective job was done that it is now impossible to be certain of the exact nature of the pre-tenth-century endowments of these two houses.

EXPANSION TO THE SOUTH AND WEST

From their base in the upper Thames Valley the Gewisse had the potential to expand in several directions, but in practice they found their options limited in the seventh century by the growth in power of the great midland kingdom of Mercia. The *Anglo-Saxon Chronicle* records for 628 that Penda fought Cynegils and Cwichelm [of the Gewisse] and that afterwards they came to terms. The terms were presumably in favour of Penda as it was the Mercians who were to exercise political influence over the Hwicce of Gloucestershire, not the West Saxons. Expansion into Gloucestershire along the Thames Valley would have been an obvious corridor for Gewissan power, and sixth-century cemeteries at Lechlade, Fairford and Kemble (the last only six miles south of Cirencester) are more characteristically Saxon than Anglian and seem to show links with the Dorchester-on-Thames area.[18] But whatever the Gewisse might have achieved in the sixth century, Mercian expansion meant that henceforth their activities in the region were largely confined south of the Thames and Avon, though, as will become apparent, several West Saxon kings endeavoured to exercise overlordship north of the rivers.

The battle at Cirencester is the first recorded instance of a rivalry between the Mercians and West Saxons in the north of our region which was to continue well into the ninth century. One of its first results was to drive the Gewisse into alliance with other powerful enemies of the Mercians. When Cynegils was baptized in 635 Oswald of Northumbria was his sponsor and their alliance was further sealed by the marriage of Oswald to Cynegils's daughter Cyneburh.[19] Cynegils's son and successor Cenwalh was married to a daughter of Penda (possibly this could have been part of the treaty arrangements after the battle of Cirencester), but he repudiated her after his accession in 642 and was subsequently driven out by Penda.[20] Another Mercian enemy, King Anna of the East Angles, gave him protection and after three years Cenwalh was able to return to Wessex. Cenwalh and his brother Centwine, who came to

---

17. Finberg, 'The Winchester Cathedral clergy: their endowments and their diplomatic crimes', in *Early Charters of Wessex*, 214–48; Edwards, *Charters of the Early West Saxon Kingdom*, 166–96 (for Abingdon). See further Ch. 5, 213–15.
18. C. Heighway, *Anglo-Saxon Gloucestershire* (1987), 22–31; D. Miles and S. Palmer, *Invested in Mother Earth: The Anglo-Saxon Cemetery at Lechlade* (1986).
19. *HE*, III, 7.
20. *HE*, III, 7.; P. Sims-Williams, *Religion and Literature in Western England, 600–800* (1990), 27.

the throne in *c.* 676, both also cultivated Northumbrian connections. Cenwalh was apparently on friendly terms with the subking Alhfrith of Deira, son of King Oswiu of Northumbria, and with Benedict Biscop, the founder of Wearmouth and Jarrow.[21] Centwine was married to the sister of Iurminburg, wife of King Egfrith of Northumbria, and because of this connection would not allow the exiled Northumbrian Bishop Wilfrid to stay in his kingdom, though Wilfrid became an important adviser of his successor Cædwalla.[22] King Aldfrith of Northumbria (686–705) married Cuthburh, sister of King Ine of Wessex, and was the godson and correspondent of Abbot Aldhelm of Malmesbury.[23]

Anti-Mercian alliances did not stop the pressure on the upper Thames from Penda (d. 655) and his son Wulfhere (658–75). Wulfhere is recorded in the *Chronicle* in 661 as harrying Ashdown, the chalk downs between Wallingford and Marlborough, and at about the same time the West Saxon bishopric was divided with a new see established at Winchester.[24] According to an account Bede was given, Cenwalh had grown tired of his Frankish bishop's poor command of the Saxon language and had wanted a bishop of his own race. The account does not sound altogether plausible, especially as Cenwalh was happy to appoint Agilbert's nephew Leuthere to Winchester a few years later. Growing Mercian power in the upper Thames is more likely to lie behind both the division of the bishopric and Agilbert's withdrawal from Dorchester shortly after, at which point it ceased to be a West Saxon see.[25] In the early 670s Thame, on a tributary of the River Thames, was being used as a Mercian royal residence[26] and by the end of the decade Dorchester briefly became a Mercian bishopric, presumably for their newly acquired lands in the upper Thames.[27]

Various considerations may have prompted the choice of Winchester for the new Gewissan bishopric, but they are likely to have included the fact that it lay only a few miles from the northern border of the Jutish kingdom in southern Hampshire.[28] Conquest of the Jutish province became a matter of priority in the second half of the seventh century for defensive reasons as much as any other.

---

21. D. Kirby, *The Earliest English Kings* (1991), 58.
22. B. Colgrave (ed.), *The Life of Bishop Wilfrid by Eddius Stephanus* (1927), Ch. 40 and 42.
23. *ASC* A *s.a.* 718; M. Lapidge and M. Herren (trans.), *Aldhelm: The Prose Works* (1979), 32.
24. *HE*, III, 7.
25. Finberg, 'The Winchester clergy', 214–15; B.A.E. Yorke, 'The foundation of the Old Minster and the status of Winchester in the seventh and eighth centuries', *PHFCAS, 38* (1982), 75–84.
26. S 1165/B 34.
27. *HE*, IV, 23; N. Doggett, 'The Anglo-Saxon see and cathedral of Dorchester-on-Thames: the evidence reconsidered', *Oxoniensia, 51* (1986), 49–61.
28. B.A.E. Yorke, 'The Jutes of Hampshire and Wight and the origins of Wessex', in *The Origins of Anglo-Saxon Kingdoms*, ed. S. Bassett (1989), 84–96.

Mercia was not only squeezing the Gewisse from the north, but from the south as well. After he had harried Ashdown in 661, Wulfhere had done the same to the Isle of Wight and then placed the kingdom and the district of the Meonware under the control of King Æthelwalh of the South Saxons.[29] The alliance between Mercia and the South Saxons was further sealed by Æthelwalh receiving baptism through the Mercian court with Wulfhere as his sponsor and marrying a princess of the Hwicce, another Mercian satellite province. The Gewisse were in danger of being surrounded on their southern and eastern flanks by provinces controlled by Mercia. Wulfhere had a free hand with the Meonware in 661, but his apparent failure to deal with the rest of the Hampshire Jutes may indicate that they were already controlled by the Gewisse. The choice of Winchester as the new diocesan centre at about this time implies that the Gewisse were determined that conversion of the bulk of the Hampshire Jutes would be through their bishop not via Mercian missionaries.

Permanent control of both Jutish provinces was achieved by King Cædwalla of the Gewisse (685–8) who, even before his accession, when he was in exile, had raised an army and had attacked and slain King Æthelwalh.[30] After he became king of the Gewisse he captured the Isle of Wight and killed its King Aruald and his two brothers. Cædwalla conquered the province of Surrey as well and was overlord of the South and East Saxons, and for a brief period his brother Mul was king in Kent before he was burnt to death by the Kentishmen.[31] Ine continued his overlordship of Surrey and the South Saxons, but the Jutish kingdoms and the district of the Basingas were the only Anglo-Saxon provinces conquered at this time which are likely to have remained West Saxon throughout the eighth century. These successes against other Germanic groups seem to have marked a significant stage in the growth of Wessex, for it is at this point that Bede begins consistently to refer to the dynasty as 'West Saxons' instead of as 'Gewisse',[32] though Cædwalla and his successor Ine (688–726) seem generally to have used the form 'king of the Saxons' in documents they issued, with the additional 'West' only becoming commonplace in the second half of the eighth century.[33] Between them, Wulfhere, Cædwalla and Ine had altered significantly the political make-up of the south-eastern quarter of England and ended the previous Jutish-Kentish link.

---

29. *HE*, IV, 13; the date of 661 comes from the *Anglo-Saxon Chronicle* entry for that year.
30. *HE*, IV, 15 and 16; Colgrave, *Life of Wilfrid*, Ch. 42.
31. F.M. Stenton, *Anglo-Saxon England* (3rd edn., 1971), 69–73; D. Kirby, *The Earliest English Kings* (1991), 118–22.
32. H.E. Walker, 'Bede and the Gewissae: the political evolution of the Heptarchy and its nomenclature', *Cambridge Historical Journal*, 12 (1956), 174–86, but for some possible earlier uses of the title 'King of the Saxons' see Kirby, *Earliest English Kings*, 20–1.
33. Edwards, *Charters of the Early West Saxon Kingdom*, 309.

Bede implies that the area to the west of the Jutish province in Hampshire was already in the hands of the Gewisse in 685;[34] however, as has already been explained, we cannot trace their expansion to the west in any detail. The fact that the large Northumbrian kingdom was anxious to ally itself with the Gewisse from the 630s implies that the latter were already considered to be in control of a substantial area. The Saxon settlements of the Avon Valley (Wilts) could have come under control of the Gewisse by the end of the sixth century and have been a launching pad for expansion into west Wiltshire and Dorset, while the growth of Mercian influence in Gloucestershire may have encouraged Gewissan expansion south into north Wiltshire and Somerset. Cenwalh (642–72) was claimed as the first Saxon patron of Sherborne (Dorset)[35] and Cenred, another Gewissan king, granted land nearby in Dorset to Abbot Bectun in the early 670s.[36] The earliest reliable charters from Malmesbury (N. Wilts)[37] and Glastonbury (N. Som)[38] date from the reign of Centwine (676–85). The *Life of St Boniface* implies that West Saxon control must have reached as far as Exeter by about 680 when the young Boniface was entered into the monastery there under an English abbot.[39] These pointers are quite inadequate for any narrative of how the Gewissan kings came to dominate the British areas of the west, but they are sufficient to show that much of the region of Wessex was at least nominally under the control of the Gewissan dynasty by the time Ine came to the throne in 688. However, it is unlikely that the whole of Devon was firmly part of Wessex this early, as battles with the British of Dumnonia continued throughout the eighth century with varying fortunes for the West Saxons including losses of territory previously gained.[40] Nor were all other borders finally established, as the history of the northern borders of Wessex shows.

---

34. *HE*, IV, 16; Yorke, 'Jutes', 90.
35. H.P.R. Finberg, 'Sherborne, Glastonbury, and the expansion of Wessex', in *Lucerna. Studies of Some Problems in the Early History of England* (1964), 95–115, especially 97–9; O'Donovan, *Charters of Sherborne*, xliii–iv, 3 and 81–8.
36. S 1164/B 107; Edwards, *Charters of the Early West Saxon Kingdom*, 229–34. The charter is preserved in a cartulary of Shaftesbury Abbey, but it is not clear where Bectun's monastery lay.
37. S 71/B 59 (681); S 1169/B 65 (685); S 1170/B 71 (676×86). S 1245/B 37, which cannot be accepted as genuine as it stands, provides the date of 675 for the appointment of Aldhelm as abbot of Malmesbury.
38. S 236/B 61; S 237/B 62.
39. W. Levison (ed.), *Vitae Sancti Bonifatii, MGH Scriptores Rerum Germanicarum* (Hanover, 1905), Ch. 1; translated in C.H. Talbot (trans.), *The Anglo-Saxon Missionaries in Germany* (1954), 28.
40. Finberg, 'Expansion of Wessex', 99–105.

THE NORTHERN BORDERS OF WESSEX

Right through the seventh and eighth centuries the Gewisse had to defend their northern borders from Mercian encroachments and their shared boundaries fluctuated depending on the relative power of the two kingdoms. Although in the ninth century the Avon and Thames served as boundaries, it would appear that they were only used as such for limited periods in the seventh and eighth centuries and that the rulers of both kingdoms aimed to control swathes of land on either side of their banks. Some significant battles are recorded in the *Anglo-Saxon Chronicle*, but the most sensitive indicators of changing fortunes are the records of grants to religious communities close to the borders.

When Christianity was spreading through the Anglo-Saxon kingdoms in the second half of the seventh century, the River Avon seems to have been the boundary between the Hwicce and the Gewisse.[41] Malmesbury on the Wiltshire bank of the Avon was founded (or taken over) by Gewissan rulers, while Bath, on the opposite bank of the Avon, was initially patronized by Hwiccian rulers and their Mercian overlords.[42] Neither camp saw the river as an immutable boundary. In the 680s Malmesbury received land grants from Baldred, a West Saxon subking,[43] and from Cenfrith and Berhtwald, respectively kinsman and nephew of King Æthelred of Mercia, who held a comparable delegated authority.[44] The patronage of religious houses in areas which they hoped to take over was a Mercian policy which can be paralleled elsewhere.[45] Although Malmesbury's position in a border zone meant that it might benefit from the patronage of both sides, there were clearly potential dangers as well. Aldhelm, abbot of Malmesbury, obtained a grant of privileges from Pope Sergius I which he got both Ine of Wessex and Æthelred of Mercia to ratify and further secured their agreement that Malmesbury should not suffer in wars between the two kingdoms.[46] Ine's grants to Glastonbury and Malmesbury imply

---

41. A.H. Smith, 'The Hwicce', in *Medieval and Linguistic Studies in Honor of Francis Peabody Magoun Jr*, ed. J.B. Bessinger and R.P. Creed (1965), 56–65; D. Hooke, *The Anglo-Saxon Landscape: The Kingdom of the Hwicce* (1985), 13–16; Sims-Williams, *Religion and Literature*, 383–5.
42. For Malmesbury see Ch. 4, 162–3. For Bath see C.S. Taylor, 'Bath, Mercian and West Saxon', *Transactions of the Bristol and Gloucestershire Archaeological Society, 23* (1900), 129–61; and P. Sims-Williams, 'Continental influence at Bath monastery in the seventh century', *ASE*, 4 (1975), 1–10.
43. S 1170/B 71; the transaction may also be referred to in a letter from Aldhelm to Wynberht – Lapidge and Herren, *Aldhelm: The Prose Works*, 151, and Edwards, *Charters of the Early West Saxon Kingdom*, 94–7.
44. S 71/B 59 (Cenfrith); S 1169/B 65 (Berhtwald). For Berhtwald see Colgrave, *Life of Wilfrid*, Ch. 40.
45. B.A.E. Yorke, *Kings and Kingdoms of Early Anglo-Saxon England* (1990), 107–11.
46. B 105 and 106; H. Edwards, 'Two documents from Aldhelm's Malmesbury', *Bulletin of the Institute of Historical Research, 59* (1986), 1–19.

that he was fully in control of northern Somerset and Wiltshire during his reign,[47] but developments in subsequent reigns show that Aldhelm's precautions were justified.

Although it seems that the Gewisse were originally based in the upper Thames Valley, as we have seen, they were forced out by the Mercian expansion in the course of the seventh century and their new north-eastern boundary is hard to establish with any precision, but for a time at least it may have been marked by 'Ashdown', the line of Marlborough/Berkshire Downs. It has generally been assumed that Ine recovered control of northern Berkshire as far as the Thames, but a major plank for this contention, his patronage of Abingdon Abbey, has been removed by a recent rereading of the relevant charters which has shown instead that they relate to a minster at Bradfield in southern Berkshire.[48] The *Chronicle* is enigmatic about the reasons and outcome of a battle Ine fought with Æthelred's son King Ceolred at Woden's barrow near Wansdyke on the southern edge of the Wiltshire Downs, but it may well have been connected with control of the Vale of the White Horse, the area between the Downs and the Thames.

West Saxon fortunes in its northern territories continued to fluctuate after the death of Ine. In 733 King Æthelbald of Mercia invaded deep into the heart of Somerset and occupied Somerton. The invasion established Mercian overlordship of the West Saxon kings Æthelheard and his successor Cuthred, who seem to have been obliged to accompany Æthelbald on military expeditions against the Welsh.[49] Æthelbald also put himself in a position to dispose of land in the north of Wessex. The monastery of Cookham in east Berkshire was given to Christ Church, Canterbury, by Æthelbald,[50] and he was a patron of Glastonbury (Som) where his confirmation seems to have been necessary for grants from West Saxons.[51] Cuthred tried to reassert his independence in the early 750s,[52] but in 757 his successor Cynewulf was obliged to witness a grant from Æthelbald to Malmesbury of land at Tockenham (N. Wilts).[53] The implication of these grants by Æthelbald in northern Wessex is that he had taken lands there directly under his control.

757 was also the year of Æthelbald's murder and Cynewulf was able to take advantage of the hiatus of power in Mercia to retrieve territory in northern Wessex and annex land in the Hwiccian province which by this time was in the process of being absorbed

47. Edwards, *Charters of the Early West Saxon Kingdom*, 23–34, 105–14.
48. Edwards, *Charters*, 168–76; an edition of the charters is being prepared by Susan Kelly. See also J. Blair, *Anglo-Saxon Oxfordshire* (1994), 59–60.
49. See S 93/B 155 and *Chronicle* A *s.a.* 743 and interpretation by Kirby, *Earliest English Kings*, 133–4.
50. S 1258/B 291.
51. S 238/B 121; S 1410/B 168.
52. *HE Continuatio s.a.* 750 records the rebellion of Cuthred against Æthelbald.
53. S 96/B 181; Sims-Williams, *Religion and Literature*, 225–8.

into Mercia. He bribed two members of the Archbishop of Canterbury's household to steal the title-deeds of Cookham for him and took over the monastery and the proceeds of its estates for himself.[54] He granted land freely in Wiltshire,[55] and his grant to Bath of land north of the Avon suggests he was trying to establish claims to that area.[56] However, in 779 Cynewulf and Offa of Mercia fought at Bensington on the Thames and Cynewulf evidently lost and was forced to cede the *tun* and other territory to the victor.[57] Offa took over Cookham for himself and, according to a later Abingdon chronicler, he ruled 'all the country between the Icknield Way from Wallingford to Ashbury on the south and the River Thames on the north', which would seem to imply that the whole of what became Berkshire was under his control.[58] An estate at Tetbury (Gloucs) which Æthelred of Mercia had granted to Malmesbury was rescinded and came into the possession of the bishop of Worcester.[59] Bath was taken back and as part of an agreement between Offa and the bishop of Worcester at the synod of Brentford in 781 came under the control of the king himself as a proprietary monastery. Its endowment included 30 hides south of the river in Somerset which Cynewulf had been obliged to sell to the bishop of Worcester. Offa's interest in Bath was no doubt stimulated by its strategic position in relation to Wessex.[60]

Beorhtric, who succeeded Cynewulf as king of the West Saxons in 786, seems to have been Offa's man and in 789 married his daughter Eadburh who, judging by the accounts Asser received in the reign of Alfred, seems likely to have been an active representative of Mercian interests at the West Saxon court.[61] He appears to have been similarly subordinate to his brother-in-law Egfrith who came to the throne in 796 and whose court at Bath he attended in that year.[62] Beorhtric used his influence to have an estate at Purton (Wilts) which had been confiscated by Offa restored to Malmesbury,[63] but also seems to have agreed that the monastery at Glastonbury should come under the control of Cynehelm, a lay

---

54. S 1258/B 291; N. Brooks, *The Early History of the Church of Canterbury* (1984), 103–4.
55. S 260/B 185.
56. S 265/B 327; Taylor, 'Bath, Mercian and West Saxon', 129–61.
57. *ASC* 779 (*s.a.* 777).
58. F.M. Stenton, *The Early History of the Abbey of Abingdon* (1913), 23–5; Blair, *Anglo-Saxon Oxfordshire*, 54–5; M. Gelling, *The Place-Names of Berkshire. Part III*, EPNS, *51* (1976), 839–40.
59. William of Malmesbury, *GP*, 388.
60. S 1257/B 241; Taylor, 'Bath, Mercian and West Saxon'; Sims-Williams, *Religion and Literature*, 159–65.
61. *ASC* 789; for Eadburh and West Saxon subordination to Mercia see Asser, Ch. 14–15.
62. S 148/B 277.
63. S 149/B 279.

member of the Mercian royal house.[64] Before the end of 796 Cynehelm's father Cenwulf had succeeded Egfrith as king of Mercia and a papal privilege confirmed Cynehelm's ownership of Glastonbury. Berkshire also remained a Mercian dependency under Cenwulf. A synod held at *Clofesho* in 798 confirmed Cynethryth (probably the widow of Offa) in possession of Cookham.[65] Two sisters of Cenwulf are said to have lived at Culham, to have left the estate to Abingdon and to have been buried in its church.[66]

Beorhtric died in 802 and, on the very same day that Egbert succeeded to the throne of Wessex, the Hwicce and the men of Wiltshire under their respective ealdormen fought a battle from which the Wilsætan emerged as victors.[67] The battle seems to have decided that north Wiltshire and Somerset would be finally recognized as part of Wessex and no more is heard of Glastonbury as a family monastery of the Mercian royal house. The boundary between Wessex and the province of the Hwicce seems to have returned to what it was in the late seventh century with Bath and its monastery remaining Mercian possessions for the time being; King Burgred of Mercia held a court there in 864.[68] Berkshire – or at least a significant part of it – remained a Mercian possession for the first half of the ninth century and was probably integrated with the rest of Wessex in the reign of Æthelwulf (839–58).[69]

THE NATURE OF CONQUEST

The sources available for the expansion of Wessex are not particularly informative on how conquest was achieved and maintained or how conquerors and the conquered coexisted. However, by viewing their information in the broader context of early Anglo-Saxon England as a whole, it is possible to understand something of the processes involved. Outright conquest, in the sense of the permanent absorption of one province by another, was rarely achieved as the result of a single battle and might only be obtained after many years of fluctuating relationships. There was a difference between establishing overlordship over a subordinate province and actually incorporating it into the parent kingdom. When an overlordship was established the underking was obliged to acknowledge his inferiority and pay tribute to his overlord, but the latter would not

---

64. S 152/B 285; W. Levison, *England and the Continent in the Eighth Century* (1946), 32, 251.
65. S 1258/B 291.
66. A.T. Thacker, 'Æthelwold and Abingdon', in *Bishop Æthelwold: His Career and Influence*, ed. B.A.E. Yorke (1988), 45.
67. *ASC* 802.
68. Taylor, 'Bath, Mercian and West Saxon': Sims-Williams, *Religion and Literature* 384–5.
69. Stenton, *The Abbey of Abingdon*, 24–9, and see Ch. 3, 95–6.

necessarily have the ability to interfere in the internal affairs of the underkingdom.[70] In the late sixth and seventh centuries the most powerful military leaders, among whom Ceawlin of the Gewisse is to be counted, seem to have been able to establish wide-ranging, but superficial, overlordships of this type.[71] But for most of the seventh and eighth centuries the West Saxon kings had to acknowledge the overlordship of more powerful kings from either Northumbria or Mercia, though Cædwalla (685–8) and Ine (688–725) were both overlords of other kingdoms in the south. Bede recounts how in 626 King Cwichelm of Wessex sent an assassin with a poisoned sword to murder Edwin of Northumbria who was currently overlord of the southern kingdoms.[72] The assassination attempt failed and, in the words of Bede:

> When in due course the king had been healed of his wound, he summoned his army and marched against the West Saxons. During the course of the campaign he either slew all whom he discovered to have plotted his death or forced them to surrender.

According to the northern recension of the *Anglo-Saxon Chronicle* five West Saxon kings were killed by Edwin. Overlords, it would seem, might act decisively to deal with any threats to their power even if it involved operating some way outside their core area. They might also in certain circumstances oblige subject kings to join with them on military campaigns. Ine took Nothhelm of the South Saxons on his campaign against King Geraint of Dumnonia in 710,[73] but in the middle decades of the eighth century when the West Saxons were subject to Mercian overlordship Æthelheard and Cuthred seem to have been obliged to serve with Æthelbald of Mercia against the Welsh.[74]

Overlords might find various opportunities to increase their hold on subject kings. When Oswald of Northumbria stood as sponsor to King Cynegils at the latter's baptism in 635, the relative status of the two men was clearly articulated and the position of godfather enhanced Oswald's hold over Cynegils.[75] According to Bede the two men were joint founders of the first West Saxon see at Dorchester-

---

70. P. Wormald, 'Bede, *Bretwaldas* and the origins of the *Gens Anglorum*', in *Ideal and Reality in Frankish and Anglo-Saxon Society*, ed. P. Wormald, D. Bullough and R. Collins (1983), 99–129; Yorke, *Kings and Kingdoms*, 157–62.
71. *HE*, II, 5.
72. *HE*, II, 9.
73. *ASC* A 710; Nothhelm is described as Ine's kinsman, but this could be through marriage.
74. See n. 49.
75. A. Angenendt, 'The conversion of the Anglo-Saxons considered against the background of the early medieval mission', *Angli e Sassoni al di qua e al di la del Mare, Spoleto Settimane di Studio, 32* (1986), II, 747–81.

on-Thames.[76] Subsequently Oswald married a daughter of Cynegils. However, links between greater and lesser kings could be more complicated than a simple one-to-one relationship. In 661 when Wulfhere of Mercia was the dominant overlord in southern England he placed the Meonware and the Isle of Wight under the intermediary overlordship of the king of the South Saxons. The result was three tiers of overlordship, with the king of Wight being subject to the king of the South Saxons who was himself the underking of the king of Mercia.[77] Although the sources do not clearly say so, it is likely that in the seventh century many of the West Saxon kings were in an analogous position in which they were obliged to recognize the authority of Northumbrian or Mercian overlords, but also had other Germanic and British leaders subject to them.

An essential prerequisite for the permanent acquisition of a subject province was the removal of the provincial royal house. In spite of many years of subjection to Mercian overlords, in the seventh and eighth centuries the West Saxon kings never seem to have been in danger of suffering such a fate; presumably the province was too large to make the attempt feasible. It was a fate though that they were prepared to deal out to their own subject areas. In 686, when Cædwalla invaded the Isle of Wight, he had the king and his two brothers put to death and the island came permanently under West Saxon control from that time.[78] No doubt other rulers, both Germanic and Celtic, suffered similar fates, but have gone unrecorded. The tactic was not always successful. Cædwalla also invaded Kent and tried to establish his brother Mul as king in place of the native royal house, but Mul was burnt to death by the Kentishmen after only a short period in power. Cædwalla's successor Ine received compensation for the murder, but had no power in Kent which was too far from his securely held territory. Ine was more successful in holding on to Surrey which had also been one of Cædwalla's conquests, but later in the eighth century Surrey was lost to Mercia, which was similarly interested in acquiring it, and had controlled it previously.[79]

Such considerations underline how hard it is to interpret correctly the enigmatic references to battles against the British in the *Chronicle* annals for the seventh century. Battles might be fought to impose overlordship, gain territory or visit retribution; they might be fought on land that was already 'West Saxon' or some way outside secure boundaries. Battles could bring permanent results,

---

76. *HE*, III, 7.
77. *HE*, IV 13; J. Campbell, *Essays in Anglo-Saxon History* (1986), 91–2.
78. *HE*, IV, 16.
79. Stenton, *Anglo-Saxon England*, 69–73. For Surrey see J. Blair, *Early Medieval Surrey. Landholding, Church and Settlement* (1991). Reconciliation of the West Saxons and Kent had been eased by Theodore's reconciliation with Wilfrid, Cædwalla's adviser – Kirby, *Earliest English Kings*, 120–1.

but success might equally be short-lived depending upon the relative strength of the two powers, the proximity of their borders and the interests of powerful neighbours. Too often we are not given enough information to establish which of these criteria applied to West Saxon battles. It would be a mistake to see the growth of Wessex as a simple linear progression; what we can trace in detail is far more complex with fluctuating borders and varying political status *vis-à-vis* other kingdoms. One should also not assume that the kings of Dumnonia were much less troublesome neighbours than the Mercians simply because we hear less about them.

One factor which does emerge clearly is that warfare was an essential ingredient of political success. Early medieval armies need not be large; the army with which Cyneheard hoped to overthrow King Cynewulf in 786 apparently consisted of 84 men.[80] The West Saxon royal army probably numbered no more than a few hundred at most, but such forces could inflict considerable damage on peoples they wished to bully into surrender. It was not just opposing kings and their armies who suffered the brutalities of war. We are told that the unfortunate inhabitants of the Isle of Wight were harried by Wulfhere of Mercia in 661, presumably to encourage them to submit to his authority.[81] Just over twenty years later they received similar treatment from Cædwalla.[82] Almost a century later King Cynewulf of Wessex made a grant to Wells to compensate for harassment from the Cornish enemy, presumably a reference to a raid into Somerset organized by the king of Dumnonia.[83] Non-combatants if they were not slain by ravaging enemy forces might be carried off to become slaves. Such may have been the fate of a Kentish girl who became a slave of the abbot of Glastonbury and was the subject of a letter to Bishop Forthhere of Sherborne from Archbishop Brihtwold of Canterbury who was trying to intervene on behalf of her family to secure her release in return for a ransom.[84]

With such small resources of manpower available, areas the West Saxons wished to conquer could not be permanently garrisoned. Bede's account of the conquest of the Isle of Wight refers to Cædwalla endeavouring 'to wipe out all the natives by merciless slaughter and to replace them by inhabitants from his own kingdom'.[85] Such actions may have been more commonplace than we would prefer to believe and Bede ascribes a similar policy to Æthelfrith of Northumbria during his expansion of territory.[86] Whether there were massacres or not, some movement of settlers

---

80. *ASC s.a.* 757; see further below.
81. *ASC s.a.* 661.
82. *HE*, IV, 16.
83. S 262/B 200.
84. *EHD*, I, 794–5.
85. *HE*, IV, 16.
86. *HE*, I, 34.

was no doubt necessary when establishing permanent control and the laws of Ine seem to envisage the likelihood of men moving from one place to another; nobles were allowed to take with them their reeve, smith and children's nurse, and guidelines were given for the state in which cultivated land should be left.[87] The parents of Boniface, who reputedly settled at Crediton in Devon in the second half of the seventh century, are presumably examples of first-generation settlers.[88] Individual families of this type would not be easy to trace archaeologically and the best hope of recognizing them is probably through their graves, though even this resource becomes less useful in the course of the seventh century as distinctive grave-goods and burial customs became less pronounced after conversion to Christianity. However, various small cemeteries of Saxon type, apparently dating to the late seventh or early eighth centuries, from north-east Dorset and the Dorchester area may well be those of Anglo-Saxon settlers.[89] The ability of West Saxon kings to move their subjects from place to place is implied by the rapid growth of Hamwic in the early eighth century.[90] This was a planned settlement likely to have numbered at least two or three thousand by the middle of the eighth century and it is inconceivable that such a large of body of people could have been brought together without royal involvement. It is situated in the centre of the former Jutish kingdom in Hampshire and within easy reach of the Isle of Wight. It is tempting to speculate that one of Ine's solutions for controlling the former Jutish lands (for the archaeological dating implies it was founded during his reign) was to concentrate some of their inhabitants in a planned settlement which could be closely supervised.

It would have been impossible to replace all Britons and subject Germanic peoples with 'Saxons' even if the West Saxon rulers had desired such a melodramatic solution. The dominance of the Old English language and Old English place-names might superficially seem to suggest a plurality of Anglo-Saxon settlers, but such an interpretation would be misleading. As in eastern Wessex, the process of place-naming was a gradual one and the majority of habitation names are not recorded until Domesday Book by which time Anglo-Saxon linguistic and administrative dominance had been established for many generations. Unfortunately there have not been any recent detailed studies of place-names in Devon, Somerset or Dorset, but it would appear that the survival of Celtic names was higher than in the three eastern shires of Wessex. This

---

87. 'Laws of Ine', in F.L. Attenborough (ed.), *The Laws of the Earliest English Kings* (1922), Ch. 63–6.
88. See n. 39.
89. C.J.S. Green, 'Early Anglo-Saxon burials at the "Trumpet Major" public house, Allington Avenue, Dorchester', *PDNHAS, 106* (1984), 148–52.
90. A.D. Morton, *Excavations in Hamwic: Volume 1*, CBA res. rep., *84* (1992), and see Ch. 7, 302–7.

is well illustrated by Kenneth Jackson's classic map of British river-names which shows a much denser concentration of Celtic river-names in western Wessex than in the east (fig. 18).[91] We also find clusters of settlements which all share the name of a British river which runs through their lands, such as the Cerne (Dorset) and Clyst (Devon) villages. They reflect the Celtic practice of naming settlements from a nearby river and may also be the remnants of large estates bearing river-names which were divided up in the late Saxon period. A comparable large estate is that of 'Pouholt' granted by King Æthelheard to Glastonbury Abbey in 729.[92] The name may be derived from Celtic *bo gwelt*, 'cattle pasture'. In the later Saxon period the estate was divided into a number of smaller units all with Old English names and that of 'Pouholt' fell out of use altogether (see fig. 70). Before Old English became the dominant language there is likely to have been a bilingual period. The bounds of another Glastonbury charter describes a hill as 'called in the British language *Cructan*, but among us *Crycbeorh*',[93] and when Asser wrote his *Life of King Alfred* he was able to provide both Celtic and Saxon names for many places in the west.

Though it is likely that even after the Saxon take-over, the majority of people living in western Wessex were of Celtic descent, so far there has been little archaeological evidence to support the contention. Much interest has focused on five inscribed memorial stones with similarities to those found in Dumnonia, which were discovered built into the piers of the south arcade of the nave when the greater part of the Saxon minster at Wareham was demolished in 1841 (fig. 19).[94] All are cut into Romano-British architectural fragments probably from a nearby Roman villa, and are usually dated to the seventh and eighth centuries, though these dates may need to be re-examined in the light of Elisabeth Okasha's reservations about being able to date the Dumnonian stones with any precision.[95] It is unlikely that they were erected to commemorate ninth-century Breton refugees as has sometimes been claimed, for the different letter-forms suggest they are of varying dates and that some must be earlier than the ninth century.[96] The Wareham stones are more likely to have come from a Celtic burial

91. K. Jackson, *Language and History in Early Britain* (1953), 219–29.
92. S 253/B 147; N. Corcos, 'Early estates on the Poldens and the origin of settlement at Shapwick', *PSANHS*, 127 (1982), 47–54.
93. S 237/B 62; M. Costen, *The Origins of Somerset* (1992), 60–1.
94. R.A.S. Macalister, *Corpus Inscriptionum Insularum Celticarum*, II (Dublin, 1949), 188–9; C.A.R. Radford and K. Jackson, 'Early Christian inscriptions', in *An Inventory of Historical Monuments in the County of Dorset, II South-East* (1970), 304–12.
95. D. Hinton, 'The inscribed stones in Lady St Mary Church, Wareham', *PDNHAS*, 114 (1992), 260; E. Okasha, *Corpus of Early Christian Inscribed Stones of South-West Britain* (1993).
96. E. McClure, 'The Wareham inscriptions', *EHR*, 22 (1907), 728–30; Hinton, 'Inscribed stones'.

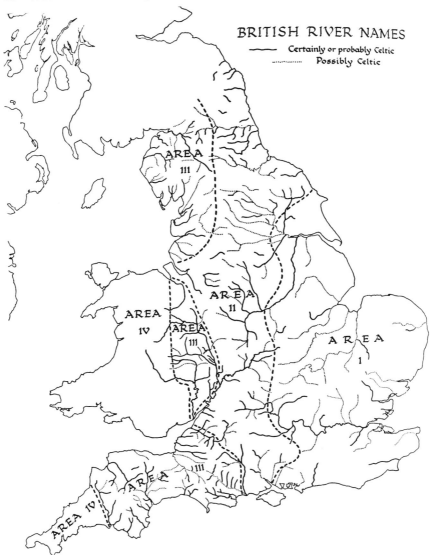

18. Distribution of British river-names [K. Jackson, *Language and History in Early Britain* (1953), 220, with permission of Edinburgh University Press]

ground which preceded the Saxon minster in existence by 802 when King Beorhtric was buried there. They imply the presence of prominent British Christians with Celtic names and commemorated in a traditional British manner after the official conquest of the area by Anglo-Saxons, and the survival of Celtic culture is

CATGUG. C...
[FI] LIUS. GIDEO

GONGORIE

IUDNNE...
FIL[I] QUI...

[D]ENIEL FI[LIUS]
...AUPRIT IA[CET]

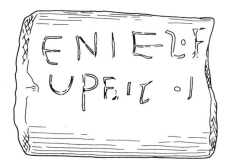

VIDCV...
FILIVS VIDA...

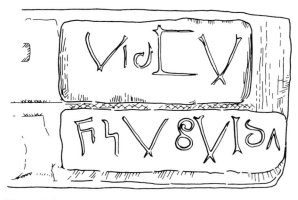

19. Memorial stones from the church of St Mary, Wareham (Dorset)
[after C.A.R. Radford and K. Jackson, 'Early Christian Inscriptions',
in *An Inventory of Historical Monuments in the County of Dorset. II,
South-East*, RCHM (1970) and R. Moorcroft in *The Church of Lady St
Mary, Wareham* (1989), 6–8]

consistent with the lack of early or middle Saxon material from the Isle of Purbeck.[97]

King Ine's laws legislate for his British as well as his Germanic subjects and reveal one stage in the process of assimilation. Ine's laws survive as an appendix to the laws of King Alfred and so the question arises of whether they were revised in the late ninth century. There are linguistic arguments in favour of some revision, but it is also the case that some of Alfred's promulgations differ from those of Ine which might suggest that Ine's original decrees have been preserved.[98] The British are second-class citizens in Ine's Wessex. Their wergilds (price payable in compensation if killed) are half that of Englishmen and their oaths also count for less.[99] On the other hand, the fact that they have wergilds shows that they were entitled to the king's protection like his other subjects and it is envisaged that they can pursue accusations against Anglo-Saxons. Their social order is presented as similar to that of the Anglo-Saxons, with slaves at the bottom, different classes of peasant and freemen, with and without land, and nobles generally owning land of five hides or more. Britons in the service of the king as horse-riding messengers had the same wergild as Anglo-Saxon freemen.[100] The potential for full integration of the two communities is there and had apparently been achieved by the laws of Alfred where no racial differences are acknowledged. No doubt royal service and inter-marriage helped blur distinctions.

Above all the West Saxons would have wanted peace and continuity from their conquered populations so that they could exploit them as a resource. A key feature of overlordship was the ability to collect tribute from conquered provinces, but when areas were brought under more permanent control kings claimed *feorm* (food rents) instead–a subtle change from payments imposed by a victorious overlord to those given 'voluntarily' to help support a ruler's duties.[101] We unfortunately have no details of what the early West Saxon rulers either paid or received as tribute, but in the tenth century King Athelstan is supposed to have exacted an annual payment from subject Welsh kings of gold, silver, hounds, hawks and oxen, which gives some idea of what is likely to have been involved.[102] Such tributes were an important means by which

---

97. B. Eagles, 'The archaeological evidence for settlement in the fifth to seventh centuries', in *Medieval Settlement in Wessex*, ed. M. Aston and C. Lewis (forthcoming).
98. M. Richards, 'The manuscript contexts of the Old English laws: tradition and innovation', in *Studies in Earlier Old English Prose*, ed. P. Szarmach (Albany NY, 1986), 171–92.
99. Attenborough, 'Laws of Ine', Ch. 23.3, 24.2, 32, 46.1, 54.2, and see Ch. 6, 259–60.
100. Attenborough, 'Laws of Ine', Ch. 33.
101. T.M. Charles-Edwards, 'Early medieval kingships in the British Isles', in *The Origins of Anglo-Saxon Kingdoms*, ed. S. Bassett (1989), 28–39.
102. William of Malmesbury, *GP*, I, 148; W. Davies, *Wales in the Early Middle Ages* (1982), 114.

kings acquired luxury materials and items which they needed to obtain the support of their military followers who enabled them to stay in power. Ine's laws define the amount of food rent payable from ten hides of land:[103]

> 10 vats of honey, 300 loaves, 12 ambers of Welsh ale, 30 of clear ale, 2 full-grown cows or 10 wethers, 10 geese, 20 hens, 10 cheeses, an amber full of butter, 5 salmon, 20 pounds of fodder and 100 eels.

Even allowing for the difficulties in interpreting the measures, it can be seen that this was not an inconsiderable amount to be paid annually from what can loosely be thought of as ten farmsteads (Bede defines a hide as *terra unius familiae*, land sufficient to support one family).[104]

The hide was used as the basic unit of assessment for all sorts of purposes throughout Anglo-Saxon England. In Wessex, as in other Anglo-Saxon provinces, estates granted in the earliest surviving charters are measured in hides and it would appear that a system of hidage assessments must have been in place before our written records begin. A document known as the 'Tribal Hidage' gives hidage assessments for the different provinces in England south of the Humber.[105] It is generally interpreted as a list drawn up to enable one of the great Northumbrian or Mercian overlords of the seventh century to exact tribute payments, but like many of our early documents it only survives copied into much later manuscripts so its date and provenance are controversial. The West Saxons are assessed at 100,000 hides which is substantially higher than the next largest assessments (30,000 each for Mercia and the East Angles) and out of line with the use of multiples of 300 which are used for most of the calculations. It has been suggested that it could be an exceptionally high penal imposition,[106] but it is also possible that it is an alteration or addition to the original text, perhaps to reflect the later greatness of Wessex, and it does not appear in one of the recensions of the text.[107] Also included in the 'Tribal Hidage' are the 'Wihtgara' assessed at 600 hides who are presumably the inhabitants of the Isle of Wight. Bede's account of the conquest of Wight by Cædwalla gives the assessment for the

---

103. Attenborough, 'Laws of Ine', Ch. 70.1.
104. T.M. Charles-Edwards, 'Kinship, status and the origins of the hide', *Past and Present*, 56 (1972), 3–33; H.R. Loyn, *The Governance of Anglo-Saxon England, 500–1087* (1984), 36–40.
105. B 297; W. Davies and H. Vierck, 'The contexts of Tribal Hidage; social aggregates and settlement patterns', *Frühmittelalterliche Studien, 8* (1974), 223–93; D.N. Dumville, 'The Tribal Hidage: an introduction to its texts and their history', in *The Origins of Anglo-Saxon Kingdoms*, ed. S. Bassett (1989), 225–30.
106. C. Hart, 'The Tribal Hidage', *TRHS, 21* (1971), 133–57; at 156–7.
107. P. Sawyer, *From Roman Britain to Norman England* (1978), 111.

island as 1,200 hides, that is exactly twice the 'Tribal Hidage' entry.[108] A doubling of the normal figure could be seen as in keeping with Cædwalla's harsh treatment of the island. It would appear that the West Saxons inherited a hidage assessment for the Isle of Wight which they used as the basis for their own exactions, and no doubt they took over similar units of assessment elsewhere.

The laws of Ine seem to envisage Wessex divided into ten-hide units for payment of food rent. In fact lands granted in early charters generally seem to have been arranged in rather larger units of assessment of which ten-hide units or similar would be component parts. One of the best examples of this type of arrangement, from an early charter whose authenticity is not in doubt, is the grant by Cædwalla in 688 of a 60-hide estate at Farnham in Surrey for the foundation of a minster.[109] The 60 hides is defined as being divided among a number of subdivisions – 10 at Binton, 2 at Churt etc. (the patience of the copyist seems to have run out at this point). Farnham had become the property of the see of Winchester by about 800 and the estate retained its integrity as a unit controlled from Farnham as its manorial and hundredal centre, but made up of a number of component settlements.[110] Surrey, of course, is not one of the shires we are primarily concerned with, though the basic similarities between the organization of western Surrey and eastern Berkshire and Hampshire have already been described.[111] Unfortunately none of our Wessex shires has surviving charters which demonstrate early estate organization and its continuity quite as clearly as that for Farnham, but an estate granted by Ine to Abbot Aldhelm of Malmesbury sounds of very similar type. Aldhelm received 45 hides just to the south of Malmesbury which consisted of 5 hides at Garsdon, 20 hides at the source of the Gauze Brook, 10 in another place by the Gauze Brook and 10 hides at Rodbourne.[112] These units of Middle Saxon civil administration (often, rather misleadingly, called 'multiple estates') also seem to have formed the earliest 'minster' parishes in many instances, and so the reconstruction of ecclesiastical boundaries has been used to help suggest their original distribution.[113] Some seem to have been identical in extent with later hundreds, but the term 'hundred' is not found before the early tenth century by which time many estates had begun to be split up.[114]

---

108. *HE*, IV, 16.
109. B 72/S 235; *EHD*, I, 445.
110. Campbell, *Essays in Anglo-Saxon History*, 110–12; Blair, *Early Medieval Surrey*, 25.
111. See Ch. 1, 40–3.
112. B 103/S 243; Edwards, *Charters of the Early West Saxon Kingdom*, 105–7.
113. P.H. Hase, 'The development of the parish in Hampshire' (Ph. D. thesis, Cambridge University, 1975); see further Ch. 4, 181–7.
114. H. Cam, *Liberties and Communities in Medieval England* (1944), 64–106; see further Ch. 3, 124–9.

The organization of settlements for purposes of assessment into large estates supervised from a central place seems not only to have been an essential feature of Anglo-Saxon Wessex. Regional studies have demonstrated the existence of a broadly similar organization of 'multiple estates' over much of early medieval Britain.[115] They are as much a characteristic of Celtic areas as Anglo-Saxon and the age and origin of the estate system is open to debate. Desmond Bonney has argued that some estate boundaries in areas of dense Iron Age settlement in Wiltshire may be pre-Roman in date because they are randomly bisected by the Roman road network in contrast to other areas of Wiltshire which have sparse Iron Age settlement where Roman roads are often used as estate and parish boundaries.[116] The latter must obviously post-date the laying out of the Roman roads and Bonney argues that the former must equally pre-date the Roman road system as any *de novo* creation of boundaries in the Roman period or later would surely have made use of such obvious landscape features as Roman roads. The putative Iron Age estates in Wiltshire are centred on the valleys of rivers, such as the Wylye and the Avon, and are typically long and thin, running from the downland ridges to the rivers themselves. Land units of similar type can be found in southern Hampshire and adjoining areas of Dorset where they are also based around river valleys and incorporate a variety of land types. Such obvious units of agricultural exploitation may also have had a long history and may have been controlled from hill-forts situated in each river valley in the Iron Age.[117] Other commentators have argued for continuity into the early Middle Ages of estates controlled from a Roman villa.[118]

The administrative estates of Wessex *could* have had a very long history before they were utilized by the West Saxons, which is not to say that all *must* have done.[119] The antiquity of estate structures cannot be proved decisively in the absence of written records indicating boundaries from Iron Age or Roman Britain. Areas of good agricultural land would have always attracted dense settlement and demands for a variety of lands for different agricultural

---

115. G.R.J. Jones, 'Multiple estates and early settlements', in *Medieval Settlement*, ed. P. Sawyer (1976), 11–40; for a critique of the 'model' as proposed by Jones, see N. Gregson, 'The multiple estate model: some critical questions', *Journal of Historical Geography*, 11 (1985), 339–51.
116. D. Bonney, 'Early boundaries in Wessex', in *Archaeology and the Landscape*, ed. P. Fowler (1972), 168–86.
117. B. Cunliffe, *Iron Age Communities in Britain* (1974), 260–3.
118. H.P.R. Finberg, 'Roman and Saxon Withington', in *Lucerna. Studies of some Problems in the Early History of England* (1964), 21–65; S. Pearce, 'Estates and church sites in Dorset and Gloucestershire: the emergence of a Christian society', in *The Early Church in Western Britain and Ireland*, ed. S. Pearce, BAR, *102* (1982), 117–43.
119. D. Hooke, 'Regional variation in southern and central England in the Anglo-Saxon period and its relationship to land units and development', in *Anglo-Saxon Settlements*, ed. D. Hooke (1988), 123–52.

purposes could have been similar in the Iron Age, Roman and Saxon periods. There is a danger in confusing similarity of land exploitation at different periods with continuity of forms of ownership or of administration of that land. The immediate inheritance of the seventh and eighth centuries was the structures which were in place during the fifth and sixth centuries which can never be fully understood. Nevertheless, as discussed in Chapter 1, there is a likelihood that during those two centuries in both eastern and western Wessex there were recognized units for the assessment of land for fiscal purposes, and, if one is correct in that supposition, it could be expected that such units would form the basis of the administrative structures which are recorded in the earliest written records of the seventh and eighth centuries.

A West Saxon administrative estate was organized from a central place which is referred to in Anglo-Saxon sources as *tun* or *villa regia* and is generally called a 'royal vill' by modern historians.[120] It is possible to identify a number of places which were the sites of royal vills in the Anglo-Saxon period. Some are specifically referred to as such in chronicles and histories, but in other cases it can be inferred because they were the centres of estates in royal wills or of royal hundreds in Domesday Book, or places from which charters were issued, at which royal councils were held and battles fought.[121] However, many of these references are from relatively late in the Anglo-Saxon period or after 1066 and, although some estate centres had a very long history, many Middle Saxon vills must have been abandoned subsequently.

It is possible that the sites of two such abandoned vills have been located and partially excavated at Cowdery's Down, near Basingstoke and Basing (presumably the centre of the Basingas),[122] and Foxley, near Malmesbury,[123] though it must be stressed that there is no documentary evidence to indicate the status of either settlement (fig. 20). However, even if they were not early administrative centres, they are, from the quality of their buildings, the highest status settlements so far uncovered in Wessex and so provide an insight into what might be expected at a royal vill. In their most extensive phases both sites were dominated by large timber halls with annexes or partitioned rooms at the gable-ends and set inside fenced enclosures which contained other substantial timber structures focused on the halls. The main halls were not only large, but also of sophisticated construction with raking timbers

120. Campbell, *Essays in Anglo-Saxon History*, 108–16.
121. P. Sawyer, 'The royal *tun* in pre-Conquest England', in *Ideal and Reality in Frankish and Anglo-Saxon Society*, ed. P. Wormald, D. Bullough and R. Collins (1983), 273–99.
122. M. Millett and S. James, 'Excavations at Cowdery's Down, Basingstoke, Hampshire, 1978–81', *Arch J, 140* (1983), 151–279; for Basingas see Ch. 1, 40–1.
123. J. Hinchcliffe, 'An early medieval settlement at Cowage Farm, Foxley, near Malmesbury', *Arch J, 143* (1986), 240–59.

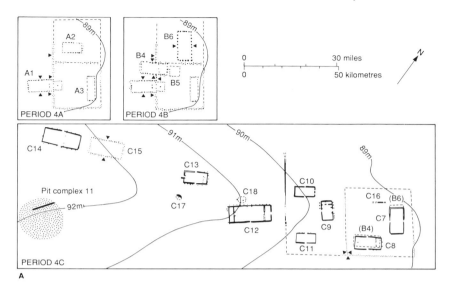

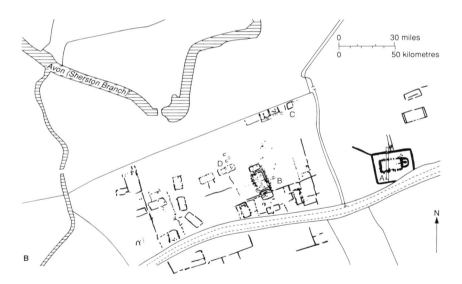

20. (a) Plans of successive Saxon halls and fenced enclosures
excavated at Cowdery's Down (Hants) [after M. Millett and S. James,
'Excavation at Cowdery's Down, Basingstoke, 1978–81', *Arch. J. 140*
(1983), 151–279 (b) Complex reconstructed from aerial photographs
and excavation at Foxley (Wilts); B appears to be the main hall and A
may be a church [after J. Hinchcliffe, 'An early medieval settlement
at Cowage Farm, Foxley near Malmesbury', *Arch. J. 143* (1986), 240–
59]

21. Hall C8 under excavation at Cowdery's Down (Hants) with several phases of fenced enclosure visible to its left [photograph: Hampshire County Museum Service]

providing additional support for the main timbers of the wall (fig. 21). It has been estimated that the great hall of the final phase of Cowdery's Down could have utilized some 70 tonnes of timber, daub and thatch. The halls are larger and of more elaborate construction than those of other Middle Saxon settlement sites such as Chalton (Hants) (see fig. 68), and are comparable in size and technique to the halls of Yeavering in Northumbria which has been identified with the *villa regalis* of *Ad Gefrin* mentioned by Bede.[124] The main hall at Foxley had walls of continuous vertical planking in which alternate baulks were deeply bedded in rock-cut slots which can be directly paralleled at Yeavering. Both West Saxon sites (again like Yeavering) produced remarkably few finds, but radio-carbon dates have helped suggest that their main period of occupation was the late sixth and seventh centuries. Cropmarks at Sutton Courtenay and Long Wittenham, just to the south of the Thames and so formerly in Berkshire, may indicate comparable sites.[125]

We also get some insight into the appearance of royal vills from the *Chronicle* account of the attack of Cyneheard on King Cynewulf in 786 at the royal residence of *Meretun* whose exact location is not known.[126] The site was enclosed as Cyneheard's forces locked its

124. B. Hope-Taylor, *Yeavering: An Anglo-British Centre of Early Northumbria* (1977).
125. D. Benson and D. Miles, *The Upper Thames Valley: An Archaeological Survey of the River Gravels* (1974); Blair, *Anglo-Saxon Oxfordshire*, 31–2.
126. *ASC* 755 for 757.

gates against an army of the king who had to break their way in. The king was visiting his mistress in a separate chamber (*bur*) when he was attacked and his retainers were not able to get to him quickly enough to prevent his death; perhaps like Beowulf's retainers they slept on benches in a hall. King Alfred in one of his additions to the *Soliloquies* of St Augustine envisaged that in the *cyninges ham* some would live in *bur*, some in *heall*, some in threshing floors and some in prison.[127] The sites at Cowdery's Down and Foxley are certainly capable of interpretation as sites which could have housed a king and his entourage for such occasional visits and there would have been ample room to store a king's food rent until he came to make use of it or had it sent on elsewhere. One might envisage that a royal official (reeve) would be permanently based in each royal vill to manage it and its dependent area.

THE WEST SAXON SUBKINGS

There was an administrative tier between the king of the West Saxons and the royal vills with their dependent districts. In the seventh century there were subkings and in the eighth century ealdormen. So far the reader has been spared many of the complexities of West Saxon political history. But in addition to the kings whose names appear in the regnal lists there were evidently other rulers who are either named as such in charters, the *Chronicle* and other historical works or who are depicted carrying out royal functions. Cwichelm, for instance, whom Bede describes as plotting the murder of Edwin of Northumbria, does not appear in any of the regnal lists.[128] In the *Chronicle* he is depicted as sharing command of the West Saxon army with Cynegils (in whose reign the attack on Edwin occurred),[129] and he is probably to be identified with the son of Cynegils who appears in one of the West Saxon genealogies.[130] The northern recension of the *Chronicle* says Edwin slew five West Saxon kings in revenge for the attempt on his life.[131] Probably not much faith should be put in that figure, but it does appear that at any point in the seventh century there might be several individuals with the title of king in Wessex though the regnal lists assert a tradition that there was always one dominant king.

Our ability to interpret the relations between different West Saxon kings is hampered by doubts about the reliability of the genealogies provided in the *Chronicle*. The only West Saxon genealogy to be preserved outside ninth-century West Saxon sources is one for King Ine in the so-called Anglian collection of

---

127. R. Waterhouse, 'Tone in Alfred's version of Augustine's *Soliloquies*', in *Studies in Earlier Old English Prose*, ed. P. Szarmach (Albany NY, 1986), 47–85.
128. *HE*, II, 9.
129. *Chronicle s.a.* 614 and 628.
130. In the genealogy of Cuthred, *Chronicle s.a.* 648.
131. *Chronicle* E *s.a.* 626.

genealogies, which was probably put together in the late eighth century in either Mercia or Northumbria.[132] When the version in the Anglian collection is compared with the version of Ine's genealogy in the *Chronicle* under the year 688 problems at once arise (see fig. 22). The Anglian version is two generations longer than the one in the *Chronicle* as a result of the inclusion of Creoda as son of Cerdic and father of Cynric and Cuthwulf as father of Ceolwold. The appearance of Creoda is particularly problematic.[133] He does not appear in the *Chronicle* annals at all which clearly assert that Cynric was Cerdic's son and this is repeated in the genealogy of Cædwalla provided in the *Chronicle* entry for 685. Yet the genealogy of Æthelwulf (father of Alfred and descendant of a brother of Ine) included in the *Chronicle* for 855 reproduces the longer version of Ine's genealogy, so clearly both versions were known in Wessex in the ninth century.

Another problem for the modern historian – and perhaps for ninth-century *Chronicle* compilers – is the similarity of many West Saxon names and particularly the fact that they may appear either in full or shortened forms. Cuthwulf of the Anglian collection genealogy, for instance, appears as Cutha in the genealogy of Æthelwulf. A problem of this type concerns the paternity of Cynegils, the first of the West Saxon kings to be baptized; in the *Chronicle* entry for 611 he is described as a son of Ceola. In the *Chronicle* entry for 676 Centwine is described as the son of Cynegils, the son of Ceolwulf, and Ceola could easily be a shortened form of this name. However, another ninth-century West Saxon production, the West Saxon Genealogical Regnal List,[134] complicates matters by identifying King Cynegils as the son of a *brother* and predecessor of Ceolwulf called Ceol. Either the two brothers Ceol and Ceolwulf both had sons called Cynegils, one of whom was baptized by Birinus in 635, or there was only one Cynegils, the son of Ceola, but the chronicles in the ninth century were confused as to whether 'Ceola' was Ceol or Ceolwulf, or a further possibility is that Ceol and Ceolwulf were in fact the same person. On the other hand, when the genealogy of Ine entered in the *Chronicle* annal for 688 says pointedly that his grandfather was the brother of Cynegils that may be an attempt to claim the first Christian West Saxon king for the family of Ine and his descendants, the West Saxon rulers of the ninth century.[135]

It appears that the genealogical information in the *Chronicle* and West Saxon Genealogical Regnal List was – like the regnal years in the same sources – subject to some misunderstandings and

---

132. D.N. Dumville, 'The Anglian collection of royal genealogies and regnal lists', *ASE, 5* (1976), 23–50.

133. K. Sisam, 'Anglo-Saxon royal genealogies' *PBA, 39*, 287–346, especially 337–8.

134. D.N. Dumville, 'The West Saxon Genealogical Regnal List and the chronology of early Wessex', *Peritia, 4* (1985), 21–66, and 'The West Saxon Genealogical Regnal List: manuscripts and texts', *Anglia, 104* (1986), 1–32.

135. For further discussion of these problems and different solutions see Kirby, *Earliest English Kings*, 53–4.

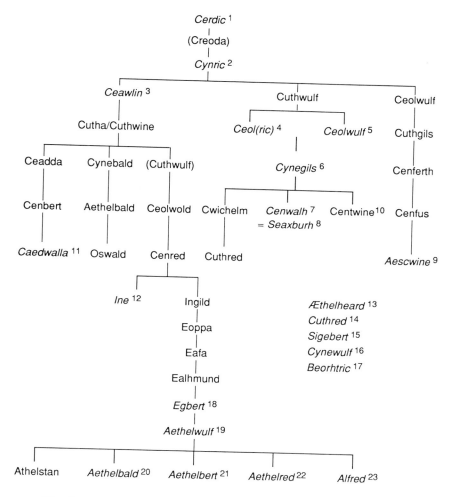

22. Genealogical table of early West Saxon kings. Kings have been numbered in the order in which they appear in West Saxon regnal lists, but nos. 13–17 lack specific genealogical information. Surviving genealogies contain conflicting information and this table is an attempt to resolve them; individuals appearing in one version, but not in another are shown in brackets

revisions in the ninth century. The exact motives for additions or concealments are hard for us to appreciate. Was Creoda really the son of Cerdic and father of Cynric and, if so, why was he eliminated from the *Chronicle* annals? Possibly there was a desire to make the different branches of the West Saxon royal house seem more closely related than was actually the case. It has even been questioned whether all the lines which claimed the right to rule in Wessex in fact had a common ancestor as the genealogies claim.[136] Such a fiction cannot be ruled out, but one factor in support of their common identity is the prevalence of names beginning in 'C' which therefore alliterate with Cerdic, the putative founding father of the royal house. A similar use of alliteration is found in the East Saxon royal house which also has examples of multiple kingship. Practically all the East Saxon kings have names beginning with 'S' and they claimed common descent from Sledd.[137]

The West Saxon genealogies seem to show a situation of competing branch lines in the seventh century which becomes clearer if we analyse the family connections of the kings who appear in the regnal lists (see fig. 22). From 592, when the *Chronicle* claims Ceawlin was driven out, to 672, the death of Cenwalh, all the dominant kings are given as descendants of Cutha/Cuthwulf, son of Cynric and brother of Ceawlin in the tradition presented to us. After Cenwalh's death, according to Bede, 'subkings took upon themselves the government of the kingdom, dividing it up and ruling for about ten years'.[138] The regnal lists give as dominant during this period Seaxburh, the widow of Cenwalh (1 year), Æscwine, who according to his genealogy in the *Chronicle* was descended from a third son of Cynric (2 years) and Centwine, who was probably the brother of Cenwalh (9 years).[139] The regnal lists depict these as successive rulers, but Bede implies a more complex situation in which no one ruler dominated 'until the subkings were conquered and removed', presumably by Centwine if his ten-year period is accepted as accurate.[140] Centwine himself was succeeded by Cædwalla who claimed descent from Ceawlin as did Ine who succeeded him.

Some of the kings who shared control with the rulers of the regnal lists were close family members. Cenwalh is recorded as delegating authority to his nephew Cuthred,[141] whose father Cwichelm had shared power with his own (and Cenwalh's) father Cynegils; although Ine appears dominant his father was also a king during his reign and is mentioned in Ine's lawcode as having assisted in the compilation of the laws.[142] Other subsidiary rulers though might be extremely distant cousins. Cenwalh must also have shared power with Cenbert, the father of Cædwalla, whose death is recorded in the *Chronicle* for 661. On the basis of the information in the genealogies they would have been third cousins. Ine's father Cenred may have been a ruler before his son's accession

---

136. D. Kirby, 'Problems of early West Saxon history', *EHR, 80* (1965), 10–29 (though see now *Earliest English Kings*, 53–9); Dumville, 'Genealogical Regnal List and chronology', 65–6.

137. B.A.E. Yorke, 'The kingdom of the East Saxons', *ASE, 14* (1985), 1–36.

138. *HE*, IV, 12.

139. For full discussion of the chronological problems see Dumville, 'Genealogical Regnal List and chronology', and Kirby, *Earliest English Kings*, 51–3.

140. Yorke, *Kings and Kingdoms*, 145–6.

141. *Chronicle s.a.* 648.

142. Edwards, *Charters of the Early West Saxon Kingdom*, 297–9.

if he is the Cenred who made a grant of land in Dorset between 670 and 676,[143] for the ability to grant land at this time is likely to have been a royal prerogative. According to the regnal lists either Cenwalh or Æscwine would have been the dominant king when the grant was made; Cenred was only distantly related to both of them.

The existence of these subsidary kings has a direct bearing on how new areas were brought under West Saxon control and subsequently governed. Cædwalla's conquests in south-eastern England began when he was in exile from Wessex and, with an army he had raised, attacked and killed the king of the South Saxons.[144] Cædwalla was soon expelled from Sussex, but his armed following, and perhaps the booty he had acquired, enabled him to take the West Saxon throne, after which he led a successful campaign against the South Saxons and their Jutish allies. Cædwalla's conquests at this time are therefore mixed up with his experiences in exile and desire to outmanoeuvure his West Saxon rivals. The savagery he showed to the South Saxons and Jutes in 686 may have been a response to the treatment meted out to him and his followers when they had been expelled from Sussex the year before.

Multiple kingship in the Anglo-Saxon period need not be associated with a physical division of the kingdom, but when true joint rulers are found they seem to be closely related, often brothers who have inherited jointly from their fathers like the sons of Sæbert of the East Saxons or the princes of the Hwicce.[145] It was common practice in early Anglo-Saxon England for a king to delegate control of a newly acquired province to one of his own family to rule and this was especially likely if the province had recently been ruled by its own kings. Supervision of potentially dangerous border areas might also be delegated. It is likely that many of the subkingships in Wessex involved such delegations of territory although the sources generally give little indication of their nature or purpose. Bede's account of the subkings of Wessex after the death of Cenwalh seems to imply a physical division of territory. Cenwalh is specifically said in the *Chronicle* entry for 648 to have given 3,000 hides of land near Ashdown to his nephew Cuthred. Ashdown was a name applied originally to the whole of the Berkshire Downs,[146] and Cuthred was receiving in effect an important border command for this was an area on which Mercia was increasingly encroaching at the time the grant was made. Baldred, who describes himself as the kinsman of West Saxon kings,[147] seems to have held an analagous position in north Somerset and Wiltshire during the reign of Centwine. Kings generally seem to have preferred to make

---

143. S 1164/B 107.
144. *HE*, IV, 15 and 16.
145. I. Wood, 'Kings, kingdoms and consent', in *Early Medieval Kingship*, ed. P. Sawyer and I. Wood (1977), 3–29; Yorke, *Kings and Kingdoms*, 167–72.
146. M. Gelling, *The Place-Names of Berkshire. Part I*, EPNS, *49* (1973), 2–3.
147. S 236/B 61.

such delegations of power to close relatives, but, as we have seen, extremely distant cousins might also be found as subkings. In these cases we might postulate that a royal branch line had successfully hung on to its position for several generations, establishing a hereditary right to rule in part of Wessex. This would help to explain the explosive situation in Wessex in 672 when several branches seem to have been in a position to launch a claim for the throne in spite of the fact that none of their immediate predecessors appear in the king-lists. Æscwine, Cædwalla and Ine, who all successfully contended for power, had fathers who had been subsidiary kings and the areas they controlled could have been power bases from which their sons could launch their claims.[148]

SHIRES AND BOUNDARIES

Subkings are not found in charters or *Anglo-Saxon Chronicle* annals after the reign of Ine and the last of them, and the only one known from Wessex during his reign, was his father Cenred. Their disappearance coincides with the use of titles such as *patricius*, *princeps* and *praefectus* by the chief lay witnesses of the charters of Ine and his successors.[149] These Latin titles are presumably the equivalent of Old English *ealdorman* which is used in Ine's laws.[150] The first appearance of a West Saxon with the title 'ealdorman' in the annals of the *Chronicle* is the entry for 750, but thereafter they appear with increasing frequency and evidently had a major part to play in the politics of eighth-century Wessex. The first reference to a named shire in the *Chronicle* is to *Hamtunscir* in the entry for 757. Other shires are not specifically mentioned until the ninth century, but as there are relatively few annals for the eighth century the lack of earlier references is not necessarily significant. In a number of instances the first reference is to the people (*-sæte*) of the shire rather than the shire itself: thus we have Wilsæte (802), Defena i.e. 'men of Devon' (825), Dornsæte (840) and Somersæte (845). *Bearruc scir* is first mentioned in 860.

The maximum number of ealdormen to appear in any one West Saxon charter of the eighth century is seven,[151] but as some additional areas such as Surrey and part of Cornwall were under West Saxon control for part of the eighth century the apparent appearance of an extra ealdorman does not require any particular explanation. However, when considering the likely relationship between the shire system as set up by Ine and that which is

148.   Yorke, *Kings and Kingdoms*, 142–8.
149.   H.M. Chadwick, *Studies on Anglo-Saxon Institutions* (1905), 282–90; A.T. Thacker, 'Some terms for noblemen in Anglo-Saxon England, c. 650–900', *Anglo-Saxon Studies in Archaeology and History*, 2 (1981), 201–36.
150.   Attenborough, 'Laws of Ine', Ch. 6.2, 36.1, 45 and 50.
151.   Chadwick, *Anglo-Saxon Institutions*, 282; Edwards, *Charters of the Early West Saxon Kingdom*, 183–4.

recorded more fully in the ninth century we must remember that not all of the territory of the six shires was under continuous West Saxon control throughout the eighth century. In the second half of the century northern parts of Somerset and Wiltshire and probably the whole of Berkshire were under Mercian control. That need not invalidate the concept of a continuity of the core areas of shires from the eighth to the ninth century, but could mean that whatever scheme was put in place in Ine's reign had to be modified in the light of subsequent events and this possibility is discussed further below with reference to eastern Wessex.

Before exploring the relationship between eighth- and ninth-century shires we need to look back to earlier arrangements and to consider Chadwick's proposition that the shires were themselves based on earlier subkingdoms or other administrative units.[152] Here we run up against the problem of not knowing precisely where the boundaries of earlier units lay, but some sections of shire boundaries do seem to have been of some antiquity. The boundaries formed by Selwood and Bokerley Dyke which separated Somerset and Dorset from the shires to their east may have come into existence in the fifth or sixth centuries (fig. 23; see also fig. 8).[153] Selwood was acknowledged as an important boundary in 705 when the bishopric of Sherborne was established for those 'west of Selwood'.[154] Part of the northern boundary of Somerset in the eighth and ninth centuries may have been delineated by West Wansdyke, also, of course, likely to be older in origin, for Bath and the territory dependent upon it was probably not added to Somerset until the tenth century.[155]

The organization implied by the names of the western shires also provides some grounds for thinking that there was some continuity between British-controlled territories and West Saxon shires. The name of Devon derives ultimately from the British kingdom name of *Dumnonia* which was rendered by the Welsh as *Dyfnaint* in the ninth century.[156] The name of Devon is therefore comparable with those of later West Saxon shires such as Sussex and Essex which were formerly kingdoms and retained their names (South Saxons and East Saxons) after incorporation into Wessex. The *Dornsæte* of Dorset derive their name from the Old English *sæte*, 'settlers', and the first element of *Durnovaria*, the Romano-British name of Dorchester from which they were presumably administered (see fig. 2).[157] Dorchester was, of course, the *civitas* capital of the southern

152. Chadwick, *Anglo-Saxon Institutions*, 288.
153. See Ch. 1, 22–4.
154. *Chronicle s.a.* 709 calls Aldhelm 'bishop west of the wood'; see Ch. 4, 179–81.
155. Taylor, 'Bath, Mercian and West Saxon'.
156. J.E.B. Gover, A. Mawer and F.M. Stenton, *The Place-Names of Devon, Part I, EPNS, 8* (1931), xiv and l.
157. K. Cameron, *English Place-Names* (1961), 54; L. Keen, 'The towns of Dorset', in *Anglo-Saxon Towns in Southern England*, ed. J. Haslam (1984), 203–47, *passim*.

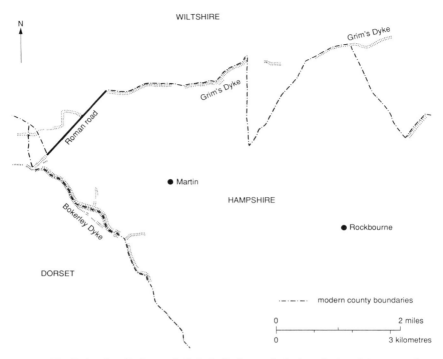

23. Bokerley Dyke and Grim's Dyke and their relationship to modern shire boundaries

Durotriges so the possibility of administrative continuity is there. Exeter (*Isca Dumnoniorum*) was the *civitas* capital of the *Dumnonii*, but we do not have any information about its status in the eighth century, other than that it was the site of an important minster church. However, in the ninth century it would appear to have been the main focus of royal administration in Devon.[158]

Somerset appears at first not to fit the pattern; the shire derives its name from the royal *tun* of Somerton which seems to be a new settlement and name of the Anglo-Saxon period. However, the large estate of Somerton included within its bounds the former Roman town of Ilchester which it has been argued was the *civitas* capital of the northern Durotriges from the third century.[159] It therefore appears possible that the three western shires are based around significant subdivisions of the late Roman or sub-Roman periods,

158.   J. Allan, C. Henderson and R. Higham, 'Saxon Exeter', in *Anglo-Saxon Towns in Southern England*, ed. J. Haslam (1984), 385–414; J.R. Maddicott, 'Trade, industry and the wealth of King Alfred', *Past and Present, 123* (1989), 3–51.
159.   R.W. Dunning, 'Ilchester', in *Victoria History of Somerset*, III, ed. R.W. Dunning (1974), 179–203, and 'Ilchester: a study in continuity', *PSANHS, 119* (1975), 44–50.

perhaps based on districts dependent upon the three *civitas* capitals of Exeter, Dorchester and Ilchester. The three western districts could have had an intervening period as West Saxon subkingdoms before being reconstituted as shires, but our evidence is not good enough to be sure of the arrangements made for them. We have seen, however, that the subking Baldred was active in Somerset (though also in north Wiltshire) in the later seventh century and that Cenred, who may have been the father of Ine, granted land in Dorset at about the same time.[160] A further link between the family of Ine and Dorset is the foundation of a nunnery at Wimborne, initially for Ine's sister Cuthburh.[161] In the ninth century the religious house there was still of great significance for the family of King Alfred who were descended from Ine's brother Ingild. One of Alfred's brothers was buried there and when a nephew launched a bid for the throne on Alfred's death one of his first actions was to seize Wimborne.[162]

How and when the boundaries between the three western shires were established is also a very difficult question and one cannot assume that boundaries remained unchanged. The boundary between Devon and Cornwall follows for much of its length the River Tamar, which may have been an ancient boundary between the Cornovii and the Dumnonii, but until relatively recently parts of some Devon parishes lay west of the Tamar, while some lands east of the river were attached to Cornish parishes, suggesting a more complex history behind the formation of the boundary.[163] The western part of Somerset containing Exmoor and the Quantocks is often assumed to have been originally part of the territory of the Dumnonii (see fig. 2). Land on the eastern edge of the Quantocks was apparently granted by a West Saxon king to Glastonbury in 682,[164] and it may be that it was ceded to West Saxon control at an earlier date than the rest of Dumnonia which would account for it ending up as part of Somerset rather than Devon. Possibly the boundary between Dorset and Somerset relates to a division between northern and southern Durotriges of Roman date, but there is no hard evidence.

Hampshire and Wiltshire are also named from places (Hamtun and Wilton) from which they were presumably administered, but neither of these had administrative roles in the Roman period. In the eastern shires the sub-Roman arrangements seem to have disrupted the Roman organizational structures of the area and the new territorial units which were created were themselves affected by Mercian and West Saxon expansion in the seventh and eighth

160. See above, 60–2.
161. *Chronicle s.a.* 718.
162. *Chronicle s.a.* 871 and 900.
163. Todd, *South-West to AD 1000*, 203–4, 216–17; C. and F. Thorn (ed.), *Domesday Book: Devon* (2 vols. 1985), II, notes: 4.
164. S 237/B 62; Costen, *Origins of Somerset*, 85–6.

centuries. Hampshire, for instance, seems to have had a very complex evolution (see fig. 13). Its southern portion consisted of the former Jutish province, which included the administrative centre of Hamwic, and the Isle of Wight.[165] That the island seems to have been regarded as part of Hampshire in the later Anglo-Saxon period is suggested by the *Chronicle* annal for 878 which refers to 'that part of Hampshire which is on this side of the sea' and by its inclusion under Hampshire in Domesday Book.[166] Southern Hampshire also contained the area around Christchurch which was thus divorced from the upper part of the Avon Valley which was in Wiltshire. It is just possible that Christchurch had been part of the Jutish province, but there is no definite evidence that it was. Hampshire's eastern boundary was formed in part by the *regio* of the Basingas,[167] and the northern part contained Winchester, the episcopal centre for eastern Wessex though the earlier administrative history of this area is not known.

Hampshire's northern boundary with Berkshire is rather different in appearance from that of the other shire boundaries which tend to undulate around fields and other negotiated boundary points. The Hampshire/Berkshire boundary runs more or less straight and cuts through ecclesiastical and estate boundaries which had presumably been established prior to its inception and also incorporated the northern boundary of Silchester, thus severing it from any surrounding territory or *oppidum* (see fig. 8).[168] As Margaret Gelling has argued it looks like an imposed rather than a negotiated boundary and is most likely to have been created during a period of Mercian domination in the seventh or eighth centuries.[169] If that boundary was imposed after the introduction of the original shire system, for instance, in the reigns of Æthelbald or Offa, it could have led to a reorganization of earlier administrative arrangements. Berkshire, like Hampshire, seems to have been composed from disparate units. Its eastern part consisted of the *regiones* of the Sunningas and Readingas with possible links with the adjoining province of Surrey,[170] and its northern boundary, which contained the territory of the Horningas and was bounded by the River Thames, had been divorced from lands on the northern bank of the Thames with which it had presumably been associated in the kingdom of the Gewisse. It may be that Berkshire took on its final

165. Yorke, 'Jutes of Hampshire and Wight'.
166. B.J. Golding, 'An introduction to the Hampshire Domesday', in *The Hampshire Domesday*, Alecto historical editions (1989), 1–27; very little is known about the island in the later Anglo-Saxon period.
167. D. Hinton, 'The place of Basing in mid-Saxon history', *PHFCAS, 42* (1986), 162–3.
168. D. Hinton, 'Hampshire's Anglo-Saxon origins', in *The Archaeology of Hampshire*, ed. S.J. Shennan and R.T. Schadla Hall, Hampshire Field Club monograph, *1* (1981), 57.
169. Gelling, *Place-Names of Berkshire. III*, 844–5.
170. Gelling, *Place-Names of Berkshire. III*, 840–3.

form when it became the only territory south of the Thames left in Mercian hands when other provinces were surrendered to Wessex in 825.[171] The western part of Berkshire must have been part of the 'three thousand hides near Ashdown' which Cenwalh gave to Cuthred and which had probably included part of Wiltshire north of East Wansdyke as well. The Celtic name *Barroc* from which Berkshire was named may have been the original name of the Berkshire Downs which was supplanted by Old English *Aescesdun*.[172]

Some additional light on the origin of the three eastern shires may come from the Burghal Hidage, a document listing the arrangements for fortifying Wessex in the late ninth and early tenth centuries which is discussed in more detail in the next chapter.[173] There appears to be a relationship between the total number of hides allocated to burhs and the shire hidages given in Domesday Book, which, as Nicholas Brooks has argued, could suggest that shire hidages remained broadly the same from the ninth century when the first burhs were built to the end of the Anglo-Saxon period.[174] There is a contrast between the hidage totals for the eastern and western shires of Wessex. In the east a 2,400 hide unit seems to have been significant and is the amount recorded in the Burghal Hidage as allocated for the defences of Winchester and Wallingford.[175] The aggregate of the Wiltshire burhs is 4,800 hides, exactly the total of the 2,400 hides allocated to Winchester and Wallingford (see fig. 29). The regularity of the assessment for northern Hampshire, northern/western Berkshire and Wiltshire raises the possibility that the hidages were imposed at the same time and this could have been in the period when the eastern shires were created, but possibly before they obtained their final forms. For the Domesday shire of Berkshire also included the Burghal Hidage burh of Sashes near Cookham in eastern Berkshire and that of Hampshire included the Burghal Hidage burhs of Portchester, Hamtun and Twynham/Christchurch (1,120 hides in total). From this a hypothesis could be presented that three shires were created in eastern Wessex in the reign of Ine: *Hamtunscir* based on the former Jutish province, Wiltshire assessed at 4,800 hides and another 4,800-hide shire consisting of territories based on Winchester and Wallingford. However, when as a result of Mercian overlordship the northern/western Berkshire lands were severed from those of northern Hampshire, adjustments had to be made. The Winchester area was joined with *Hamtunscir* to make medieval

171. Gelling, *Place-Names of Berkshire. III*, 841–2.
172. Gelling, *Place-Names of Berkshire. I*, 2–3.
173. See Ch. 3, 115–20.
174. Sawyer, *From Roman Britain to Norman England*, 227–8; N. Brooks, 'The administrative background of the Burghal Hidage', in *The Burghal Hidage*, ed. D. Hill and A. Rumble (forthcoming).
175. See Fig. 28 and Brooks, 'Administrative background', from which all Domesday Book figures have been taken.

Hampshire, and Berkshire was ultimately formed from the Wallingford district plus the *regio* of the Sunningas probably with Cookham as its administrative centre.

The figures of 2,400 and 4,800 hides are reminiscent of those of the Tribal Hidage which contained many multiples of 300 and it is possible that the 2,400/4,800 hide units are older than the shires. However, given the fact that the shires seem to have been created from what had been disparate territories in the seventh century, it would seem unlikely that an aggregate of existing hidage assessments would produce identical round numbers. The administrative changes of the ninth century would be another possible context for the hidages to have been imposed. The creation of the burhs could be a plausible period for a revision of hidage assessments, though it would have been a formidable undertaking against a background of Viking wars. It is also harder to explain why the aggregate of four Wiltshire burhs should be identical with the amount allocated to Winchester and Wallingford in those circumstances. As Nicholas Brooks has argued, some of the Burghal Hidage information could be seen as indicating a system adapted to fit with existing hidages rather than one which was dictating the hidage assessments.[176]

In contrast in western Wessex the hidage assessments as represented in Burghal Hidage and Domesday Book are neither as regular nor as substantial as those for eastern Wessex. For Devon the aggregate of the hidage allocations of its four burhs is 1,534 hides of which 415 hides, as the Domesday Book figures make clear, was the hidage total for Cornwall.[177] Somerset (excluding Bath which was not incorporated into the shire until the tenth century) also had four burhs, giving a hidage total of 1,613 hides, while the total for the three Dorset burhs was 3,060 hides. Even allowing for some low-quality farmland, Devon and Somerset seem to have been assessed lightly compared to the three shires of eastern Wessex, and one might conclude that Ine (if he was indeed responsible for recalculating hidages in the latter) was not sufficiently secure in the west to attempt the same process, but instead accepted assessments already in place or imposed new ones in an *ad hoc* manner. However, in Somerset at least, many large manors were kept in royal hands and were never assessed in hides for public services and payments, so the impression that all of western Wessex was underassessed compared to the east may be partly due to more land being in non-royal ownership in the east.[178]

We can learn something of the roles of the ealdormen, the royal officials in charge of the shires, from the *Chronicle* annals. The activity with which they are most frequently associated is the leading of the shire forces in battle. For instance, in 802 Ealdorman

---

176. Brooks, 'Administrative background', and see Ch. 3, 116–18.
177. Brooks, 'Administrative background'.
178. D. Hill, *An Atlas of Anglo-Saxon England* (1981), 101 and 106.

Weohstan led the Wilsætan into battle against the Hwicce under their ealdorman at Kempsford (Gloucs) on the border between the two peoples. Both ealdormen were killed, but the people of Wiltshire were victorious and the battle probably marked the final detachment of northern Wiltshire from Mercian overlordship (and also implies a consciousness of Wiltshire as a distinct territory before 802). It is a hotly debated issue whether all those of free status living in Wessex were liable to military service in some form (not necessarily just as fighting men)[179] – which is what one reading of Ine's laws would seem to suggest – or whether only those specially commended to the king.[180] Military service in a shire unit would seem to be an ideal way for giving the men of higher status a regional identity under West Saxon leadership. At the same time the shires were a suitable size to be managed as delegated units, a delegation which was necessary if kings were successfully to control local violence which might be a threat to their position and ability to collect tribute and food rents. Ealdormen of the eighth century probably had, like their later counterparts, responsibility for local justice, especially if they can be equated with the *scirmen* of Ine's laws who seem to have presided over local courts.[181]

The delegation of power to ealdormen was presumably preferable, from the point of view of dominant kings like Ine, to the creation of subkingdoms whose rulers might show a tendency to become too independent. But the disappearance of subkingdoms did not bring an end to disputes over the kingship within the royal house which seem to have been just as prevalent in the eighth century as in the seventh and in which ealdormen might play a prominent role.[182] In 757 Cynewulf and the *witan* of the West Saxons, that is the chief men of the kingdom which presumably included the ealdormen, deposed King Sigebert 'because of his unjust acts', which allowed Cynewulf to succeed to the throne.[183] Sigebert was initially left in charge of *Hamtunscir*, but was driven out after he had murdered 'the ealdorman who stood by him longest'. The exile led to Sigebert's death as he was killed in revenge by one of the ealdorman's retainers. Some twenty-nine years later Cynewulf wished to expel Cyneheard, Sigebert's brother, but the latter pre-empted him by attacking and killing Cynewulf at the royal vill of *Meretun*. Cyneheard was potentially in a position to make himself king instead, but failed to win over either Cynewulf's entourage at *Meretun* or a relieving force led by Ealdorman Osric which attacked and killed him.

---

179. E. John, *Orbis Britanniae and Other Studies* (1966), 133–8.
180. R. Abels, *Lordship and Military Obligation in Anglo-Saxon England* (1988), 11–25.
181. Attenborough, 'Laws of Ine', Ch. 8.
182. D.N. Dumville, 'The ætheling: a study in Anglo-Saxon constitutional history', *ASE, 8* (1979), 1–33.
183. *Chronicle s.a.* 755.

The Cynewulf/Cyneheard incident is extremely informative about the importance of powerful lords in eighth-century Wessex. Ties of lordship cut across ties of kinship for kinsman faced kinsman in the rival armies of Cynewulf and Cyneheard. Ine's laws recognized that the demands of lordship took precedence over the rights of kin,[184] and also seem to acknowledge the existence of private armies which needed to be curbed.[185] Although subkingships had been abolished, rival groups within the royal house seem to have remained in a position to attract support and organize substantial entourages. The necessity of allying oneself with a prominent lord, who must often have been a member of the West Saxon royal house, was another way, like the shire structure, in which men of disparate background who lived in Wessex came to see themselves as West Saxons. One problem facing West Saxon kings was to ensure that such lords and their entourages were united behind them.

In 800 Wessex was one of the four major kingdoms of Anglo-Saxon England. The province had been created from a number of disparate Germanic and British units by the military conquests of the Gewissan kings, but provided with coherence by its obligations to the royal house and the common administrative framework imposed to allow the kings to exact these. The opportunities for enrichment through royal service would have been another unifying factor, and although many Britons of western Wessex no doubt suffered during the period of conquest, the means existed for them to be incorporated in the West Saxon state and to retain something of lands and position through recognition of the West Saxon king. A similar assimilation was achieved in the Church with key positions passing to Anglo-Saxons, but with a British infrastructure surviving.[186] The reign of King Ine stands out as being of special significance. Initially one has some reservations about singling out Ine because some of the key sources for his reign (the *Chronicle* annals and the lawcode) have been transmitted through the actions of King Alfred, who was descended from Ine's brother Ingild and may have wanted to aggrandize the achievements of apparently the only member of his family to rule since the sixth century. But Ine's achievements seem to speak for themselves and, in the words of Sir Frank Stenton, Ine's lawcode was 'the work of a responsible statesman'.[187] It would appear to be in Ine's reign that the shires were created, drawing in part on existing administrative arrangements, but also involving some major reorganizations, especially in eastern Wessex. But the future dominance of Wessex was by no means assured in 800. Ine may have removed the subkings, but

---

184. Attenborough, 'Laws of Ine', Ch. 39, 50, 70, 74 and 76.
185. Attenborough, 'Laws of Ine', Ch. 13.1, 14, 15 and 34.
186. See Ch. 4, 177–81.
187. Stenton, *Anglo-Saxon England*, 72.

that did not put an end to rivalries between different branches of the royal house, and civil wars may have been one of the factors which weakened Wessex in the eighth century in the face of the military might of Mercia in the reigns of Æthelbald and Offa. In 800 northern areas of Wessex and the religious houses within them were under Mercian control and, although there was still an independent king of the West Saxons, it was also the case that the province had a Mercian queen, Eadburh, the daughter of King Offa.

3 Wessex and England, 802–1066

EGBERT AND THE EXPANSION OF WEST SAXON POWER

In the course of the ninth century the kings of the West Saxons were able finally to consolidate control of the six shires and also became rulers of an enlarged Wessex consisting of all the provinces south of the Thames and the former East Saxon kingdom. The first major advances were made under King Egbert; he took the throne in 802 on the death of King Beorhtric, having previously been in exile in Francia at the court of Charlemagne who may have assisted his return.[1] The *Anglo-Saxon Chronicle* reports that on the same day on which he succeeded to the throne, the Wilsætan defeated the Hwicce of western Mercia, a battle which was probably influential in deciding that the River Avon would be the boundary between Mercia and Wessex in the west.[2] Little else is recorded for Egbert's reign until 825 when a major battle was fought with King Beornwulf of Mercia at *Ellendun* (Wroughton, Wilts) on the north Wiltshire Downs which had been the scene of so much conflict between the Mercians and the West Saxons. A major defeat was imposed by the West Saxons, which Egbert followed up by despatching an army led by his son Æthelwulf to Kent to expel its ruler Baldred who was subking and probably kinsman of Beornwulf.[3] As a result, in the words of the *Anglo-Saxon Chronicle*, 'the people of Kent and of Surrey and the South Saxons and the East Saxons submitted to him'. In 829 Egbert conquered Mercia itself and received the submission of the Northumbrian king when he led an army to the Mercian/Northumbrian border.[4] Egbert may have

---

1. D. Kirby, *The Earliest English Kings* (1991), 189–94.
2. See Chapter 2, 64.
3. N. Brooks, *The Early History of the Church of Canterbury* (1984), 136–7.
4. *Chronicle s.a.* 829; F.M. Stenton, *Anglo-Saxon England* (3rd edn., 1971), 232–5.

overplayed his hand for in 830 the Mercian king Wiglaf returned to power. But the gains in the south-east proved permanent. To begin with the new provinces were managed as a subkingdom under Æthelwulf and, when he succeeded his father as king of the main part of Wessex in 839, control passed first to his son Athelstan and then to another son, Æthelbert. When Æthelbert succeeded to the main kingdom, on the death of his brother Æthelbald in 860, the south-eastern districts and the main kingdom were united to form an enlarged Wessex.[5]

Egbert's reign may also have been important for consolidating control of Devon and beginning the imposition of overlordship on Cornwall. The *Chronicle* records a battle in 825 between 'the Britons and the men of Devon' where the clear implication is that Devon was now seen as 'West Saxon' and divorced from the other Dumnonian province of the *Cornovii*.[6] But Egbert was not ruler of all the land south of the Thames, for Berkshire apparently remained a Mercian province and was not united with the other shires of Wessex until the reign of Æthelwulf (839–858). The transfer of Berkshire from Mercian to West Saxon control does not seem to have been the result of any battle and may have been achieved diplomatically as part of the co-operation between Mercia and Wessex in the middle of the century in the face of mutual harassment from Vikings and the Welsh and Cornish. There is no one point at which a transfer can be seen to have been made. In 844 the bishop of Leicester granted an estate at Pangbourne to King Beorhtwulf of Mercia,[7] but in 849 the future king Alfred was born at Wantage.[8] Æthelwulf, who was ealdorman of Berkshire in 844, still held the position in 871 when he died fighting with King Æthelred of Wessex against the Vikings. Although he was killed at Reading, Æthelwulf's body was taken to Derby for burial,[9] thus confirming the implication of the Pangbourne charter that he was in origin a Mercian ealdorman. As Sir Frank Stenton suggested, the marriage between King Burgred of Mercia and Æthelswith, daughter of King Æthelwulf, in 853 may have played a significant part in the negotiations.[10] Æthelswith granted land in Berkshire in her own right,[11] and it may have been the case that Mercian royal estates there were ceded to her as part of her dowry and subsequently passed to her male kinsmen in Wessex, thus easing the transfer of authority. Berkshire was definitely part of Wessex in

---

5. D.N. Dumville, *Wessex and England from Alfred to Edgar* (1992), 1–23.
6. The *Chronicle* also records a victory for Egbert over a combined 'West Welsh' and Viking force at Hingston Down in 838; M. Todd, *The South-West to AD 1000* (1987), 273–5.
7. S 1271/B 443.
8. Asser, Ch. 1.
9. Æthelweard, 37.
10. F.M. Stenton, *The Early History of the Abbey of Abingdon* (1913), 28–9.
11. S 1201/B 522.

the reign of Alfred who, like some at least of his Mercian predecessors, took over lands formerly allocated to the abbey of Abingdon for his own use.[12]

The marriage of Burgred and Æthelswith was the first of several such unions between the royal families of the two kingdoms of which ultimately the most significant was the marriage of Alfred's daughter Æthelflæd to Æthelred, ruler of western Mercia, that is the part of Mercia left under native control after Vikings settled in the east following their expulsion of Burgred in 874.[13] After Æthelflæd's death in 918, Alfred's son Edward the Elder (899–924) was able to annex western Mercia, having already won much of eastern Mercia ('the Danelaw') from Viking control in a brilliant series of military campaigns. By the end of his reign Edward was ruler of both Wessex and Mercia. His sons Athelstan (924–39), Edmund (939–46) and Eadred (946–55) were responsible for establishing West Saxon control of the southern Northumbrian province of Deira, and the last Viking king of York, the infamous Eric Bloodaxe, was killed in 954. Their successes enabled Edmund's son Edgar (959–75) not only to describe himself as king of the English, but ruler of Britain as well.[14] In 973 a second coronation formed part of the process by which Edgar's superiority was recognized by the remaining Celtic and Scandinavian rulers of the British Isles.[15]

THE WESSEX HEARTLANDS AND THE KINGDOM OF ENGLAND

But our concern here is with what was happening to the original West Saxon provinces while its ruling house was so dramatically expanding its territory. In particular, did the core provinces of Wessex retain any distinct identity once they became part of a wider England? The distinctiveness of the West Saxons from other major groups within England, such as the Northumbrians and the Mercians, is made clear in a number of ways in the later Saxon period. When Edward the Elder died in 924, it seems to have been his original intention that his eldest son Athelstan should succeed him in Mercia and that his second son Ælfweard (half-brother to

12. A.T. Thacker, 'Æthelwold and Abingdon', in *Bishop Æthelwold: His Career and Influence*, ed. B.A.E. Yorke (1988), 45; see also Ch. 5, 194–7.
13. F.T. Wainwright, 'Æthelflæd, Lady of the Mercians', in *Scandinavian England*, ed. H.P.R. Finberg (1975), 305–24.
14. F.M. Stenton, *Anglo-Saxon England* (3rd ed. 1971), 239–52, 320–72; P. Stafford, *Unification and Conquest: A Political and Social History of England in the Tenth and Eleventh Centuries* (1989), *passim*.
15. J.L. Nelson, 'Inauguration rituals', in *Early Medieval Kingship*, ed. P. Sawyer and I.N. Wood (1977), 50–71; A. Jones, 'The significance of the regal consecration of Edgar in 973', *Journal of Ecclesiastical History*, 33 (1982), 375–90.

Athelstan) should become king in Wessex.[16] The death of Ælfweard a few days after his father helped Athelstan to become king of both provinces, but at the battle of *Brunanburh* in 937 the West Saxon and Mercian armies fought as two separate units, possibly one led by Athelstan and the other by his half-brother Edmund.[17] In 957, in mysterious but apparently peaceful circumstances, England was divided between the two sons of Edmund, with Eadwig the eldest, who had been ruling since 955, remaining king of the West Saxons, while his brother Edgar became king of the Mercians and Northumbrians.[18] The death of Eadwig in 959 meant that Edgar could unite the country again, but in his epitaph in the 'D' version of the *Chronicle* there is a careful distinction drawn between his role as 'friend of the West Saxons' and that of 'protector of the Mercians'.[19] The different provinces of Wessex and Mercia were still distinguished on occasion in the *Chronicle* entries for the reign of Æthelred Unræd (978–1016) and when the country was divided between his son Edmund and the Danish Cnut in 1016 'Edmund succeeded to Wessex and Cnut to Mercia'.[20]

In the reign of Eadwig the River Thames was regarded as the boundary between Wessex and Mercia,[21] and it is not possible to distinguish in references to the 'West Saxons' a distinction between the original West Saxon provinces and more recently acquired south-eastern districts. Nevertheless, there are a number of pointers to suggest that the West Saxon core area largely kept its identity and that long-standing administrative subdivisions within it were retained. To begin with, as we have seen, the newly conquered eastern provinces were kept as a separate subkingdom whose holder was in effect the nominated heir of the royal house. When Æthelwulf decided to go on pilgrimage to Rome in 855 he left his eldest surviving son, Æthelbald, in charge of Wessex itself, while the next eldest, Æthelbert, seems to have been appointed ruler of the eastern provinces.[22] The terms of Æthelwulf's will, as cited in the will of Alfred, could be taken to imply that it was envisaged that Æthelbert would establish his own dynasty there.[23] However, when Æthelbert succeeded Æthelbald in 860, he reunited

16. A. Williams, 'Some notes and considerations on problems connected with the English royal succession, 860–1066', in *Anglo-Norman Studies*, 1, ed. R.A. Brown (1978), 149–51; B.A.E. Yorke, 'Æthelwold and the politics of the tenth century', in *Bishop Æthelwold: His Career and Influence*, ed. B.A.E. Yorke (1988), 70–3.
17. *Chronicle s.a.* 937.
18. Stenton, *Anglo-Saxon England*, 366–7; Yorke, 'Æthelwold and politics', 75–9.
19. *Chronicle* D *s.a.* 975.
20. *Chronicle* C,D,E *s.a.* 1016.
21. W. Stubbs (ed.), *Memorials of St Dunstan, Archbishop of Canterbury*, Rolls series (1874), 36, translated *EHD*, I, 901.
22. S 315; D.N. Dumville, 'The ætheling: a study in Anglo-Saxon constitutional history', *ASE, 8* (1979), 22–4; Kirby, *Earliest English Kings*, 200–2.
23. S. Keynes and M. Lapidge (trans.), *Alfred the Great* (1983), 173–8, 314.

Wessex and the eastern provinces. The eastern provinces were never again treated as a separate subkingdom, but, apart from Surrey which was in the Winchester diocese and had been ruled by West Saxon kings in the later seventh century, they were not closely integrated with the older West Saxon provinces either. The future of Essex lay with the other shires of eastern England; Sussex seems often to have had its own ealdorman during much of the tenth century and in Kent many of the responsibilities which elsewhere lay with ealdormen seem to have been undertaken by the Archbishop of Canterbury.[24]

Within Wessex the long-established division of the kingdom into two separate provinces east and west of Selwood seems to have remained of the greatest significance.[25] The continuing importance of the division into east and west Wessex emerges in the circumstances surrounding Æthelbald's resistance to his father's return from Rome in 856. There is no reference to these events in the *Anglo-Saxon Chronicle*, though the statement under the year 855 that Æthelbald (who died in 860) had ruled five years implies that his reign was reckoned to have continued unbroken from 855. Our sole authority is Asser's *Life of King Alfred*, where the account of Æthelbald's rebellion is one of several stories which place Alfred's brothers in a less favourable light than Alfred himself.[26] It may have been that Æthelbald had not expected his father to return from Rome. It was a notoriously unhealthy place and two previous West Saxon kings, Cædwalla and Ine, who had made the pilgrimage had died there.[27] But Æthelwulf seems to have come back positively rejuvenated and on his return journey stopped off in the western Frankish kingdom and married Judith, the young daughter of Charles the Bald. Æthelbald attempted to resist his father's return; the second marriage and the threat of rival heirs which might result from it may have been major motives.[28] But according to Asser, Æthelbald had co-conspirators, Ealhstan, bishop of Sherborne, and Eanwulf, ealdorman of Somerset, and the plot was hatched 'in the western part of Selwood'. Asser does not explain why there should have been particular resistance to Æthelwulf in the west, but the answer may lie in the political changes of the first half of the ninth century which made what had been the eastern provinces of Wessex central to the newly enlarged kingdom. The

---

24. N. Banton, 'Ealdormen and earls in England from the reign of King Alfred to the reign of King Æthelred II' (D. Phil. thesis, University of Oxford, 1981), 197–205.
25. See Ch. 1, 23–4.
26. Asser, Ch. 11–13; see also Ch. 17, 22, 23, 37, 38 and 42.
27. *HE*, V, 7. Though Bede does not specifically say that Ine died in Rome this seems likely as there is no separate record of his return and death.
28. P. Stafford, 'Charles the Bald, Judith and England', in *Charles the Bald: Court and Kingdom*, ed. M. Gibson and J. Nelson, BAR International series, *101* (1981), 137–51. See also M.J. Enright, 'Charles the Bald and Æthelwulf of Wessex: the alliance of 856 and the strategies of royal succession', *Journal of Medieval History, 5* (1979), 291–302.

family connections of Æthelwulf's house seem to have lain west of Selwood and there may have been resentment from the leading nobles of the district to the patronage shown to Winchester and Bishop Swithun.[29]

The matter was resolved by a compromise and 'the eastern districts were assigned to the father, but the western districts assigned to the son'.[30] Asser's words are not without ambiguity and it is not clear whether 'the eastern districts' are Kent, Sussex, Surrey and the East Saxons or the eastern portion of the Wessex heartlands. It has usually been assumed that Æthelwulf took back the former from his son Æthelbert (whom Asser does not mention in this context), but as David Kirby has argued, it may be that Æthelbald's control was confined to Wessex west of Selwood, that Æthelbert retained his kingdom in the east and that Æthelwulf for the last two years of his life ruled the central area, Wessex east of Selwood, between the territories of his two sons.[31] When Æthelwulf died in 858 he was buried at Steyning in Sussex which would have lain in the area controlled by Æthelbert;[32] perhaps Æthelbald was not prepared to allow him to be buried in the main kingdom of Wessex, all of which had come under his control again on his father's death. By the time the *Anglo-Saxon Chronicle* was compiled, Æthelwulf's body had been moved to Winchester.[33]

The division east and west of Selwood remained of underlying importance throughout the ninth century. After Alfred was forced to flee for his life when the Vikings seized Chippenham in 878, it appears that the Vikings received the submission of much of eastern Wessex while Alfred was supported in the west, a division which recalls the practice of the 'great heathen army' elsewhere in England of taking over one half of the kingdoms they conquered while leaving the other half under native control.[34] When the author of the *Chronicle* entry for 893 wished to convey that thegns turned out from every part of Wessex, he described them as coming from 'both west and east of Selwood'. The importance of this internal division within Wessex was recognized in the reorganization of the ealdormanries in the early tenth century. Whereas in the reign of Alfred there had been an ealdorman for each shire and bishoprics east and west of Selwood, in the tenth century the positions of ealdormen and bishops were reversed. In 909 Edward the Elder

---

29. B.A.E. Yorke, 'The bishops of Winchester, the kings of Wessex and the development of Winchester in the ninth and early tenth centuries', *PHFCAS, 40* (1984), 61–70.

30. Asser, Ch. 12.

31. Kirby, *Earliest English Kings*, 201.

32. D.N. Dumville and M. Lapidge (eds.), *The Annals of St Neots with Vita Prima Sancti Neoti* (1984), *s.a.* 858.

33. *Chronicle s.a.* 855; D. Whitelock, *The Genuine Asser* (1968), 9.

34. Asser, Ch. 52 and 53; A.P. Smyth, *Scandinavian Kings in the British Isles 850-880* (1977), 247.

1. Ealdormen in Wessex 871–924

Hampshire	*Dorset*	*Somerset*
Cuthred 871/7	Ælfstan 867/8–871/7	Eadulf? 868–871/7
Wulfred 879–894/6	Beorhtnoth? 882	Æthelnoth 878–894
Heahferth? 900–9	Beorhtulf 891–909	Ordgar? 900-926

Wiltshire	*Berkshire*	*Devon*
Wulfhere 854–c. 880	Æthelwulf 836–871	Odda 878
Æthelhelm 887–897	Æthelstan? 871/7	Æthelred 892–899
Ordlaf 898–909	Wulflaf 882–898	
	Deormod? 901	

2. Ealdormen in Wessex 924–1016

Western Wessex (Dorset, Somerset and Devon)	*Eastern Wessex* (Hampshire, Berkshire and Wiltshire)
Osferth? 909–934	Ælfwold? 925–938
Ælfhere 939–940	Wulfgar 939–949
Eadric 942–949	Æthelsige 951–958
Edmund 949–963	Ælfheah 959–970
Ordgar 964–970	Æthelmær 977–982
Æthelweard 976–998	Ælfric 982–1016
Æthelmaer 1012/3–1014	

[Where it is not possible to give the exact duration of office, years are given for which the ealdorman is known to have been in post. Question marks indicate ealdormen who are known, but cannot definitely be linked with a particular shire or group of shires.]

24. The ealdormen of Wessex, 871–1016 [N. Banton, 'Ealdormen and earls in England from the reign of King Alfred to the reign of King Æthelred II', (ph.D. thesis, University of Oxford, 1981)]

reorganized episcopal provision so that there was a bishop for each of the West Saxon shires, except Berkshire which was included in the Ramsbury diocese of Wiltshire, while the bishop of Winchester also had control of Surrey. Edward also began to reduce the number of ealdormanries, and his policy was continued by Athelstan, so that by the end of the latter's reign there were only two ealdormanries within Wessex.[35] It is possible to draw up complete lists for the two West Saxon ealdormanries from *c.* 924 to 1016 (see fig. 24). Unfortunately the ealdormen did not regularly use titles which reveal the exact areas they controlled, but the indications we do have suggest the division of east and west of Selwood was maintained, that is one ealdorman controlling Devon, Dorset and Somerset, plus Cornwall, and the other Wiltshire, Berkshire and Hampshire (and probably Surrey which was in the Winchester

---

35. That is, excluding Kent and Sussex. H.M. Chadwick, *Studies on Anglo-Saxon Institutions* (1905), 194–7; Banton, 'Ealdormen and earls', especially 197–214.

diocese). Æthelweard the Chronicler, who was an ealdorman from 975/6 to *c.* 998, is described as *Occidentalium provinciarum dux,* 'ealdorman of the western provinces', in one charter.[36] His son Æthelmær is generally assumed to have succeeded to the same position and in 1013 carried the submission of the western thegns to the Danish King Swein at Bath. Both he and Æthelweard's predecessor Ordgar are described as controlling the province of *Domnania* in the twelfth-century *Chronicon ex Chronicis* compiled at Worcester.[37] All three were major patrons of West Country religious houses. Holders of the other ealdormanry, if they are given a title at all, are described as ealdormen of Hampshire. Ælfric, *Wentaniensium provinciarum dux,*[38] is shown as leading an army from Wiltshire and Hampshire in 1003. As Wiltshire and Berkshire formed one diocese it is reasonable to assume that he had control of that shire as well, a hypothesis which can receive support from the fact that Ælfric bought the position of abbot of Abingdon for his brother Edwin and was remembered as one of the despoilers of the abbey.[39]

There are additional factors which also mark out the Wessex provinces from other areas of England in the later Anglo-Saxon period. The greatest preponderance of royal estates lay within the West Saxon shires as the Domesday Book entries recording the lands of Edward the Confessor indicate.[40] It was not just that there was more royal demesne land in Wessex, but that it seems to have been more highly prized. In the will of King Eadred (946–55) the only named estates lay within Wessex, though his mother also received unspecified booklands in Sussex, Surrey and Kent (fig. 25).[41] As far as we can tell from the limited references available to indicate royal itineraries, the later Anglo-Saxon kings spent more time in Wessex than in other parts of their kingdom and travelled with their court from estate to estate as their predecessors had done (fig. 25); many of these estates paid a compounded food rent ('the farm of one night') and were never assessed in hides.[42] Many of the leading nobility of the tenth century also seem to have been West Saxon in origin and to have retained estates there even if they were in charge of ealdormanries in other parts of the country. The great ealdorman Athelstan 'Half King', who controlled much of eastern England in the first half of the tenth century, seems still to

36. S 891; *The Chronicle of Æthelweard*, ed. A. Campbell (1962), xii–xvi.
37. B. Thorpe (ed.), *Florentii Wigorniensis Chronicon ex Chronicis* (2 vols, 1849), I, 142 and 146.
38. S 891; the title presumably implies a district administered from Winchester.
39. S. Keynes, *The Diplomas of King Æthelred 'The Unready' 978–1016* (1980), 177–8.
40. D. Hill, *An Atlas of Anglo-Saxon England* (1981), 100–1.
41. S 1515; translated *EHD*, I, 554–6.
42. Hill, *Atlas of Anglo-Saxon England*, 87-91; P. Sawyer, 'The royal *tun* in pre-Conquest England', in *Ideal and Reality in Frankish and Anglo-Saxon Society*, ed. P. Wormald *et al.* (1983), 273–99.

▲
Tanshelf
947

Abingdon
955

Frome
Died 23 Nov 955

Kingston
Consecrated 946

Glastonbury

Old Minster
Buried

Somerton 949 ▲
Easter crown-wearing

▲ Witan

A

0   60 miles

0   100 kilometres   THE MERCIANS

Dorchester
Wantage
WILTSHIRE   BERKSHIRE
Calne○   Thatcham
Bradford○ Shalbourne○ ○ Kingsclere
Andover   ● Basing   SURREY
Glastonbury ○ Wherwell
SOMERSET   Amesbury ● New Minster   KENT
Wilton ■   Old Minster
Shaftesbury   Nunnaminster
Damarham Downton SUSSEX
DEVON   HAMPSHIRE
DORSET

Christchurch ■

■ houses receiving bequests   DEVON named shires receiving relief
○ lands to churches   KENT shires with booklands donated
● lands to King's mother

B

25. (a) Known itinerary of King Eadred (b) places mentioned in the will of King Eadred [after D. Hill, *Atlas of Anglo-Saxon England* (1981), figs. 158–9]

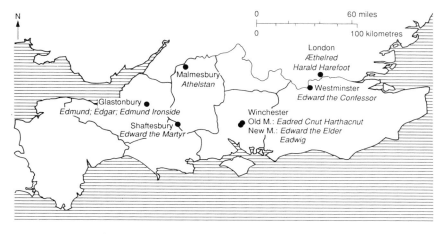

26. Burial places of the kings of Wessex and England from Edward the Elder to Edward the Confessor

have considered himself 'West Saxon', for when he retired he entered the monastery of Glastonbury of which he and other members of his family were major patrons.[43] Royal patronage meant that the religious houses of Wessex were particularly favoured and, until the reign of King Æthelred, all kings of the West Saxon royal house were buried in Wessex (fig. 26).[44] The nunneries which their daughters and other female relatives entered were all within Wessex, and Barking and Leominster are the only nunneries listed in Domesday Book which lay outside the Wessex heartlands (see fig. 53).[45]

THE VIKING WARS OF THE NINTH CENTURY: ALFRED AND THE WRITTEN SOURCES

Of all the developments in West Saxon affairs in the ninth century, the one which received most attention in the surviving narrative sources was the successful resistance to Viking attackers and invaders. The basic framework of events is provided by the *Anglo-Saxon Chronicle*. This work has often been referred to before as it contains information relating to earlier West Saxon reigns, and it also linked Wessex with earlier British and world history with, for instance, its first annal recording the conquest of Britain by Julius Caesar. However, the work of compilation of the *Chronicle* belongs

---

43. C. Hart, 'Athelstan "Half King" and his family', *ASE, 2* (1973), 115–44; see also A. Williams, '*Princeps Merciorum gentis*: the family, career and connections of Ælfhere, ealdorman of Mercia, 956–983', *ASE, 10* (1982), 143–72.
44. See Chapter 5, 203–5.
45. Hill, *Atlas of Anglo-Saxon England*, 154 and see Ch. 5, 206–8.

to the ninth century and the text seems to have been officially 'published' in the early 890s when there was a widespread copying and circulation of manuscripts from which the surviving versions all ultimately descend.[46] Unfortunately nothing is known about the circumstances of compilation or of the history of any of the component parts except what can be inferred from the surviving manuscript witnesses. Various attempts have been made to infer different stages in its composition from the form of the text which emerged in the 890s, but detailed linguistic analysis suggests that all the earlier material, including annals for the reigns of Egbert and Æthelwulf, was edited and revised during the reign of Alfred.[47] A team of compilers seems likely and the annals for the 870s were written by a different individual from those for the 880s. The great nineteenth-century historian of the *Chronicle*, Charles Plummer, was convinced that Alfred initiated the compilation,[48] but Sir Frank Stenton, reacting to such arguments, saw it as uncharacteristic of a court production and argued for it being the private work of a West Country nobleman.[49] Respect for the views of Stenton has meant that there is still reluctance to seeing the *Chronicle* as a work commissioned by the king,[50] even though it is hard to see who else could have organized the substantial copying and distribution of manuscripts which evidently took place and which seems to be paralleled by the arrangements for the distribution of the king's translation of Pope Gregory's *Pastoral Care* at about the same time.[51] From what Alfred says in the preface to this translation, it seems unlikely that anyone was producing substantial written works in Old English in late ninth-century Wessex except the king and those working for him.[52] Study of the vocabulary shows that the *Chronicle* was not 'written' by the king himself or any of his close associates who have compositions in Old English surviving,[53] but that does not mean it could not have been a court production, though some commentators have preferred to see it as a work commissioned by the king from one of his favoured religious communities such as Athelney.[54]

---

46. Keynes and Lapidge, *Alfred*, 275–81.
47. J. Bately, 'The compilation of the Anglo-Saxon Chronicle, 60 BC to AD 890: vocabulary as evidence', *PBA, 64* (1978), 93–129.
48. *Chronicle*, II, civ–ix.
49. F.M. Stenton, 'The south-western element in the Old English Chronicle', in *Preparatory to Anglo-Saxon England*, ed. D.M. Stenton (1970), 106–15.
50. Bately, 'Compilation', 127–9; Keynes and Lapidge, *Alfred*, 40.
51. *Chronicle*, II, cviii–ix; R.H.C. Davis, 'Alfred the Great: propaganda and truth', *History, 56* (1971), 174–5.
52. Keynes and Lapidge, *Alfred*, 124–6.
53. Bately, 'Compilation', 116–29.
54. J. Campbell, 'Asser's Life of Alfred', in *The Inheritance of Historiography 350–900*, ed. C. Holdsworth and T.P. Wiseman (1986), 115–35. The absence of any identification by the author(s) with the interests of a specific house or region could be an argument in favour of court production.

Although, again following Sir Frank Stenton, there is still some reluctance to describe the *Chronicle* as propaganda, the case for so seeing it has been strongly argued by Professor Davis,[55] and, as James Campbell has remarked, *'prima facie* the *Chronicle* does appear to be Alfredian propaganda, to the extent that the *onus probandi* would seem to lie principally upon those who hold that it was not'.[56] The *Chronicle* texts were circulated at a time when Wessex was facing renewed Viking attacks and the need to urge the people to further resistance by reminding them of past successes under Alfred and his forbears are a convincing motivation for the great effort involved in getting the text widely disseminated. However, one should not overlook the possibility that the compilation may also have had some connection with Alfred's desire to secure the succession for his son rather than one of his nephews.[57] Not only does the *Chronicle* dwell upon Anglo-Saxon successes and diminish those of the enemy by such devices as giving the number of Vikings killed in battle, but not the Anglo-Saxon casualties,[58] it also magnifies the achievements of Alfred himself at the expense of other West Saxon leaders. The annals for the reigns of Egbert and Æthelwulf frequently refer to the role of ealdormen and other leaders in battle, and it is clear that the armies which met the Vikings during their reigns were not always led by a king, but in the entries between 871 and 892 only Alfred is mentioned by name, which creates quite a different impression. Further annals were produced for the wars against the Vikings between 893 and 896 which seem to have been added to the circulated copies of the original *Chronicle*.[59] They are quite different in style from those of the original composition and much more detailed.

In 893, just after the circulation of *Chronicle*, Asser wrote his biography of King Alfred and used a version of the *Chronicle* annals to 887 to provide the framework for his text. Asser interspersed the annalistic account with detailed discussions of Alfred's character and behaviour as king and with information about the royal house which seems to have been provided by the king himself and which often placed his predecessors, and especially his brothers, in a poor light. Asser also expanded the *Chronicle* annals' accounts of the Viking wars. He was in an excellent position to gather information as he was in frequent attendance at the royal court from 885 when he first came from the bishopric of St David's in Wales and found favour with Alfred.[60] Asser's account of events in the crucial year of 878 reveals that he had actually visited the site of the siege at *Cynuit* (perhaps Countisbury) in north Devon, and his description

---

55. Davis, 'Alfred the Great', 169–82.
56. Campbell, 'Asser's Life of Alfred', 124.
57. See the will of King Alfred–Keynes and Lapidge, *Alfred*, 173–8; and see below.
58. E.g. in the account of the siege of *Cynuit* in 878.
59. Keynes and Lapidge, *Alfred*, 114–19 and 279–80.
60. Keynes and Lapidge, *Alfred*, 48–58.

of how the Devon force was caught by surprise and without adequate provisions contains the type of circumstantial details which suggests it was based on an eye-witness account. On the other hand, Asser was not in the business of writing an objective account of Alfred's reign. Alfred was his lord and patron and Asser lovingly records the generous gifts he received from the king, including the minsters of Banwell, Congresbury and Exeter.[61] Asser in return produced a biography which has ensured Alfred's high reputation in subsequent generations. His subject emerges as part ideal Carolingian king, part saint and, some way behind, part traditional warrior king.[62] Although Asser occasionally allows himself some tart comments about the Anglo-Saxons as a whole, no word of criticism is made of the king. It is not clear whether Asser wrote because he had been specifically commissioned. In places he appears to be addressing his fellow countrymen, and it has been suggested that he wrote to encourage Welsh kingdoms to accept Alfred's overlordship.[63] However, there is no evidence that the work was ever circulated in Wales and it is possible that the biography, which ends abruptly and has some internal inconsistencies, was never completed.

Also of use in reconstructing events during the wars against the Vikings is the Latin version of the *Chronicle* made by Æthelweard, ealdorman of the western shires from 975/6 to *c*. 998. Unlike Asser, Æthelweard did not have the opportunity to interrogate veterans of the campaigns against the Vikings, but he nevertheless supplies convincing additional information such as the names of ealdormen. Stenton suggested that Æthelweard made use of annals compiled in the West Country which formed the basis of the *Chronicle* entries for Alfred's reign, but were in a fuller form, extraneous matter such as the names of ealdormen having been edited out when the final version of the 'national' chronicle was produced.[64] Alternatively Æthelweard could have had a version of the *Chronicle* which had been annotated in the ninth or early tenth centuries, for Æthelweard has additions to the annals for 893–6 as well. Such a text of the *Chronicle* could have been passed down within Æthelweard's family (he was descended from Alfred's brother King Æthelred I) or between holders of west country ealdormanries. However, identification of the origin of Æthelweard's additions is complicated by the fact that he did not provide a straight translation of the *Chronicle* text and his Latin is often extremely hard to comprehend. Interpretation is also not helped by the almost complete destruction

61. Asser, Ch. 81.
62. Campbell, 'Asser's Life of Alfred'.
63. M. Schütt, 'The literary form of Asser's *Vita Alfredi*', *EHR, 62* (1957), 209–20; D. Kirby, 'Asser and his Life of King Alfred', *Studia Celtica, 6* (1971), 12–35.
64. Stenton, 'South-western element'; see also E.E. Barker, 'The Anglo-Saxon Chronicle used by Æthelweard', *Bulletin of the Institute of Historical Research, 40* (1967), 74–91.

of the only known version of his text, an eleventh-century copy, in the disastrous Cottonian fire of 1731; the modern printed edition has had to be based on a sixteenth-century transcript.[65] Nevertheless Æthelweard's version of the *Chronicle* is of interest as it occasionally seems to diverge from the 'official' version of events. Otherwise we have few sources, of which charters are probably the most useful, through which to see the Viking wars through eyes other than those of Alfred and his court.[66] The Vikings, not being Christian and literate at this time, have not left their version of events and even later sagas do not touch upon their activities in Wessex in the ninth century.

THE VIKING ATTACKS OF THE LATE EIGHTH AND NINTH CENTURIES

[During the reign of King Beorhtric 789–802] there came for the first time three ships of Northmen and then the reeve rode to them and wished to force them to the king's residence, for he did not know what they were; and they slew him.[67]

Thus the *Chronicle* baldly reported the first Viking attack on Wessex which may well have been the first raid on any of the Anglo-Saxon kingdoms. The murder of the king's reeve while going about his official business seems to have made a considerable impact, for additional details about the event are recorded in different texts of the *Anglo-Saxon Chronicle*. The manuscripts of the northern recension (D and E) include the important information that the Scandinavians came from Hörthaland in Norway, and the *Annals of St Neots*, which utilized a lost text of the *Chronicle*, add that they landed at Portland (Dorset).[68] Æthelweard knew the name of the reeve and that he was based at Dorchester where 'in an authoritative manner' he ordered the men to be taken for 'he thought they were merchants rather than marauders'.[69] However, in spite of the alarm that the attack may have caused there are no more raids recorded on Wessex until the 830s.

Wessex was exposed to Viking attacks from two main directions. Its western shores which bordered the Bristol Channel were liable to raids from the so-called 'Hiberno-Norse' who settled in Ireland, the Isle of Man and the islands off the west coast of Scotland, and

---

65. *The Chronicle of Æthelweard*, ed. A. Campbell (1962), ix–lxiii.
66. Though Alfred was also patron and lord of Scandinavians; see Asser, Ch. 94, and N. Lund, *Two Voyagers at the Court of King Alfred: Ohthere and Wulfstan* (1984).
67. *Chronicle s.a.* 789. References to Viking attacks in this section are taken from the *Chronicle* unless otherwise stated.
68. Dumville and Lapidge (eds), *Annals of St Neots*.
69. Æthelweard, 26–7.

perhaps in Wales as well, in the course of the ninth century. However, the places of origin of the attackers are rarely identified in the *Chronicle* which tends to use the blanket term 'Danish' for all Scandinavian forces. As we have seen, the three ships which arrived off Portland in the reign of Beorhtric seem to have contained predominantly Norse adventurers, but some way from their normal raiding grounds in Britain; perhaps they had been blown off course or were exploring the possibilities of further raiding or settlement. Attacks on the north Devon and Somerset coasts, presumably by Hiberno-Norse, began in earnest in the 830s and 840s. Carhampton (Som) was attacked in 836 and 843, and in 838 Vikings joined with the Cornish against King Egbert at Hingston Down (Corn), but the West Saxons won. A great victory for the men of Somerset and Dorset over a Viking army at the mouth of the River Parrett (Som) is recorded for 845 and for the men of Devon at the unidentified site of *Wicganbeorg* in 851. These are the last recorded ninth-century raids which can plausibly be identified as those of Hiberno-Norse, though we should not discount the possibility of unrecorded hit-and-run raids. However, it would appear that decisive defeats had discouraged the Norse from attempting to establish permanent bases on the north-west coast of Wessex.[70]

The parts of Wessex bordering the Channel were subject to raids by predominantly Danish fleets which also operated in western Francia where Danish bases had been established. When the Frankish kings and other leaders were successful against them they turned their attention to England, but would then return to Francia if they were beaten off by Anglo-Saxon armies.[71] The parts of Wessex we are concerned with seem to have been only marginally affected to begin with, unlike Kent which seems to have borne the brunt of the early Danish attacks. The first serious raids recorded for the main part of Wessex occurred in 840 when a fleet of 33 ships attacked first Hamwic/Hamtun and then Portland where the ealdorman of Dorset was killed; the Frankish historian Nithard records an attack on Hamwic in 842, but this may be a reference to the raid the *Chronicle* dated to 840.[72] In 851 Wessex faced a serious threat when a fleet estimated at 350 ships sailed into the Thames and defeated the Mercian king. A combined West Saxon army defeated and dispersed it at *Aclea* in Surrey. In 860 what is described as 'a great naval force' stormed Winchester, but was successfully attacked by the shire armies of Hampshire and Berkshire as its men were returning to the ships with their booty.

---

70. Hill, *Atlas of Anglo-Saxon England*, 36–7; J. Richards, *Viking Age England* (1991).
71. Hill, *Atlas of Anglo-Saxon England*, 36–9.
72. G.H. Pertz and E. Muller (eds), *Nithardi Historiarum Libri III, MGH Scriptores Rerum Germanicarum, Separatim Editi* (Hanover, 1956), 42; A.D. Morton (ed.), *Excavations in Hamwic: Volume I*, CBA res. rep., *84* (1992), 76–7.

Up to this point Viking raids on Wessex seem to have been few and generally targeted on individual centres. The Viking forces seem to have been satisfactorily dealt with by one or two shire contingents serving under their own ealdormen and a 'national' West Saxon army had rarely been called out. Most of Wessex had not even been ridden over by Viking forces.

The real Viking threat to Wessex was the 'great heathen army' which landed in Thanet in 865, but which did not come to the main part of Wessex until 870/1, by which time it had already defeated the armies of Northumbria and the East Angles and established control of parts of those provinces.[73] This was an army which intended political conquest and settlement and so posed a much greater threat to the West Saxon leadership than any previously encountered. It was led in 870/1 by Bagsecg and Halfdan who are described in the *Chronicle* as kings; Halfdan appears to have been the son of the Viking ruler Ragnar Lothbrook who figures prominently in saga literature.[74] The leaders had already demonstrated their prowess in Northumbria and East Anglia, and in Wessex showed a similar grasp of tactics and local knowledge. Their major engagements in 870/1 were fought at royal vill centres presumably because the Viking leaders knew that these were the centres from which the surrounding countryside was managed and where the king's *feorm* would be collected and stored.[75] The Viking army entered Wessex at Reading and this seems to have formed their main base in the campaign season of 870/1 (fig. 27). King Æthelred, aided by his brother Alfred whose role the *Chronicle* and Asser were keen to stress, tried to dislodge them and failed. Four days later they met again at Ashdown where the West Saxons seem to have had the greater success and killed Bagsecg. Asser is particularly careful to give much credit to Alfred who, he says, had to take full command at the start of the battle when Æthelred was still in his tent praying for victory.[76] The *Chronicle* emphasizes the large numbers of Vikings slain at Ashdown, but there were still sufficient surviving to defeat the West Saxons at Basing two weeks later. Two months on the armies met at the unidentified *Meretun* and the Danes again had the victory.[77] At this point the Viking army was joined at Reading by reinforcements, the 'great summer army' led by Guthrum which, according to Asser, had previously been campaigning overseas.[78] After its arrival King Æthelred died, after Easter on 15 April, and Alfred at once took over as king. His succession seems to have been agreed in advance, presumably so that there would be no hiatus in the command against the invasion

---

73. Smyth, *Scandinavian Kings, passim*.
74. Smyth, *Scandinavian Kings*, 1–67.
75. Sawyer, 'The royal *tun*', 273–99.
76. Asser, Ch. 37–9.
77. For a discussion of possible identifications see J. Peddie, *Alfred the Good Soldier* (1989), 91–3.
78. Asser, Ch. 40; Smyth, *Scandinavian Kings*, 240–2.

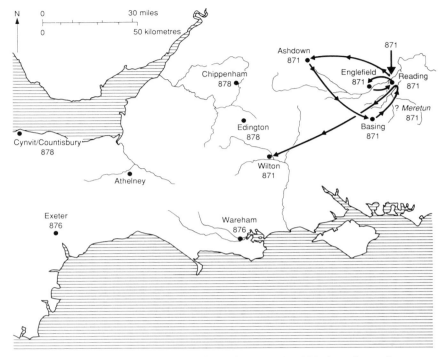

27. The 'great heathen army' in Wessex 871–878, based on the annals of the *Anglo-Saxon Chronicle*

force; Æthelred had two sons but both were still children in 871.[79] A month later Alfred was defeated by the enlarged Danish army at Wilton. The writer of the *Chronicle* annal for 871 estimated that there had been nine major battles fought in Wessex, plus many minor engagements fought by individual ealdormen with their forces, but neither side had established a clear advantage. Alfred made peace with the army, which probably means that a substantial tribute was paid, in order to make them leave the kingdom.[80]

An army led by Guthrum returned in 876, though this would have been smaller than the army Alfred had confronted at Wilton, as many of Halfdan's followers had chosen to settle on lands already won in eastern England.[81] Guthrum's army had been based in Cambridge and apparently outmanoeuvred the West Saxon forces and traversed the whole of Wessex to occupy Wareham. Æthelweard describes how the Vikings ravaged the countryside and

79. Asser, Ch. 29, 38 and 42; though see discussion in Dumville, 'The ætheling', 1–33.
80. Smyth, *Scandinavian Kings*, 242.
81. Smyth, *Scandinavian Kings*, 242–5.

had to be bought off by Alfred,[82] but the *Chronicle* refers only to how they swore oaths to the king that they would leave the kingdom and gave him hostages. In the event they left Wareham, but only to occupy Exeter instead; however, this time Alfred was able to persuade them to withdraw to Mercia. In 878 Guthrum tried to take Alfred by surprise by attacking him at the royal vill of Chippenham shortly after Christmas.[83] It is at this point that Alfred escaped to the marshes around Athelney which is the reputed site of the famous cake-burning episode which first appears in written form in the late Anglo-Saxon *Life of St Neots* (see fig. 31).[84] The impression the legend conveys of the king's fortunes being at a low ebb is valid enough because at this time a large number of the inhabitants of the eastern part of the Wessex apparently submitted to Guthrum.[85] Wulfhere, who was probably ealdorman of Wiltshire, may have been among them, for a later charter records how he forfeited estates for deserting 'without permission both his lord King Alfred and his countrymen in spite of the oath which he had sworn to the king and all his leading men'.[86] But the ealdormen of Somerset and Devon remained loyal and free, and the latter performed a major service in intercepting a second Viking force led by Ubbe, the brother of Halfdan, which sailed from Wales to *Cynuit* (Countisbury?) in north Devon presumably intending to join up with Guthrum's forces.[87] Alfred was able to rally sufficient forces from all over Wessex to meet and decisively defeat Guthrum at Edington (Wilts) in May. A new treaty was established and Guthrum was converted to Christianity and was baptized at Aller near Athelney (Som) with Alfred as sponsor.[88]

This treaty with Guthrum proved binding, though Alfred presumably could not have assumed that it would be and there was still the threat of attack by other Viking armies and particularly from a Viking group active in western Francia which probably included men who had fought with Halfdan and Guthrum and whose movements are carefully detailed in the *Chronicle*.[89] There were clashes between Alfred and this Viking force in the 880s, though none of these are said specifically to have affected the main part of Wessex. But in 892 the army established itself in bases in

82. Æthelweard, 41.
83. *Chronicle*, II, 92; Smyth, *Scandinavian Kings*, 246–8.
84. Keynes and Lapidge, *Alfred*, 197–202; Dumville and Lapidge (eds), *The Annals of St Neots*, 75–81.
85. D. Whitelock, *The Importance of the Battle of Edington* (1978); for a sceptical interpretation of the 878 annal see Davis, 'Alfred the Great', 170–2.
86. S 362; *EHD*, I, no. 100. R. Darlington, 'Anglo-Saxon Wiltshire', in *VCH Wiltshire, 2*, ed. R.B. Pugh (1955), 6–7.
87. Asser, Ch. 54; Smyth, *Scandinavian Kings*, 248–9.
88. *EHD*, I, no. 34; Whitelock, *Battle of Edington*; R.H.C. Davis, 'Alfred and Guthrum's frontier', *EHR*, 97 (1982), 803–10; D.N. Dumville, 'The treaty of Alfred and Guthrum', in *Wessex and England from Alfred to Edgar* (1992), 1–28.
89. Hill, *Atlas of Anglo-Saxon England*, 40–2.

eastern England, was joined by men from the Danish settlements within England and over the next four years raided widely within Wessex by land and sea, often splitting up into different subgroups which complicated the West Saxon resistance. Nevertheless, the West Saxons kept them on the move, and though they took booty they do not seem to have posed the same threat of political conquest as Guthrum's army.[90] In the summer of 896 the army divided up and its men either returned to settlements in East Anglia and Northumbria or sailed to the Seine and the burgeoning Viking colony in Normandy.

THE VIKING IMPACT ON WESSEX

The Viking attacks on Wessex are relatively well recorded in comparison to many previous events in West Saxon history and so it is not surprising that they have often been seen as having a major impact on the development of the province. The contrast that Alfred appears to draw in the Preface to his translation of Pope Gregory I's *Pastoral Care* between the cultural poverty of his own day and the happier times 'before everything was ravaged and burnt'[91] has been taken as a convenient explanation for why some early Saxon monasteries, such as Nursling on Southampton Water, seem to have failed to survive into the later Saxon period.[92] The disappearance of the settlement at Hamwic on the Itchen side of the Southampton peninsula has also been attributed by some writers to the effects of the Viking raid of 840/842 and the more general disruption Viking attacks caused to cross-Channel trade.[93] In fact, of course, it is extremely difficult to determine conclusively from archaeological evidence the reasons why sites were abandoned – as many were – in the course of the Anglo-Saxon period. No signs of enemy action have been discovered during the excavations at Hamwic, though occupation does seem to have contracted by the middle of the eighth century.[94] Even when buildings, such as a stone building associated with the watermill at Old Windsor (Berks), do seem to have been destroyed by fire during this period it cannot be proved that Vikings were responsible for the

---

90. Keynes and Lapidge, *Alfred*, 41–4.
91. Keynes and Lapidge, *Alfred*, 124–6; H. Sweet (ed.), *King Alfred's West Saxon Version of Gregory's Pastoral Care*, EETS, o.s., 45 and 50 (2 vols, 1871–2).
92. P. Hase, 'The development of the parish in Hampshire' (Ph. D. thesis, University of Cambridge, 1975), 73–95, and see Ch. 4, 181–5.
93. P. Holdsworth, 'Saxon Southampton', in *Anglo-Saxon Towns in Southern England*, ed. J. Haslam (1984), 331–43, especially 336–7; R. Hodges, 'State formation and the role of trade in Middle Saxon England', in *Social Organisation and Settlement*, ed. D. Green, C. Haselgrove and M. Spriggs (2 vols), BAR International series, 47 (1978), II, 439–53; R. Hodges, *Dark Age Economics: The Origins of Towns and Trade, AD 600–1000* (1982).
94. Morton, *Excavations in Hamwic*, 71–7.

destruction.[95] For every site where there is a lack of continuity between the pre- and post-Viking periods, one can point to another where occupation was not interrupted. Thus the monastery of Nursling may have disappeared, but the early Saxon minster church at Titchfield, which was just as exposed to attackers in the Solent, is still standing today (see fig. 47).[96] Hamwic was raided in 840/842, but Winchester was stormed by a 'great naval force' in 860 which seems to have done nothing to stem the rapid expansion of that town.[97]

Direct evidence for the Viking presence in ninth-century Wessex is slight. There is a burial from close to the banks of the Thames at Sonning (Berks) of two bodies with a sword of Viking type, a knife, six arrowheads, a Celtic ring-headed pin and miscellaneous iron fragments which has generally been accepted as Scandinavian.[98] There are also two possible, but poorly recorded, burials from Reading.[99] Other possible Viking burial sites in Wessex have been rejected by modern scholarship. Nor does the invasion of Viking armies seem to have panicked the inhabitants of Wessex into depositing their wealth in hoards. Of 39 hoards listed by Dolley as being buried in Britain between c. 865 and 879, the only one from the central West Saxon shires is from the minster site at Reading and that may have been a burial deposit rather than an actual hoard; what is known of the coins is consistent with it being connected with the occupation of the royal vill by the 'great heathen army' in 870–1.[100] The correspondence between the distribution of the hoards recorded by Dolley and the recorded activities of Viking armies in the ninth century is good and suggests that there were no major Viking incursions into Wessex which do not appear in the written sources.[101] The negative evidence of place-names supports

95. D. Wilson and J. Hurst (eds), 'Medieval Britain in 1957', *Med Arch, 2* (1958), 183–5; cited as possible evidence for a site destroyed in a Viking raid in D. Wilson, 'The Scandinavians in England', in *The Archaeology of Anglo-Saxon England*, ed. D. Wilson (1976), 393–403, at 375.

96. M.J. Hare, 'The Anglo-Saxon church of St Peter, Titchfield', *PHFCAS, 32* (1976), 5–48, and 'Investigations at the Anglo-Saxon church of St Peter, Titchfield, 1982–9', *PHFCAS, 47* (1992), 117–44.

97. M. Biddle, 'The study of Winchester: archaeology and history in a British town', *PBA, 69* (1983), 93–135.

98. V. Evison, 'A Viking grave at Sonning, Berkshire', *Ant J, 49* (1969), 330–45.

99. Evison, 'Viking Grave'; M. Biddle and J. Blair, 'The Hook Norton hoard of 1848: a Viking burial from Oxfordshire?', *Oxoniensia, 57* (1987), 186–95. One of the putative burials is believed to have accompanied the coin hoard of n. 100.

100. R.J. Sherlock, 'A nineteenth-century manuscript book on coins', *BNJ, 28* (1956), 394–6; R.H.M. Dolley, *The Hiberno-Norse Coins in the British Museum* (1966); M. Blackburn and H. Pagan, 'A revised check-list of coin hoards from the British Isles c. 500–1100', in *Anglo-Saxon Monetary History*, ed. M. Blackburn (1986), 291–313; N. Brooks, and J. Graham-Campbell, 'Reflections on the Viking-Age silver hoard from Croydon, Surrey', in *Anglo-Saxon Monetary History*, ed. M. Blackburn (1986), 91–110 (the Croydon hoard may also have been deposited as a result of the great army wintering at Reading).

101. Dolley, *Hiberno-Norse Coins*, 15–40.

the conclusion that there were no Viking colonies established within Wessex.

The archaeological and numismatic evidence highlights the Reading area, where the Viking army based itself during the campaign of 870/871, as the part of Wessex where positive evidence survives for a Viking presence. But that does not mean that the rest of Wessex was unaffected by the Viking wars. The lack of material evidence for the Vikings in Wessex is testimony to the effectiveness of the defence organized by the West Saxon kings, and it was these defensive measures, as much as the Viking attacks, which had a major impact on Wessex. The building of fortified sites known as 'burhs' has sometimes been regarded as a particular achievement of Alfred, but the process of providing fortified centres in Wessex is likely to have begun before his accession and to have continued after his death. The first West Saxon charters which specifically refer to fortress-work as one of the 'common burdens' which all the landowning populace had to perform date from the reign of King Beorhtric (786–802) and probably reflect the influence in Wessex of Mercia during his reign.[102] Beorhtric's father-in-law Offa had played a major role in enforcing fortress-work in Mercia and had introduced the obligation into Kent, following his conquest of that province, specifically in response to Viking attacks.[103] When the West Saxons took over as lords of Kent they would have inherited the system of fortifications initiated by the Mercians. However, references to fortress-work, and to the other 'common burdens' of military service and the building of roads and bridges, only became a regular feature of West Saxon charters during the reign of Alfred's brother Æthelbald (855–60), though that need not rule out an earlier date for the introduction of the new obligations.[104] The revival of Winchester, which may well have included refurbishment of the defences, seems to have been under way around the middle of the ninth century.[105] Asser's account of the Viking seizure of Wareham in 876 seems to imply that Wareham already had its defensive circuit by that date, and Viking occupation of other burh sites may point in the same direction.[106] The defences at Wareham are still an impressive sight and have been excavated, but earthworks are notoriously difficult to date through excavation. The best

---

102. N. Brooks, 'The development of military obligations in eighth and ninth-century England', in *England Before the Conquest: Studies in Primary Sources Presented to Dorothy Whitelock*, ed. P. Clemoes and K. Hughes (1971), 69–84.

103. Brooks, 'The development of military obligations', 78–80.

104. N. Brooks, 'The administrative background of the Burghal Hidage', in *The Burghal Hidage*, ed. D. Hill and A. Rumble (forthcoming).

105. Biddle, 'Study of Winchester', 119–26.

106. N. Brooks, 'England in the ninth century: the crucible of defeat', *TRHS, 29* (1979), 1–20, at 9–10; for a contrary view see C.A.R. Radford, 'The pre-Conquest boroughs of England, ninth to eleventh centuries', *PBA, 64* (1978), 131–53, at 140.

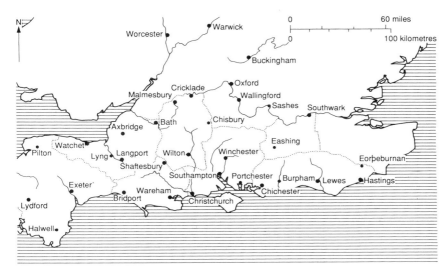

28. The burhs listed in the Burghal Hidage [after D. Hill, *Atlas of Anglo-Saxon England* (1981), fig. 150]

which the archaeological evidence could do was to demonstrate that they were post-Roman in date and similar in form to other West Saxon burhs listed in the Burghal Hidage.[107]

The document known as the 'Burghal Hidage' is central to any discussion of the West Saxon defences against the Vikings.[108] It contains a list of burhs with an assessment in hides for each from which, as a formula included with one version of the text explains, the length of defences to be maintained and manned can be worked out.[109] The burhs lie mostly within central Wessex, but the circuit begins at *Eortheburnan*, probably Castle Toll, Newenden, on the edge of Romney Marsh, and ends with Southwark (fig. 28).[110] Like many Anglo-Saxon texts it only survives in later manuscripts, and there is some uncertainty about the original date of compilation and about which variant readings should be preferred between the two main versions which have survived. Both main versions include a burh at Buckingham, and it is generally assumed that the document, in the form in which it has survived, dates to after 914 when the *Chronicle* records Edward the Elder built a double burh

---

107. RCHM, 'Wareham west walls', *Med Arch, 3* (1959), 120–38, and see further below.

108. D. Hill, 'The Burghal Hidage: the establishment of a text', *Med Arch, 13* (1969), 84–92; Keynes and Lapidge, *Alfred*, 193–4 and 339–41.

109. In version A it is explained that each pole (5½ yards) of wall was to be defended by four men and that every hide of land was to provide one man.

110. N. Brooks, 'The unidentified forts of the Burghal Hidage', *Med Arch, 8* (1964), 74–90; B.K. Davison, 'The Burghal Hidage fort of Eorþeburnan: a suggested identification', *Med Arch, 16* (1972), 123–7.

there;[111] a case for dating the Burghal Hidage list and all its fortifications to soon after Alfred's occupation of London in 886 has not met with general support.[112] It would appear that the burhs do not relate to just one campaign of building, and that the Burghal Hidage document records the system at only one stage in its evolution.

The scale of provision for the defences of the burhs varied considerably and in a way that does not always seem to have corresponded with the actual length of ramparts on the ground (fig. 29). Winchester has a very close correspondence between the length of its Roman walls at 3,318 yards and its hidage allocation of 2,400 hides which allowed for defence and maintenance of 3,300 yards.[113] None of the other hidage allocations fit quite so well (though differential survival of ramparts makes the original length uncertain in many cases),[114] and it may be that Winchester provided the template for the whole scheme with the hidage formula worked out from relating the length of its Roman walls to the number of hides available for their maintenance and defence from its catchment area of northern Hampshire. The fact that, as Nicholas Brooks has argued, hidage allocations for the burhs were likely to have been based on existing shire hidages,[115] explains why some burhs seem to have been woefully underprovided for in the Burghal Hidage arrangements. The inadequate provision for Devon's burhs can be directly related to the fact that it was very lightly assessed in hides compared to the other shires of Wessex, even when boosted by fortress-work allocations from Cornwall.[116] Exeter was only allocated 734 hides which would man 1,009 yards of wall, although the circuit of its Roman defences was some 2,566 yards (see fig. 87).[117] Lydford's 140 hides or 193 yards was insufficient for even the bank and ditch of 350 yards across the neck of the promontory on which it was situated (fig. 30).[118] Halwell and Pilton, the other two Devon burhs, had allocations of 300 and 360 hides respectively.[119] What is not clear is whether the provisions for the

---

111. Also relevant is Portchester, purchased by Edward in 904 – S 372/B 613.
112. Davis, 'Alfred and Guthrum's frontier', 803–10; criticized by Dumville, *Wessex and England*, 24–7, and Brooks, 'Administrative background'.
113. M. Biddle and D. Keene, 'Winchester in the eleventh and twelfth centuries', in *Winchester in the Early Middle Ages*, ed. M. Biddle, Winchester Studies, *1* (1976), 272–3.
114. Brooks, 'Administrative background'.
115. Brooks, 'Administrative background'; see also P.H. Sawyer, *From Roman Britain to Norman England* (1978), 227–9.
116. Brooks, 'Administrative background' and see Ch. 2, 90.
117. J. Allan, C. Henderson and R. Higham, 'Saxon Exeter', in *The Anglo-Saxon Towns of Southern England*, ed. J. Haslam (1984), 385–414, at 396–7.
118. A.D. Saunders, 'Lydford Castle, Devon', *Med Arch, 24* (1980), 123-86; J. Haslam, 'The towns of Devon', in *Anglo-Saxon Towns in Southern England*, ed. J. Haslam (1984), 249–83, at 256-9.
119. Haslam, 'Towns of Devon', 251–6 and 259–67; T. Slater, 'Controlling the South Hams: the Anglo-Saxon *burh* at Halwell', *Dev Assoc, 123* (1991), 57–78.

	Assessment (hides)	Equivalent (feet)
Portchester	500	2062
Southampton	150	619
Winchester	2400	9900
Wilton	1400	5775
Chisbury	700	2887
Shaftesbury	700	2887
Christchurch	470	1939
Wareham	1600	6600
Bridport	760	3135
Exeter	734	3028
Halwell	300	1237
Lydford	140	577
Pilton	360	1485
Watchet	513	2116
Axbridge	400	1650
Lyng	100	412
Langport	600	2475
Bath	1000	4125
Malmesbury	1200	4950
Cricklade	1500	6187
Wallingford	2400	9900
Sashes	1000	4125

29. The burhs of Wessex as listed in the Burghal Hidage with assessments in hides and their equivalent in feet, in accordance with the formula given in the text [after D. Hill, *Atlas of Anglo-Saxon England* (1981), fig. 152]

defences from the shire allocations were boosted by other means such as from royal resources or by requiring some landowners to contribute more. Nicholas Brooks has pointed out that some of the smaller 'emergency' burhs appear to have been additional to the burhs supported from the hidages available for their shires.[120] The system it would appear could not have worked unless some extra

120. Brooks, 'Administrative background'.

provisions were made. For instance, at Wareham only the three ramparts surrounding the settlement to north, west and east seem to have been provided for by the Burghal Hidage arrangements which would have left the southern boundary, marked by the River Frome, quite undefended, although the Vikings could be expected to use the river to gain access to the settlement.[121]

The Burghal Hidage included places of different status. Some were already important royal or ecclesiastical centres, including Winchester, Exeter, Wareham, Malmesbury and Shaftesbury, although there are some surprising omissions such as Sherborne and Dorchester (Dorset). Some established administrative centres were not themselves defended, but had a burh in their vicinity to which possibly some functions were temporarily transferred; examples include Langport for Somerton (Som), Chisbury for Bedwyn (Wilts) and Sashes for Cookham (Berks).[122] Most of these 'emergency' burhs were subsequently abandoned, though Langport continued to function as the trading centre ('port') of the Somerton estate (see fig. 83). The status of some places, including Wallingford and Cricklade (fig. 30), before their use as burhs is not known. Some of the burhs already had defences from an earlier period in their history. Refurbished sites included former Roman towns (Winchester, Exeter, Bath), Roman forts (Portchester and, possibly, the fort at Bitterne for Southampton) and Iron Age forts (Watchet (Som), Chisbury and Malmesbury (Wilts), Pilton and Halwell (Devon)). Among the *de novo* constructions, the most substantial were the rectangular fortified sites of Cricklade (fig. 30), Wareham and Wallingford which were allocated 1,500, 1,600 and 2,400 hides respectively. Other newly defended sites had substantially smaller allocations. A form particularly favoured for the smaller burhs was the promontory fort of which Lydford (Dev) (fig. 30), Langport (fig. 83) and Lyng (Som) are examples. The modest hidages provided for Portchester and for Southampton (if this entry is identified as the fort at Bitterne) have given rise to the suggestion that what was actually being provided under the Burghal Hidage scheme was a bank to cut off the promontories on which they were situated.[123] Some other types of site are also found; Sashes is an island in the Thames,[124] and Lyng may have been used in conjunction with Athelney to block access down the River Yeo and through the marshes (fig. 31).[125]

At Roman sites the walls were presumably repaired, but work

121. As they presumably did in 876; see also n. 106–7 above.
122. For more on these burhs and their relations to royal vills see Ch. 7, 309–16. For recent overviews of the system see M. Biddle, 'Towns', in *The Archaeology of Anglo-Saxon England*, ed. D. Wilson (1976), 99–150; R. Abels, *Lordship and Military Obligation in Anglo-Saxon England* (1988), 58–78; Richards, *Viking Age England*, 52–4.
123. D. Hill, 'The Burghal Hidage–Southampton', *PHFCAS, 24* (1967), 59–61.
124. Brooks,'The unidentified forts', 74–90.
125. M. Aston, 'The towns of Somerset', in *Anglo-Saxon Towns in Southern England*, ed. J. Haslam (1984), 167–202, at 183–5.

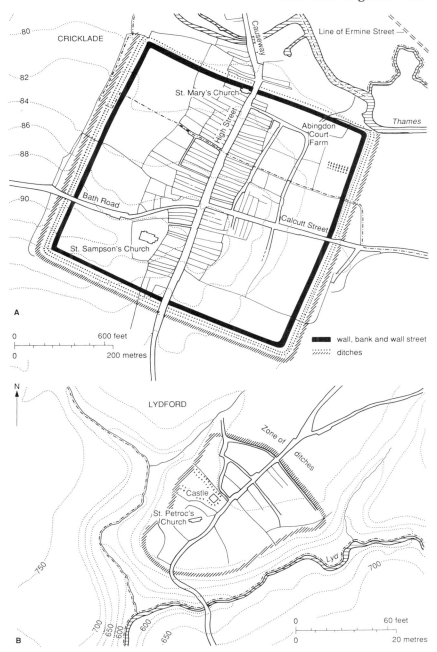

30. The burhs at (a) Cricklade (Wilts) and (b) Lydford (Devon) [after J. Haslam (ed.), *Anglo-Saxon Towns in Southern England* (1984), figs. 44 and 88]

31. Aerial photograph of Lyng and Athelney (Som) during flooding in January 1980. Lyng is in the right-hand foreground and is linked to Athelney in the top left-hand corner by a causeway rising above the flood-plain [photograph: M. Aston]

dating to this period has not definitely been identified. At Winchester the walls were supplemented by a substantial double ditch for at least part of the circuit.[126] Newly defended sites which have been excavated mostly share common characteristics of ramparts constructed of clay and turf with timber reinforcements which would probably have been surmounted by timber palisades,[127] though Watchet (Som) seems to have had ramparts topped with mortared stone walls.[128] Additional defences at Cricklade consisted of a triple ditch system of two small and one wide outer ditch separated from the rampart by a 20-foot-wide berm (fig. 30).[129] Some of the burhs were provided with a system of interconnecting streets. The most notable evidence comes from Winchester, where a combination of written and excavated evidence suggests that a substantial part of the gridded street system of the town (much of it still in use today) was laid out by the end of the ninth century,[130] and with great precision using a four-pole unit, also to be detected

126. Biddle and Keene, 'Winchester in the eleventh and twelfth centuries', 272–7.
127. See RCHM, 'Wareham west walls'; Saunders, 'Lydford Castle', and Richards, *Viking Age England*, 52–4.
128. F. McAvoy, 'Excavations at Daw's Castle, Watchet, 1982', *PSANHS, 130* (1986), 47–60.
129. J. Haslam, 'The towns of Wiltshire', in *Anglo-Saxon Towns in Southern England*, ed. J. Haslam (1984), 87–147, at 106–111.
130. M. Biddle and D. Hill, 'Late Saxon planned towns', *Ant J*, 51 (1971), 70–85.

elsewhere including in the laying out of Cricklade's defences.[131] The refurbishment of Winchester's defences may have pre-dated the laying out of the streets which can be seen as a secondary development, perhaps connected, as Nicholas Brooks has suggested, with the arrangements for garrisons which may have been a new departure during Alfred's reign.[132]

The burhs could have served varying defensive functions and the idea of a defensive circuit around Wessex may only have evolved gradually. Cricklade and Wallingford controlled key crossing-points on the Thames, while Portchester, Southampton, Christchurch, Wareham, Bredy, Exeter and Watchet were all either on the coast or controlled important routes inland from the sea. The provision of garrisons would have greatly extended the defensive and offensive roles of the burhs. In 893 a Viking force failed to take Exeter, presumably because of the effectiveness of its garrison, and when it moved round to the Severn estuary it was intercepted by Anglo-Saxon forces assembled from all the burhs east of the River Parrett.[133] Another function of burhs may have been to protect the foodstuffs and other valuable commodities which would be rendered to the royal vills.[134] In the campaigns of 870/1 the Vikings had focused their energies on attacking royal vills presumably because they knew payments of the royal *feorm* would be found there. It has been estimated that no part of Wessex was more than 20 miles from a burh and the regularity of provision may reflect that they were to have a key role in the maintenance of royal administration.[135]

It will be apparent that the burghal system placed a considerable burden on the population of Wessex. Many of the burhs involved substantial construction works, and Nicholas Brooks has estimated that almost one in five of the able-bodied adult male population of Wessex would have been required to furnish the garrisons as laid out in the Burghal Hidage.[136] The garrisons were in addition to the fyrd, the main army, for which one man may have been drawn from every five hides of land and in which most lay men of noble birth would fight.[137] Alfred divided the army into two halves so that 'always half its men were at home, half on service',[138] but even when at home its men might be required to turn out for a local emergency, as in 893 when 'the king's thegns who were then at home' in Somerset and Wiltshire were called out to join the army which defeated the Vikings at Buttington (Cheshire).

131. P. Crummy, 'The system of measurement used in town planning from the ninth to the thirteenth centuries', *ASSAH, 1*, BAR, 72 (1979), 149–64; J. Haslam, 'The metrology of Anglo-Saxon Cricklade', *Med Arch, 30* (1986), 100–2.
132. Brooks, 'England in the ninth century', 17–20.
133. *Chronicle* 893.
134. Sawyer, 'The royal *tun*', 273–99.
135. Hill, 'Burghal Hidage'.
136. Brooks, 'England in the ninth century', 18–19.
137. C. Warren Hollister, *Anglo-Saxon Military Institutions* (1962), especially 49–52; Abels, *Lordship and Military Obligation*, 58–79, 97–115.
138. *Chronicle* 893; Keynes and Lapidge, *Alfred*, 285–6.

West Saxon kings had been entitled for some time to call upon their subjects for military service and probably other public works, but the demands made by Alfred and his brothers for military service and fortress-work would have far exceeded anything that people would have experienced previously, and it is not surprising to find that it was resented. Asser wrote of the problems Alfred had in getting his subjects to work *pro communi regni neccessitate*, 'for the common needs of the kingdom', and in particular of the reluctance to work on fortifications.[139] Nor are Alfred's demands likely to have stopped with military service and fortress-work. The Viking wars must have involved a great expense in keeping the army in the field, not to mention the tributes which Alfred sometimes seems to have been obliged to pay, and it is only to be expected that Alfred would seek to recoup some of his costs. The Church in particular seems to have been obliged to help him out. Bishop Ealhferth of Winchester (*c.* 862–871×877) was unable to pay his portion of a heavy tribute demanded by the Vikings and so was obliged to ask the king to pay it for him and in return to surrender to him two estates which had been left to the Old Minster in the will of Alfred's father. Ealhferth's successor Denewulf was later able to negotiate a reversionary interest in the estates (and a sum of money), but only at the cost of surrendering an estate of comparable size in Berkshire.[140] In another lease Denewulf promises to pay an annual render unless it is not possible because of the stress caused by a raid;[141] whether it was the actions of the Vikings or the king's defensive measures which caused the stress he does not say! In Wessex it would appear that religious foundations were more at risk from the depredations of the West Saxon kings than the Vikings.[142] The estates that had been given to support the religious community at Abingdon were apparently seized by King Alfred, who is compared to Judas in the Abingdon *Chronicle*. Alfred may have made some provision for the continuation of a community of priests, but most of the lands seem to have been annexed to the royal fisc.[143]

Wessex escaped serious damage at the hands of the Vikings, but only at the price of increased royal demands. Naturally there was resistance and resentment; some preferred subjection to Viking rule to the tyranny of Alfred. But Alfred seems to have been able to command sufficient support to quell any opposition and was in the enviable position of being able to claim that all he did was for the protection of the kingdom. The large number of surviving written

---

139. Asser, Ch. 91.
140. S 354/B 565.
141. S 385/B 622.
142. R. Fleming, 'Monastic lands and England's defence in the Viking age', *EHR*, *100* (1985), 247–65; D.N. Dumville, 'Ecclesiastical lands and the defence of Wessex in the first Viking Age', in *Wessex and England*, 29–54.
143. A.T. Thacker, 'Æthelwold and Abingdon', in *Bishop Æthelwold: His Career and Influence*, ed. B.A.E. Yorke, 45–6.

sources which seem to have emanated from Alfred's court show how he sought to win the support of his subjects by appeals to national and religious unity. The revival in Old English culture and the Christian religion which Alfred seems to have sponsored in Wessex may have been driven by the desire to persuade his subjects that their religious duty lay in carrying out his commands in the wars against the heathen Vikings. People should remember that the Vikings were God's punishment because the West Saxons were such poor Christians, he urged in the preface to his translation of *Pastoral Care*.[144] In that work he also held out the carrot that 'wealth and wisdom' went together,[145] that those whom God favoured prospered in worldly affairs, and no doubt there were sufficient people who felt they were prospering in Alfred's service to offset those who resented the growth in royal demands. The inevitable deaths in battle of major office-holders would have given Alfred the opportunity to promote those who were sympathetic to his ambitions. The wars with the Vikings do mark a turning-point in the history of Wessex, but not because the Vikings destroyed so much that new beginnings had to be made nor even because they provided the opportunity for the West Saxon kings to become kings of England. Arguably, the major development for Wessex was that their kings emerged with greater rights over their subjects than ever before.

DEVELOPMENTS IN ROYAL ADMINISTRATION

Alfred and his successors inherited Carolingian concepts of the duty of Christian kings to rule 'with justice' and like the Carolingians appreciated that an association of royal with divine justice could be to their advantage.[146] Alfred prefaced his laws with quotations from the Old and New Testaments to emphasize the context in which his own legislation should be viewed,[147] and in 962 Edgar issued a lawcode in which it was declared that a recent outbreak of plague was the result of divine displeasure because of the withholding of tithes, but also that 'secular rights [should] be in force in every province, as good as they can be devised, to the satisfaction of God and for my full royal dignity'.[148] Some late Saxon governmental

---

144. Keynes and Lapidge, *Alfred*, 124–6; Sweet (ed.), *King Alfred's Pastoral Care*; and see Ch. 5.
145. T.A. Shippey, 'Wealth and wisdom in King Alfred's *Preface* to Old English *Pastoral Care*', *EHR*, 94 (1979), 346–55.
146. J. Wallace-Hadrill, *Early Germanic Kingship in England and on the Continent* (1971), 98–109; R. McKitterick, *The Frankish Church and the Carolingian Reforms 789–895* (1977), 1–44.
147. F. Liebermann, *Die Gesetze der Angelsachsen* (3 vols, Halle, 1903–16), I, 15–89; F.L. Attenborough (ed.), *The Laws of the Earliest English Kings* (1922), 62–94; Keynes and Lapidge, *Alfred*, 163–70.
148. Liebermann, *Gesetze*, I, 206–15; *EHD*, I, 434–7.

innovations may be direct borrowings from Carolingian legislation, such as the imposition of an oath of loyalty to the king on all adult males which is first clearly recorded in Edmund's Colinton code of *c.* 943.[149] Such legislation was intended to apply to all the areas controlled by the later Anglo-Saxon kings, not just to Wessex, and was imposed through a system of local governmental structures which was broadly the same throughout the whole country, but with some local variations. The administrative structures of Wessex were largely in place before the accession of Alfred and to a certain extent served as a blueprint which the West Saxon dynasty sought to impose on the other provinces of England as they conquered them. But although the structures were of some antiquity, the financial and public service demands and degree of supervision imposed through them greatly increased and partly explain why the late Saxon kings felt the need to underpin their extension of royal authority by linking together obligations to king and God.

The shire remained the basic unit for organization of fiscal and military demands with control organized through the shire courts in which the major landowners met four times a year under the presidency of the ealdorman and bishop. The shire courts did not just serve as law courts, but as places where a variety of public transactions, such as transfers of land, could be recorded. Through their officials kings could publicize judgements of legal cases and provide notification of decisions; by the end of the Saxon period this was increasingly done through a written document called a writ which was authenticated by a royal seal.[150] However, important though the shire courts were, a major reason for the success of late Saxon royal government (from the royal point of view) was the control it could exercise through the main subdivisions of the shire, the hundreds. The hundreds are first mentioned by name in the 'Hundred Ordinance' which was probably issued sometime between 945 and 961.[151] Its main concern was with the hundred courts which were to be held every four weeks and were to ensure the maintenance of local law and order, through the prevention of theft and pursuit of law-breakers.[152] Although there are no earlier references to hundreds as such, laws of Edward the Elder also refer to courts held every four weeks under the supervision of a royal reeve.[153] It is likely that there was no one point at which hundreds were created in Wessex, rather they were a natural evolution from

---

149. J. Campbell, 'Observations on English government from the tenth to the twelfth centuries', *TRHS*, 25 (1975), 39–54; A.J. Robertson (ed.), *Laws of the Kings of England from Edmund to Henry I* (1925), 12.
150. F. Harmer (ed.), *Anglo-Saxon Writs* (1952).
151. Liebermann, *Gesetze*, I, 192–5; *EHD*, I, 429–30.
152. H.R. Loyn, 'The hundred in England in the tenth and early eleventh centuries', in *British Government and Administration: Studies Presented to S.B. Chrimes*, ed. H. Hearder and H.R. Loyn (1974), 1–15.
153. Loyn, 'The hundred in England', 2–3.

earlier administrative arrangements whereby estates were grouped together for fiscal and other royal demands and supervised from a king's *tun* or royal vill.[154] A substantial number of the hundreds defined in Domesday Book were centred on, or named from, places which were or had been royal vills. Other hundreds were known from their meeting-places, many of which show signs of some antiquity, being prominent natural or man-made features such as trees, stones, fords, crossroads, barrows or other eminences, and could imply that royal vill districts were themselves based on older units for the regulation of local affairs.[155] In Devon in Domesday Book and later a number of hundreds seem to have had alternative names, one being that of the manor from which they were controlled and the other that of the traditional meeting-place of the district.[156]

It is unlikely that the West Saxon shires were ever divided into uniform hundred-hide units as Chadwick and Corbett tried to argue from the Domesday Book hidages for the shires.[157] The name 'hundred' is likely to have been borrowed, together with much royal legislation, from Carolingian Francia where the *centena* was a comparable local administrative unit and so it need not be interpreted as a literal measurement.[158] On the other hand, the districts dependent on the king's *tun* had commonly been assessed in hundreds of hides so it is not surprising that some hundreds were literally one hundred hides in size, but most 'hundreds' were larger or smaller. Although many of the more substantial districts dependent on royal vills had been subdivided by the late Saxon period, some continued to exist as distinctive groupings of hundreds in Domesday Book or later, such as the six hundreds of Basingstoke which survived until 1225 or the seven hundreds of Cookham and Bray which was still an administrative unit at the end of the Middle Ages.[159] Some such groupings may preserve early *regiones* which existed as administrative units before they were incorporated into Wessex, but it was also the case that hundreds might be grouped together for certain administrative purposes in the later Saxon period. Pre-eminent among these was the organization of hundreds into groups of three as shipsokes to pay for the cost of a new ship for the king's fleet. Shipsokes were possibly introduced in the reign of Edgar, and seem certainly to have been in existence

154. H. Cam, *Liberties and Communities in Medieval England* (1944), 64–90; Stenton, *Anglo-Saxon England*, 300–1.
155. O.S. Anderson, *English Hundred Names* (Lund, 1939); L.V. Grinsell, 'Barrows in Anglo-Saxon land charters', *Ant J*, 71 (1991), 46–63.
156. F. Thorn, 'The hundreds of Devonshire', in *The Devonshire Domesday*, ed. A. Williams and R. Erskine (1991), 26–42, at 38.
157. Chadwick, *Anglo-Saxon Institutions*, 208–10.
158. F.L. Ganshof, *Frankish Institutions under Charlemagne* (New York 1965, reprinted 1970), 32–3, 79–80; Campbell, 'Observations on English government', 45–6.
159. Cam, *Liberties and Communities*, 98–100.

before 1008 when Æthelred II was able to raise a new fleet of over a hundred ships to combat the Vikings.[160] The shipsokes are a good example of the increasing demands kings made on their subjects under the guise of it being necessary for the public good.

What was probably a relatively regular and coherent system of hundreds in the early tenth century, based on earlier territorial subdivisions of shire units, had become much more complex and fragmented by the time Domesday Book was compiled. Some territorially coherent hundreds still existed, especially the large royal manors paying a food render, 'the farm of one night', to the king, which in organizational terms had probably not changed since they came under the control of the West Saxon royal house.[161] But some estates once organized on similar lines had been split among different owners, and by 1086 had come to be divided between different hundreds because major landowners had been allowed to group together their lands in a particular shire in so-called 'private' hundreds. Most of these hundreds were held by ecclesiastial foundations, but some were owned by other major lay landowners besides the king, such as Queen Edith, Countess Gytha (widow of Earl Godwine) and Harold Godwineson.[162] Component parts of such a hundred might be scattered within the shire. The trend was for hundreds to become more numerous and more varied in size; Somerset, for instance, had a number of hundreds under 10 hides in the late eleventh century as well as some which were more than a hundred hides.

These developments can be illustrated from the history of the Worthy estate near Winchester. In Domesday Book there are four contiguous settlements called Worthy which can be equated with the four villages later known as King's, Abbot's, Headbourne and Martyr Worthy.[163] Their common name elements suggest they originally formed one estate,[164] probably controlled from King's Worthy which was a royal vill at which King Athelstan held an assembly in 931.[165] and which was still contributing to 'the farm of one night' in Domesday Book. One might have expected the Worthy estate to have become a hundred managed from King's Worthy, but parts of the estate were granted away to lay and ecclesiastical

160. E. John, *Land Tenure in Early England* (1960), 115–23; Hollister, *Military Institutions*, 108–15; N. Hooper, 'Some observations on the navy in late Anglo-Saxon England', in *Studies in Medieval History Presented to R. Allen Brown*, ed. C. Harper-Bill, C. Holdsworth and J. Nelson (1989), 203–13. See further below.

161. However, P. Stafford, 'The "farm of one night" and the organization of King Edward's estates in Domesday', *Economic History Review, 33* (1980), 491–502, argues that the arrangements were periodically reviewed.

162. H. Cam, *Law-Finders and Law-Makers in Medieval England* (1962), 59–70.

163. J. Munby (ed.), *Domesday Book: Hampshire* (1982), 1, 17; 3, 13; 6, 17; 29, 3–4; 39, 3.

164. R. Coates, *The Place-Names of Hampshire* (1989), 182–4.

165. S 413/B 675.

recipients from the ninth century. That in itself would not have been sufficient to prevent the Worthys remaining a unit for purposes of royal administration (i.e. a hundred), for the different estates that made up a hundred might well have several different owners by the late Saxon period. But Abbot's Worthy and Martyr Worthy had come into the hands respectively of New Minster and the bishop of Winchester, who had been able to detach them from King's Worthy and incorporate them into their own private hundreds. The two remaining estates, King's Worthy and Headbourne Worthy, were too small to constitute a hundred on their own and so were attached to the nearest royal manor, that of Barton Stacey.

Abbot's Worthy was part of the New Minster hundred of Micheldever. By great good fortune we can reconstruct fairly exactly the extent of this hundred, because in addition to the entries for it in Domesday Book, we have a charter in which the component estates of the hundred are listed and all, with the exception of Abbot's Worthy, provided with bounds. The charter claims to be a grant of these lands to New Minster from Edward the Elder in 900, but, as Nicholas Brooks has shown, seems in fact to be a forgery of the eleventh century, though we need not doubt that it accurately describes the estates in New Minster's possession by that time which formed the hundred of Micheldever.[166] As can be seen from fig. 32, although the core of the hundred is a block of territory at Micheldever itself, other component parts are some distance away. The hundred had no territorial coherence, it was only the fact that all the estates were owned by New Minster which led to them being brought together.

By the time Domesday Book was compiled most of the major religious communities in Wessex seem to have had hundreds of this type. The hundreds were 'private' only in the sense that they had one owner. Royal officials were not excluded and might continue to hold hundred courts, but the hundred owners probably received some profits of justice which would otherwise have gone to the royal coffers, as well as enjoying the administrative convenience of having all their estates in one hundred.[167] Ecclesiastical ownership was probably conceived as assisting royal government, and the creation of private ecclesiastical hundreds would seem to belong to the ambience of the tenth-century reformation which began in the reign of Edgar and which saw an emphasis both on the rights of the

---

166. S 360/B 596. N. Brooks, 'The oldest document in the college archives? The Micheldever forgery', in *Winchester College: Sixth-Centenary Essays*, ed. R. Custance (1982), 189–228.

167. Uncertainty exists over just what rights private hundred owners possessed and there is little relevant information from Wessex to match that from other parts of the country. See Cam, *Law-Finders and Law-Makers*, 22–43, and W.L. Warren, *The Governance of Norman and Angevin England 1086–1272* (1987), 46–9.

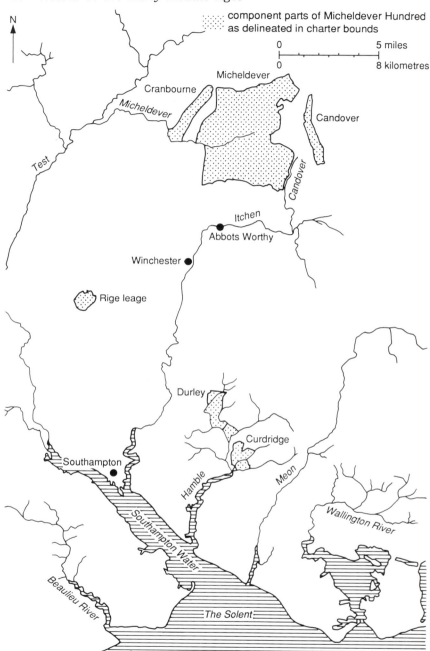

32. The component parts of Micheldever hundred [after N. Brooks, 'The oldest document in the college archives? The Micheldever forgery', in *Winchester College: Sixth-Centenary Essays*, ed. R. Custance (1982), 189–228]

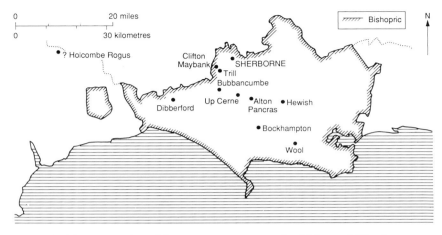

33. Estates owing ship-scot payments to the bishop of Sherborne as listed in S 1383 [after D. Hill, *Atlas of Anglo-Saxon England* (1981), fig. 166]

Church and on ways in which the Church could be used to underpin royal government.[168] The ecclesiastical hundreds may have been established at the same time as the shipsokes, for the provision of ships for the king seems to have been a major concern of a number of bishops during the reign of Æthelred. Archbishop Ælfric gave a ship for the people of Wiltshire in his will of 1003/4,[169] and Bishop Ælfwold of Crediton bequeathed a *scegth* of 64 oars to King Æthelred when he died in 1012.[170] But the most important evidence comes from a writ from Bishop Æthelric of Sherborne to Æthelmær (probably the son of Ealdorman Æthelweard), in which the bishop complains that he is not able to collect all the ship-scot which his predecessors had done because thirty-three hides had been alienated and the community feared it would lose more land as well.[171] Æthelric refers to the 'three hundred hides that other bishops had formerly for their dioceses' perhaps referring to a major reordering of diocesan hundreds coinciding with the creation of the new obligation of ship provision. The thirty-three hides which the bishop claims to have lost are widely dispersed in a manner which recalls the scattered estates of New Minster's hundred in Hampshire (fig. 33). Perhaps shipsokes were the price major ecclesiastical communities had to pay for being allowed to group their estates in private hundreds.

The hundreds were subdivided into tithings. These have some-

---

168. See further Chapter 5, 210–18.
169. S 1488; D. Whitelock (ed.), *Anglo-Saxon Wills* (1930), 160–3.
170. S 1492; *EHD*, I, 580–2.
171. The writ has the date range 1002–1007×14. Harmer, *Anglo-Saxon Writs*, 266–70; M.A. O'Donovan, *Charters of Sherborne* (1988), 46–8.

times been assumed to be groupings of ten men, but it seems more likely that the tithing of late Saxon Wessex was an administrative subdivision of the hundred, literally 'a tenth', and was a natural development from the vills into which the estates dependent upon royal *tun* had been divided.[172] As we saw in Chapter 2, such units were typically conceived as being of ten hides; for instance, Ine's laws defined the amount of *feorm* payable from ten hides.[173] Royal legislation was particularly concerned with the policing duties of the hundred, and each freeman over the age of twelve had to be assigned to a tithing after taking an oath at the hundred court to keep the king's peace and assist in the apprehension of malefactors when called out to do so. In addition, each man needed to produce sureties, either a lord or neighbours (probably twelve in number) who would vouch for his good behaviour at the hundred court and either bring him to justice or be accountable for financial penalties should be default. Late Saxon government put considerable emphasis on local policing, supervised by royal officials, and, although no doubt matters were not perfect, there is no reason to believe that Wessex was a particularly lawless state in the later Saxon period, though it must also be appreciated that punishments for offences were often harsh and could include heavy fines, confiscation of property, exile and mutilation, as well as a variety of forms of a judicial death penalty.[174] An oppressive government was the price to be paid for relative peace and security.

The structures of local administration also provided an effective means for the collection of royal dues and enforcement of policy decisions, which were also good reasons, as far as the king was concerned, for controlling lawlessness. The effectiveness of royal administration in these matters is suggested by the large amounts of money that kings were able to collect in gelds in the late tenth and early eleventh centuries to pay tribute to Viking armies and by the effectiveness of the regular recoinages which seem to have been obeyed and respected.[175] Of course, an incentive for obeying royal commands was the threat of punishment for defaulters. Failure to carry out public service duties or to make geld payments could lead to confiscation of property, especially of bookland (land originally granted by charter from the royal fisc) over which the king claimed ultimate ownership. Judging by the frequency by which land which had been granted out found its way back into royal possession, the threat of confiscation must have been carried out when necessary and may have been especially widespread in the reigns of Æthelred and Cnut when considerable financial demands were made on

---

172. Warren, *Governance of Norman England*, 39–42; W.A. Morris, *The Frank-pledge System* (New York, 1910), Ch. 1.
173. See Ch. 2, 72–3.
174. S. Keynes, 'Crime and punishment in the reign of King Æthelred the Unready', in *People and Places in Northern Europe 500–1600. Essays in Honour of Peter Hayes Sawyer*, ed. I. Wood and N. Lund (1991), 67–81.
175. See further below, 140–1.

landowners.[176] However, the effectiveness of the whole system depended, both from the king's point of view and from that of his humbler subjects, on the probity of the royal officials, who imposed the law and collected the gelds, and were rewarded by a share in the profits. Laws throughout the tenth and eleventh centuries reiterate the necessity for royal officials to protect the king's interests, to be honest and impose his laws justly, which suggests that these desiderata were frequently not met and the temptations for abuse must have been considerable. Corruption among royal officials was one of the sins of the English in the reign of Æthelred II to which Archbishop Wulfstan took particular exception.[177]

But royal officials were not the only instruments of government in the localities. The system of local administration was designed to work hand in hand with the developing powers of lordship which later Anglo-Saxon kings seem to have seen as preferable to kindred obligations. Lords exercised minor policing functions over their dependent peasants and had some responsibilities for the behaviour through the shire and hundred courts of freemen and lesser nobles who were commended to them.[178] Local lords and royal officials should have provided mutual checks on each others' behaviour, but there was obviously also the possibility of collusion between them. The profits and status of royal service helped bind the nobles to their king, but when substantial royal powers were delegated there was a danger that some subjects might become overpowerful. In the middle years of the tenth century, following the death of King Athelstan, Edmund, Eadred, Eadwig and Edgar all came to the throne young and had short reigns. The ealdormen were important in providing stability and continuity, but the two major families, those of Athelstan 'Half King' and Ælfhere of Mercia, who between them filled a large number of the ealdormanries in Wessex and elsewhere, developed unassailable positions.[179] The rivalries between these two families and their supporters threatened to destabilize the country and was probably a factor in the division of the kingdom between Eadwig and Edgar in 957.[180] Open hostility broke out after the death of King Edgar in 975 when rival factions developed around his two surviving sons, Edward and Æthelred, from different marriages. Edward was crowned in 975, but on 18 March 978 he was murdered at Corfe (Dorset) while on a visit to his half-brother Æthelred and stepmother Ælfthryth.[181] No one was

176. Keynes, 'Crime and punishment'; M.K. Lawson, 'The collection of Danegeld and Heregeld in the reigns of Æthelred II and Cnut', *EHR, 99* (1984), 721–38.
177. D. Whitelock (ed.), *Sermo Lupi ad Anglos* (3rd edn., 1963); *EHD*, I, 928–34; Keynes, 'Crime and punishment', 74–6.
178. Warren, *Governance of Norman England*, 44–52; for lordship see further in Ch. 7, 254–5.
179. Hart, 'Athelstan "Half King"'; Williams, *'Princeps Merciorum gentis'*.
180. Stenton, *Anglo-Saxon England*, 366–7; Yorke, 'Æthelwold and politics', 75–9.
181. *Chronicle s.a.* 978; Keynes, *Diplomas of King Æthelred*, 163–76,

ever arraigned for the murder and a contemporary, Byrhtferth of Ramsey, hints that this was because the murderers were closely associated with the new king Æthelred.[182] He implies the guilt of Ælfhere of Mercia, by association at least, but by the end of the Anglo-Saxon period the main burden of guilt had been assigned to Ælfthryth, who was portrayed with all the archetypal trappings of the 'wicked stepmother'.[183] The unfortunate circumstances of his succession are important background for understanding the reign of Æthelred in which relations between king and leading nobles seem to have been particularly troubled, though it was the strains imposed by a renewal of Viking attacks which brought them to the fore.

THE REGIN OF ÆTHELRED II AND THE RENEWAL OF VIKING ATTACKS

Viking attacks began again in earnest in the reign of Æthelred II Unræd (978–1016), but it is likely that the threat of more Viking incursions was felt to be a reality during the earlier part of the tenth century as well. Wessex was invaded twice by Viking armies during the reign of Edward the Elder. His cousin Æthelwold disputed the succession on Alfred's death and, after being unable to withstand Edward in Wessex, sought the support of the predominantly Danish settlers in eastern and northern England. An army from East Anglia crossed the Thames at Cricklade, ostensibly in his support, and plundered in Wiltshire in 903.[184] In 914 a Viking force from Brittany sailed into the Severn and, after raiding in Wales, turned its attention to Somerset, but the king was ready for the attack and had stationed men all along the coast. Although men from the Viking army twice came ashore, at Watchet and Porlock, they were beaten back. These are the only Viking attacks on Wessex recorded in the *Chronicle* before the reign of Æthelred, but as the various manuscripts of the *Chronicle* have very few entries for the reigns between Athelstan and Edgar, one cannot be entirely sure that further minor raids did not occur. The will of King Eadred (946–55) is suggestive, for he left sums of money to various leading churchmen specifically to redeem the West Saxon and other southern shires 'from famine and from a heathen army'.[185] It sounds as if Eadred thought that a Viking attack on Wessex was a possibility. The successes of Eadred and his immediate predecessors

---

182. J. Raine (ed.), *The Historians of the Church of York and its Archbishops*, Rolls series (3 vols, 1879–94), I, 448–52.
183. C. Fell, *Edward King and Martyr* (1971); S. Ridyard, *The Royal Saints of Anglo-Saxon England* (1988), 154–71.
184. *Chronicle s.a.* 900 and 903; all references to events are taken from the *Chronicle* unless otherwise indicated.
185. S 1515; *EHD*, I, 554–6.

in the Danelaw and further afield (in which many West Saxons must have been involved) would have acted as a discouragement to potential Viking aggressors, but the Hiberno-Norse colonies were a continuing threat to the north coast of Wessex, and Viking settlers in Brittany and Normandy to that of the south.

Edward the Elder may not only have built new burhs in the Danelaw. His acquisition of estates such as Portchester and Plympton in strategic positions, but ecclesiastical ownership, could be interpreted as a desire to expand the burghal system in Wessex.[186] Athelstan's laws issued at Grately enforced the by now traditional duty of *burhbot* and insisted that every burh had to be repaired annually by a fortnight after Rogation Day.[187] The mounted men in the boroughs who helped round up law-breakers, according to other decrees of the same king, may have been the same men who would garrison the burhs if they were attacked.[188] However, the economic and administrative roles of the burhs became increasingly important and it is unlikely that some of the 'emergency burhs', like Sashes, Chisbury, Athelney, Lyng, Pilton and Halwell, whose location better suited them for military needs rather than frequent visits by the populace, continued to fulfil a role. Certainly they did not become 'boroughs' in the sense that they had a mint. Instead from the mints named on coins from the reign of Athelstan onwards we can see new centres emerging, such as Ilchester, Taunton, Crewkerne, Totnes and Barnstaple, most of which are not known to have had defences in the Anglo-Saxon period, though presumably Ilchester's Roman walls may still have been standing.[189] The new settlement at Southampton on the Test side of the peninsula, established in the early tenth century, was provided with a substantial bank and ditch, with a second circuit laid down as the town expanded during the course of the century.[190] Timber and earth defences have a limited life-span unless the timber is renewed and archaeological evidence suggests that the defences were not kept in peak condition throughout the first three-quarters of the tenth century. Some decay of the burghal system therefore seems likely by the time of Æthelred's accession, but not complete atrophy, and the king's right to claim the three 'common burdens' for the defence of the realm remained in place and had probably been recently reinforced by the arrangement of hundreds into shipsokes to provide ships for the king's fleet.

186. Haslam, 'The towns of Devon', 267–79; Fleming, 'England's defence in the Viking age'.
187. Attenborough, II Athelstan, Ch. 13; Liebermann, *Gesetze*, 150–67; *EHD*, I, 417–22.
188. Abels, *Lordship and Military Obligation*, 88–9.
189. D. Hill, 'Trends in the development of towns during the reign of Æthelred II', in *Ethelred the Unready*, ed. D. Hill, BAR, *59* (1978), 213–26.
190. Holdsworth, 'Saxon Southampton', and personal comment on recent excavations by Andy Russell.

As in Alfred's reign, it is the *Chronicle* which provides the main narrative account for the wars against the Vikings, but the *Chronicle* annals for Æthelred's reign are very different in tone and style from those of his predecessor. Whereas the annals for Alfred's reign were written while the king was alive and in a way favourable to his interests, those for the reign of Æthelred, which are preserved in manuscripts C, D and E of the *Chronicle*, were written after the king's death in 1016 and outside Wessex, possibly in London.[191] The unknown chronicler wrote with the benefit of hindsight and in the knowledge that the English were conquered by the Danish kings Swein and Cnut. One of his purposes seems to have been to apportion blame for the defeat, and he is scathing in his condemnation of the conduct of the war and the behaviour of certain (dead) ealdormen in particular. His annal entries are longer and more discursive than most of those for the reign of Alfred, but that does not mean he has provided accounts which are more reliable or more objective and we do not know what materials he drew upon for his version of Æthelred's reign. The A manuscript of the *Chronicle* provides an alternative account of events for the year 1001 which was probably written at the Old Minster in Winchester. It includes a battle between the men of Hampshire and the Viking invaders, which the CDE chronicler does not mention at all, and puts the defeat of the Anglo-Saxon forces in Devon, which the CDE seems to ascribe to half-hearted resistance by local forces, in a quite different context. For only the A chronicler explains that the Viking army which went from Hampshire into Devon was joined there by the Danish leader Pallig and his men who had been recruited by King Æthelred to fight on his behalf. The men of Devon and Somerset who gallantly tried to resist the enlarged army (in A) would originally have been expecting Pallig to be fighting with them not against them. Unfortunately 1001 is the only year for which such a comparison can be made, but it suggests that the CDE chronicler either did not know all the facts or chose to manipulate them to serve his overall aims.

These reservations about the objectivity of the CDE chronicler are particularly important for any assessment of the role of Wessex in the Viking wars, for the six main Wessex shires are frequently portrayed by the chronicler as not offering an effective resistance to the Vikings, and Ælfric, the ealdorman of eastern Wessex who was in post throughout the war, is one of the commanders of whom the chronicler is most critical. Ælfric stands accused of betraying the Anglo-Saxon cause on two occasions. In 992 he is said to have warned the Danish army of the Anglo-Saxon fleet which was

---

191. C. Clark, 'The narrative mode of the *Anglo-Saxon Chronicle* before the Conquest', in *England Before the Conquest*, ed. P. Clemoes and K. Hughes (1971), 224–30; S. Keynes, 'A tale of two kings; Alfred the Great and Æthelred the Unready', *TRHS*, 36 (1986), 195–217.

gathered at London to trap them and to have withdrawn on the night before the planned attack. In 1003 when Ælfric was leading the forces of Hampshire and Wiltshire towards the enemy, he is said to have 'feigned him sick, and began retching to vomit, and said that he was taken ill'. Should we see these as justified accusations or malicious gossip? Ælfric was the longest serving of Æthelred's ealdormen (982–1016) and died fighting for King Edmund (son and successor of Æthelred) at the battle of *Assandun*. On the other hand, separate evidence shows that Æthelred did fall out with Ælfric and his family. In 993 Ælfric's son Ælfgar, who previously seems to have been a favoured thegn, was blinded, and in the same year Æthelred renounced Ælfric in a charter for having bribed him to allow his brother to become abbot of Abingdon and for various other offences against the abbey's interest.[192] Final judgement on Ælfric is difficult to make when so much hinges on one man's point of view.

Nor was Ælfric's the only prominent West Saxon family to fall in and out of favour with Æthelred. Until his death in 998, Ealdorman Æthelweard, translator of the *Chronicle* and distant cousin of the king, was the king's most senior ealdorman and his son Æthelmær was a favoured thegn. However, not only was Æthelmær passed over for his father's position as ealdorman of west Wessex which Æthelred apparently did not fill, but in 1005 he was obliged to withdraw from active life to the monastery at Eynsham.[193] The king's uncle Ordulf, also a previously favoured thegn, withdrew to his own monastery at Tavistock at about the same time.[194] Æthelmær, however, seems eventually to have re-emerged and in 1013 submitted to Swein as ealdorman of the western shires. Jealousies among the leading nobles at Æthelred's court and the king's apparent willingness to see potential plots against him (a paranoia perhaps occasioned by the murder of his half-brother Edward) have to be taken into account in the history of the Viking wars of his reign and the CDE chronicler's version of it.

Court factions may have been complicated further by the problem of regional affiliations. One of the major differences between the reign of Æthelred and that of Alfred is that the latter had only had to be responsible for the defence of Wessex whereas the former had to co-ordinate activities in all the Anglo-Saxon provinces. The CDE chronicler does refer on occasion to the whole English army being called out, but he is often vague on details of how it was commanded. The ill-fated expedition of 992, which Ealdorman Ælfric is said to have betrayed, was apparently under the command

---

192. S 876; Keynes, *Diplomas of King Æthelred*, 177–8.
193. Keynes, *Diplomas of King Æthelred*, 209–13; B.A.E. Yorke, 'Æthelmær: the foundation of the abbey at Cerne and the politics of the tenth century', in *The Cerne Abbey Millennium Lectures*, ed. K. Barker (1988), 15–26.
194. C. Hart, *The Early Charters of Northern England and the North Midlands* (1975), 352–3.

of Ælfric himself, Earl Thored of Northumbria and the bishops Ælfstan and Æscwig. Æthelred rarely led an army himself, which seems to have occasioned some contemporary criticism.[195] Some national campaigns were embarked upon, about which the CDE chronicler is generally scathing, but at other times the Vikings seem to have been met in different localities by the relevant local shire contingents commanded either by their ealdorman or by high reeves who seem to have been in charge of individual shires under the regional ealdorman. So in 1003 Ealdorman Ælfric called out the army from both Hampshire and Wiltshire to intercept the Danish army which was moving from Devon into Wiltshire, but in 1001 the men of Hampshire, apparently led by high reeves and king's thegns, tried to intercept the Danes as they were on the point of crossing from Sussex into Hampshire. One can see that in these situations there could be a conflict between regional and national interests which might put the local commanders in particular in the difficult position of having to choose between obedience to Æthelred's orders and protecting the interests of local thegns bound to them by the ties of lordship. In his annal for 1010 the CDE chronicler observed that 'in the end no shire would even help the next' and one can see how this could have been the case. The solution of one shire's problems could be the creation of new problems for its neighbour. In 1001 the failure of the Hampshire army to turn back the Danes enabled them to move on to raid Devon, while in 1003 the reverse occurred and the Danish army was able to move from the successful capture of Exeter to the raiding of Wiltshire.

By any standards it is clear that Wessex suffered substantially from the Viking armies during the reign of Æthelred (though not necessarily more than other regions) and to a much greater extent than it had during the reign of Alfred. However, attacks did not really become serious until the 990s. The CDE chronicler often does not explain who was in charge of raiding armies and so it is not always clear whether attacks are coming from the same or different groups, but Simon Keynes has recently provided a convincing overview of events.[196] Raids on the north coasts of Devon and Cornwall in 981 and on Watchet in 988 may have been made from established Hiberno-Norse colonies that were also bothering Wales at that time, but the attacks on Southampton in 980 and on Portland in 982 are perhaps more likely to have been the work of fleets from Scandinavia and the precursors of those which were to cause so much trouble. The first really serious challenge for the armies of Wessex came in 993/4 from the fleet led by Olaf Trygvasson of Norway and various Danish commanders, including

195. S. Keynes, 'The declining reputation of King Æthelred the Unready', in *Ethelred the Unready*, ed. D. Hill, BAR, *59* (1978), 227–53, espec. 235. It was of the utmost importance for the king to stay alive.
196. S. Keynes, 'The historical context of the Battle of Maldon', in *The Battle of Maldon AD 991*, ed. D. Scragg (1991), 81–113.

probably King Swein of Denmark, which may previously have been involved in the celebrated battle of Maldon in 991. Eastern Wessex was badly ravaged in 993 and matters only concluded when the two Wessex ealdormen, Æthelweard and Ælfric, negotiated a truce and agreed to pay tribute. The army spent the winter at Southampton and was provided with provisions from the West Saxon shires. A national treaty was negotiated in which the bulk of the fleet would remain in England and provide protection against any other invaders. Olaf, however, returned to Norway after he had been confirmed at Andover (Hants) with King Æthelred as his sponsor.

The truce held until 997 when the unfortunate Watchet was again attacked and there was considerable ravaging and booty-taking in Devon and, in the following year, in Dorset, ending with the fleet staying on the Isle of Wight, the first of a number of occasions when the island was used as a base by the Vikings. It was probably the same fleet which (after an interlude in Normandy) fought in Hampshire and Devon in 1001 and then retreated back to the Isle of Wight where another treaty was made and further tribute paid. In 1002 Æthelred attempted to deal with the problem by ordering the massacre on St Brice's Day of all the Danes in England, but the result was further ravaging for both Wessex provinces in 1003; that fleet, now led by King Swein, returned to Denmark in 1005. In 1006 'the whole nation from Wessex and Mercia' was called out to counteract an army newly arrived from Denmark, but apparently with little success. That army over-wintered on the Isle of Wight and the chronicler recounts an expedition it made inland to Cuckhamsley Barrow, a prominent hundred and shire meeting-place on the Berkshire Downs, 'and waited there for what had been proudly threatened for it had often been said that if they went to Cuckhamsley, they would never get to the sea'. Needless to say they did return with their booty and further tribute had to be paid to buy them off.

1009 saw the arrival of a formidable fleet led by Thorkell the Tall to counteract which a new fleet was raised through the shipsoke levy and three days of penitential prayers and fasting imposed on the whole country.[197] Wessex suffered savage attacks, along with the rest of the nation, until Æthelred agreed to pay tribute in 1011, and in 1012 recruited Thorkell and part of his fleet to fight for him in return for substantial payments. King Swein returned in 1013, perhaps in response to Thorkell's defection, and seems to have quickly received submissions from the various regions, including that of the two parts of Wessex which he took at Winchester and Bath respectively. King Æthelred spent Christmas on the Isle of Wight and then fled to Normandy, only to return the following year after Swein's death. Swein's army in England chose his son Cnut to

---

197. 'VII Athelred' in Liebermann, *Gesetze* I, 260–2 and *EHD*, I, 447–51.

be their new leader and in 1015 he was raiding in Wessex. According to the CDE chronicler, when Æthelred died in 1016 Wessex declared for his son Edmund Ironside and there was a major battle between the two leaders and their supporters at Penselwood near Gillingham (Dorset). But the twelfth-century Worcester chronicle, which seems to have additional sources of information for Æthelred's reign, records that at a second battle in the same year at Sherston, on the border of Wessex and the province of the Hwicce, only the men of western Wessex were fighting for Edmund, eastern Wessex being on the side of Cnut.[198] Whatever the truth of this, it is usually assumed that Ealdorman Ælfric of eastern Wessex was fighting for Edmund when he was killed at the battle of *Assandun* (Essex) the following year in 1016. By the terms of the treaty made between Edmund and Cnut after the battle, the former was to be king in Wessex and the latter in Mercia, but the death of Edmund later the same year enabled Cnut to become king of all England.

Æthelred's ultimate failure which led to England's conquest by a Danish king and the scathing tone of the CDE chronicler has meant that he and his commanders have received little credit for the defence they mounted against the Vikings. Yet even from the references to the war in Wessex it can be seen that a number of strategies were adopted and that many of them were comparable to the policies followed by Alfred who generally receives favourable comment for them. The confirmation of Olaf at Andover parallels the baptism of Guthrum organized by Alfred after the battle of Edington. In both cases the religious ceremony and bonds of spiritual affinity between the Scandinavian and English leaders helped to underscore the terms of a treaty. As even the CDE *Chronicle* acknowledged, Olaf kept his promise to Æthelred not to return to England with hostile intent, and, as Æthelred may have intended, by his ambitions in Norway temporarily distracted Swein from an interest in England.[199] The payment of tribute has been much criticized, but was a policy which Alfred had also been obliged to adopt.[200] Tribute was only paid to prevent further devastation when military action had failed (always paid too late according to the CDE chronicler) and was probably, as in 994, accompanied by a negotiated treaty, though some Viking leaders such as Pallig do not seem to have felt obliged to honour the terms. Æthelred's retaliation – the St Brice's Day massacre – was the type of hard-hitting reply that was necessary in a world inhabited by Vikings.

Not all Æthelred's strategies are reflected in the account of the CDE chronicler who, as we have seen, does not always seem to have

---

198. B. Thorpe (ed.), *Florentii Wigorniensis Chronicon ex Chronicis* (2 vols, 1849), I, 174–5.
199. T. Andersson, 'The Viking policy of Ethelred the Unready', *Scandinavian Studies*, 59, (1987), 284–98.
200. Keynes, 'A tale of two kings'.

been well-informed about details of events in Wessex. Although we do not have a document comparable to the Burghal Hidage, it appears that Æthelred overhauled the burghal system which he inherited. Most of the West Saxon burghal defences which have been excavated have a secondary pre-Norman Conquest phase of defences when ditches have been recut, ramparts reinforced and provided with stone revetments and walls. Æthelred's reign provides the most likely context and the deliberate slighting of the defences which has been discerned in a number of cases could have been on the orders of Cnut.[201] It can also be more conclusively shown that Æthelred ordered two new burhs to be built in Wessex. After Wilton had been burnt by Swein in 1003, its minters were moved to the Iron Age hill-fort of Old Sarum where the defences seem to have been renovated.[202] Excavations at South Cadbury (Som) have revealed an even more impressive refurbishment of defences, with the whole inner rampart repaired and provided with a mortared wall, while the south-west gate was rebuilt with high quality masonry (see fig. 7).[203] Moneyers from Ilchester were transferred there in 1010 according to the numismatic evidence, perhaps while Thorkell's army was occupied in East Anglia.[204] Even at this late stage in Æthelred's reign new defensive measures were being undertaken and there are other emergency mint sites which have not been identified.[205]

Even when Æthelred's burhs have been acknowledged, it has generally been assumed that they were not garrisoned and were merely places of refuge for a civilian population.[206] The chief grounds for such an assumption seem to be that there are no specific references to forces stationed in the burhs and the Vikings were able to take several of them. It is true that Watchet was taken in 988 and 997, Exeter and Wilton in 1003 and Wallingford in 1006, but it also appears that in 997 the Vikings were stopped at Lydford and in 1001 were stoutly resisted and turned aside at Exeter, which, according to the CDE chronicler they only got into in 1003 because its Norman reeve betrayed the city. When the Vikings marched back to the coast from Cuckhamsley in 1006, the citizens were able to watch them march past their walls which they made no attempt to take. Did the fact that no garrison came out to

201. RCHM, 'Wareham west walls'; Haslam, 'Towns of Wiltshire', 109–10; Richards, *Viking Age England*, 92–4.
202. R.H.M. Dolley, 'The sack of Wilton in 1003 and the chronology of the "Long Cross" and "Helmet" types of Æthelred II', *Nordisk Numismatisk Unions Medlensbled* (1954), 152–6; Haslam, 'Towns of Wiltshire', 122–8.
203. L. Alcock, *'By South Cadbury is that Camelot . . .' Excavations of Cadbury Castle 1966–70* (1972), 194–201.
204. R.H.M. Dolley, 'The emergency mint of Cadbury', *BNJ*, 28 (1955–7), 99–105.
205. Hill, 'Trends in the development of towns', 223–5; D.M. Metcalf, 'The ranking of boroughs: numismatic evidence from the reign of Æthelred II', in *Ethelred the Unready*, ed. D. Hill, BAR, *59* (1978), 159–212, espec. 160.
206. For example, Abels, *Lordship and Military Obligation*, 91–2.

intercept them mean that there was none there or that 'the great fleet' was too large to make it practical to try to take them on? The truth is that we do not know as much about the organization of the army in the time of Æthelred as in the time of Alfred and it seems unwise to conclude that a king who could command substantial resources and took pains to have his army better equipped[207] and burhs provided with stronger defences, left his fortified sites without a garrison.

The temporary abandonment of Wilton and Ilchester as minting sites underlines the short-term damage which raids could cause; the mint at Wallingford also seems to have had to be suspended after the raid on it in 1006.[208] But there is no need to think that the damage caused was serious in the long term – Wallingford appears as a flourishing borough in Domesday Book.[209] Accounts of attacks on monasteries, admittedly written after the Norman Conquest, tend to make light of Danish raids and the emphasis is on the outwitting of the raiders rather than the destruction they caused. At Malmesbury the monks are said to have removed everything of value except the shrine of St Aldhelm, and when a Dane tried to remove one of the gems embedded in it he was struck down and his companions fled in terror.[210] Danish raiders on Abingdon were claimed to have been fought off by the crucifix hanging on the walls of the refectory whose figure came to life and 'with marble arms and flexible fingers' began pelting the intruders with stones it extracted from the refectory walls.[211] What the monastic writers did complain of, however, was the financial hardship caused by the various tribute payments. The *Chronicle* records some £158,000 paid between 991 and 1014 and a further £82,500 after Cnut's final victory.[212] In addition to 'national' payments, individual districts seem to have bought off Viking armies on occasion as Wessex was obliged to do in 994. There has been much debate about whether the *Chronicle* figures are to be taken as realistic or not,[213] but they

---

207. N. Brooks, 'Arms, status and warfare in late-Saxon England', in *Ethelred the Unready*, ed. D. Hill, BAR, *59* (1978), 81–104.

208. M. Blackburn, 'Æthelred's coinage and the payment of tribute', in *The Battle of Maldon in AD 991*, ed. D. Scragg (1991), 156–69, at 162.

209. P. Morgan (ed.), *Domesday Book: Berkshire* (1979), fol. 56 b–c; Astill, 'Towns of Berkshire', 62–3.

210. *GP*, 409–10.

211. J. Stevenson (ed.), *Chronicon Monasterii de Abingdon* (2 vols, 1858), I, 47; Thacker, 'Æthelwold and Abingdon', 60.

212. Lawson, 'The collection of Danegeld and Heregeld', 721–38.

213. Lawson, 'Collection of Danegeld and Heregeld'; J. Gillingham, '"The most precious jewel in the English crown": levels of Danegeld and Heregeld in the early eleventh century', *EHR*, *104* (1989), 373–84; M.K. Lawson, '"Those stories look true": levels of taxation in the reigns of Æthelred II and Cnut', *EHR*, *104* (1989), 385–406; J. Gillingham, 'Chronicles and coins as evidence for levels of tribute and taxation in late tenth and early eleventh century England', *EHR*, *105* (1990), 939–50; M.K. Lawson, 'Danegeld and Heregeld once more', *EHR*, *105* (1990), 951–61.

appear feasible in terms of the country's wealth and the amount of coinage in circulation.[214] Nor is it certain how the large payments were raised, but it seems that the churches had to contribute substantial amounts. Malmesbury had to sell estates or mortgage them on unfavourable terms to meet its geld commitments,[215] while Glastonbury may have had estates confiscated by royal officials which it was later able to redeem.[216] These monasteries were sufficiently wealthy to survive the demands, but smaller religious houses may have been more severely hit. The nunnery of Horton (Dorset) seems to have been disbanded during the reign of Æthelred, though whether this was due to financial demands or the general unsettled situation is not clear.[217] Small lay landowners are also likely to have had trouble meeting continual demands and the heavy gelds may have helped hasten social and economic changes in later Anglo-Saxon England.[218]

ROYAL GOVERNMENT IN THE ELEVENTH CENTURY

The succession of Cnut did not lead to substantial changes in royal administration; Cnut was anxious to enjoy the benefits and profits of Anglo-Saxon kingship and stressed his desire to maintain Anglo-Saxon laws and to rule in the traditions of his English pre-decessors.[219] The structure of shires, hundreds and tithings remained unchanged though some of their functions were more vigorously defined in Cnut's lawcodes. However, the new king's desire to be secure in his conquered land naturally caused some changes and the introduction of new personnel which then led to other developments. Many of the leading Anglo-Saxon aristocracy had died in the hard fighting of the last few years as is perhaps indicated by several items concerning windows in Cnut's laws. Other leading nobles were put to death or exiled on various pretexts following Cnut's accession. The families of the two Wessex ealdormen at the end of Æthelred's reign were among those who

---

214. Keynes, 'Historical context', 100–2; D.M. Metcalf, 'Large Danegelds in relation to war and kingship; their implications for monetary history and some numismatic evidence', in *Weapons and Warfare in Anglo-Saxon England*, ed. S. Chadwick Hawkes (1989), 179–89.
215. *GP*, 411.
216. J. Scott (ed.), *The Early History of Glastonbury. An Edition, Translation and Study of William of Malmesbury's De Antiquitate Glastonie Ecclesie* (1981), 140; Lawson, 'Danegeld and Heregeld', 724.
217. O'Donovan, *Charters of Sherborne*, lviii–lx.
218. W. Runciman, 'Accelerating social mobility: the case of Anglo-Saxon England', *Past and Present, 104* (1984), 3–30; and see Ch. 6, 269–74.
219. P. Stafford, 'The laws of Cnut and the history of Anglo-Saxon royal promises', *ASE, 10* (1982), 173–90; A. Kennedy, 'Cnut's law code of 1018', *ASE, 11* (1983), 57–81; M.K. Lawson, *Cnut. The Danes in England in the Early Eleventh Century* (1993).

suffered. Ealdorman Ælfric died at the battle of *Assandun* and nothing further is heard of his family. Ealdorman Æthelmær (son of Ealdorman Æthelweard) is not heard of after he gave the submission of the south-western thegns in 1016. His son Æthelweard was one of those whom Cnut had put to death with Eadric Streona in 1017 and his son-in-law Æthelweard, who seems initially to have succeeded to what can be described as the family ealdormanry, was outlawed in 1020.[220] The fall of the highest ranking members of this family, which could claim descent from King Æthelred I, may have affected other relatives. All the estates mentioned in the will of Ealdorman Æthelweard's sister Ælfgifu (who had been married briefly to King Eadwig) were in other hands than those which she had intended in Domesday Book, perhaps indicating a general confiscation of lands of the family.[221]

However, not all the leading families suffered the same fate and that of Ordgar, the father-in-law of King Edgar and ealdorman of western Wessex before Æthelweard, seems to have maintained its position.[222] A second Ordgar, who may have been a grandson of Ealdorman Ordgar, was a prominent *minister* in Cnut's charters of 1030s and 1040s. Ordulf, who is likely to have been a member of the same family, attested charters between 1044 and 1050 and was one of the great landowners of Devon according to Domesday Book. Cnut needed the co-operation of such men to run the country, but it is not surprising to find that he also introduced new men, especially Scandinavians, into the local landowning elites. A key group was the housecarls, broadly the equivalent of the earlier kings' thegns, who after service in the royal entourage would be settled on rural estates to help represent royal interests in the localities.[223] We are particularly well-informed about a group of housecarls in Dorset, where a levy for the support of housecarls is mentioned in the Domesday Book entries for Dorchester, Bridport, Wareham and Shaftesbury, the four main boroughs of Dorset.[224] Three housecarls with Scandinavian names, Urk, Bovi and Agemund, regularly appear as witnesses in Cnut's Dorset charters. They can also be seen working hard at laying down local roots. Bovi seems to have been associated with Ordgar II or Ordulf II in the refoundation of Horton Abbey,[225] and Urk, together with his wife, Tola, founded and handsomely endowed a

---

220. *Chronicle s.a.* 1017 and 1020; Æthelweard, xvi.
221. R. Fleming, *Kings and Lords in Conquest England* (1991), 43–4.
222. H.P.R. Finberg, 'The house of Ordgar and the foundation of Tavistock abbey', *EHR, 58* (1943), 190–201.
223. N. Hooper, 'The housecarls in England in the eleventh century', *Anglo-Norman Studies, 7* (1984), 161–76; J. Campbell, 'Some agents and agencies of the late Anglo-Saxon state', in *Domesday Studies*, ed. J.C. Holt (1987), 201–18, at 201–5.
224. Thorn (ed.), *Domesday Book: Dorset*, 75a.
225. Finberg, 'House of Ordgar'; O'Donovan, *Charters of Sherborne*, lx–lxii, 68–80.

monastery at Abbotsbury where he also helped to organize a local guild.[226]

Traces of Scandinavians and Scandinavian styles which may have come to England with Cnut have been found in Winchester, pointing again to a small number of immigrants at the higher end of society. A fragment of a Scandinavian runestone, which is believed to date to the first half of the eleventh century, was found built into one of Winchester's later medieval churches and may well represent one of Cnut's followers who wished to be remembered in traditional fashion.[227] Gunni, the earl's companion, on the other hand, was buried in the Old Minster cemetery with some ceremony. His burial was in a wooden coffin, with his head resting on a pillow of flint and limestone. The burial was covered with a coped grave-cover recording his name and position, and with a finely carved footstone with the Hand of God holding a cross (fig. 34). Only the inclusion of a Roman coin with the burial perhaps looks to different traditions of honouring the dead.[228] The Old Minster was Cnut's burial place as well and the choice can be seen as typical of his desire to follow in the footsteps of his West Saxon predecessors which made him a generous patron of West Saxon churches and saints-cults.[229] Martin Biddle has associated a fragment of a sculptured frieze, found during his excavation of the eastern crypt of Old Minster, with Cnut's patronage of the foundation (fig. 35).[230] The stone shows a mail-clad soldier walking to the left and the head and shoulders of a bound man who seems to be being attacked by a wolf who is inserting his tongue into the man's mouth. Martin Biddle has suggested that the stone represents an incident from the story of Sigmund in the Volsunga saga. It would appear a strange choice for the decoration of Old Minster (if that indeed was where the sculpture stood originally). Due probably to King Alfred's interest in attracting Danish support, the West Saxon pedigree incorporated the names of some traditional Danish heroes,[231] so the sculpture could have been part of a campaign to demonstrate Cnut's 'legitimate' claims to the English throne. Cnut was also a patron of New Minster, and an illustration in its *Liber Vitae* shows Cnut with his queen Emma/Ælfgifu presenting a magnificent gold cross to the

---

226. S. Keynes, 'The lost cartulary of Abbotsbury', *ASE, 18* (1989), 207–43, espec. 208–9, 230–3; for the Abbotsbury guild regulations see *EHD*, I, 606–7.

227. B. Kjølbye-Biddle and R.I. Page, 'A Scandinavian rune-stone from Winchester', *Ant J, 55* (1975), 389–94.

228. Kjølbye-Biddle and Page, 'A Scandinavian rune-stone', 390–2.

229. Ridyard, *Royal Saints*, 150–1, 168–9; D. Rollason, *Saints and Relics in Anglo-Saxon England* (1989), 157–60.

230. M. Biddle, 'A late Saxon frieze sculpture from the Old Minster', *Ant J, 66* (1966), 329–32. The date has proved controversial; see summary in J. Backhouse, D.H. Turner and L. Webster, *The Golden Age of Anglo-Saxon Art* (1984), 133–5.

231. A.C. Murray, '*Beowulf*, the Danish invasions and royal genealogy', in *The Dating of Beowulf*, ed. C. Chase (Toronto, 1981), 101–12.

34. Gravecover and footstone of Gunni as excavated in the cemetery of Old Minster, Winchester [photograph: M. Biddle, Winchester Research Unit]

foundation.[232] A panel of a finely decorated casket in the Ringerike style found during the underpinning of the cathedral nave in 1910 may also be evidence of Scandinavian patronage of Winchester's minsters.[233]

Winchester was probably the place in Wessex where the greatest concentration of Danish settlers was to be found and there are only slight indications of their presence in other boroughs such as Exeter where a church was dedicated to the Norwegian saint St Olaf and patronized by Gytha (sister-in-law of Cnut).[234] In the survey of Winchester made in the reign of Edward the Confessor, just over 6 per cent of the personal names recorded were Scandinavian, and some of those probably represented a fashion for Scandinavian names rather than people of Scandinavian descent.[235] The Danes or other Scandinavians who settled in Wessex as a result of Cnut's conquest were a small, but influential, minority, who seem to have soon merged their life-styles with those of Anglo-Saxons of

232. British Library, Stowe MS 944; W. de Gray Birch (ed.), *Liber Vitae: Register and Martyrology of New Minster and Hyde Abbey, Winchester* (1892).
233. Kjølbye-Biddle and Page, 'Scandinavian rune-stone', 392.
234. Allan *et al.*, 'Saxon Exeter', 385–414, at 397.
235. Olof von Feilitzen, 'The personal names and bynames of the Winton Domesday', in *Winchester in the Early Middle Ages. An Edition and Discussion of the Winton Domesday*, ed. M. Biddle, Winchester Studies, 1 (1976), 143–229, at 187–91.

35. Panel from a late Saxon frieze excavated from Old Minster, Winchester, possibly illustrating a scene from the saga of Sigmund [photograph: Winchester Museums Service; Winchester Research Unit; Dean and Chapter of Winchester Cathedral]

comparable rank. Housecarls like Bovi and Urk continued to enjoy their estates under Edward the Confessor and a small number of landowners with Scandinavian names are recorded throughout Wessex in Domesday Book.

What had a more significant impact on the history of the six West

Saxon shires as an administrative grouping was Cnut's abolition of the two ealdormanries of eastern and western Wessex and his appointment of Godwine as earl of Wessex, that is of all England south of the Thames. The *Chronicle* records that after his accession in 1017 Cnut divided England into four and kept Wessex for himself, but Godwine appears as earl in 1018, and perhaps held some special coastal defence command in the Solent region which seems to have been a key area for his family in years to come and where they had extensive estates.[236] His father Wulfnoth seems to have been a South Saxon thegn whose quarrel with another noble was responsible for the débâcle in which Æthelred's newly raised fleet was lost in 1009, at least according to the CDE chronicler.[237] By 1020 Godwine was earl of all Wessex and had been brought into Cnut's family nexus by marriage to Cnut's sister-in-law Gytha. From this point the family went from strength to strength, and Edward the Confessor was in the unenviable position of being indebted to Godwine for his accession in 1042, and their alliance was sealed by Edward's marriage to Godwine's daughter Edith. When Godwine died in 1053, the position of earl of Wessex went to his son Harold.

The family were assiduous in building up a network of estates in the six Wessex shires where Godwine is not known to have had any landed interest before he became earl.[238] By 1065, the land holdings of the Godwine family as a whole in Hampshire, Wiltshire, Devon and Somerset were as substantial, and in some shires perhaps greater, than those of the king. Many of these estates were attached to the office of earl, though some of these, and other payments due to Godwine and Harold as earls of Wessex, seem to have been assigned to support other members of the family; for instance, Domesday Book records that it was Gytha who received the earl's payment of the third penny from the six hundreds of Wallop (Hants).[239] Some lands seem to have been appropriated from local churches which were still trying to reclaim them in Domesday Book. The office of earl also gave Godwine and Harold considerable powers through the shire courts, which enabled them to influence the outcome of cases and made their support worth wooing. Wessex was undoubtedly an important power base of the Godwine family, but, apart from southern Hampshire and the Isle of Wight, it was not an area where they were really secure. When Edward tried to end the power of the family by having them exiled in 1051, the Isle of Wight and neighbouring coastlands in Hampshire and Sussex

236. Fleming, *Kings and Lords*, 92–5.
237. D. Raraty, 'Earl Godwine of Wessex: the origins of his power and his political loyalties', *History, 74* (1989), 3–19.
238. A. Williams, 'Land and power in the eleventh century: the estates of Harold Godwineson', *Anglo-Norman Studies, 3* (1980), 171–88; Fleming, *Kings and Lords*, 54–103.
239. Munby (ed.), *Domesday Book: Hampshire*, I, 19, fol. 38c.

had an important part to play in the Godwines' counter-attack and Godwine waited off the Isle of Wight for Harold to arrive with more ships in 1052. However, Harold was fiercely resisted by the men of Somerset and Devon when he attempted a landing at Porlock in the same year.

The Godwines were not a West Saxon family and the six shires of Wessex was only one of the areas of the country in which they had a substantial landed interest; there were also major holdings in Sussex and Kent, in eastern England (where Harold had been earl before he became earl of Wessex) and western Mercia. Major royal officials called stallers, first appointed by Cnut and continued by Edward, also tended to hold estates scattered through several shires, and most of them seem to have been outsiders rather than West Saxon men, as was Odda of Deerhurst, the king's kinsman, who may have been earl of western Wessex between 1051 and 1056.[240] Edward did visit Wessex and Winchester in particular for official 'crown wearings' at major religious festivals, but he is more often recorded as being in Gloucester or London.[241] Edward's major building programme was his great palace and abbey at Westminster where he was to be buried.[242] The royal and aristocratic preference for Wessex over other areas of England was at an end.

By the middle of the eleventh century – that is before the Norman Conquest – the six Wessex shires had lost the distinctiveness which they had enjoyed in the tenth century when they had been divided between two ealdormanries and had continued to be treated as the homelands of the West Saxon dynasty. Even when the West Saxon kings became kings of England, they spent most of their time in Wessex and made it the major centre of their patronage. The change seems to have begun during the reign of Æthelred II, who came to distrust some of the most powerful of the West Saxon nobility and rarely visited the three western shires.[243] With his burial in St Paul's, London, he became the first of his line to be buried outside Wessex.[244] However, the shift away from Wessex should not be seen so much as personal preference as an inevitable outcome of the creation of the kingdom of England which made London with its good communications to all parts of the country a desirable centre of government.

Æthelred II seems to have based himself in London towards the

240. K. Mack, 'The stallers: administrative innovation in the reign of Edward the Confessor', *Journal of Medieval History*, 12 (1986), 123–34.
241. M. Biddle, 'Seasonal festivals and residence: Winchester, Westminster and Gloucester in the tenth to twelfth centuries', *Anglo-Norman Studies*, 8 (1985), 51–72.
242. R. Gem, 'The Romanesque rebuilding of Westminster abbey', *Anglo-Norman Studies*, 3 (1980), 33–64.
243. Hill, *Atlas of Anglo-Saxon England*, 91.
244. W. Stubbs, (ed.), *Willelmi Malmesbiriensis Monachi De Gestis Regum Anglorum* (2 vols, 1887–9), II, 179.

end of his reign, possibly for strategic reasons in the war with the Vikings. As in a number of cases, it may not have been so much what the Vikings did, but the measures adopted to counteract Viking threats which were a major force for change in late Saxon Wessex. The damage caused by the Vikings should not be underestimated, though it was in the reign of Æthelred II that the worst damage was inflicted on Wessex, not in the reign of Alfred, in spite of the Vikings being traditionally seen as major agents of change in the ninth century. However, it was ultimately the Vikings who provided the opportunity for the kings of Wessex to become kings of England and supplied much of the *raison d'être* for new royal legislation and demands which helped to break down distinctions between the organization of Wessex and other English regions. When Cnut became king it was natural he should be less attuned to regional differences than his Anglo-Saxon predecessors and less concerned, in spite of his patronage of West Saxon ceremonial sites, to preserve them. As a result, by the eleventh century it becomes much more difficult to provide the area with its own regional history and to distinguish it as a distinctive region from the rest of England.

4 The spread of Christianity 400–800

Royal administration, taxation and other demands were key elements in ordering the lives of the Anglo-Saxon inhabitants of Wessex and the landscape in which they lived. The administrative framework of the state was mirrored by that of the Church which also had a distinct role to play in the lives of the inhabitants of Wessex from the cradle to the grave, as well as making its own demands on their pockets. As the main vehicle of literacy in Anglo-Saxon Wessex, the Church is naturally one of the best recorded facets of that society though it should always be remembered that churchmen were not necessarily objective observers and that they were not above altering or adapting records to suit changing needs.[1]

THE CHRISTIAN LEGACY FROM ROMAN BRITAIN

The question of the extent to which Britain had been converted to Christianity by the end of the fourth century is a controversial one on which it has been possible to reach quite different conclusions. Professor Frend has pointed to the paucity of evidence for Christian worship in Roman Britain when compared to other areas of the western Roman Empire and so has questioned whether there was any significant continuity of Christianity from the Roman to the early medieval periods.[2] It is certainly the case that throughout our region there are hardly any structures of the Roman period which can unequivocally be interpreted as churches. The strongest candidate is the small basilican structure at Silchester whose plan can be paralleled by known early churches and which, it has been argued, may have had an adjoining baptistery.[3]

---

1. See discussion of Wells and Glastonbury below, p. 162.
2. W.H.C. Frend, 'Romano-British Christianity in the west: comparison and contrast', in *The Early Church in Western Britain and Ireland*, ed. S. Pearce, BAR, *102* (1982), 5–16.
3. S. Frere, 'The Silchester church: the excavation by Sir Ian Richmond in 1961', *Archaeologia*, *105* (1975), 277–302; C. Thomas, *Christianity in Roman Britain to AD 500* (1981), 214–16.

However, many of its features are also shared by pagan temples and the dating evidence from the site could mean that the building was erected before the official recognition of Christianity in 313, in which case it is unlikely to have been founded as a Christian church.[4] On the other hand, finds suggest that there were Christians within Silchester in the fourth century and the discovery of a lead seal with a chi-rho monogram from within the basilica provides some support for the traditional identification.[5]

There may not be good evidence yet for public buildings for Christian worship, but recent work on burials provides more positive evidence for the spread of the Christian religion in late Roman Britain. A few burials have produced good evidence that they are those of Christians, such as the mausolea with wall-paintings and a lead-lined coffin with an inscription, probably to be read as *In Nomine Domini*, on its lid from Poundbury, Dorchester (Dorset),[6] and a burial with a pendant in the form of a silver cross inscribed with a chi-rho from Shepton Mallet (Som) (fig. 36).[7] But in most instances the case for Christian burial depends upon the recurrence of certain traits compatible with Christian belief and often in sharp counterdistinction to other late Roman practices. The traits include inhumation; burial with the head facing to the east; an absence of grave-goods; care taken to protect the body through use of coffins, cists, stone-lined graves and mausolea and even perhaps to slow down decay in the case of plaster burials from Poundbury; and burial in family groups with the use of the same rites for infants and neo-natals as for adults.[8] None of these features on their own are enough to indicate adoption of Christianity, but when several are found together in one cemetery without other forms of burial being present it does seem reasonable to draw that conclusion. On these grounds Christian cemeteries established within the fourth century have been identified throughout the Wessex region (except Devon), including those at Poundbury (Dorset), Cannington and Ilchester

4. A. King, 'The Roman church at Silchester reconsidered', *Oxford Journal of Archaeology, 2* (1983), 225–38.
5. G.C. Boon, *Silchester: The Roman Town of Calleva* (2nd edn., 1974), 173–84.
6. C.J.S. Green, 'The cemetery of a Romano-British Christian community at Poundbury, Dorchester, Dorset', in *The Early Church in Western Britain and Ireland*, ed. S. Pearce, BAR, *102* (1982), 61–76; but for a rather more sceptical discussion of the lead inscription see now R. Tomalin, 'An inscription from the lead lining in Grave 350', in *Excavations at Poundbury 1966–80, Volume II: The Cemeteries*, eds D.E. Farwell and T.I. Molleson, DNHAS monograph, *11* (1993), 132–3.
7. BUFAU (Birmingham University Field Archaeology Unit), *Romans in Shepton Mallett: Excavations at Fosse Lane 1990* (1990).
8. E.W. Black, 'Romano-British burial customs and religious beliefs in south-east England', *Arch J, 143* (1986), 201–39; D.J. Watts, 'Infant burials and Romano-British Christianity', *Arch J, 146* (1989), 372–83; and D.J. Watts, *Christians and Pagans in Roman Britain* (1991).

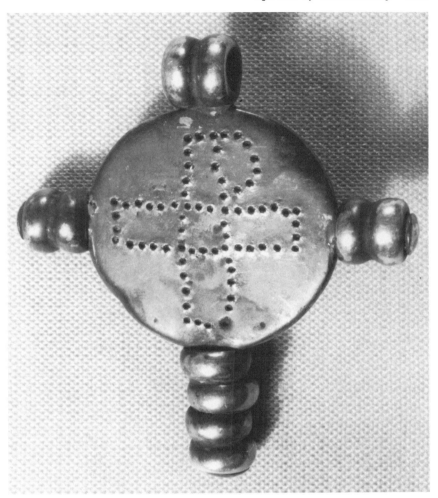

36. Silver alloy pendant with incised chi-rho emblem from a late
Roman burial at Shepton Mallet (Som) [photograph: the University of
Birmingham Field Archaeology Unit]

(Som),[9] Victoria and Chester Road, Winchester,[10] and possibly
Queenford Farm, near Dorchester-on-Thames.[11]

---

9. P. Rahtz, 'Pagan and Christian by the Severn Sea', in *The Archaeology and History of Glastonbury Abbey*, ed. L. Abrams and J.P. Carley (1991), 3–37.

10. J.L. Macdonald, 'Religion', in *Pre-Roman and Roman Winchester: Part II, The Roman Cemetery at Lankhills*, ed. G. Clarke, Winchester Studies, *3* (1979), 424–33 (Lankhills may have included a few Christian burials inside an enclosure); Black, 'Romano-British burial customs'.

11. R.A. Chambers, 'The late and sub-Roman cemetery at Queenford Farm, Dorchester-on-Thames, Oxon.', *Oxoniensia, 52* (1987), 35–69; for doubts on its Christian nature see Watts, 'Infant burials'.

The suburban Christian cemeteries are what we might expect, but the location of the rural cemetery of Cannington inside a hill-fort is more surprising. Hill-forts were favoured locations for pagan temples in Somerset in the fourth century and it is possible that a circular rock-cut structure on the hill above the cemetery at Cannington was a late Roman shrine.[12] The use of Cannington hill-fort for Christian burials may therefore show a desire to continue the religious associations of the site and to replace clearly one religious practice by another. It is even possible that some temples or their sites were reused as sites of Christian churches. Towards the end of the fourth century a temple on Brean Down (Som) was demolished and some of its stone used to erect a small rectangular building close by, which was oriented east-west and for which parallels can be found among known early churches: subsequently a cemetery of east-west burials was founded nearby (fig. 37).[13] A phase of conversion to Christian use before the end of the fourth century has also been argued for a pagan temple at Nettleton Scrubb (Wilts).[14]

Such sites may convey an important message about the reception of Christianity in late Roman Britain, namely that there was no sudden break with former cults, but rather an adaptation of existing practices. Such syncretism can be seen at a number of different levels and is also apparent, for instance, in the mosaics from the Dorset Roman villas of Frampton, Fifehead Neville and Hinton St Mary where Christian motifs have been combined with those from classical mythology; the rooms in which the mosaics have been found may have been used as chapels by the villa owners.[15] There now seems to be evidence to suggest that Christianity could be found at all levels of society in late Roman Wessex and not just among the urban and rural elites represented by the Roman villas in Dorset and the mausolea of Poundbury. Roger Leech's excavations of a cemetery associated with a small farmstead at Bradley Hill (Som) have revealed there the shift from burials of pagan to Christian type in the course of the fourth century.[16] Finds such as Roman tiles inscribed with Christian graffiti from Exeter, Winchester and Gatcombe villa (Som),[17] or of a tablet from Bath with a casual reference to the

12. Rahtz, 'Pagan and Christian', espec. 14–15.
13. R. Leech, 'Religion and burials in South Somerset and North Dorset', in *Temples, Churches and Religion: Recent Research in Roman Britain*, ed. W. Rodwell, BAR, *77(i)* (1980), 329–66.
14. W.J. Wedlake, *The Excavation of the Shrine of Apollo at Nettleton, Wiltshire, 156–1971*, Soc. of Antiquaries research report, *40* (1982).
15. Thomas, *Christianity in Roman Britain*, 104–6.
16. R. Leech, 'The excavation of a Romano-British farmstead and cemetery on Bradley Hill, Somerset', *Britannia, 12* (1981), 177–252.
17. Thomas, *Christianity in Roman Britain*, 88–90; R. Foot, 'An early Christian symbol from Winchester?', *Winchester Museums Service Newsletter, 13* (July 1992), 6–8.

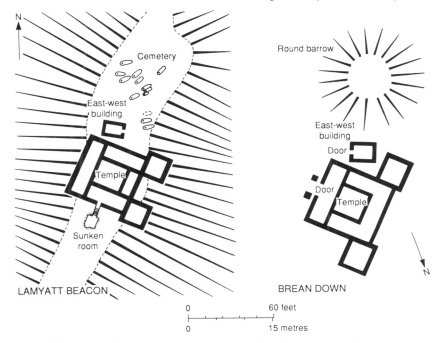

37. Plans of late Roman temples and probable early Christian churches at Brean Down and Lamyatt Beacon (Som) [R. Leech and P. Leach, 'Roman town and countryside', in *The Archaeology of Somerset*, ed. M. Aston and I. Burrow (1982), figs. 8.18 and 8.19]

new religion,[18] suggest that Christianity may have made more impact on Romano-British Wessex than was once believed possible. However, it is unlikely that Christianity was ever more than a minority religion. Many pagan temples in western Wessex at least, such as those at Maiden Castle (Dorset), Nettleton (Wilts) and Pagan's Hill (Som), underwent a revival in the late fourth century.[19] However, damage to Pagan's Hill and Nettleton, and a possible short phase of adaptation to Christian use at the latter, may suggest increasing hostility to the old religions.[20]

THE CONVERSION OF DUMNONIA

There is at present no evidence that the area of Dumnonia west and north of Exeter was converted to Christianity by the end of the

18. Tablet no. 98 in B. Cunliffe, *The Temple of Sulis Minerva at Bath, vol. 2 The Finds from the Sacred Spring* (1988).
19. P. Rahtz and L. Watts, 'The end of Roman temples in the west of Britain', in *The End of Roman Britain*, ed. P.J. Casey, BAR, 71 (1979), 183–201.
20. Wedlake, *Nettleton*, espec. 81–2; P. Rahtz and L. Watts, 'Pagan's Hill revisited', *Arch J, 146* (1989), 330–71.

Roman period[21] – though it would be equally hard to prove the converse of that statement. The question of the development of the Christian Church in non-Romanized Devon and western Somerset really belongs with that of Cornwall, for which fuller sources of information survive, but which is beyond the scope of this study.[22] One visible sign of the links between this area and Cornwall is the distribution of inscribed memorial stones. As discussed in Chapter 1, the greatest concentration of the memorial stones is in Cornwall, but there is a substantial group from the south and west of Dartmoor, four from the island of Lundy and a small group in north Devon and the adjoining area of Somerset (fig. 5). A group of five at Wareham are very much outliers (fig. 19).[23] Some stones may originally have stood in churchyards and be associated with burials, like those on Lundy,[24] but most have been removed from their original locations. It is generally agreed that the inscribed memorial stones of the south-west are ultimately derived from Christian memorials developed on the Continent in the early fifth century, but several different sources of influence may have been in operation on the Dumnonian group.[25] The stones which lie outside Cornwall do not belong to the earliest phase of their introduction to Britain and the earliest are probably of late fifth or sixth-century date. The majority of the stones have vertical, Latin inscriptions of the *filius* type recording the descent of the commemorated person. Some of the stones have Christian symbols, a chi-rho or inscribed cross within a circle, and although it cannot be automatically assumed that all those commemorated on the stones were Christians, the stones do seem to have been linked with the assimilation of Christianity by the Dumnonian aristocracy.[26]

The distribution of the inscribed stones in Dumnonia and their absence (apart from Wareham) in the Durotrigean province may indicate different patterns in the Christianization of the two areas, and perhaps a later date for the assimilation of Christianity among the ruling classes of Dumnonia. On the other hand, Gildas drew no distinction between the ecclesiastical provision in Dumnonia and that for the other provinces which he castigates, so any variations

21. S. Pearce, *The Kingdom of Dumnonia: Studies in History and Tradition in South-Western Britain AD 350–1100* (1978), 60–4; Thomas, *Christianity in Roman Britain*, 136–40.

22. See n. 21 and L. Olson, *Early Monasteries in Cornwall* (1989); A. Preston-Jones, 'Decoding Cornish churchyards', in *The Early Church in Wales and the West*, ed. N. Edwards and A. Lane, Oxbow monographs, *16* (1992), 104–24.

23. See Ch. 1, 16–18. For Devon stones see E. Okasha, *Corpus of Early Christian Inscribed Stones of South-West Britain* (1993), and for Wareham see RCHM, *Dorset II: West* (1970), 304–12.

24. C. Thomas, P. Fowler and K. Gardner, 'Lundy', *Current Archaeology, 16* (1969), 138–42; Okasha, *Corpus*, 154–66.

25. J. Knight, 'The early Christian Latin inscriptions of Britain and Gaul: chronology and context', in *The Early Church in Wales and the West*, ed. N. Edwards and A. Lane, Oxbow monographs, *16* (1992), 45–50; Okasha, *Corpus*, 31–42.

26. Okasha, *Corpus*, 14–30, 50–60.

in ecclesiastical experience in the fourth or early fifth centuries may not have been of much significance by the time he was writing. The Church in Dumnonia may not have evolved from foundations laid down in the late Roman period, but the Christian practices introduced to Dumnonia would have been derived ultimately from the same late Roman background. In addition, continuity with facets of traditional Celtic religion is likely to have been common to all the western provinces.

CHRISTIANITY IN WESTERN WESSEX IN THE FIFTH AND SIXTH CENTURIES

Professor Frend argued that the type of syncretism to be seen in the Dorset villa mosaics meant a superficial reception of Christianity that was unlikely to survive the separation of Britain from the Roman Empire.[27] However, the archaeological evidence suggests both continuity of site use from the fourth century into the fifth century and later, as at Cannington where radio-carbon dating and artefacts suggest the cemetery was in use from the fourth to the late seventh or early eighth centuries, and also continuation of the practice which seems to have begun in the late Roman period of adaptation of temples and hilltop sites for Christian worship or burial.[28] At Lamyatt Beacon (Som) a small rectangular masonry building accompanied by east-west burials has been found overlying a Roman temple, and there are close parallels with the sequence and arrangement at Brean Down (Som), except that there seems to have been a greater hiatus between disuse of the temple and erection of the putative church at Lamyatt Beacon (fig. 37).[29] Similar sequences of pagan temples being succeeded by Christian chapels and burials have been proposed for Nettleton (Wilts), Pagan's Hill (Som) and Uley (Gloucs), close to the Somerset border.[30] There are other examples where hilltop temple sites have subsequently been used for Christian burial at Henley Wood (Som) and at Maiden Castle (Dorset).[31] If the late fifth or sixth century occupation of Glastonbury Tor is that of a religious community, as Philip Rahtz would now argue (fig. 40),[32] then it suggests that the strength of the association of hilltop sites with ritual practices was such that they might be favoured locations for sites of Christian worship even where there is no sign of previous pagan ritual use.

27. Frend, 'Romano-British Christianity'.
28. Rahtz, 'Pagan and Christian'.
29. Leech, 'Religion and burials', 329–32.
30. See n. 20; A. Ellison, 'Natives, Romans and Christians on West Hill, Uley: an interim report on the excavation of a ritual complex of the first millennium AD', in *Temples, Churches and Religion: Recent Research in Roman Britain*, ed. W. Rodwell, BAR, 77(i) (1980), 303–28.
31. Rahtz and Watts, 'The end of Roman temples', 190–5.
32. Rahtz, 'Pagan and Christian', 19–34.

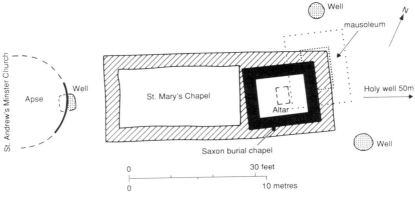

38. Sequence of religious structures beneath St Mary's Chapel, Wells
[W. Rodwell, 'From Mausoleum to Minster: the early development of
Wells Cathedral', in *The Early Church in Western Britain and
Ireland*, ed. S. Pearce (1982), 49–59]

Also of great importance in Romano-Celtic religion were the sites
of natural springs or wells, and it seems likely that these are
another facet of traditional ritual practice which was absorbed by
the early Christian Church in western Wessex,[33] though the
evidence is perhaps more nebulous than that for hilltop sites. Of
course, one must beware of seeing every church built near a natural
spring as evidence for continuity of religious cults; churches had
need of water, not least for baptisms, and so a perfectly practical
explanation for the association can be made in a number of cases.
Nevertheless some sites seem suggestive. Excavations at Wells in
Somerset have revealed a mausoleum of late Roman type as the
first in a sequence of Christian buildings aligned on the most
important of the spectacular natural springs which was later known
as the holy well of St Andrew (fig. 38).[34] At Bath the sacred spring
in its Roman reservoir seems to have been an important component
of the monastic complex established by Anglo-Saxons in the seventh
century; however, there is at present no detailed evidence for cult
practices there between the late fourth and the seventh centuries.[35]

The medieval Church in western Wessex abounded in holy wells
some of which were associated with British or other Celtic saints.[36]
Some like the holy well in the former abbey churchyard at Cerne
Abbas with its neat kerbing of stones have been carefully preserved

33. A. Ross, *Pagan Celtic Britain* (1967), 46–59; R. Morris, *Churches in the
Landscape* (1989), 85–92.
34. W. Rodwell, 'From mausoleum to minster: the early development of Wells
cathedral', in *The Early Church in Western Britain and Ireland*, ed. S. Pearce,
BAR, *102* (1982), 49–59.
35. B. Cunliffe, 'Saxon Bath', in *The Anglo-Saxon Towns of Southern England*, ed. J.
Haslam (1984), 345–58.
36. J. and C. Bord, *Sacred Waters* (1985); J. Scherr, 'Springs and wells in Somerset',
Nomina, 10 (1986), 79–91.

39. Holy well in the churchyard at Cerne Abbas (Dorset) [photograph: author]

to this day and were the focus of ritual practices into modern times (fig. 39).[37] The stories associating saints with their wells are often only recorded in later medieval accounts which are dubious in the extreme and follow stock hagiographical conventions. Decuman (Watchet), Sidwell (Exeter), Juthwara (Sherborne) and Urith (Chittlehampton) were all saints who were said to have died by decapitation and were associated with healing wells; the healing springs either appeared where the head was struck off or were natural springs which acquired miraculous powers after the saint carried his or her head to them.[38] What is interesting about these hagiographic conventions is the continuity they may imply with Romano-Celtic practices in which healing shrines associated with natural springs and severed heads played an important part.[39] Like the continued use of hilltop sites, they suggest that the Christian Church in western Wessex experienced a natural evolution from religious practices of the Roman period which was unaffected by the severance with Rome.

The concept of Christian practices in the Romanized south-west in the fifth and sixth centuries evolving from late Roman foundations is compatible with what Gildas has to say about the

37. R. Legg, *Cerne's Giant and Village Guide* (1986), 16–17.
38. N. Orme (ed.), *Nicholas Roscarrock's Lives of the Saints: Cornwall and Devon*, Devon and Cornwall Record Society, new series, *35* (1992), *passim*.
39. Ross, *Pagan Celtic Britain*, 94–171; A Woodward, *Shrines and Sacrifice* (1992), 51–65.

Church in his day in *De Excidio*.[40] Gildas conceived of the audience for which he wrote as being completely Christian. He makes various complaints about standards of behaviour among his contemporaries, but a tendency towards paganism is not among them. The Church Gildas writes about is sufficiently well established to have become corrupt and he complains bitterly of the greed of bishops, priests and deacons. It would seem that the financial rewards from church office were well worth having and might be purchased from the kings (or tyrants as Gildas preferred to call them) at whose sins the office-holders then had to connive. His portrait of a sixth-century Church firmly entrenched in society and closely linked with secular powers is what one might expect from Christianity having become established among the aristocracy of late Roman Britain. As elsewhere in the late Roman world, the aristocracy no doubt found the new religion useful in reinforcing their position,[41] and it would seem that those who rose to power following the ending of formal links with Rome wished to continue the association.

Gildas writes of the normal church hierarchy of bishops, priests and deacons.[42] The episcopal structure may have survived into the seventh century as two British bishops helped Bishop Wine of Wessex to consecrate Chad as bishop in 664,[43] and presumably they are most likely to have come from the south-west. Bishops from the same area may have taken part in Augustine's meeting with British bishops on the border of the provinces of the West Saxons and the Hwicce, though at least some of these bishops were from Wales.[44] Although these sources imply a structured British Church continuing in the western shires until the period of the Anglo-Saxon take-over, there are no clear indications of where the bishoprics were located at that time. Charles Thomas has argued that all the *civitas* capitals are likely to have contained bishoprics in the late Roman period,[45] and on this basis one would expect Exeter, Dorchester and probably Ilchester to have been episcopal centres. However, even if these places were Roman episcopal centres, they may not have continued to be so in the immediate post-Roman period. In the neighbouring kingdom of the Hwicce, for instance, neither Gloucester nor Cirencester which had been *civitas* capitals became early medieval bishoprics; instead it was the smaller walled town of Worcester which was chosen for this purpose.[46] The decline of towns and rise of new centres of secular power in the post-Roman

40. M. Winterbottom (ed.), *Gildas. The Ruin of Britain and other documents* (1978), Ch. 65–92 *passim*.
41. P. Brown, *The Cult of the Saints: Its Rise and Function in Latin Christianity* (Chicago, 1981).
42. Gildas, *Ruin*, Ch. 65 and 67.
43. *HE*, III, 28.
44. *HE*, II, 2.
45. Thomas, *Christianity in Roman Britain*, 195–215.
46. S. Bassett, 'Churches in Worcester before and after the conversion of the Anglo-Saxons', *Ant J, 69* (1989), 225–56.

period may have caused episcopal centres to be relocated. However, as the West Saxons, unlike some of the other Anglo-Saxon peoples, do not seem to have placed their own bishoprics in established British episcopal centres, the latter have yet to be identified.

The nature of parochial arrangements beneath episcopal level are also difficult to establish with any certainty. There are no churches still surviving which can be dated to this period. Presumably many would have been built of timber, like the church which has been postulated at the former temple site of Uley (Gloucs),[47] but possible stone churches have been identified at Brean Down and Lamyatt Beacon (both Som) where they were constructed from masonry from the abandoned temples (fig. 37).[48] The larger stone mausolea would have been big enough to hold a small number of worshippers and to act as small private chapels. The mausoleum at Wells evidently remained a significant structure (fig. 38),[49] and two of the mausolea at Poundbury seemed to have been frequently visited, though it would be difficult to suggest over what period of time or for what purposes.[50]

Another important category of early Christian site in the western Wessex region was the enclosed cemetery.[51] Reused hill-forts like Cannington (Som) were already provided with an encircling rampart, but newly created sites were likely to be provided with their own curvilinear enclosure (generally considerably smaller than that of the hill-fort sites). Many of these enclosed graveyards are preserved as churchyards today in the south-west, their outlines often reinforced by a surrounding perimeter road and raised interior. Lustleigh in Devon provides a very good example, and a memorial stone, subsequently incorporated in the later medieval church, may once have stood in the churchyard.[52] Such church enclosures seem to have been known by the Celtic word *lan* and its use in place-names like Landkey and Landcross (Devon) presumably indicates the former existence of such enclosures. It is possible that the word *stow* was also applied to them in place-names in Devon.[53] However, it must also be emphasized that the building of curvilinear graveyards was not limited to the fifth and sixth centuries nor to the Celtic world.[54]

47. Ellison, 'West Hill, Uley', 314–8; Woodward, *Shrines and Sacrifice*, 101–3.
48. Leech, 'Religion and burials', 331–4.
49. Rodwell, 'Mausoleum to minster', 49–59.
50. Green, 'Poundbury', 72–5.
51. Pearce, *Kingdom of Dumnonia*, 67–71; Preston-Jones, 'Decoding Cornish churchyards'.
52. M. Swanton and S. Pearce, 'Lustleigh, South Devon: its inscribed stone, its churchyard and its parish', in *The Early Church in Western Britain and Ireland*, ed. S. Pearce, BAR, *102* (1982), 139–44; Okasha, *Corpus*, 167–70, modifies some of their conclusions.
53. S. Pearce, 'The early church in the landscape: the evidence from north Devon', *Arch J, 142* (1985), 255–75, at 259–61.
54. J. Blair, 'Anglo-Saxon minsters: a topographical review', in *Pastoral Care Before the Parish*, ed. J. Blair and R. Sharpe (1992), 226–66, at 231–5.

An enclosed graveyard could become what Charles Thomas has called a 'developed churchyard' by the addition of a church or other ecclesiastical buildings.[55] Cannington cemetery may have had a timber church, but it did not become the site of the later medieval church which was more conveniently sited in the village beneath the hill-fort. Lustleigh, on the other hand, may be an example of an enclosed cemetery which became the site of a medieval church and the focus of medieval settlement, but more work is needed to confirm the hypothesis. It is impossible to know how many local churches had been established before Anglo-Saxon settlement in western Wessex and whether they should be seen as staffed with Gildas's priests and deacons in a similar way to that proposed for many of the minster churches of Anglo-Saxon England. The close proximity of major minster churches such as Banwell, Halstock (Devon), Cheddar (Som), Tarrant Crawford and Whitchurch Canonicorum (Dorset) to the sites of Roman villas has encouraged the suggestion of some form of continuity between villa ownership and subsequent use of estates and the foundation of local churches, for which the mausoleum and subsequent church building at Wells, apparently in close proximity to a Roman villa, could be a model.[56] Without excavation at other sites it is impossible to know the exact nature of any such link nor what structures were in place by the time of Saxon conquest in the seventh century.

MONASTERIES

An emphasis on the development of a British Church in the south-west from origins established in the Roman period does not mean that there were no foreign influences on the developing Christian Church in western Wessex. Gildas tells us that British priests might be ordained abroad.[57] Finds of imported pottery demonstrate contacts between western Britain and various parts of Gaul and the Mediterranean in the fifth and sixth centuries, and it has been argued that the same routes would have enabled British Christians to keep in touch with developments in the Church elsewhere in the former Roman Empire.[58] The inscribed memorial stones of Dumnonia may be an example of a new form of Christian commemoration adopted in Gaul which was copied in the south-west.

55. C. Thomas, *The Early Christian Archaeology of North Britain* (1971), 51–3.
56. S. Pearce, 'Estates and church sites in Dorset and Gloucestershire: the emergence of a Christian society', in *The Early Church in Western Britain and Ireland*, ed. S. Pearce, BAR, *102* (1982), 117–43: R. Morris and J. Roxon, 'Churches on Roman buildings', in *Temples, Churches and Religion: Recent Research in Roman Britain*, ed. W. Rodwell, BAR, *77(i)* (1980), 175–209.
57. Gildas, *Ruin*, Ch. 67.
58. C. Thomas, '"Gallici nautae de Galliarum provinciis" – a sixth/seventh century trade with Gaul reconsidered', *Med Arch, 34* (1990), 1–26.

The western sea-routes would also have provided a means of linking the British of the south-west with fellow Celtic Christians in Wales, northern Britain and Ireland.

The introduction of monasticism has been seen as another example of a new Christian form which spread from the Christian areas of mainland Europe to the 'free' Celtic areas of Britain in the fifth and sixth centuries. However, the question of its reception in the south-west has been complicated by the belief, which was prevalent until recently, that the introduction of monasticism was the point at which the true conversion of the south-west to Christianity began.[59] It was partly because this view was so entrenched that there was an unwillingness to believe in any substantial survival of 'Roman' Christianity in the more Romanized areas of the south-west. The old orthodoxy is not supported by Gildas, who in *De Excidio* wrote for a society serviced by a secular church structure of bishops, priests and deacons in which monasteries were few in number and by implication a relatively recent introduction for which he had great hopes for the eventual emergence of a purer, less corrupt Church.[60]

Belief in the primacy of a monastic Church responsible for missionizing the south-western communities came from a reading of the *Lives* of Celtic saints which seemed to show a number of monks from Wales, Ireland and Brittany active in the conversion of the south-west and in establishing monasteries there. There are a few genuine early saints' *Lives* which do show some contacts between churchmen in different Celtic areas, such as the *Life of St Samson* who seems to have visited Cornwall from his native Brittany, but the majority of saints' *Lives* were written at a much later date and are of doubtful value for the history of the fifth and sixth centuries.[61] Susan Pearce has shown that the majority of dedications to Celtic saints in Devon and Somerset are not genuine survivals from the 'age of the saints', but the result of later cult activities.[62] The cults of Breton saints were probably introduced in the early tenth century when Breton refugees came to Britain, while many Welsh and Irish dedications are likely to date from after a period of Welsh hagiographic activity in the late eleventh

---

59. For example, C.A.R. Radford, 'The Celtic monastery in Britain', *Archaeologia Cambrensis, 111* (1962), 1–24; E.G. Bowen, *Saints, Seaways and Settlements in the Celtic Lands* (1969). Recent critiques include W. Davies, 'The myth of the Celtic church', in *The Early Church in Wales and the West*, ed. N. Edwards and A. Lane, Oxbow monographs, *16* (1992), 12–21; H. Pryce, 'Pastoral care in early medieval Wales', in *Pastoral Care Before the Parish*, ed. J. Blair and R. Sharpe (1992), 41–62.
60. Gildas, *Ruin*, Ch. 65; M.W. Herren, 'Gildas and early British monasticism', in *Britain 400–600: Language and History*, ed. A. Bammesberger and A. Wollmann (Heidelberg, 1990), 65–83.
61. Olson, *Early Monasteries in Cornwall*, *passim*.
62. S. Pearce, 'The dating of some Celtic dedications and the hagiographical traditions in South Western Britain', *Dev Assoc, 105* (1973), 95–120.

century. Glastonbury Abbey seems to have been particularly active in mining Welsh hagiographical works to enhance its own history and that of its dependent churches.[63]

These pseudo-historical developments may sometimes conceal genuine traditions about early monastic saints in the south-west. One monastic founder generally accepted as 'genuine' is St Congar. Cadbury Congresbury preserves the name of his monastic enclosure or 'bury', and the late Saxon list of saints' resting-places records its possession of his body.[64] However, the twelfth-century *Life of St Congar* is a complete fabrication which attempts to equate Congar with Docco, a well-attested sixth-century saint from Wales. The main purpose of the *Life*, which was written by a canon of Wells, seems to have been to help with jurisdictional claims of the bishop of Wells.[65] It is also likely that Irish monastics did establish themselves in south-western Britain in the sixth and early seventh centuries, as has been traditionally claimed, even though the best-known traditions, such as the activities of Patrick and Bridget at Glastonbury, must be rejected. An Irish monk who is more reliably attested is St Maildub of Malmesbury, a place-name which Bede renders as *Maildubi Urbs*,[66] and in which the element *burh* seems to be used, as in the case of Congresbury, in its sense of 'monastic foundation'. According to William of Malmesbury, the Anglo-Saxon Aldhelm who became abbot of Malmesbury had been educated by Maildub.[67] The contacts seen in Aldhelm's letters between his circle and Ireland may well continue links first established before the Anglo-Saxon take-over of the south-west and its churches.[68] Perhaps it was through such links that a relic of St Patrick reached Glastonbury by the tenth century,[69] and eventually inspired the fanciful stories of his role in the foundation of Glastonbury.

Archaeology is at present of limited use in helping with the identification of early monastic sites as there is some uncertainty as

---

63. V. Lagorio, 'The evolving legend of St Joseph of Glastonbury', *Speculum, 46* (1971), 209–31; A. Gransden, 'The growth of Glastonbury traditions and legends in the twelfth century', *Journal of Ecclesiastical History, 27* (1976), 337–58; J. Scott (ed.), *The Early History of Glastonbury: An Edition, Translation and Study of William of Malmesbury's De Antiquitate Glastonie Ecclesie* (1981).

64. Asser, Ch. 81; I.C.G. Burrow, *Hillfort and Hill-Top Settlement in Somerset in the First to Eighth Centuries AD*, BAR, *91* (1981), 58–60; D. Rollason, 'Lists of saints' resting-places in Anglo-Saxon England', *ASE, 7* (1978), 61–93, at 92.

65. C.A.R. Radford, 'The church in Somerset down to 1100', *PSANHS, 106* (1962), 28–45, at 38–40.

66. *HE*, V, 18.

67. *GP*, V, 333–5; see further below.

68. M. Lapidge and M. Herren (trans.), *Aldhelm: The Prose Works* (1979), letter 6, 146–7; P. Sims-Williams, *Religion and Literature in Western England, 600–800* (1990), 108–9.

69. M. Lapidge, 'The cult of St Indract at Glastonbury', in *Ireland in Early Medieval Europe*, ed. D. Whitelock, R. McKitterick and D.N. Dumville (1982), 179–212; L. Abrams, 'St Patrick and Glastonbury abbey: *nihil ex nihilo fit?*', in *Saint Patrick AD 493–1993*, ed. D.N. Dumville (1993), 233–44.

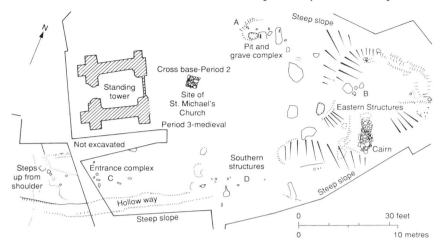

40. Occupation on the summit of Glastonbury Tor; with the exception of the Saxon cross-base and the later medieval tower, features are thought to date from the sixth century [P. Rahtz, 'Pagan and Christian by the Severn Sea', in *The Archaeology and History of Glastonbury Abbey*, ed. L. Abrams and J.P. Carley (1991), 3–37]

to what these sites would have looked like. Some sites have been suggested as likely locations of monasteries because of their topography. In other Celtic areas islands or other remote sites were used, especially by the more ascetic communities. The island of Lundy has been seen as a possible candidate and has at least one, and probably two, early Christian cemeteries, though there is at present nothing from them to support a monastic identification.[70] Hilltop sites, such as that of Malmesbury which was probably originally a hill-fort, could also be seen as possible remote monastic locations, and it has been suggested that the settlements with Christian cemeteries and putative churches at Lamyatt Beacon and Brean Down could have been monasteries (fig. 37).[71] Cadbury Congresbury could be a possible candidate for the 'bury' of St Congar (fig. 7), but it seems more likely that his foundation was in the vicinity of the church and well in the modern village.[72] Glastonbury Tor with putative rock-cut cells and timber church is another possible candidate, and its excavator, Philip Rahtz, now favours the Tor as the most likely site for a pre-Saxon monastery at Glastonbury (fig. 40; see also fig. 45).[73]

Professor Rahtz initially preferred a secular interpretation for the

---

70. Thomas *et al.*, 'Lundy'; Rahtz, 'Pagan and Christian', 11–12.
71. Burrow, *Hillfort and Hill-Top Settlement*, 16–66; Rahtz, 'Pagan and Christian', 11–12.
72. P. Rahtz *et al.*, *Cadbury Congresbury 1968–73* (1992), BAR, *223*, 242–6.
73. Rahtz, 'Pagan and Christian', 19–34.

settlement on Glastonbury Tor, partly because the large number of meat bones he excavated there did not seem in keeping with the asceticism which received wisdom attributed to religious communities in the Celtic south-west.[74] However, it is now appreciated that that element of early Celtic monasticism has been overstressed.[75] Although in his *De Excidio* Gildas refers to some monasteries which he admires, he also writes of a monastery into which King Constantine of Dumnonia had retired and in which 'in the habit of a holy abbot' he had stabbed two kinsmen to death in front of the altar.[76] In a later work known as 'Epistolary Fragments', Gildas appears more disillusioned with monasteries and sees similar shortcomings in them to those which he had traced formerly in the secular church.[77] Monasteries, it would appear, could also be closely associated with the secular power structure. It is therefore likely to be difficult to distinguish in the archaeological record between a monastic site and that of a community of priests, or even between monasteries and the contemporary secular establishments of their patrons.

CHRISTIANITY IN EASTERN WESSEX IN THE FIFTH AND SIXTH CENTURIES

The continuous development of Christianity from late Roman foundations cannot at present be demonstrated convincingly within eastern Wessex during the fifth and sixth centuries. A case for some continuity of Christian worship has been argued for Dorchester-on-Thames, the site of the first West Saxon bishopric founded in 635. The cemetery at Queenford Farm, 0.7 km north of Dorchester, resembles the late and sub-Roman cemeteries found in western Wessex, such as Cannington (Som), and radio-carbon dates suggest it was founded in the fourth century, continued in use in the fifth century and perhaps into the sixth century.[78] Nothing overtly Christian has been excavated, but the burials inside a ditched enclosure, without grave-goods and aligned west-east, could be compatible with that of a Christian community. Nicholas Doggett has proposed, on rather slender evidence, that there may have been another Christian burial ground beneath the abbey church which lay just outside the line of the Roman defences.[79] The first Anglo-Saxon cathedral is presumed to be on the same site as the abbey church, which may incorporate remains of a late Saxon church.

74. P. Rahtz, 'Excavations on Glastonbury Tor', *Arch J, 127* (1971), 1–81.
75. Davies, 'The myth of the Celtic church', 12–21.
76. Gildas, *Ruin*, Ch. 28.
77. Herren, 'Gildas and British monasticism', 65–83.
78. Chambers, 'Queenford Farm'; and see n. 11 above.
79. N. Doggett, 'The Anglo-Saxon see and cathedral of Dorchester-on-Thames: the evidence reconsidered', *Oxoniensia, 51* (1986), 49–61.

Doggett speculates that there could have been a sequence of Christian buildings on this site similar to that excavated at Wells, whereby a prominent Saxon church was founded on the site of the mausoleum of a revered member of a late Roman Christian community. Dorchester-on-Thames may have parallels with Worcester, as a small walled Roman town which seems to have become a centre of secular power in the fifth and sixth centuries which was then chosen as the site of an Anglo-Saxon bishopric,[80] but the interesting possibility that it was also a place of continuing Christian worship needs further support from archaeological investigations.

Juxtapositions of medieval churches and significant Roman sites have been noted elsewhere in eastern Wessex. In Winchester, the Old Minster, the second West Saxon cathedral, was built over the site of the forum of the Roman town, probably in about 660.[81] However, in the absence to date of substantial evidence for occupation of the town site between the end of the Roman period and the foundation of the bishopric, it seems more likely that Winchester was chosen in accordance with an expectation that bishoprics should be sited in former Roman towns – a factor which may also be relevant for the choice of Dorchester-on-Thames.[82] Other factors which could lead to medieval churches being built on or close to the sites of Roman buildings were desire to reuse Roman enclosures, building materials and even buildings themselves.[83] The present parish church of Silchester, for instance, whose visible fabric seems to be of twelfth-century date, lies just inside the defences of the Roman town, on the site of a temple.[84] If, as seems likely, the church had an Anglo-Saxon predecessor, it may have been built on that site for any or all of those three reasons. Possibly some individual Christian communities did exist in eastern Wessex in the fifth and sixth centuries, but it is unlikely that there was an organized Church of the type Gildas describes in western Britain without the British-based power structures with which he was also familiar. Nor is there surviving from eastern Wessex the range of evidence for the practice of Christianity from archaeological remains, church dedications and written remembrances which is to be found in the western region.

---

80. Bassett, 'Churches in Worcester'.
81. M. Biddle, 'The study of Winchester: archaeology and history in a British town', *PBA*, 69 (1983), 93–135.
82. D. Hill, 'Continuity from Roman to Medieval: Britain', in *European Towns*, ed. M. Barley (1977), 293–302; B.A.E. Yorke, 'The foundation of the Old Minster and the status of Winchester in the seventh and eighth centuries', *PHFCAS*, 38 (1982), 75–84.
83. Blair, 'Anglo-Saxon minsters', 235–46.
84. Boon, *Silchester*, 155–7.

NON-CHRISTIAN RELIGION IN WESSEX IN THE FIFTH TO SEVENTH CENTURIES

It is unlikely even in western Wessex that Christianity was the only religion practised between the fifth and the seventh centuries. Use of pagan temples continued in the West Country beyond 400 and some sites may still have been in use in an attenuated form in the seventh century; for instance, the discovery of various objects, including a blue squat glass jar of seventh-century date in a well-shaft at Pagan's Hill (Som) has suggested a continuing use of the site for ritual deposition.[85] At Cadbury Congresbury Philip Rahtz has argued that one of the penannular, rock-cut structures in the reoccupied hill-fort was a shrine (fig. 7) and that a pagan cult was transferred there from the adjacent hilltop temple of Henley Wood, which may have then been used for burial by the inhabitants of the hill-fort.[86] But Philip Rahtz is also at pains to stress the difficulty of correctly identifying and interpreting cult practices; should the objects from the well-shaft at Pagan's Hill be seen as ritual deposits or as evidence for a formal desecration of the site, for instance? Nevertheless, it would appear that although the presumably upper-class audience Gildas addressed in *De . Excidio* considered themselves to be Christians, there were still adherents of pagan practices among the British community. When Aldhelm wrote of places 'where once the crude pillars of the same foul snake and the stag were worshipped with coarse stupidity in profane shrines',[87] he may not have been referring to Anglo-Saxon shrines, but to those of British pagans who would have come under his jurisdiction as bishop of Sherborne. Antler-headed gods were a feature of pagan Celtic religion and might be associated with a ram-horned serpent; antlers have been found at a number of West Country temples.[88]

In eastern Wessex the Anglo-Saxons brought their own cult practices to supplement those of the Romano-British community. It is only through place-names that we can have any suggestion that the main gods of the Germanic pantheon were worshipped in eastern Wessex.[89] Margaret Gelling's work on heathen place-names has revealed a notable concentration incorporating the name of the god Woden (from whom the West Saxon royal house claimed descent) in north Wiltshire in the vicinity of Wansdyke (Woden's

---

85. Rahtz and Watts, 'End of Roman temples in the west' and 'Pagan's Hill revisited'.
86. Rahtz *et al.*, *Cadbury Congresbury*, 242–46.
87. Lapidge and Herren (trans.), *Aldhelm: The Prose Works*, 143–6, 160–4.
88. Ross, *Pagan Celtic Britain*, 172–201; Leech, 'Religion and burials', 334–5.
89. M. Gelling, 'Place-names and Anglo-Saxon paganism', *University of Birmingham Historical Journal*, 8 (1961–2), 7–25; M. Gelling, 'Further thoughts on pagan place-names', in *Place-Name Evidence for Anglo-Saxon Invasion and Scandinavian Settlement*, ed. K. Cameron (1975), 99–114; for some differing interpretations, see L.J. Bronnekant, 'Place-names and Anglo-Saxon paganism', *Nomina, 8* (1984), 72.

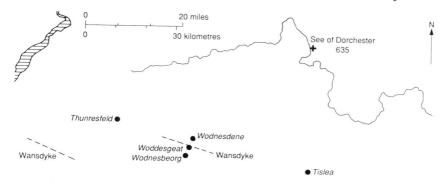

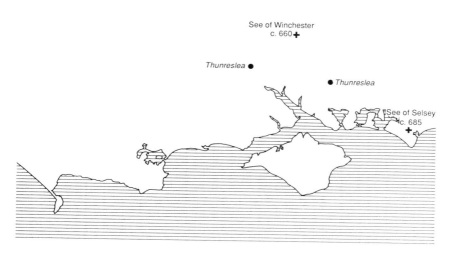

41. Place-names from eastern Wessex whose first elements appear to derive from the names of Germanic gods [M. Gelling, *Signposts to the Past* (1978), 160]

dyke) (fig. 41). Thunor is represented by *Thunresfeld* in Wiltshire and two examples of *Thunreslea* in Hampshire, and Tiw, who is rare generally in the Anglo-Saxon place-name evidence, may be commemorated at Tislea (Hants). There are possible derivations from the name of the goddess Frig at Freefolk, Frobury and Froyle (all Hants), but none of these identifications is considered very secure. A number of the names include *lea*, 'grove', as their second element, with the implication of worship at sacred groves within woods. Wheely Down (Hants) combines *lea* with *weoh*, one of the Old English words for 'temple' or 'shrine'. This haul of pagan place-names might appear meagre, but it must be remembered that such names are likely to be chance survivals; a number of the West

42. Cremation urn from the cemetery at Portway, Andover (Hants) [photograph: Hampshire County Museum Service]

Saxon examples are from remote locations or on the bounds of estates. There may have been a deliberate policy of substituting other names for pagan place-names; a rare demonstration of this may be the neolithic long barrow *Wodnesbeorg*, one of the several Woden names in north Wiltshire, which was subsequently called Adam's Grave.

The other main potential source for a knowledge of Anglo-Saxon paganism is Anglo-Saxon burials (fig. 42). It is, however, difficult to discern how far burial practices were governed by religious beliefs.[90] Archaeologists have moved away from simplistic explanations of grave-goods being included for use in an afterlife to more complex sociological interpretations which draw upon anthropological parallels. For instance, the weapons in some male burials and the complex costumes in which some women were buried may have signalled the free status of the dead people and of the families who buried them. Nevertheless, there are some practices associated with burial which suggest the performance of ritual, such as the inclusion of charcoal or other burnt items which is a feature of a number of West Saxon cemeteries.[91] Inclusion of charcoal was noted for instance in several burials at Chessell Down (I of W) and Camerton, one of the few cemeteries of Anglo-Saxon type in Somerset. At Frilford (Berks) a number of graves had been lined with stones which had been in contact with fire, while at Broad Chalke (Wilts) all of the nineteen graves excavated contained burnt or unburnt flints and pieces of iron pyrites (the unburnt flint and iron pyrites could have been used for fire-lighting). We may not be able to explain the beliefs behind rituals such as these, but they do serve to show that religious rituals were likely to be important in the everyday lives of the Germanic immigrants in Wessex. Some dead ancestors may themselves have been the focus of cults – some of the cremations at Alton (Hants), Carisbrooke (I of W) and Berinsfield (Oxon) appear to have had small shrines erected around them[92] – but it is difficult find any obvious links between burials and the worship of the gods represented in the place-names.

The Anglo-Saxons who settled in Wessex evidently continued to worship the gods and follow the burial rituals of their homelands, and such things were presumably important in reinforcing their group identity. However, that does not mean that they would have been indifferent to Romano-British cult practices which they encountered. Although their pantheons of gods and goddesses differed, there were many parallels between Celtic and Germanic religion whose main festivals followed the agricultural year and were particularly concerned with control of the elements and fertility of the soil.[93] Both religions recognized many localized deities or other supernatural beings, and the Anglo-Saxons would presumably have felt the need to win over those that were established in the places in which they settled. The fact that Anglo-Saxons often chose places for burial which had earlier cult

---

90. See further below, and M. Welch, *Anglo-Saxon England* (1992), 71–87.
91. D.M. Wilson, *Anglo-Saxon Paganism* (1992), 113–28, including references to sites cited in text.
92. V. Evison, *An Anglo-Saxon Cemetery at Alton, Hampshire*, Hampshire Field Club monograph, *4* (1988), 34–6; A. Down and M. Welch, *Chichester Excavations 7: Apple Down and the Mardens* (1990), 25–33.
93. H.E. Davidson, *Myths and Symbols in Pagan Europe* (1988).

43. Bronze Age barrow and ditch cut by Anglo-Saxon burials,
probably of late sixth/seventh century date, at Christchurch (Dorset)
[photograph: Hampshire County Museum Service]

associations may show such a desire to fit into a landscape which
already had lines of communication with an otherworld. Anglo-
Saxons were buried alongside Romano-British at the former Roman
temple at Frilford (Berks),[94] and it has been suggested that the
term *weoh* may have been applied by Anglo-Saxons to Romano-
British temples which they encountered (though this has yet to be
demonstrated as fact).[95] Prehistoric barrows might also act as a
focus for Anglo-Saxon burials or be reused for interments. Both
practices are in particular a feature of Anglo-Saxon settlement in
central and northern Wiltshire, but are also found elsewhere in
Wessex, such as Christchurch in Dorset (fig. 43), wherever prehistoric barrow burial was practised.[96] Reuse of barrow mounds or
burial in their vicinity may also show a desire to claim the barrows'
occupants as 'ancestors' and so reinforce claims to their land.[97]

94. G. Rolleston, 'Researches and excavations carried on in an ancient cemetery at
    Frilford, near Abingdon, Berkshire, in the years 1867–1868', *Archaeologia, 42*
    (1869), 417–85.
95. Bronnekant, 'Place-names', 72.
96. Morris, *Churches in the Landscape*, 46–92, *passim*; Wilson, *Anglo-Saxon
    Paganism*, 67–71; K.S. Jarvis, *Excavations in Christchurch 1969–1980*, DNHAS
    monograph, 5 (1983).
97. J. Shephard, 'The social identity of the individual in isolated barrows and
    barrow cemeteries in Anglo-Saxon England', in *Space, Hierarchy and Society,
    Interdisciplinary Studies in Social Area Analysis*, ed. B.C. Burnham and J.
    Kingsbury, BAR Int ser., *59*, 47–79.

CONVERSION OF THE WEST SAXONS TO CHRISTIANITY

For a narrative of the conversion of the West Saxons to Christianity we have to rely upon the information given by Bede in his *Historia Ecclesiastica*, whose main focus for Wessex is the conversion of the kings and the episcopal succession. The earliest reliable charters date from the 670s and 680s, and no earlier traditions seem to have survived about the foundation of individual churches in eastern Wessex.[98] Bede's main informants for West Saxon affairs were Bishop Daniel of Winchester, who sent him a written account of the early history of the Church in Wessex and the neighbouring provinces, and Pehthelm, sometime bishop of Whithorn, who had been a monk at Malmesbury in the time of Aldhelm.[99] Neither informant seems to have provided Bede with much in the way of dates and his chronology for the early West Saxon bishops is vague. Bede no doubt faithfully reported in many respects the information he received, but the accounts were subordinated to his overall aims in writing and adapted to particular themes in the conversion of the English which he wished to stress.

The initial conversion of a West Saxon king was apparently achieved independently of any of the missions already established in England. The first West Saxon bishop Birinus was consecrated in Italy with the approval of Pope Honorius and given a generalized commission to convert pagan Anglo-Saxons.[100] Birinus's own nationality is uncertain, but he could, from the form of his name, have been a Frank. Bede says that he found the Gewisse 'completely heathen' and among those he converted through his preaching was King Cynegils, who was baptized in 635 according to the *Anglo-Saxon Chronicle*. Bede records that King Oswald of Northumbria was godfather at the baptism and that the two kings together gave Dorchester-on-Thames to Birinus for his episcopal seat.[101] There has been much speculation about the significance of Oswald's presence. The bond between godparent and godson probably strengthened an alliance between the two kingdoms in the face of a common enemy, the pagan Penda of Mercia, which was later confirmed by the marriage of Oswald to Cynegils's daughter.[102] However, it is

---

98. S 1164/B 107; S 71/B 59; S 1169/B 65; S 1170/B 71; S 231/B 63; see P. Wormald, *Bede and the Conversion of England: The Charter Evidence* (Jarrow lecture 1984), *passim*.

99. Bede, *HE*, Preface, and V, 18; D. Kirby, 'Bede's native sources for the *Historia Ecclesiastica*', *Bulletin of the John Rylands Library*, 48 (1966), 341–71, at 364–6.

100. *HE*, III, 7.

101. See in particular E. John, *Orbis Britanniae and Other Studies* (1966), 16, and H. Vollrath-Reichelt, *Königsgedanke und Königtum bei den Angelsachsen* (Cologne, 1971), 102–8.

102. A. Angenendt, 'The conversion of the Anglo-Saxons considered against the background of the early medieval mission', in *Angli e Sassoni al di qua e al di la del Mare*, Spoleto Settimane de Studio, 32 (1986), II, 747–81.

probably not appropriate to see Oswald enforcing baptism on Cynegils in his capacity as overlord; the conversion was through an independent agent and not via a mission from Northumbria. Nor should too much weight be put on Bede recording that both kings endowed Birinus with his bishopric, as both Bede and his informant wrote a considerable time after the event; no doubt Bede was eager to make the most of the role of the king who became St Oswald and whose cult he enthusiastically promotes in his history.

Cynegils's successor, his son Cenwalh, had apparently not been baptized (although his brother Cwichelm and Cwichelm's son, Cuthred, had been) and only became a Christian when in exile (c. 645–8) at the court of King Anna of the East Angles.[103] The *Chronicle*'s date for Birinus's death is 649/650. Bede represents Cenwalh on his return from exile as a king in need of a bishop and the vacancy was filled by the apparently fortuitous arrival of the Frankish Agilbert who had been studying in Ireland and was already consecrated as bishop. Bede then recounts how Cenwalh grew tired of Agilbert's 'barbarous speech', and appointed as a second bishop based in Winchester Wine, who had been consecrated in Gaul, but was a Saxon speaker. Deeply offended, Agilbert returned home and became bishop of Paris; Bede is vague on dating, but the *Chronicle* dates Agilbert's departure to 660. As Finberg argued, Bede's explanation lacks conviction (particularly as Cenwalh appointed another Frank a few years later) and the decision to found a new bishopric at Winchester is more likely to have been because Mercian conquests in the Thames Valley were making Dorchester untenable as a seat of West Saxon power.[104] With the departure of Agilbert, Winchester became the sole West Saxon bishopric and Dorchester served for a few years as a Mercian episcopal centre.[105]

Wessex was soon without a bishop again as Wine was expelled by Cenwalh; the reasons are not given, but as Wine seems to have moved to the court of Wulfhere and purchased the see of London from him, they may already have been in collusion.[106] The West Saxon see remained vacant until Cenwalh realized that his kingdom was suffering enemy attacks because it was not under divine protection and invited Agilbert to return. Agilbert sent instead his nephew Leuthere, but Bede is careful to stress that Leuthere was consecrated as bishop by Archbishop Theodore of Canterbury (in 670 according to the *Chronicle*). From this time onwards the Church in Wessex accepted the authority of Canterbury, and Leuthere's successor Hædde, appointed in 676, was also consecrated by Theodore.[107] However, the battle for the

103. *HE*, III, 7
104. H.P.R. Finberg, *The Early Charters of Wessex* (1964), 214–5.
105. *HE*, IV, 23; Doggett, 'Dorchester-on-Thames', 49–61.
106. *HE*, III, 7.
107. *HE*, IV, 12.

souls of the West Saxon kings was not over. Cædwalla, who began campaigning for the throne of Wessex in 685, had not been baptized. After a successful campaign in Sussex, he came under the spell of the charismatic Northumbrian Bishop Wilfrid who, in exile from his own kingdom, was acting as bishop of the South Saxons. Under the influence of Wilfrid, Cædwalla vowed a quarter of the Isle of Wight (300 hides) to God (and Wilfrid) if he conquered the island.[108] Bede reports the bloody campaign with some satisfaction as it eliminated one of the last strongholds of paganism, and he records that two brothers of the king of Wight had the good fortune to be converted to Christianity before Cædwalla had them executed. Cædwalla resigned his throne in 688 apparently so that he could receive baptism in Rome, where he fell ill and died before he could commit any more sins.[109] He was the last West Saxon king to whom any taint of paganism can be attached.

Bede's account, which is largely concerned with the spiritual health of the major West Saxon kings, is obviously inadequate as an account of the conversion of the West Saxons as a whole. He does though make it clear that it took fifty years before the accession of a baptized king of the West Saxons could be assured, and it would appear that there was some reluctance among some sectors of the royal house to abandon the pagan gods. The unusual, and unfortunately poorly recorded burial, at Cuddesdon (Oxon) which seems to have consisted of a cremation with rich grave-goods under a barrow surrounded by perhaps ten subordinated inhumations, may have been the burial of a Gewissan prince of the early seventh century,[110] and has been proposed as one of those that may have been 'aggressively' pagan in the face of encroaching Christianity.[111] Whatever the truth of Cuddesdon, one would suspect that the final conversion of all the non-Christian inhabitants of Wessex would have taken rather longer than that of their royal house, especially as a sequence of unbroken episcopal succession only began with the appointment of Leuthere in 670. There must have been a shortage of priests to undertake conversion in the early years. Wilfrid seems to have appointed just two priests to oversee the conversion of the inhabitants of the Isle of Wight who apparently were not introduced to Christianity until 686.[112] The laws of Ine (688–94) show a province which was officially Christian, but in which infant

108. *HE*, IV, 15 and 16.
109. *HE*, V, 7.
110. T.M. Dickinson, *Cuddesdon and Dorchester-on-Thames*, BAR, *1* (1974), 3–24; see also Ch. 1.
111. H. Geake, 'Burial practice in seventh and eighth-century England', in *The Age of Sutton Hoo*, ed. M. Carver (1992), 83–94; see also M. Carver, 'Ideology and allegiance in early East Anglia', in *Sutton Hoo: Fifty Years After*, ed. R. Farrell and C. Neuman de Vegvar (Kalamazoo, 1989), 173–82.
112. *HE*, IV, 16.

baptism, church payments and sabbath observance had to be enforced through the threat of large fines.[113]

One way in which it may be possible to discover more of the reception of Christianity among the ordinary population is through study of changes in burial practice in the seventh century. A key site in the discussion of this issue has been that of Winnall, just outside Winchester, which has produced two Anglo-Saxon cemeteries a few hundred yards apart.[114] The earlier cemetery, Winnall I, was uncovered in the late nineteenth century and not properly excavated; such finds which do survive date to the late sixth or early seventh centuries. At Winnall II 45 graves were excavated in 1957–8 by Audrey Meaney and Sonia Chadwick Hawkes. A number of graves were unfurnished and those that were furnished contained only a small number of grave-goods, in several cases only a knife. Grave-goods which could be dated fell into the second half of the seventh century. The excavators proposed that the people buried in Winnall II were Christian, and that, after the inhabitants were introduced to Christianity, the old pagan cemetery was abandoned and a new Christian one founded until such time as burial beside a church became a possibility. The implication was that the Church began to affect the lives of ordinary villagers only a short while after the introduction of Christianity to Wessex.

Since the publication of the report no further examples of double cemeteries have been discovered in Wessex and it has been suggested that the reason for the abandonment of Winnall I and the foundation of Winnall II may be found in 'settlement drift', the focus of burial moving when settlement shifted to a new site in the same general locality.[115] It has also been suggested that changes in the provision of grave-goods in the seventh century may be linked to other factors besides, or in addition to, the introduction of Christianity.[116] The problem is that among ordinary burials the decline in provision of grave-goods and abandonment of certain categories of grave-goods, such as weapons, seems to pre-date the introduction of Christianity.[117] On the other hand, at the top end of society burials seem in some cases to have become more elaborate, with a strong likelihood that those buried with a rich array of grave-goods at the end of the seventh century considered themselves to be Christian. Typical of these rich 'Final Phase' burials is that of the young female inserted into a Bronze Age Barrow on

113. F.L. Attenborough (ed.), *The Laws of the Earliest English Kings* (1922), 36–61, Ch. 1–4; *EHD*, I, 399.
114. A. Meaney and S. Chadwick Hawkes, *Two Anglo-Saxon Cemeteries at Winnall, Winchester, Hampshire* (1970).
115. A. Boddington, 'Models of burial, settlement and worship: the final phase reviewed', in *Anglo-Saxon Cemeteries: A Reappraisal*, ed. E. Southworth (1990), 177–99, *passim*.
116. Boddington, 'Models of burial'; Geake, 'Burial practice'.
117. H. Härke, 'Changing symbols in a changing society: the Anglo-Saxon weapon burial rite in the seventh century', in *The Age of Sutton Hoo*, ed. M. Carver (1992), 149–66.

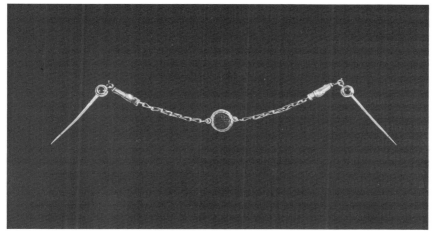

44. Pin-suite from a rich female burial in a barrow on Roundway Down (Wilts); the central blue-glass stud is decorated with a cross and has its closest parallels in Ireland. Note also the boars' head terminals at the end of the chains [photograph: Wiltshire Archaeological and Natural History Society, Devizes Museum]

Swallowcliffe Down (Wilts) at some point in the second half of the seventh century.[118] The body was laid out on a bed and, although the burial had been robbed, it was still accompanied by a rich array of grave-goods, including a satchel decorated with a roundel containing a double-armed cross (see fig. 73), a Celtic bronze sprinkler, a bronze-mounted bucket and four silver brooches. Another female burial in a barrow of similar date at Roundway Down (Wilts) (possibly also a bed burial) was wearing a linked pin-set, for fastening a veil, with a central roundel containing a cross (fig. 44).[119] It seems likely that the burials of the women of Swallowcliffe and Roundway Down, like comparable examples from elsewhere in the country, should be seen as Christian.

It therefore appears that the social functions of burial with grave-goods may have been more important than the religious connotations, and that social changes within the seventh century, linked, for instance, with the development of kingship, may have been in large part responsible for the decline in the grave-good custom among ordinary inhabitants, while making it desirable for the ruling classes to continue with ostentatious display in burial. A transitional period seems indicated in which the Church had to a certain extent to adapt itself to the expectations of the people whose support it needed if Christianity was to be firmly established in Wessex. It is also possible that the introduction of Christianity and

---

118. G. Speake, *A Saxon Bed Burial on Swallowcliffe Down*, English Heritage arch. rep., *10* (1989).
119. Meaney and Hawkes, *Winnall*, 36–7, 47–9; Speake, *Swallowcliffe*, 107–110.

the varying attitudes to it from the West Saxon kings may have created a state of some anxiety and uncertainty on religious matters within seventh-century Wessex, reflected as Audrey Meaney has argued, in the increased provision of amulets – animal bones and teeth, shells, fossils and stones – in sites like Winnall II.[120] Later burials also seem to have a higher number of decapitated burials or those in which stones have been deliberately placed over the body, and possibly these could indicate fears that certain matters pertaining to control of the dead were not being dealt with adequately as new Christian rituals replaced those of the old dispensation.

On the whole the cemetery evidence supports the indications of the historical sources that, although some individuals responded quickly to the new religion, Christianity was only gradually absorbed into Wessex as a whole in the course of the second two-thirds of the seventh century. However, something of a mystery still remains about what burial practices were adopted when the pre-Christian burial grounds were abandoned. Obviously once burial with grave-goods ceased towards the beginning of the eighth century it becomes difficult to date graves. But it is hard to believe from the number of unfurnished graves in the known pre-Christian cemeteries that they could have continued much beyond the middle of the eighth century, and many must have gone out of use earlier. Certainly some churchyard burials did begin in the later seventh century, as is shown by burials clustering around the seventh-century Old Minster in Winchester. There were at least two other burial sites in Winchester, probably without accompanying churches, a small late-seventh century burial ground at Lower Brook Street and the rather more substantial cemetery at Staple Gardens.[121] At Hamwic, whose main period of occupation was the eighth century, eight separate small burial grounds have so far been located (though not all were in use at the same time); most were unfurnished and any grave-goods were restricted to individual items in the earlier cemeteries.[122] One, or possibly two, of the cemeteries may have contained chapels, and there may also have been burials at the site of St Mary's Church which would have been obliterated by later interments, but most of the Hamwic cemeteries were not associated with a building. If the equivalent of Hamwic's cemeteries existed in the countryside, they have yet to be located and the burial practices of the rural population before the growth of villages and local churches in the later Saxon period are unknown.

120.   Meaney and Hawkes, *Winnall*, 29–33; A. Meaney, *Anglo-Saxon Amulets and Curing Stones*, BAR, 96 (1981).
121.   B. Kjølbye-Biddle, 'Dispersal or concentration: the disposal of the Winchester dead over 2000 years', in *Death in Towns*, ed. S. Bassett (1993), 210–47. Staple Gardens may not have come into use until the late eighth or ninth century.
122.   A Morton (ed.), *Excavations in Hamwic: Volume 1*, CBA res. rep., *84* (1992), 48–53, and A. Morton, 'Burial in Middle Saxon Southampton', in *Death in Towns*, ed. S. Bassett (1993), 68–77.

THE ANGLO-SAXONS AND THE BRITISH CHURCH

Bede presents a picture whereby a West Saxon Church was shaped by people representing the orthodox forms of Christianity of which he approved – Birinus, whose mission was authorized by Pope Honorius, the Franks Agilbert and Leuthere, Archbishop Theodore and Bishop Wilfrid. However, that may not have been the whole story, and Bede himself provides grounds for thinking that when he writes of two British bishops who assisted Wine in the consecration of Chad; Bede was obliged to include the information to explain why Archbishop Theodore later found Chad's consecration to have been irregular.[123] Historians working on the Anglo-Saxon provinces established in the West Midlands have been struck by the lack of pagan burial rites in the area and of traditions of conversion achieved through Italian, Irish or Frankish missionaries. They have concluded that the Anglo-Saxon settlers in the region are most likely to have been converted through contact with the native British Christian population.[124] Something similar may have occurred in western Wessex where only a small number of pre-Christian cemeteries of Anglo-Saxon type are known from Dorset and Somerset, and most of those from the fringes of the later shires, in spite of the Anglo-Saxon take-over of those areas having begun before the custom of burial with grave-goods had been abandoned in the east.[125]

If for no other reason, a rapid conversion to Christianity must have seemed desirable by those responsible for establishing Anglo-Saxon power in the west so that they could take over the churches which were an integral feature of the British aristocratic regime. There is increasing evidence that the most significant churches in western Wessex under Anglo-Saxon rule had their origins in the period before the Anglo-Saxon conquest. The evidence comes in a variety of forms, some of which have already been reviewed. At Exeter and Wells there is evidence from excavation for continuity of cult use from the British to Anglo-Saxon periods,[126] and the same may be implied by clusters of inscribed stones from Wareham, Tavistock and Buckland Monachorum (Devon), all dominant regional ('minster') churches in the Anglo-Saxon period.[127] For Dorchester and Ilchester the evidence is rather more circumstantial;

---

123. *HE*, III, 28.
124. K. Pretty, 'Defining the Magonsæte', in *The Origins of Anglo-Saxon Kingdoms*, ed. S. Bassett (1989), 171–83; Bassett, 'Churches in Worcester'; Sims-Williams, *Religion and Literature*, 54–86.
125. See above Ch. 1.
126. C.G. Henderson and P.T. Bidwell, 'The Saxon minster at Exeter', in *The Early Church in Western Britain and Ireland*, ed. S. Pearce, BAR, *102* (1982), 145–75; Rodwell, 'From mausoleum to minster'.
127. D. Hinton and C.J. Webster, 'Excavations at the church of St Martin, Wareham, 1985–6, and "minsters" in south-east Dorset', *PDNHAS, 109* (1987), 47–54; Pearce, 'Church and society in South Devon'.

Dorchester was undoubtedly a major centre for Christianity in the Roman period and an important minster church in the Anglo-Saxon period, but what happened in the intervening period is uncertain.[128] Ilchester is also beginning to produce comparable evidence for a late Roman Christian community, and its minster church, St Andrew at Northover, is suggestively sited on the outskirts of the town in close proximity to a late Roman cemetery.[129] In the case of Malmesbury and Congresbury, place-names containing the names of Celtic saints, who are also listed in the late Saxon list of saints' resting-places, imply some form of continuity.[130] *Some* (but not all) Celtic church dedications may also be evidence for continuity, including those to Nectan at Hartland (Devon) and Decuman at Watchet (Som).[131] There are also a remarkable number of cases in western Wessex where the site of an Anglo-Saxon minster church and a Roman villa or other substantial Roman building coincide, which could suggest some form of continuity for Christian worship from the post-Roman to the period of Anglo-Saxon conquest.[132]

Sherborne, which was chosen as the site of the see for western Wessex when the single West Saxon bishopric was divided in 705, is also likely to have been a pre-existing church foundation. The late medieval list of royal benefactors and the lands they gave to Sherborne is headed by the statement that King Cenwalh gave a hundred hides at Lanprobi.[133] Cenwalh was regarded as the founder of Anglo-Saxon Sherborne, as a forged foundation charter also makes clear,[134] and the name preserved in Sherborne tradition implies that the foundation included the transfer of the *lan* ('enclosed cemetery') of St Probus. That the *lan* lay in the vicinity of Sherborne itself is suggested by a reference in a papal bull of 1163 to a *capella sancti Probi* which seems to have lain in the vicinity of the castle, about a kilometre to the east of the site of Sherborne Abbey.[135] Although a spirited case has been made by Katharine Barker for equating the topography of the town of Sherborne with that of the Celtic *lan*,[136] it seems more likely that *Lanprobi* lay in the area of the later castle and that the Anglo-Saxon abbey was founded on a new site nearby.[137] Something similar may have

128. L. Keen, 'The towns of Dorset', in *Anglo-Saxon Towns in Southern England*, ed. J. Haslam (1984), 203–47; Farwell and Molleson, *Poundbury*, 237–9.
129. R.W. Dunning, 'Ilchester: a study in continuity', *PSANHS, 119* (1975), 44–50.
130. Rollason, 'Lists of saints' resting-places'.
131. For the problems see Pearce, 'Dating of some Celtic dedications'.
132. See n. 56.
133. M.A. O'Donovan (ed.), *Charters of Sherborne* (1988), 81–2.
134. S 228/B 26; O'Donovan, *Charters of Sherborne*, 1–3.
135. H.P.R. Finberg, 'Sherborne, Glastonbury and the expansion of Wessex', *Lucerna* (1964), 95–115, at 98–9; O'Donovan, *Charters of Sherborne*, 83–8.
136. K. Barker, 'The early Christian topography of Sherborne', *Antiquity, 54* (1980), 229–31, and 'The early history of Sherborne', in *The Early Church in Western Britain and Ireland*, ed. S. Pearce, BAR, *102* (1982), 77–116.
137. D. Hinton, 'The topography of Sherborne – early Christian?', *Antiquity, 55* (1981), 222–3; Keen, 'Towns of Dorset', 209–12.

occurred at Glastonbury, if the Tor is accepted as the site of a pre-Saxon religious community, for so far nothing has been found in excavation of the nearby abbey site which could not be accommodated by a Saxon foundation in the second half of the seventh century (fig. 45).[138] A list of lost Glastonbury charters included one by a Dumnonian king which gives the pre-Saxon name of Glastonbury as *Ineswitrin* and would, if genuine, help support the idea of a pre-existing British monastery superseded by a Saxon one.[139] Unfortunately there are grounds for doubting the validity of the charter, and it is worth stressing again that, in spite of Glastonbury's reputation as a site of Celtic monasticism, the surviving written evidence for such an interpretation is less than satisfactory.

Bede was full of contempt for the British Church because some of its practices did not accord with those of Rome, and he praised Aldhelm who, even before his appointment as bishop of Sherborne in 705 seems to have played a major role in incorporating the British Church of western Wessex under Anglo-Saxon rule, for reforming such errors.[140] A letter sent from Aldhelm as abbot of Malmesbury to King Geraint and his bishops in Dumnonia (which is likely to have included at that time the western part of Devon) reveals the calculation of the dates of Easter and the form of the tonsure as the main 'errors' with which he was concerned.[141] The tone of the letter is firm, but not disrespectful, and Aldhelm seems to imply that the attitude of Geraint's clergy was rather different from that of churchmen in Dyfed who would not even sit down to eat with Anglo-Saxon priests and would ritually cleanse any ecclesiastical vessels they touched. Aldhelm was even able to travel to Cornwall,[142] and Geraint was remembered among the benefactors of Sherborne.[143] These indicators of attitudes to and from British clergy are valuable because so little survives. They imply that Anglo-Saxon churchmen did assume attitudes of superiority to their British counterparts, which consciously or unconsciously must have helped them to justify annexation of their churches, but they do not suggest the same outright hostility between the churchmen of the two races which Bede exemplifies. It can only be an assumption that there was a place for British priests and monks who were prepared to adapt in the Anglo-Saxon church structure because no firm indicators of their presence exist. If they did, they must soon have abandoned British names as these do not appear in

---

138. Rahtz, 'Pagan and Christian', 19–34.
139. Scott (ed.), *The Early History of Glastonbury*, 88; Edwards, *Charters of the Early West Saxon Kingdom*, 64–5.
140. *HE*, V, 18.
141. Lapidge and Herren (trans.), *Aldhelm: The Prose Works*, 155–60 – this may be the 'book' referred to by Bede.
142. Aldhelm, 'Carmen Rhythmicum', in M. Lapidge and J. Rosier (trans.), *Aldhelm: The Poetic Works* (1985), 171–80.
143. O'Donovan, *Charters of Sherborne*, 81–2; xlviii–ix.

45. Aerial photograph with the site of Glastonbury abbey in the foreground with the Tor beyond [photograph: M. Aston]

witness-lists. Catwali, who was abbot of an unnamed monastery probably in Dorset in the late seventh century, has a name which could be British, but the issue is not clear-cut as the West Saxon ruling house used British name-elements.[144]

Whatever their attitudes to the British churches and churchmen, there seems little doubt that the structure of the Anglo-Saxon Church in western Wessex owed much to its British inheritance. Although the West Saxons imposed attitudes and orthodoxies that were a result of the pattern of conversion in eastern Wessex, one should not assume that they did not also benefit from their Celtic heritage. It may be no coincidence that the two most learned West Saxon churchmen of the late seventh and eighth centuries, Aldhelm and Boniface, seem to have received their initial education in western Wessex. Boniface, according to his *Life*, was entered as an oblate in the monastery at Exeter; the chronology of his life implies a date in the 680s.[145] One might be inclined to give little credence to Malmesbury traditions that Aldhelm received his early education from Maildub were it not for a letter to Aldhelm from someone who appears to be Irish which refers to him being 'nourished by a certain holy man of our race'.[146] Both Aldhelm and Boniface went east to complete their training, and, although Aldhelm was somewhat disparaging about his early education after a period with Theodore and Hadrian at Canterbury,[147] nevertheless it would appear both men must have received a thorough grounding in the Latin language. Under Aldhelm (appointed abbot *c.* 675) Malmesbury seems to have been a major educational centre for churchmen in Wessex and further afield,[148] no doubt benefiting from foundations laid by Maildub. Aldhelm's correspondence also reveals that he had many Irish contacts, and that some West Saxons travelled to Ireland to study – Aldhelm warned Wihtfrith before he set out to beware of the blandishments of pagan classical mythology and of Irish prostitutes![149]

MINSTER CHURCHES IN WESSEX

The term 'minster church' has already been introduced in the context of major churches in western Wessex taken over by the West Saxons, and it occurs in a number of place-names in Devon

---

144. S 1164/B 107.
145. W. Levison (ed.), *Vitae Sancti Bonifatii, MGH Scriptores Rerum Germanicarum* (Hanover, 1905), 5–6; C.H. Talbot (trans.), *The Anglo-Saxon Missionaries in Germany* (1954), 28.
146. Lapidge and Herren, *Aldhelm: The Prose Works*, 146–7; Sims-Williams, *Religion and Literature*, 108–9.
147. Lapidge and Herren, *Aldhelm: the Prose Works*, 137–9, 160–3.
148. E.g. Wihtfrith, Heahfrith and Æthilwald who appear among his correspondents; Bishop Pehthelm of Whithorn (*HE*, V, 18).
149. Lapidge and Herren, *Aldhelm: The Prose Works*, 139–40.

and Dorset in particular, such as Axminster, Beaminster, Charminster etc. The word 'minster' derives from OE *mynster* which is itself a borrowing from Latin *monasterium*, and both terms in the Anglo-Saxon period could be applied to any type of collegiate church foundation and not just to a male monastery.[150] It has come to be used by modern commentators to refer to the class of superior or mother churches which formed the main unit of church organization below the level of bishopric. The rights and functions of minster churches can be more clearly seen in the later Anglo-Saxon period, when the foundation of substantial numbers of local churches made it necessary to define the relative status of different classes of church and the rights minster churches had over other churches founded in the *parochiae* which they had previously administered.[151] Often the relationship between minster and daughter churches is only revealed through later ecclesiastical records; for instance, the links between Thatcham (Berks) and its dependent chapels can be established from later medieval disputes over tithes.[152] Remnants of these rights could persist in some cases into the nineteenth century. The minster church of St Mary's, Southampton, retained its right to be the place of burial for the citizens of Southampton up to 1846, in spite of the fact that it stood apart from the medieval walled city on the site of the Middle Saxon *wic* and corpses had to be transported across an intervening common.[153] A papal ruling in 1225 had confirmed that St Mary's was entitled to claim not only burial rights and fees in Southampton, but also tithes and other payments from its dependent churches in the city.[154] From information of this type it has proved possible to reconstruct the original areas of jurisdiction of many of the minster churches of Wessex.

A high proportion of minster churches can be shown to have their origin in the seventh or eighth centuries, while some in western Wessex, as we have seen, may have been founded even earlier. Patrick Hase, for instance, has been able to demonstrate that a group of minster churches around the Solent in Hampshire was founded in the late seventh or early eighth century (fig. 46).[155] Bede refers to the monastery at *Hreutford* ('Reed Ford', later Redbridge),

---

150. S. Foot, 'Anglo-Saxon minsters: a review of terminology', in *Pastoral Care Before the Parish*, ed. J. Blair and R. Sharpe (1992), 212–25.
151. J. Blair, 'Secular minster churches in Domesday Book', in *Domesday Book: A Reassessment*, ed. P.H. Sawyer (1985), 104–42; J. Blair, 'The local church in Domesday Book and before', in *Domesday Studies*, ed. J.C. Holt (1987), 265–78.
152. B.R. Kemp, 'The mother church of Thatcham', *Berkshire Archaeological Journal, 63* (1967–8), 15–22.
153. Morton, *Excavations in Hamwic*, 50–1.
154. E.O. Blake (ed.), *The Cartulary of the Priory of St Denys near Southampton* (2 vols, 1981), 168–74.
155. P.H. Hase, 'The development of the parish in Hampshire' (Ph. D. thesis, Cambridge University, 1975); P.H. Hase, 'The mother churches of Hampshire', in *Minsters and Parish Churches*, ed. J. Blair, OUCA, *17* (1988), 45–66.

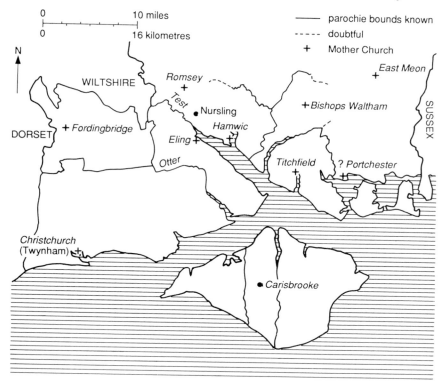

46. Minster churches in southern Hampshire [after P. Hase, 'The mother churches of Hampshire', in *Minsters and Parish Churches*, ed. J. Blair (1988), 45–66]

on the west bank of the River Test, as being in existence when Cædwalla began his conquest of the Isle of Wight in 686.[156] On the opposite bank of the Test was the minster of Nursling to which Boniface went to study, probably at the end of the seventh century.[157] Its *parochia* adjoined that of Southampton, whose minster church of St Mary's stood, as we have seen, in the Middle Saxon *wic* which was founded in the late seventh or early eighth century. East of the Southampton *parochia* was that of Bishop's Waltham, whose minster was in existence by about 710 when St Willibald was educated there.[158] The next *parochia* is that of Titchfield, whose minster church is not actually recorded until the later Saxon period, but here the minster church still stands and

---

156. *HE*, IV, 16.
157. Levison (ed.), *Vitae Sancti Bonifatii*, Ch. 2, 8–9; Talbot (trans.), *Missionaries in Germany*, 29–30.
158. O. Holder-Egger (ed.), *Vitae Willibaldi et Wynnebaldi*, *MGH Scriptores*, 15.i (Hanover, 1887), 80–117; Talbot *op cit.*, 152–77, at 155.

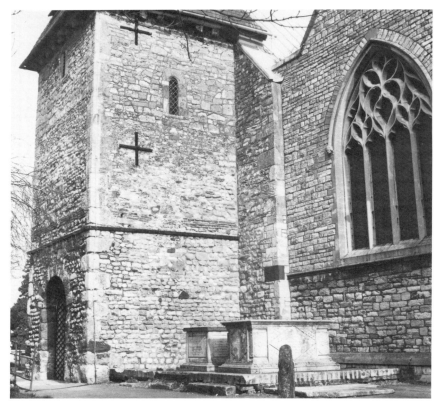

47. Titchfield church (Hants) from the south-west. Note straight-joint between Saxon nave and later aisle on the right and change in masonry where Saxon porch has been raised later in the middle ages to form a tower [photograph: M. Hare]

Michael Hare has shown that the closest parallels for its form and fabric are to be found in churches of the late seventh or early eighth century (figs. 47 and 48).[159] There therefore seems very good evidence for the systematic foundation of churches in the Southampton area from the later seventh century. The foundation can be linked with the West Saxon conquest of the former Jutish province which seems to have been accompanied by enforcing Christianity on the Jutes.

Patrick Hase was also able to demonstrate in a number of cases that the *parochiae* of minster churches corresponded with territories administered from a *villa regalis*. Other studies and evidence seem to point in a similar direction. For instance, a high

---

159. M.J. Hare, 'The Anglo-Saxon church of St Peter, Titchfield', *PHFCAS, 32* (1976), 5–48; M.J. Hare, 'Investigations at the Anglo-Saxon church of St Peter, Titchfield, 1982–9', *PHFCAS, 47* (1992), 117–44.

proportion of the places named in Alfred's will because they were places from which large royal estates were administered, can be shown to have also been the sites of minster churches.[160] In other instances the minster churches and the royal administrative centres seem to have been on different sites, but administering the same territorial area.[161] Obviously the information does not survive in every instance, but it seems a reasonable working hypothesis that in eastern Wessex secular and ecclesiastical administration mirrored each other and that by the end of the eighth century territories administered from a *villa regalis* normally contained a minster church. In eastern Wessex the foundation of minster churches was part of the process by which the West Saxon kings turned themselves from being military overlords to being territorial rulers. In western Wessex they may in a number of instances have taken over from British control large estates which already possessed churches.

However, restraint must be exercised in transferring all facets of the later Saxon minster system back into the seventh and eighth centuries. Although probably the majority of minster churches had a continuous history from their foundation, the network was subject to modification and minster churches could disappear. For instance, Nursling, named as the monastery of Wynbert under whom Boniface studied, shows no sign of having had minster jurisdiction in later periods. Instead the dominant church was at nearby Romsey where a nunnery was founded by Edward the Elder in 907. Hase has suggested that Wynbert's monastery was at Romsey as well and that Nursling should be seen as the district name which eventually became attached to an individual location in the *parochia*,[162] but another explanation could be that the minster church functions were transferred from Nursling to Romsey, which had probably been the site of the royal vill, when Edward the Elder decided to found a nunnery there. Minster rights are not necessarily a guarantee of a Middle Saxon foundation. The church of Winfrith Newburgh (Dorset) can be seen possessing many of the attributes of a minster church from the eleventh century, but David Hinton has shown that it was originally part of the very large *parochia* dependent on Wareham and was probably only given minster status shortly before it was recorded in Domesday Book.[163]

The minsters of the later Saxon period were characteristically served by small groups of secular priests, but the Middle Saxon minsters were probably a more diverse group. Some may have been purely monastic, some purely secular; others a mixture of the two –

---

160. S. Keynes and M. Lapidge (trans.), *Alfred the Great* (1983), 173–8, 313–26.
161. J. Blair, 'Minster churches in the landscape', in *Anglo-Saxon Settlements*, ed. D. Hooke (1988), 35–58.
162. Hase, 'The mother churches of Hampshire', 46.
163. Hinton and Webster, 'Excavations at the church of St Martin, Wareham', 47–54.

the evidence generally does not exist to be entirely sure of each one's composition. Some were certainly nunneries. Wessex does not seem to have possessed as many nunneries as some of the other Anglo-Saxon kingdoms, and all the ones which can be located were in western Wessex. We know of nunneries at Wimborne, Wareham and in the vicinity of Glastonbury; the name Beaminster has the female name 'Bebba' as its first element and so could possibly have been a female monastic foundation.[164] Aldhelm wrote a poem celebrating a church of St Mary's founded by Princess Bugga, daughter of King Centwine, which the poem makes clear was part of a monastic foundation.[165] The church at Wareham was dedicated to St Mary, but it was a common dedication and so not necessarily Bugga's church. Aldhelm's poem for Bugga's church and the references to Wimborne in the *Life of St Lioba* make it clear that they were 'double monasteries' in which a joint community of nuns and monks were presided over by an abbess;[166] both were also royal foundations with princesses as their first abbesses.

The minster churches may well have actively carried out parochial functions for their dependent districts, though it is hard to demonstrate that they actually did so and the topic is currently the subject of academic debate. However, one can say that many of the West Saxon minsters which seem to have been 'monastic', including the nunneries, played an active role in supporting and providing personnel for the missions to convert the continental Germans and so it is likely that they would previously have been concerned to 'missionize' closer to home.[167] The minster churches were no doubt nominally under the supervision of the bishops, but it is doubtful if bishops in the eighth century exercised the same control as their later counterparts. For even if the provision of minster churches was as systematic as some scholars have argued, there is evidence to suggest that some were assigned to individual branches or members of royal and noble houses who might then tend to regard them as their own property. The only narrative concerning the foundation of a minster church is that recounted in charters relating to the minster of Bradfield (Berks).[168] The minster subsequently came into the possession of Abingdon monastery and its charters were adapted to serve as a history for the foundation of Abingdon itself, with a resultant confusion for later historians and distortion of their contents.[169] There are many problems with the interpretation of the Bradfield charters, but they do appear to show

164. B.A.E. Yorke, 'The identification of Boniface's female correspondents and of "double monasteries" in early Wessex' (forthcoming).
165. Lapidge and Rosier, *Aldhelm: The Poetic Works*, 47–9.
166. G. Waitz (ed.), *Vita S. Leobae, MGH Scriptores*, 15.i (Hanover, 1887), 118–31; Talbot, *Missionaries in Germany*, 207–10.
167. W. Levison, *England and the Continent in the Eighth Century* (1946), *passim*.
168. B 29/S 1179; B 74/S 252; B 100/S 241; B 101/S 241; Edwards, *Charters of the Early West Saxon Kingdom*, 168–77.
169. F.M. Stenton, *The Early History of the Abbey of Abingdon* (1913).

the setting up of a minster for members of a royal house with a church passed from one royal kinsman, Eadfrith, to two others, the brother and sister Hean/Haeha and Ceolswith/Cille. King Ine's sister, Cuthburga, founded the minster at Wimborne (Dorset) and the foundation apparently remained an important possession of their branch of the royal house, for King Æthelred I (d. 871) (a descendant of Ine's and Cuthburga's brother Ingild) was buried there, and when his son Æthelwold made a bid for the throne on the death of his uncle King Alfred, Wimborne was one of the two residences he seized and he further demonstrated his lordship of the nunnery by removing a nun from it.[170]

Among the correspondence preserved because of its connections with Boniface and fellow missionaries abroad we can see networks of kin-groups holding positions within the church. Many members of Lul's family, for instance, seem to have held positions in the church and, a number of them, like him, left Wessex to work in the missions in Germany. These included his aunt Cynehild and her children Berhtgyth and Baldhard; Denehard and Burghard who worked with Lul in Germany may have been his brothers, but one kinsman who did not leave Wessex was Cyneheard, who became bishop of Winchester in 756.[171] Another family who made a notable contribution to the German missions was that of Willibald, who was entered into the minster of Bishop's Waltham (Hants) at the age of five. As a young man he desired to make a pilgrimage to Jerusalem and, significantly, is depicted not seeking the permission of his abbot or bishop, but that of his father. Subsequently, Willibald worked in the Germanic missions with his brother Winnebald and sister Walburga who ruled in turn the monastery Willibald founded at Heidenheim.[172]

Bede did not approve of family minsters and some arrangements in eighth-century Wessex were irregular according to the canons of the Church,[173] but the letters of the Boniface circle from both men and women show an impressive mastery of Latin and enthusiasm for the study and promulgation of Christianity. High standards of learning had been set by Aldhelm who was praised by Bede for his 'wide learning', 'polished style' and 'for his erudition in both ecclesiastical and in general studies'.[174] Aldhelm is in fact the most considerable scholar of the early Anglo-Saxon church, after Bede himself, and his surviving corpus of work includes his 'dual' work 'On Virginity' in prose and verse, a treatise on the composition of

---

170. *Chronicle s.a.* 718, 871 and 900.
171. Levison, *England and the Continent*, 238; Sims-Williams, *Religion and Literature*, 241–2.
172. See n. 158.
173. C. Cubitt, 'Pastoral care and conciliar canons: the provisions of the 747 Council of *Clofesho*', in *Pastoral Care Before the Parish*, ed. J. Blair and R. Sharpe (1992), 193–211; Sims-Williams, *Religion and Literature*, 115–43.
174. *HE*, V, 18; Aldhelm's Latin is extremely complex, uses obscure vocabulary and grammatical forms and is difficult to translate.

Latin verse and dedicatory inscriptions and riddles in verse.[175] William of Malmesbury cited King Alfred as his authority for Aldhelm having composed poems in Old English as well and described how he would stand on the bridge at Malmesbury chanting secular poems to attract the attention of passers-by and then intersperse them with verses on biblical themes.[176] Aldhelm seems to have been an important influence on succeeding generations in Wessex. Both Berhtgyth and Lul, among others, show the influence of his style in their own writings; Lul seems to have been educated at Malmesbury after Aldhelm's death and in one of his letters from Germany wrote requesting 'some works of Aldhelm, either in prose or metre or rhythmical verse'.[177] Boniface was also a notable scholar and his work is represented by a Latin grammar and a set of riddles in addition to his well-crafted letters.[178]

We therefore have many examples of high standards in learning among churchmen and churchwomen in eighth-century Wessex. But we unfortunately have no major illuminated manuscripts which have been identified with a West Saxon house. We know such manuscripts were produced because Boniface requested Abbess Eadburga (almost certainly a West Saxon abbess, probably of Wimborne, rather than the contemporary abbess of Thanet) to copy the epistles of St Peter in letters of gold.[179] Nor has much survived of the minster churches themselves. Many, of course, would have been built of wood like the church, probably in Devon, which Aldhelm visited on his return from Cornwall and from which the congregation had to flee during divine office when a great wind shook 'the entire wooden structure with its mighty beams' and removed the roof.[180] The only substantial standing remains which have been identified with some certainty as being of this period are parts of the church at Titchfield (Hants).[181] Michael Hare's careful examination of the surviving fabric has shown that the nave and bottom part of the western tower are Anglo-Saxon work, and the scar of the roof of the original eastern arm of the church has also been located (fig. 48). The church appears to be constructed of stones from a variety of sources, probably robbed from Roman

---

175. See Lapidge and Rosier, *Aldhelm: The Poetic Works*; and Lapidge and Herren, *Aldhelm: The Prose Works*.

176. *GP*, 336; for a suggestion that Aldhelm could have been the author of the poem 'Dream of the Rood' see D. Howlett, 'Inscriptions and design of the Ruthwell Cross', in *The Ruthwell Cross*, ed. B. Cassidy (Princeton, 1992), 71–93, at 92–3.

177. Tangl, no. 71; trans. *EHD*, I, no. 176, 815–6; for Lul see n. 171.

178. G. Greenaway, 'Saint Boniface as a man of letters', in *The Greatest Englishman*, ed. T. Reuter (1980), 31–46; V. Law, 'The study of Latin grammar in eighth-century Southumbria', *ASE*, 12 (1983), 43–71, espec. 62–8.

179. Tangl, no. 35 (see also 30); trans. *EHD*, I no. 172, 811–12; S. Hollis, *Anglo-Saxon Women and the Church* (1992), 276.

180. 'Carmen Rhythmicum' in Lapidge and Rosier, *Aldhelm: The Poetic Works*, 171-9.

181. See n. 159.

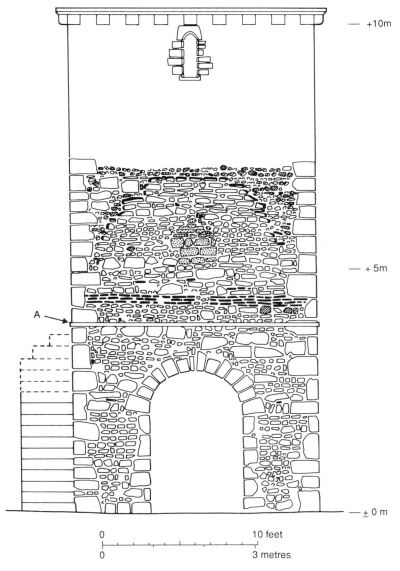

48. Stone-by-stone recording of Anglo-Saxon fabric in west tower at Titchfield (Hants); note string-course of re-used Roman tiles also visible in fig. 47 [M. Hare, 'The Anglo-Saxon church of St Peter, Titchfield', *PHFCAS 32* (1976), 5–48]

buildings, and a bonding-course of Roman tiles is included in all the visible external walls of the nave and those of the western arm. The most notable surviving feature is a window in the western gable of the nave which was built entirely of through stones. Although the date cannot be established with absolute certainty, there are no obvious late Anglo-Saxon features and the closest parallels are with churches of late seventh or eighth-century date.

The full plan of Titchfield church is not known, but the foundations of the greater part of that of the Old Minster in Winchester have been excavated, though somewhat obscured by the later Anglo-Saxon building operations which incorporated it into a much larger church.[182] The original Old Minster consisted of nave, a square eastern arm, which was replaced in the course of the eighth century by an apse, and a square northern porticus which contained a well and presumably served as a baptistery (fig. 49). It appears to have been matched by a corresponding porticus on the south (which could not be excavated in its entirety because of its proximity to the present cathedral). The nave was of double square plan and at 21.90 × 10.95m was larger than that at Titchfield (17.38 × 8.36m), which was also formed from a double square. None of the walls of Old Minster survived *in situ* to be excavated, but fragments of oolitic limestone may have come from lost features. It is possible that fragments of a baluster frieze found during the excavations may have come from the seventh-century church.[183] However, to get some idea of the original appearance of these churches we must turn to Aldhelm's poem on the church of Princess Bugga, which refers to its glass windows, a gold and silver cross decorated with jewels, a golden chalice covered with jewels, a silver patten, an altar cloth made from threads twisted with gold and a thurible hanging from on high in which frankincense was burnt.[184]

It would seem that surviving remains do not do justice to the achievements of the early West Saxon Church and that in the century and half after its introduction Christianity had had a considerable impact on West Saxon society, among the upper echelons at least. Its rapid progress no doubt owed much to the British foundations on which it could build, but there is no acknowledgement of this fact in the sources produced in eighth-century Wessex itself. What is even more difficult to assess is the impact of Christianity on the lower levels of society who receive little attention in the written sources. The laws of Ine evidently envisaged that all children would be baptized, everyone would pay church-scot and that even slaves would not work on Sunday.[185] Pre-Christian burial practices and burial grounds appear to have been abandoned by the early eighth century. However, it is not possible to know the degree of pastoral care ordinary peasants received from the minsters of Wessex. The interest in missionary work amongst

182. B. Kjølbye-Biddle, 'The 7th century minster at Winchester interpreted', in *The Anglo-Saxon Church*, ed. L. Butler and R. Morris, CBA res. rep., *60* (1986), 196–209.

183. L. Webster and J. Backhouse (eds), *The Making of England: Anglo-Saxon Art and Culture AD 600–900* (1991), 239.

184. *Aldhelm: The Poetic Works*, 47–9.

185. F.L. Attenborough (ed.), *The Laws of the Earliest English Kings* (1922), Ch. 2–4.

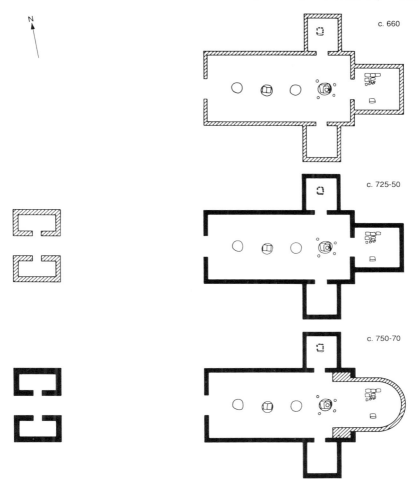

49. The development of Old Minster, Winchester in the seventh and eighth centuries as revealed by excavation [after M. Biddle, 'Archaeology, architecture and the cult of the saints in Anglo-Saxon England', in *The Anglo-Saxon Church*, ed. L. Butler and R. Morris (1986), 1–31]

the pagan Germanic peoples of mainland Europe shown by many West Saxon churchmen and churchwomen could be taken to suggest a similar phase of missionary endeavour in Wessex itself. However, until more local churches were founded, it is possible that there were limits to the degree of regular involvement in Christian worship open to the majority of the population in Wessex. Outward conformity with various Christian norms may have masked a good deal of muddled thinking and imperfect knowledge of the new religion.

5 Renewal and Redirection: The West Saxon Church 800–1066

DECLINE IN THE NINTH CENTURY

In view of the evidence for a vibrant Church in eighth-century Wessex, it is surprising to find that there were apparently major problems in church provision in the ninth century. In the prefatory letter which accompanied his translation of Pope Gregory's *Pastoral Care*, King Alfred wrote that:

> Learning had declined so thoroughly in England that there were very few men on this side of the Humber who could understand their divine services in English, or even translate a single letter from Latin into English . . . There were so few of them that I cannot recollect even a single one south of the Thames when I succeeded to the kingdom.[1]

A certain amount of hyperbole must be allowed for here,[2] but Alfred's statement receives some support from a grant of privileges to Sherborne from King Æthelbert which was recorded in the vernacular rather than in the Latin which would normally have been used.[3] At Winchester Old English was used to record leases to laymen in the late ninth century, but land transactions which were intended to be permanent were still written in Latin and so the leases cannot be securely used as evidence for the type of general decline in knowledge of Latin which Alfred claims.[4]

Asser noted the decay of monasticism among the West Saxons:

> For many years past the desire for the monastic life had been totally lacking in that entire race . . . even though quite a number of monasteries which had been built in that area still

---

1. S. Keynes and M. Lapidge (trans.) *Alfred the Great* (1983), 124–7, at 125.
2. J. Morrish, 'King Alfred's letter as a source on learning in England', in *Studies in Earlier Old English Prose*, ed. P. Szarmach (Albany NY, 1986), 87–107.
3. S 333/B 510; M. O'Donovan, *Charters of Sherborne* (1988), 18–24.
4. S 1275/B 543; S 1285/B 599; S 1287/B 617.

remain but do not maintain the rule of monastic life in any consistent way.[5]

The witness-lists of charters suggest that a number of places, such as Malmesbury, which had been monastic were now staffed by priests.[6] Of course, a decline in monasticism need not necessarily have led to a decline in learning, but Alfred seems to have linked both facets together in a letter, written in about 886, to Archbishop Fulk of Rheims in which he requested his help in reviving the Church in Wessex.[7] Both Asser and Fulk, in his reply to Alfred's letter, raised the possibility that the Viking attacks could have been responsible for problems in the West Saxon Church. But while Kent and Essex which formed part of Alfred's domains may have been seriously affected by Viking raids, the attacks on the Wessex heartlands were hardly on a sufficient scale to have caused widespread disruption to the Church, even if the need to counter attacks may have diverted royal and episcopal wealth away from investment in the Church. Both Asser and Fulk were prepared to believe that there were other explanations. Asser blamed 'the people's enormous abundance of riches of every kind' for causing a disinclination for the rigours of monastic life. Fulk pinpointed neglect by bishops and 'the ignorance of those subject to them'. Alfred himself makes it clear that he believed the problems stretched beyond his lifetime.[8] In his youth, or perhaps even earlier in the ninth century, the libraries had been stocked with books, but the churchmen could not make use of them because they had already lost the ability to read Latin. The Viking attacks could, according to Alfred, be seen as divine punishment for the neglect of Christian teachings which had resulted from this inability to study key texts. To understand the crisis which Alfred believed existed in his own day we must look back to developments at the end of the eighth century and early in the ninth century.

In 747 the two West Saxon bishops attended the synod of *Clofesho*, which was primarily concerned with the responsibility of bishops and priests for the provision of pastoral care and is likely to have reflected the influence of reforming councils in Francia attended, or made known to, Boniface and other Anglo-Saxons working as missionaries in areas subject to Francia.[9] A major concern of the council seems to have been to strengthen episcopal

---

5. Asser, Ch. 93; Keynes and Lapidge, *Alfred the Great*, 103.
6. For Malmesbury see S 356/B 568 and S 363/B 589.
7. Keynes and Lapidge, *Alfred the Great*, 182–6; the contents of Alfred's letter can only be inferred from Fulk's reply.
8. In the preface to *Pastoral Care*, n. 1 above; for analysis of its chronology see T.A. Shippey, 'Wealth and wisdom in King Alfred's *Preface* to Old English *Pastoral Care*', *EHR, 94* (1979), 346–55.
9. Haddan and Stubbs, III, 360–85; C. Cubitt, 'Pastoral care and conciliar canons: the provisions of the 747 council of *Clofesho*', in *Pastoral Care Before the Parish*, ed. J. Blair and R. Sharpe (1992), 193–211.

authority, and the right of bishops to visit and discipline the various *monasteria* in their dioceses is stressed, as well as the authority they could exercise over those they had ordained as priests. The synod of *Clofesho* seems to have marked an important stage in bringing all parochial provision under the supervision of the bishops, and it may indicate a shift to a preference for active work amongst the laity being carried out by secular clerks rather than by monks. In Mercia and Kent there seem to be indications of bishops actively carrying out the provisions by reforming their households (*familiae*), and establishing control over previously monastic minsters and perhaps replacing them with communities of secular clerks.[10] The quality of evidence from Wessex is not so good, but both Sherborne and Winchester, judging from the witness-lists of their charters, were served by comparable communities of secular clergy.[11] It would also appear that bishops of Winchester established ownership of some of the minsters in their diocese; the former monastery at Nursling (*Nhutscelle*), where Boniface had studied, had come into Winchester's possession by 874,[12] and by the early tenth century Old Minster possessed Portchester, Alresford, Whitchurch and Hurstbourne Priors which are likely all to have been the sites of minsters in Hampshire.[13]

However, bishops were not the only people interested in acquiring control of minsters, and archbishops of Canterbury and bishops of Worcester in the late eighth and early ninth centuries were involved in major struggles with kings over the right to possess minster churches and their dependent lands. Bishops of Wessex seem to have faced similar competition from their kings, and it would appear that a number of minsters and their estates came under royal control in the ninth century or early tenth century. Thus although the bishop of Winchester controlled Portchester, he did not control the neighbouring minster centre of Bishop's Waltham which seems to have been in royal hands, as in 904 the bishop exchanged the one for the other with King Edward the Elder, probably because Portchester was wanted by the king as one of the defended burhs.[14] Alfred is accused in the Abingdon tradition of taking over the monastery and its estates; it would appear that a group of secular clergy was still supported, but that the bulk of the estates were added to the royal demesne.[15] There are two separate points at issue here to which bishops could object; firstly that the

10. N. Brooks, *The Early History of the Church of Canterbury* (1984), 129–208; P. Sims-Williams, *Religion and Literature in Western England, 600–800* (1990), 144–76.
11. See n. 3–4 and 20.
12. S 1277/B 544.
13. P. Hase, 'The mother churches of Hampshire', in *Minsters and Parish Churches*, ed. J. Blair, OUCA, *17* (1988), 45–66, at 48–9.
14. S 372/B 613; see Ch. 3.
15. J. Stevenson (ed.), *Chronicon Monasterii de Abingdon* (2 vols. 1858), I, 50; A. Thacker, 'Æthelwold and Abingdon', in *Bishop Æthelwold: His Career and Influence*, ed. B.A.E. Yorke (1988), 43–64, at 44–8.

kings were annexing lands for their own use which had been granted at some point to churches for ecclesiastical purposes. An exasperated Bishop Denewulf of Winchester reminded King Edward of the impropriety of such actions when obliged to lease an estate at Bedington (Surrey) to the king:

> The bishop and community at Winchester beg that in charity for the love of God and for the holy church you desire no more land of that foundation for it seems to them an unwelcome demand; so that God need blame neither you nor us for the diminishing in our days; for there was a very great injunction of God about that when men gave those lands to the foundation.[16]

The second issue is that kings might be the 'lords' of minsters on their estates and so presumably challenge the effectiveness of the bishops' ability to supervise their inmates. Royal lordship of minsters is made clear in Alfred's will where the community at Cheddar is urged 'to choose [Edward the Elder] on the terms we have previously agreed', although the community at Damerham (Wilts) were to be allowed possession of their charters and the right to select whatever lord they desire.[17] Kings might also, perhaps particularly, be lords of nunneries, and ætheling Æthelwold's seizure of a nun from Wimborne after the death of Alfred may have been to make clear his lordship of the nunnery and of the estates it commanded.[18]

Kings might grant churches under their control to others as a reward for services rendered, and in this way Asser received the minsters at Congresbury and Banwell (Som) from a grateful King Alfred.[19] Alfred's father Æthelwulf had granted 15 hides at Halstock (Dors) to an individual deacon called Eadberht who may have been in royal service.[20] The charter was preserved in the archives of Sherborne Abbey and the land seems to have come into its possession; possibly Eadberht was also associated with the Sherborne community. However, when individual clergy could hold estates, it was not inevitable that estates granted to them would come to their community; they might be claimed by secular kinsmen and there was even a danger that lands lent from a community's possessions to support clergy would be claimed by relatives. Whatever the reasons it would appear that by the end of the ninth century the community of Old Minster, Winchester, was trying to reclaim lands which had come into lay hands. A particular concern was a large 40-hide estate at Alresford (Hants)

---

16. S 1444/B 618; trans. *EHD*, I, 543–4.
17. Keynes and Lapidge, *Alfred the Great*, 173–8.
18. M. Clunies Ross, 'Concubinage in Anglo-Saxon England', *Past and Present, 108* (1985), 3–34, at 31–2.
19. Asser, Ch. 81; Keynes and Lapidge, *Alfred the Great*, 97.
20. S 290; O'Donovan, *Charters of Sherborne*, 5–11.

which was leased by Bishop Tunbeorht (871×77–878×79) to a married couple with reversion to Winchester – such leases in the Anglo-Saxon period often seem to have been the result of a compromise when an estate was disputed between a church and a lay family. Tunbeorht's successor Denewulf was obliged to renew the lease to the couple's son Alfred,[21] but retrieved the estate when it was forfeited to King Edward on account of Alfred's sexual misconduct, though only through payment of a gold dish.[22] However, in the reign of King Eadwig, Alfred's son Ælfric was able to take back the estate.[23]

From this information we can understand something of how the nature of the Church in Wessex was transformed between the time of Boniface and that of Alfred. Monastic minsters (an important though probably not the only element in earlier parochial provision) declined in fortune because secular priests were favoured for active pastoral work and both bishops and kings saw an opportunity to increase their own holdings by taking over monastic lands and replacing their communities with small bodies of priests who could be supported on a smaller portion of the estates. Kings may have had other motives as well for, if one is right in seeing some of the monastic minsters as being closely associated with branches of the royal house, suppression of them could have been linked with elimination of collateral lines who might be rivals for the throne. The decline or disappearance of monastic communities could have had serious consequences for the Church in Wessex for some of them had been major centres of learning in the eighth century, including Nursling which seems to have passed to the control of the Old Minster in Winchester. Problems could have begun in the late eighth century when Mercia was in control of the northern part of Wessex including Glastonbury and Malmesbury; the latter in particular seems to have been a major educational establishment for Wessex. Glastonbury for a while became an *eigenkloster* of the family of Cenwulf of Mercia,[24] and may have passed from them to control by the West Saxon royal house as it is referred to as a 'royal island' in descriptions relating to the early tenth century.[25] Malmesbury still supported an important religious house in the ninth century when it received grants from West Saxon kings,[26] though it lost some estates when the border was finally established between Wessex and Mercia, and William of Malmesbury records that Bishop Ealhstan of

---

21. S 1287; A.J. Robertson, *Anglo-Saxon Charters* (2nd edn., 1956), no. 15, 28.
22. S 375/B 623 – the charter is dubious, but circumstantial detail suggests an authentic tradition behind it; see also S 814/B 1150.
23. S 589/B 938; S 814/B 1150.
24. For Mercian control of Glastonbury see Ch. 2, 61–4.
25. W. Stubbs (ed.), *Memorials of St Dunstan, Archbishop of Canterbury* (1874), 7–12; N. Brooks, 'The career of St Dunstan', in *St Dunstan: His Life, Times and Cult*, ed. N. Ramsay and M. Sparkes (1992), 1–23, at 5–6, 11.
26. S 301/B 457 seems genuine; S 305/B 470; S 306/B 481; S 320/B 444; S 322/B 447 are more dubious, but with some authentic basis possible.

Sherborne (816×25–867) tried to appropriate some of its lands and revenues;[27] one of its estates seems to have come somehow into royal possession and was leased by King Alfred to one of his thegns.[28]

The decline of monastic schools would not have mattered if the bishops had founded comparable episcopal schools to take their place; the comments examined above perhaps suggest that they neglected to do so. When apportioning blame, however, one must remember that it was kings who appointed bishops and we do not know what priorities they had when making appointments. Possibly bishops like Swithun of Winchester and Ealhstan of Sherborne, who seem to have been closely involved with the politics of the royal house, were chosen more for their connections than their reforming zeal.[29] Kings of the house of Egbert before, and to a certain extent including, Alfred seem to have been concerned to liberate ecclesiastical lands for their own use and that of their nobles, and even major churches like that of Winchester seem to have felt under pressure from the acquisitiveness of kings and their followers. Certainly kings made some grants to favoured ecclesiastics and communities, but behind these we can sometimes detect other motives than desire to promote the well-being of churches. Egbert granted an estate to Old Minster, Winchester, on condition that it supported the succession of Æthelwulf;[30] West Saxon churches benefitted from Æthelwulf's 'decimation' in 855, a surrender of the tenth of his lands, but grants were made to thegns as well and a prime purpose may have been to ensure the loyalty of the country on the eve of his departure to Rome.[31]

REVIVAL IN THE NINTH CENTURY

Although West Saxon kings of the ninth century seem sometimes to have manipulated church lands and appointments to their own advantage, there were other pressures which would have encouraged them to become patrons of the Church. The movements in Francia which inspired English bishops in the latter part of the eighth century to reform, were ultimately harnessed by the Carolingian dynasty to buttress their newly achieved power. The Carolingian rulers became role models to leaders throughout Europe who desired to emulate their formidable military and political successes. From the beginning of their rise to power the

---

27. *GP*, 176.
28. S 356/B 568.
29. See Ch. 3, 98–9; B.A.E. Yorke, 'The bishops of Winchester, the kings of Wessex and the development of Winchester in the ninth and early tenth centuries', *PHFCAS, 40* (1984), 61–70.
30. S 281/B 423; see also Brooks, *Church of Canterbury*, 145–7.
31. H.P.R. Finberg, *The Early Charters of Wessex* (1964), 187–213; Keynes and Lapidge, *Alfred the Great*, 232–4.

house of Egbert had close connections with Francia. Egbert of Wessex had been in exile at the court of Charlemagne during the reign of Beorhtric (786–802) and it is not inconceivable that his return to take the throne was achieved with Frankish help. Egbert's son Æthelwulf maintained contacts with Francia and had a Frankish scribe called Felix. Æthelwulf would have had a chance to see some of the splendours of the Carolingian Renaissance for himself when he went on pilgrimage to Rome in 855 with his youngest son Alfred. His route to Rome lay through Francia, and Charles provided him with an escort through his territories. On his return in 856 Æthelwulf was formally betrothed to Judith, daughter of Charles the Bald, in the Frankish palace of Verberie. When Æthelwulf died in 858 Judith was married to Æthelwulf's son and successor Æthelbald (d. 860).[32]

However, direct Frankish contacts were not the only route by which Carolingian and reforming influences could have come to Wessex. The Mercians also had their contacts with the Franks. King Offa had been in correspondence with Charles the Great and had introduced a number of innovations from Francia.[33] During the latter part of Offa's reign northern Wessex had been under direct Mercian rule and Mercian influences may have been pervasive in Wessex, for King Beorhtric was beholden to Offa and married to his daughter, Eadburh, who was reputedly a powerful presence in the kingdom.[34] A lasting legacy of this period of Mercian overlordship may be sculptures in the form of cross-shafts, gravecovers and grave-markers which are particularly to be found in Wiltshire and Somerset, but with outliers more widely distributed in Wessex.[35] Many of them carry decoration in the form of zoomorphic interlace which has its closest parallels in south-west Mercian sculpture and decorated manuscripts. One of the finest of the West Saxon pieces is the cross-shaft fragment from Codford St Peter (Wilts) showing the lively figure of a man in secular dress, perhaps a representation of King David (see cover photo).[36] The date of the Codford piece and of related West Saxon sculptures has been much discussed, but Dominic Tweddle has made a good case for dating the earliest of them to the late eighth and early ninth centuries. They imply a widespread patronage for Christian arts in the West

---

32. D. Kirby, *The Earliest English Kings* (1991), 176–7, 198–201; see Ch. 3 for the family politics of this time.
33. B.A.E. Yorke, *Kings and Kingdoms of Early Anglo-Saxon England* (1990), 115–17.
34. Asser, Ch. 14–15; Keynes and Lapidge, *Alfred the Great*, 71–2.
35. D. Tweddle, 'Anglo-Saxon sculpture in south-east England before *c.* 950', in *Studies in Medieval Sculpture*, ed. F.H. Thompson (1983), 18–40; S. Foster, 'A gazetteer of the Anglo-Saxon sculpture in historic Somerset', *PSANHS, 131* (1987), 49–80.
36. D. Tweddle, 'Sculpture', in *The Making of England*, ed. L. Webster and J. Backhouse (1991), 239–44; M. Swanton, 'The "dancer" on the Codford cross', *ASSAH, 1*, BAR, 72 (1979), 139–48. I am also indebted to Professor Rosemary Cramp for advice on the interpretation of the figure.

Saxon provinces, perhaps beginning under Mercian influence, but gathering its own momentum.

Beorhtric of Wessex was buried at Wareham,[37] and may have been responsible for the erection of the substantial church dedicated to St Mary. Unfortunately the church was demolished in 1841–2 and is known only from nineteenth-century illustrations, but it would appear to have been not unlike the surviving church at Brixworth (Northants), with a spacious nave some 64 feet long flanked by a series of *porticus* and lit by a clerestory.[38] The lost Wareham church is architecturally much more ambitious than that at Titchfield or the original Old Minster at Winchester, and may show the influence of Carolingian church building mediated through Mercia. It is difficult to relate any surviving architecture to Alfred's immediate predecessors in his own family, but a possible candidate is the church at Britford (Wilts), a royal estate centre, where the archway to a north *porticus* has exceptionally fine carvings of plant scrolls which Richard Gem believes may date to the early ninth century and show influences from contemporary Italian work (fig. 50).[39] However, it is obviously difficult to date such work exactly, let alone relate it to the patronage of individuals. There are some written references (though these tend to be from post-Conquest sources) to support the erection of churches and other patronage of the Christian arts in ninth-century Wessex before the reign of Alfred: for instance, Bishop Swithun of Winchester (852×3–862×5) is associated with the building and restoration of several churches,[40] while King Æthelwulf is said to have given Malmesbury a shrine for the remains of St Aldhelm which was decorated with miracles of the saint.[41] There has been a tendency, because there were some evident problems in the West Saxon Church in the second half of the ninth century, not to mention the Viking attacks, to dismiss the whole century as one in which no interest in or patronage of the Church occurred before the time of Alfred. The concentration of works from the reign of Alfred, and Alfred's own emphasis on his achievements, may have led to an underestimation of his immediate predecessors' involvement with the Church. When he recruited Mercians and Franks to help rejuvenate the West Saxon Church, Alfred was following a 'track' of influences already established in Wessex.[42]

Alfred's most pressing concern seems to have been the decline of learning in the West Saxon Church, and Asser presents this as arising from the king's desire to learn to read and study books for

37. *Chronicle s.a.* 786.
38. H.M. and J. Taylor, *Anglo-Saxon Architecture* (2 vols. 1965), 634–9.
39. Taylor, *Anglo-Saxon Architecture*, 105–8; R. Gem, 'Church architecture', in *The Making of England*, ed. Webster and Backhouse (1991), 185–8.
40. E.P. Sauvage (ed.), 'Goscelin, *Vita Sancti Swithuni*', *Analecta Bollandiana*, 7 (1888), 373–80, at 379.
41. *GP*, 389–90.
42. In his preface to *Pastoral Care* Alfred uses the hunting metaphor of following a track.

50. East jamb of the north *porticus* of Britford church (Wilts)
[RCHME Crown Copyright]

himself.[43] To this end he recruited scholars from Mercia, including
Bishop Wærferth of Worcester, in the early 880s, followed by
Grimbald of St Bertins and John the Old Saxon from the Frankish
empire around the middle of the decade. Asser seems to have paid
his first visit to the West Saxon court in 886. The scholars read
books in Latin to the king and discussed their meaning with him.
Eventually the king learnt to read and with the help of his advisers
began to translate certain works from Latin into Old English in
rather free renditions with illustrative digressions apparently
drawn from his own experiences. Translations of Pope Gregory's
Pastoral Care, Boethius's *Consolation of Philosophy*, St Augustine's
Soliloquies and of the first fifty psalms have been identified as the

43. Asser, Ch. 77–9; Keynes and Lapidge, *Alfred the Great*, 26–8, 92–4.

king's work, and he also commissioned translations from others, including the *Dialogues* of Pope Gregory from Wærferth, and Orosius's *Histories against the Pagans*.[44] Another work in English with which the king is likely to have been associated is the production of the *Anglo-Saxon Chronicle*.[45]

Alfred seems to have felt that others might benefit from the same path of self-improvement he had followed. His translation of *Pastoral Care* was circulated to his bishoprics with a clear statement in a prefatory letter written by the king that they should implement its provisions, that is train and supervise priests[46] – a restatement in fact of the aims of the Council of *Clofesho* of 747. Alfred also let it be known to royal officials such as ealdormen that he expected them to read and study, and he established a school at the royal court.[47] He also had a formidable patronage to disperse which could ensure that those receiving secular and ecclesiastical office were men who would promote his views. For instance, he appointed to Sherborne first Wulfsige, evidently a man of some learning who composed an Old English verse preface to Wærferth's translation of the *Dialogues*,[48] and then Asser, who may have served as a suffragan bishop to Wulfsige in Devon before the latter's death.[49] Alfred could use carrot and stick to get what he wanted; the preface to *Pastoral Care* intimates that bishops will carry out its provisions if they wish to keep Alfred's favour, but provides an inducement to do so by the gift of an *æstel* worth fifty mancuses, perhaps a book-pointer, of which the gold and enamel Alfred Jewel and comparable pieces found near Weymouth (Dorset) and Minster Lovell (Oxon) may be examples.[50] The *Anglo-Saxon Chronicle* seems also to have been widely circulated among religious houses in Wessex and disseminated what is likely to have been a royally approved view of West Saxon successes under their kings. The *Chronicle* and *Pastoral Care* can be seen to have mutually supporting messages in the royal interest, for doing one's duty as a Christian would also have meant doing one's patriotic duty in supporting Christ's deputy on earth, the king himself.

Alfred founded two monastic houses, apparently the first new monastic foundations in Wessex since the early eighth century. A nunnery was founded at Shaftesbury with Alfred's daughter Æthelgifu as its first abbess,[51] and a monastery at Athelney where

---

44. Keynes and Lapidge, *Alfred the Great*, 28–35.
45. See Ch. 3, 103–5.
46. H. Sweet (ed.), *King Alfred's West Saxon Version of Gregory's Pastoral Care*, EETS, o.s. 45 and 50 (1871–2); Keynes and Lapidge, 124–30, 293–6.
47. Asser, Ch. 102 and 106; Keynes and Lapidge, *Alfred the Great*, 107, 109–10.
48. Keynes and Lapidge, *Alfred the Great*, 187–9.
49. Asser, Ch. 81, says Alfred gave him the *parochia* of Exeter; on problems of interpretation see Keynes and Lapidge, *Alfred the Great*, 264–5.
50. J. Clarke and D. Hinton, *The Alfred and Minster Lovell Jewels* (3rd edn., 1971); Webster and Backhouse (eds), *The Making of England* (1991), 281–3.
51. Asser, Ch. 98; Keynes and Lapidge, *Alfred the Great*, 105.

51. Fragment of wall-painting from New Minster foundation trench, Winchester [photograph: Winchester Museums Service; Winchester Research Unit; Dean and Chapter of Winchester Cathedral]

Alfred had held out when nearly overthrown by the Vikings in 878.[52] According to Asser, Athelney was initially filled with foreign monks as there were no Anglo-Saxons prepared to live under the rigours of true monasticism, though it is not clear whether Asser had in mind the Benedictine Rule advocated in the Carolingian reform councils or the type of *regula mixta* with which he would have been familiar in Wales. However, this foundation of exiles (some of the Frankish monks may have been uprooted by Viking attacks) does not seem to have been very harmonious. Asser reports that some of the Franks resented being under the command of John the Old Saxon as abbot and attempted to have him murdered. Alfred may also have provided a small establishment for Grimbald in Winchester which was subsequently refounded by Edward the Elder as the New Minster.[53] A fragment of a wall-painting from the foundation trench of New Minster church may have come from buildings, perhaps those provided for Grimbald, known to have been demolished when the church was built. The fragment shows part of a frieze of figures, and they and the geometric decoration recall the work of the so-called 'palace school' of Charlemagne (fig. 51).[54] If it was from a building commissioned by Alfred, it could be evidence for the high quality buildings in stone which Asser says Alfred had built.[55]

52. Asser, Ch. 92–7; Keynes and Lapidge, *Alfred the Great*, 102–5.
53. P. Grierson, 'Grimbald of St Bertin's', *EHR*, 55 (1940), 529–61.
54. M. Biddle, 'Excavations at Winchester 1966: fifth interim report', *Ant J*, 7 (1967), 251–79, at 277–9; F. Wormald, 'The "Winchester School" before St Æthelwold', in *England Before the Conquest*, ed. P. Clemoes and K. Hughes (1971), 305–13.
55. Asser, Ch. 91; Keynes and Lapidge, *Alfred the Great*, 101.

However, Alfred was not necessarily concerned with bringing about a broader monastic revival in Wessex. Shaftesbury and Athelney belong to a well-established early medieval tradition of establishing houses for female relatives or to commemorate circumstances in which God's deliveration had been particularly felt. Alfred's main achievements were the re-establishment of standards of education in the Church and among the secular aristocracy, and his promotion of Old English as a literate language.

ROYAL PATRONAGE AND THE CHURCH IN THE FIRST HALF OF THE TENTH CENTURY

Alfred's successors in the tenth century continued the types of patronage we can see operating during his reign. Although they came to be rulers of all England, Wessex was their favoured centre of ecclesiastical patronage. The conquest of other areas of the country by the West Saxons was emphasized by removing relics of saints from northern to southern churches and Glastonbury seems to have been one recipient. In the post-Conquest period Glastonbury claimed to have the relics of Aidan, Bede, Begu, Ebba and Boisil. Glastonbury made many unlikely claims about its early history, so its relic lists have to be treated with some scepticism, but the eleventh-century 'list of saints' resting-places' includes Aidan among Glastonbury's saints.[56] Some of the profits from the kings' expansion of territory were invested in the Church in Wessex. The most notable new foundation was New Minster in Winchester built by Edward the Elder adjacent to Old Minster and used by him as a burial church for his parents, immediate family and ultimately himself (fig. 52).[57] Edward's actions in founding New Minster demonstrate the powers kings could exercise on behalf of the churches they favoured. New Minster not only cut across Old Minster's near monopoly of royal and other burials within Winchester, but some of the estates with which it was endowed were ones to which Old Minster had a claim.[58] The church of New Minster has not been fully excavated, but enough has been uncovered to show that it had a large aisled nave and transepts.[59] It was built immediately adjacent to Old Minster and would have dwarfed the seventh-century building which was only provided with

56. D. Rollason, 'The shrines of saints in later Anglo-Saxon England: distribution and significance', in *The Anglo-Saxon Church*, ed. L. Butler and R. Morris (1986), 32–43, at 36–8.
57. W. de Gray Birch (ed.), *Liber Vitae: Register and Martyrology of New Minster and Hyde Abbey, Winchester* (1892), 5–6.
58. S 1443/B 605; S 359/B 594 (see also S 354/B 565); H.P.R. Finberg, 'The churls of Hurstbourne', in *Lucerna: Studies of Some Problems in the Early History of England* (1964), 131–43, at 133–6.
59. M. Biddle, *'Felix Urbs Winthonia*: Winchester in the age of monastic reform', in *Tenth-Century Studies*, ed. D. Parsons (1975), 123–40, at 128–31.

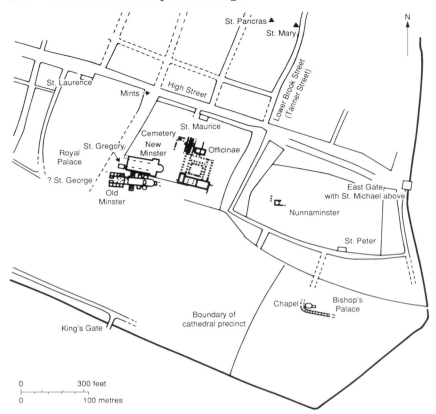

52. Late Saxon churches and other ecclesiastical foundations in the eastern sector of Winchester [after B. Kjølbye-Biddle, 'Old Minster, St Swithun's Day 1093', in *Winchester Cathedral Nine Hundred Years*, ed. J. Crook (1993), 13–20]

a new western façade at this time. King Eadwig was also buried at New Minster, but his uncle Eadred returned to using Old Minster as a place of royal burial and it was subsequently to be the choice of Cnut.[60]

Athelstan's foundation at Milton Abbas (Dorset), which is said to have been made in thanksgiving for the victory at *Brunanburh* and for the soul of his half-brother Edwin (whom Athelstan may have had murdered) may also have been a new creation.[61] However, most of the male religious houses favoured by the tenth-century kings, principally Malmesbury, Glastonbury, Muchelney, Bath and Abingdon, were pre-existing minsters which had been founded originally as monasteries. Like the new foundations of New Minster,

---

60. Birch, *Liber Vitae de Hyde*, 7; *Chronicle* D s.a. 955; *Chronicle* C and D s.a. 1035.
61. *GP*, 186.

Winchester and Milton Abbas, these minsters were staffed, as far as we can tell, by secular clergy (canons). The earliest *Lives* of Dunstan and Æthelwold make it clear that Glastonbury in Dunstan's youth and Abingdon before the arrival of Æthelwold contained *clerici*.[62] The community at Bath was reinforced by clerks from St Bertin, who were allowed to settle there by King Edmund when they fled to England rather than accept the Benedictine Rule which was being imposed on their community.[63] We know very little about the way of life in the major minsters at this time, and it is not clear, for instance, whether any of them followed the *Rule of Chrodegang* which was prescribed in Carolingian legislation for communities of secular clergy. A description of Abingdon before the abbacy of Æthelwold suggests that it contained separate houses and chapels for twelve priests.[64] The clergy probably drew individual incomes from the communal endowments and would be likely to come from well-born families, like those of Dunstan and Æthelwold, both of whom served among the young nobles in the royal entourage before beginning their ecclesiastical careers.[65] Some of the clergy would have been married, earning them the epithet of 'lascivious clerks' from those who believed celibate monasticism to be the better way of life for men of the cloth.[66] The reputation of the secular clergy was ruthlessly blackened in documents emanating from the reformed monastic communities, especially those associated with Æthelwold. However, we must remember here that, apart from the prejudices of their monastic training, it was in the interests of the monastic reformers to stress the corruptness of those they hoped to dispossess.

No doubt there were abuses amongst the secular minsters, but they should not be exaggerated. Kings felt they were appropriate places for royal ceremonial and for the commemoration of themselves and their families after death, and endowed them with lands and other gifts. Many of them were closely associated with adjacent or nearby royal palaces. The great embassy sent from Duke Hugh of the Franks was received at Abingdon in 926,[67] while Malmesbury

62. Stubbs, *Memorials of St Dunstan*, 7–12; M. Lapidge (ed.), *Wulfstan of Winchester. Life of St Æthelwold* (1991), 30–3.
63. J. Armitage Robinson, *The Times of St Dunstan* (1923), 62.
64. Stevenson, *Chronicon Monasterii de Abingdon*, II, 272–3; Thacker, 'Æthelwold and Abingdon', 47–8.
65. B.A.E. Yorke, 'Æthelwold and the politics of the tenth century', in *Bishop Æthelwold, His Career and Influence*, ed. B.A.E. Yorke (1988), 65–88, at 66–9, though see also Brooks, 'Career of St Dunstan', for a different view of Dunstan's origins.
66. Lapidge, *Wulfstan, Æthelwold*, 30–3; also the tract 'King Edgar's establishment of monasteries', now generally thought to have been writen by Æthelwold; D. Whitelock, M. Brett and C.N.L. Brooke (eds), *Councils and Synods and other Documents relating to the English Church, I, 871–1204*, Part I, 871–1066 (1981), 142–54; *EHD*, I, 920–3.
67. W. Stubbs (ed.), *Willelmi Malmesbiriensis Monachi De Gestis Regum Anglorum* (2 vols, 1887–9), I, 150–1.

was the choice of Athelstan as the burial place both for himself and for two cousins who died during his reign at the battle of *Brunanburh*.[68] John the Old Saxon may have retired to Malmesbury after his unsuccessful period at Athelney and has been proposed as the author of a Latin poem addressed to and praising Athelstan.[69] It would appear that minsters of secular clergy could be centres of learning and the ecclesiastical arts in the first half of the tenth century. The upsurge in the copying of texts and tentative experiments in ecclesiastical art which took place in the aftermath of Alfred's attempts to raise Christian awareness must have taken place in minster communities, including those in Winchester and Glastonbury, even if the place of origin of many manuscripts is uncertain or disputed.[70] Dunstan, a skilful poet in later life, seems to have received a thorough grounding in Latin in his youth in the minster of Glastonbury,[71] whose notable library was referred to by Æthelwold's biographer Wulfstan.[72]

Kings promoted a monastic way of life for their daughters and aristocratic women who went into the Church. Only two nunneries are known to have survived from the time of the double monasteries: Wimborne, which had been founded by St Cuthburh whose brother Ingeld was a direct ancestor of the family of Egbert,[73] and Wareham, which in the late tenth century had an abbess who may have been related to the family of Ealdorman Æthelweard (the chronicler) which claimed descent from Alfred's brother Æthelred.[74] The new foundations of Alfred and his descendants seem on the whole to have been more significant. In addition to Shaftesbury, Nunnaminster (Winchester) was founded by Alfred's widow Ealhswith (fig. 52), and Romsey and Wilton for daughters of King Edward the Elder (fig. 53).[75] The new nunneries are often seen as quite distinct from the earlier double monasteries, but they were still likely to have parochial duties attached to them and priests in close association.[76] We know little of the realities of life in the

68. Stubbs, *Willelmi Malmesbiriensis*, I, 151 and 157.
69. M. Lapidge, 'Some Latin poems as evidence for the reign of Athelstan', *ASE, 9* (1981), 61–98, at 72–83.
70. M.B. Parkes, 'The palaeography of the Parker manuscript of the Chronicle, Laws and Sedulius and historiography at Winchester in the late ninth and tenth centuries', *ASE, 5* (1976), 149–71; J. Higgitt, 'Glastonbury, Dunstan, monasticism and manuscripts', *Art History, 2* (1979), 275–90; R. Gameson, 'The decoration of the Tanner Bede', *ASE, 21* (1992), 115–59.
71. M. Lapidge, 'St Dunstan's Latin poetry', *Anglia, 98* (1980), 101–6.
72. Wulfstan, *Æthelwold*, ed. Lapidge, 14–17.
73. *Chronicle s.a.* 718, 900 and 962.
74. *Chronicle C s.a.* 982; L. Whitbread, 'Æthelweard and the Anglo-Saxon Chronicle', *EHR, 74* (1959), 577–89, at 583.
75. M.A. Meyer, 'Patronage of the West Saxon royal nunneries in late Anglo-Saxon England', *Revue Bénédictine, 91* (1981), 332–58.
76. B.A.E. Yorke, '"Sisters under the skin?" Anglo-Saxon nuns and nunneries in southern England', in *Medieval Women in Southern England, Reading Medieval Studies, 15* (1989), 95–117.

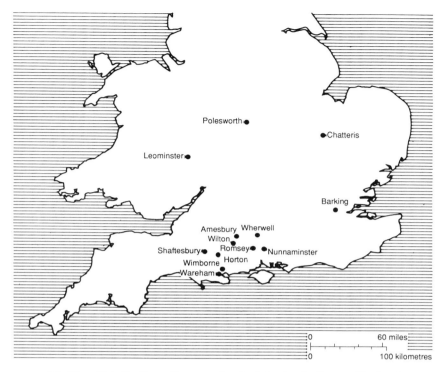

53. The distribution of nunneries in late Anglo-Saxon England

nunneries. The biographers of St Eadburga of Nunnaminster (daughter of Edward the Elder) represent the nuns conforming to aspects of the Benedictine Rule, but, although probably drawing on pre-Conquest sources, the earliest *Life* dates only from the twelfth century and may project a later perspective on to monastic life in the early tenth century.[77] Different degrees of strictness might apparently be followed by female religious; William of Malmesbury drew a contrast between two daughters of Edward the Elder who 'vowing celibacy to God renounced the pleasure of earthly nuptials: Æthelflæda in a religious and Æthelhilda in a lay habit'.[78] Vowesses might take a vow of celibacy, but could continue to own and live on their own property like the wealthy widow Wynflæd, mother-in-law of King Edmund, who was described as *religiosa femina* and associated with the nunnery of Shaftesbury.[79] However, some female religious did not live in nunneries, but were associated with male religious communities. One example is Æthelflæda, a

77. S. Ridyard, *The Royal Saints of Anglo-Saxon England* (1988), 96–139, 253–308.
78. Stubbs, *Willelmi Malmesbiriensis*, I, 137.
79. S 485/B 775; S 1539. D. Whitelock (ed.), *Anglo-Saxon Wills* (1930), 10–15.

kinswoman of King Athelstan, who had taken a religious vow and lived in her own house in Glastonbury where other relatives were members of the minster community.[80]

The choice of monastic life for princesses and a series of grants from kings to 'religious women' testify to the popularity of nunneries in Wessex in the first half of the tenth century. Sometimes motives for support may have been less than pure; the entry of Edward the Elder's wife Ælfflæd into the nunnery of Wilton enabled the king to remarry, and the same nunnery later provided an appropriate residence for a discarded mistress of King Edgar and her daughter.[81] Kings also were probably not unaware that people's perceptions of kingship could be heightened by the existence of saints from the royal house of Wessex who, at this point, were exclusively princesses or queens who had entered the Church. The cults of Eadburga of Nunnaminster, daughter of Edward the Elder (d. 924) and Ælfgifu of Shaftesbury, first wife of King Edmund (d. 944) were added to that of the only certain royal West Saxon saint from the pre-Alfredian period, St Cuthburh of Wimborne.[82] In the first half of the tenth century nunneries may have been the most monasticized communities in Wessex and, with a wealth of patronage concentrated upon them, are likely to have been important centres for cultural revival. The proposal that a number of manuscripts, which may have a Winchester association, were produced at Nunnaminster has not commanded general support,[83] but a set of embroideries probably commissioned by Queen Ælfflæd for Bishop Frithestan, but later presented to the shrine of St Cuthbert, are likely to have been produced in one of the West Saxon nunneries,[84] and their plant and figural decoration have parallels in contemporary manuscript art.[85]

Other princesses married foreign rulers which resulted in exchanges of gifts and embassies that brought foreign art works to England and English churchmen into contact with their European counterparts. Particularly significant were the marriages of daughters of Edward the Elder to Charles the Simple, Duke Hugh of the Franks and Emperor Otto I.[86] Religious books were

---

80. Stubbs, *Memorials of St Dunstan*, 17–18; D.N. Dumville, *Wessex and England from Alfred to Edgar* (1992), 177–8.

81. P. Stafford, *Queens, Concubines and Dowagers. The King's Wife in the Early Middle Ages* (1983), 175–90; Ridyard, *Royal Saints*, 140–8.

82. See D. Rollason, 'Lists of saints' resting-places in Anglo-Saxon England', *ASE, 7* (1978), 61–93, and for some other possible candidates, Meyer, 'Patronage of West Saxon royal nunneries', 333, n. 3.

83. Parkes, 'Palaeography of the Parker manuscript', 149–71; for criticism see D.N. Dumville, 'English square minuscule script: the background and earliest phases', *ASE*, 16 (1987), 147–79, and Gameson, 'Tanner Bede', 140–8.

84. E. Plenderleith, C. Hohler and R. Freyhan, 'The stole and maniples', in *The Relics of Saint Cuthbert: Studies by Various Authors*, ed. C.F. Battiscombe (1956), 375–432.

85. Wormald, 'The "Winchester School"', 305–13.

86. F.M. Stenton, *Anglo-Saxon England* (3rd edn., 1971), 344–6.

among the gifts which might be presented and then deposited in
English religious houses; that may be the route through which Old
Minster, Winchester, acquired the so-called Athelstan Psalter (BL
Cotton Galba A xviii) which was made in the Liège area, and
Glastonbury the gospel book known as the *Textus Sancti
Dunstani*.[87] Relics might also be presented and their cult seems
to have become increasingly important in later Anglo-Saxon
Wessex. Kings, especially Athelstan, were enthusiastic collectors,
but they also passed on relics to favoured ecclesiastical communities. Malmesbury received fragments of the Cross and the
crown of thorns and Abingdon a nail used at the Crucifixion and a
finger of St Denis from the gifts presented by the embassy of Duke
Hugh to Athelstan in 926.[88] Such gifts were probably responsible
for a number of the cults of continental saints recorded in the 'list of
saints' resting-places', such as that of the martyr Justus recorded at
Old Minster; King Athelstan is said to have given the martyr's head
to the foundation.[89]

Tenth-century West Saxon kings continued to appoint some
foreign churchmen to positions within Wessex. The German
presbyter Godescalc was appointed to Abingdon by Athelstan and
there also seem to have been Germans in the household of the
bishop of Winchester.[90] Churchmen in exile, like the clerks from St
Bertin, might be given sanctuary by the West Saxon kings. David
Dumville has drawn attention to the importance of Breton exiles,
fleeing from Viking occupation in Brittany, in bringing essential
texts from the Carolingian reform movement.[91] They were probably
also responsible for the spread of the cults of Breton saints
particularly notable in western Wessex which, of course, had long-
established links with Brittany.[92] Athelstan's new foundation at
Milton Abbas was dedicated to the Breton saints Samson and
Branawaldr and claimed to have their relics; both Athelstan and his
father Edward were in confraternity with the monastery of St
Samson at Dol in Brittany.[93] The demand for Breton saints
apparently continued through the tenth century as Ordulf acquired
the body of the Breton saint Rumon for his foundation at Tavistock
in the reign of Æthelred.[94]

---

87. Robinson, *Times of St Dunstan*, 51–71; M. Wood, 'The making of King
    Athelstan's empire', in *Ideal and Reality in Frankish and Anglo-Saxon Society*,
    ed. P. Wormald *et al.* (1983), 250–72, at 259–65; S. Keynes, 'King Athelstan's
    books', in *Learning and Literature in Anglo-Saxon England*, ed. M. Lapidge and
    H. Gneuss (1985), 143–201.
88. Robinson, *Times of St Dunstan*, 71–80; Wood, 'Athelstan's empire', 266–8.
89. Rollason, 'Lists of Saints' resting-places', and 'Shrines of saints', 36.
90. Dumville, *Wessex and England*, 159–60.
91. Dumville, *Wessex and England*, 156–9.
92. S. Pearce, 'The dating of some Celtic dedications and the hagiographical
    traditions in South Western Britain', *Dev Assoc, 105* (1973), 95–120.
93. Robinson, *Times of St Dunstan*, 73–4.
94. H.P.R. Finberg, *Tavistock Abbey* (1953), 278–83.

The power the kings exercised over the Church enabled Edward the Elder to carry out a major reform of episcopal provision in *c.* 909 when he divided the two large West Saxon sees of Winchester and Sherborne.[95] With the exception of Berkshire which was grouped with Wiltshire, the West Saxon shires were now each provided with their own bishopric with new sees created at Ramsbury for Wiltshire and Berkshire, Wells for Somerset and Crediton for Devon (and Cornwall). Ramsbury and Wells had pre-existing minster churches, and Ramsbury at least seems to have been the site of an important royal vill.[96] The choice of Crediton at first seems surprising when nearby Exeter would appear the more obvious location, for Exeter may have been the site of a British bishopric and had been held by Asser, possibly while acting as suffragan bishop of Devon and Cornwall. It is often stated that Crediton was chosen because it was the place of St Boniface's birth, but the tradition is not recorded before the fourteenth century.[97] However, what may have been more significant is that Bishop Forthhere of Sherborne had apparently been granted 20 hides by King Æthelheard in 739 to build a minster at Crediton, to which further land in the vicinity may later have been added, and it may have been felt that it had a better landed endowment from which to support a bishop's household.[98] The new western bishoprics were at least in part endowed by lands formerly held by Sherborne. In addition to the loss of Crediton, a late medieval list of estates granted to Sherborne includes several in Somerset which subsequently were held by the bishopric of Wells (see fig. 17).[99] One might expect that Winchester would have had to surrender some estates in Wiltshire and Berkshire to the new see of Ramsbury, but, if so, it did not lose all its holdings in these shires and retained (or reacquired) a major estate at Downton (Wilts) which was an episcopal hundred in the late tenth century.[100]

THE MONASTIC REFORM MOVEMENT

In the first half of the tenth century kings do not seem to have had any particular interest in promoting monastic reform; instead the

---

95. S 1296; A.S. Napier and W.H. Stevenson, *The Crawford Collection of Early Charters and Documents* (1895), 18–19; Stenton, *Anglo-Saxon England*, 438–40.

96. J. Haslam, 'A Middle Saxon smelting site at Ramsbury, Wiltshire', *Med Arch*, *24* (1980), 1–68.

97. N. Orme, 'The church in Crediton from Saint Boniface to the Reformation', in *The Greatest Englishman*, ed. T. Reuter (1980), 97–131.

98. S 255/B 1331; O'Donovan, *Charters of Sherborne*, xlvii–viii.

99. J. Armitage Robinson, *The Saxon Bishops of Wells; A Historical Study in the Tenth Century*, British Academy supplemental papers, *4* (1918), 18–24, 52–5; O'Donovan, *Charters of Sherborne*, xlvi–lii.

100. Finberg, *Charters of Wessex*, 235–44.

desire for a more ascetic and regular religious life developed within the Church itself. But, royal support was essential if there were to be more than a few isolated individual monastic enthusiasts. Royal patronage was initially obtained because many of the early supporters were or had been royal chaplains or had other associations with the royal house. By the reign of Athelstan some among the senior clergy of Wessex were beginning to promote monastic ideals. Ælfheah the Bald, bishop of Winchester (934×5–51) and Oda, bishop of Ramsbury (909×927–41) seem to have been particularly significant.[101] Both are described as monks; the circumstances of Ælfheah's profession are not known, but Oda made a profession of obedience to the Benedictine community at Fleury-sur-Loire, which he may have visited when he went as ambassador from Athelstan to Duke Hugh of the Franks in 936.[102] Ælfheah is said to have been a kinsman of Dunstan and to have persuaded the latter to become a monk while a priest in his *familia* at Winchester.[103] Just how Ælfheah, Dunstan and Oda lived a life as monks when their communities were largely composed of secular clergy is not clear, but Dunstan's biographer 'B' describes Ælfheah and Dunstan attending compline at St Gregory's, one of the subsidiary churches attached to New Minster in Winchester, suggesting that some attempt was made to observe the monastic office privately.[104]

Benedictine monasticism was introduced into a non-episcopal minster community when Dunstan was appointed abbot of Glastonbury by King Edmund (940–6). According to Dunstan's biographer 'B', Edmund had been intending to exile Dunstan following intrigue at the royal court, but was persuaded that a narrow escape, when his horse nearly went over Cheddar Gorge, was a warning of divine displeasure with his decision.[105] Following this change of heart Edmund seems to have become a particular patron of Glastonbury and was buried there, as were his son Edgar and great-grandson Edmund Ironside.[106] Royal favour was echoed by that of the high aristocracy; Athelstan 'Half King' is said to have retired there and several members of his family gave generous grants of land.[107] With such support behind him, Dunstan introduced the Benedictine Rule to Glastonbury, and Æthelwold, who had been with Dunstan in Ælfheah's household in Winchester, joined the community and took

101. Robinson, *Times of St Dunstan*, 82–4, 94–6, 127–8; Dumville, *Wessex and England*, 164–5.
102. J. Armitage Robinson, *St Oswald and the Church of Worcester* (1919), 38–51.
103. Stubbs, *Memorials of St Dunstan*, 13–15.
104. Stubbs, *Memorials of St Dunstan*; M. Biddle (ed.), *Winchester in the Early Middle Ages*, Winchester Studies, 1 (1976), 316.
105. Stubbs, *Memorials of St Dunstan*, 23–6; Brooks, 'Career of St Dunstan', 11–14.
106. Stubbs, *Willelmi Malmesbiriensis*, I, 159–60; Stubbs, *Willelmi Malmesbiriensis*, I, 180; *Chronicle* D and E *s.a.* 1016.
107. C. Hart, 'Athelstan "Half King" and his family', *ASE*, 2 (1973), 115–44.

his vows as a monk.[108] Nevertheless, as Nicholas Brooks has stressed in a recent assessment of Dunstan's career, Glastonbury was not a wholly monastic community and contained many clerks (including possibly Dunstan's biographer 'B') as well as some like Æthelwold who were trying to live life according to the Rule.[109] Æthelwold is reported by his biographer Wulfstan as wanting to leave Glastonbury for one of the reformed monastic communities in Europe 'to receive a more perfect grounding in a monk's religious life', but King Eadred (946–55) refused permission.[110] Instead he made Æthelwold abbot of the minster at Abingdon to which he restored lands which had previously been taken into the royal demesne. Eadred and his mother Eadgifu, who seems to have been an influential supporter of monasticism, also gave large amounts of money and other gifts.[111]

Abingdon was the first of the communities to be completely reformed according to the Benedictine Rule. Æthelwold sent Osgar, one of the *clerici* who had come with him from Glastonbury, to Fleury 'to learn there the way of life according to the Rule and show it to his brothers when he taught them back at home'.[112] No more is heard of the unfortunate clerks who had presumably been in residence when Æthelwold acquired the foundation. Eadred's nephew and successor, Eadwig (955–9), granted a wood as building materials for the new church,[113] and also seems to have sent his brother Edgar to be tutored by Æthelwold.[114] After his accession, Edgar (959–75) appointed Æthelwold as bishop of Winchester when the see fell vacant in 963 and thus enabled him to promote monasticism within a broader remit. In the following year Æthelwold with the aid of a king's thegn expelled the clerks from the Old Minster in Winchester while they were hearing mass and replaced them with monks from Abingdon.[115] In the same year the clerks were expelled from the royal minsters of Milton Abbas and New Minster in Winchester. Edgar, like some of his continental counterparts, was providing unequivocal backing for the introduction of Benedictine monasticism, but it was Æthelwold who was setting the agenda.[116]

---

108. *Wulfstan, Æthelwold* (ed. Lapidge), Ch. 9, 14–17.
109. Brooks, 'Career of Dunstan', 11–14.
110. *Wulfstan, Æthelwold* (ed. Lapidge), Ch. 10–11, 16–23.
111. M.A. Meyer, 'Women and the tenth-century English monastic reform', *Revue Bénédictine*, 87 (1977), 34–61, at 37–46; Thacker, 'Æthelwold and Abingdon', 51–2.
112. Lapidge, *Wulfstan, Æthelwold*, Ch. 14, 25–9.
113. S 607/Stevenson, *Chronicon Abingdon*, I, 183–5; see Thacker, 'Æthelwold and Abingdon', 52, for a different perspective on Eadwig's relationship with Abingdon.
114. E. John, *Orbis Britanniae and Other Studies* (1966), 159–60; M. Lapidge, 'Æthelwold as scholar and teacher', in *Bishop Æthelwold: His Career and Influence*. ed. B.A.E. Yorke (1988), 89–117, at 98.
115. Lapidge, *Wulfstan, Æthelwold*, Ch. 16–18, 28–33.
116. *Chronicle A s.a.* 964.

Following a synod held in Winchester some time between 970 and 973, Æthelwold drew up the *Regularis concordia*, an agreed customary for the newly reformed communities in England. The *Regularis concordia* supplemented the Benedictine Rule, and drew on practices at Fleury and Ghent (where Dunstan had spent a brief period in exile following the accession of Eadwig) as well as making allowance for English customs.[117]

It should perhaps be stressed at this point just how extreme Æthelwold's espousal of monasticism was compared to his counterparts in England and Europe. Dunstan as archbishop of Canterbury and Oswald as bishop of Worcester had mixed communities of monks and priests, and in Europe it was generally considered appropriate for episcopal *familia* to be staffed by secular clergy. Patrick Wormald has suggested that Æthelwold's vision of a fully monastic Church was inspired by his reading of the days of Bede when many leading bishops and their foundations were monastic.[118] Edgar too may have been attracted by what King Alfred had described as those 'happy times' when Kings and monks had worked together to the mutual advantage of both.[119] Certainly Æthelwold's vision demanded substantial commitment from the king, for part of his desire to return to earlier times included reconstructing the original landed foundations of his West Saxon communities, even though that might mean reacquiring land which had passed out of ecclesiastical control several generations before. The restoration to Old Minster of its large estate at Taunton (Som) involved dispossessing king's thegns who had held the land as bookland and could produce royal charters to prove it. No doubt some compensation was provided, but the concession that one couple might continue to hold their estate for their lifetime was clearly only granted because of an intervention by Queen Ælfthryth; the couple subsequently complained that undue pressure had been applied to get them to surrender their title-deed.[120] Such repossessions were only possible because the king authorized them, and Edgar and his wife Ælfthryth seem to have been rewarded with substantial gifts of money from Æthelwold for their assistance in the recovery of the Old Minster's lost rights in Taunton.[121]

Æthelwold supported his claims to the lost estates by producing a formidable array of charters; unfortunately many of them seem to have been newly written although purporting to be of greater

117. T. Symons (ed.), *Regularis concordia Angliae nationis monachorum sanctimonialumque* (1953); Lapidge, 'Æthelwold as scholar', 98–100.
118. P. Wormald, 'Æthelwold and his continental counterparts', in *Bishop Æthelwold: His Career and Influence*, ed. B.A.E. Yorke (1988), 13–42.
119. Keynes and Lapidge, *Alfred the Great*, 124–6 (Alfred's preface to *Pastoral Care*).
120. F. Harmer (ed.), *Anglo-Saxon Writs* (1952), no. 108, 396–7; John, *Orbis Britanniae*, 154–80.
121. S 806/Robertson, *Anglo-Saxon Charters*, no. 45, 92–5.

antiquity. To enforce his claims to Taunton Æthelwold was able to produce four charters in the names of earlier rulers whose contents are summed up in Edgar's own confirmation of the estate to the bishopric of Winchester: an estate at Taunton is said to have been first granted to Winchester by Frithugyth, wife of King Æthelheard (726–40), to have been augmented by King Æthelwulf, to have received further exemptions from Edward the Elder and to have been restored by King Eadred 'after forcible seizure by certain other kings'.[122] The claim to the estate is likely to be genuine, and Queen Frithugyth would be an unlikely choice as donor in a completely fictitious case, but many of the charters do not conform to the diplomatic features that one would expect to find in genuine charters of the same date. Similar sets of documents culminating in confirmation by Edgar also exist for Old Minster estates at Downtown (Wilts), Alresford (Hants), Farnham (Surrey) and Chilcombe (Hants), as well as for Æthelwold's foundation of Abingdon.[123]

It would appear that when Æthelwold examined the Winchester and Abingdon archives he found some genuine documents which were allowed to stand, such as the Old English leases dating from the ninth century, but perhaps others which although genuine needed some rewriting because, for instance, the estates recorded in them did not match precisely what was being claimed by the later tenth century. However, Æthelwold is also likely to have found serious gaps in the archives which were remedied by, what seem to us, to be more obviously fraudulent productions. None of the Wessex minsters has a convincing foundation charter and it would appear that the first grants were either conveyed purely symbolically or were perhaps held by some tenure less absolute than bookland. Winchester claimed that its hundred of Chilcombe had been granted originally by King Cynegils, but that the gift had not been put in writing.[124] Historians are divided between seeing this as a genuine tradition, perhaps a granting of the original *territorium* of Roman Winchester to the new church,[125] and those with a suspicion that Cynegils might have granted something less than the full extent of the later hundred whose lands were likely to have been acquired more gradually.[126] Æthelwold's claim that Alfred had

---

122.   S 254/B 158; S 311/B 476; S 373/B 612; S 521/B 831; S 825/B 1149.
123.   E. John, 'The church of Winchester and the tenth-century reformation', *Bulletin of the John Rylands Library, 74* (1964–5), 404–29; Finberg, *Early Charters of Wessex,* 214–48; Thacker, 'Æthelwold and Abingdon', 51–4.
124.   S 325/B 493.
125.   Finberg, *Charters of Wessex,* 215–6; M. Biddle and D. Keene, 'Winchester in the eleventh and twelfth centuries', in *Winchester in the Early Middle Ages,* ed. M. Biddle, Winchester Studies, *1* (1976), 254–8; P. Hase, 'The development of the parish in Hampshire' (Ph. D. thesis, Cambridge University, 1975), 250–65.
126.   Harmer, *Writs,* 373–80; John, 'Church of Winchester', Some of the estates claimed to be part of Chilcombe in S 817 and S 1820 are known to have been acquired by Old Minster at some point after its foundation (e.g. Nursling, Bishop's Waltham).

allowed the Chilcombe estate to be beneficially assessed at one hide because of Viking attacks has also been received with varying degrees of belief.[127] Assessment of the charters is made more difficult by the fact that most of them are only known from their enrolment in post-Conquest cartularies, and some of the charters seem to have been improved further after the Norman Conquest. The twelfth-century *Codex Wintoniensis* seems to have been a careful and faithful transcription of the cathedral's charters as they existed at that time.[128] However, the three cartularies produced at Abingdon in the twelfth and thirteenth centuries are not straight-forward registers, but rather narratives interspersed with charters from the archives.[129] One result was the attempt to turn the charters of the early minster of Bradfield into a history of the foundation of Abingdon itself.[130] The Glastonbury cartularies and histories have comparable problems.[131]

Æthelwold also sought to buttress his foundations through use of saints' cults. According to the 'resting-places of saints' six pre-Æthelwoldian bishops were venerated as saints in Winchester,[132] but the cult which Æthelwold promoted most assiduously was that of Swithun whose body, after visitations from the dead bishop demanding he be appropriately honoured, was first translated in 971. The event and the many miracles attributed to Swithun were recorded by Lantfred, a monk from Fleury recruited to Winchester by Æthelwold, in *Translatio et miracula S. Swithuni* (*c.* 975), which was subsequently rendered in poetic form by Æthelwold's biographer Wulfstan.[133] Swithun's miracles helped make Winchester a major centre of pilgrimage, but were also seen as providing heavenly endorsement of Æthelwold and his actions: 'what Æthelwold preached by the saving encouragement of his words, Swithun won-derfully ornamented by display of miracles', observed Wulfstan.[134] Swithun is perhaps a surprising choice for Æthelwold's patronage for he does not seem to have been a monk, but his cult provided a means of reconciling the former clerks to the new regime. Swithun is reported to have appeared in a dream to a smith who was to report

127. Harmer, *Writs*, no. 107, 373–80, 395–6.
128. A. Rumble, 'The purposes of *Codex Wintoniensis*', *Anglo-Norman Studies, 4* (1981), 153–66.
129. Stenton, *Early History of Abingdon*, 1–6; M. Biddle, M.T. Lambrick and J.N.L. Myres, 'The early history of Abingdon and its abbey', *Med Arch, 12* (1968), 26–69.
130. H. Edwards, *The Charters of the Early West Saxon Kingdom*, BAR, *198* (1988), 167–77; see Ch. 4, 186–7.
131. Edwards, *Charters of West Saxon Kingdom*, 3–6; J. Scott (ed.), *The Early History of Glastonbury: An Edition, Translation and Study of William of Malmesbury's De Antiquitate Glastonie Ecclesie* (1981).
132. Rollason, 'Lists of saints' resting-places'.
133. *Wulfstan, Æthelwold* (ed. Lapidge), xx–xxii, xciv–xcv; the texts will be printed and discussed in Professor Lapidge's forthcoming *Cult of St Swithun*.
134. Lapidge, *Wulfstan, Æthelwold*, Ch. 26, 42–3.

what he said to a former clerk, Eadsige, a kinsman of Æthelwold, who was to pass the message to Æthelwold himself. As a result Eadsige and Æthelwold were reconciled, Eadsige became a monk and was appointed sacrist of Swithun's shrine.[135] Æthelwold himself was recognized as a saint some twelve years after his death in 984, and his cult was zealously promoted by his former pupil Wulfstan, who composed various liturgical works in the saint's honour as well as a *Life of St Æthelwold*, which was subsequently abridged by another pupil, the homilist Ælfric.[136] However, Æthelwold's cult never seems to have become particularly widespread or popular.

Æthelwold's rebuilding of his cathedral church reflects the honour which he wished to pay to the cult of Swithun and his emphasis on links between his monastic foundations and those of the early Christian period in Wessex. Rather than pull down the small seventh-century church, Æthelwold made it the centre-piece of a much grander building which was extended westwards to incorporate a previously free-standing tower of St Martin which had originally been erected in the eighth century (fig. 54).[137] Swithun's tomb had stood between the west end of the original church and the tower and so was now incorporated within the new church. The tomb was surrounded by a flint-walled chamber and remained a focus of cult activity throughout the Middle Ages.[138] A vast structure was built over and around the grave consisting of a central tower flanked by two large apses to north and south. However, not long after its completion a decision was taken to remodel the western part of the church, retaining the central tower but demolishing the apses, and building at the west end a massive westwork which was dedicated in 980. Its ground-plan was revealed by excavation, but information about its appearance also comes from Wulfstan's dedicatory epistle to his *Narratio metrica de S. Swithuno*.[139] The westwork lay adjacent to the royal palace in Winchester and may have held the king's throne like the westwork in Charlemagne's chapel at Aachen.[140] It may have been one of several ways, including through the *Regularis concordia* and manuscript decoration, in which the special religious role and status of the king as Christ's deputy on earth was emphasized.[141]

---

135. D.J. Sheerin, 'The dedication of the Old Minster in Winchester in 980', *Revue Bénédictine, 88* (1978), 261–73.
136. Lapidge, *Wulfstan, Æthelwold*, cxii–cxliii.
137. B. Kjølbye-Biddle, 'Old Minster, St Swithun's Day 1093', in *Winchester Cathedral: Nine Hundred Years*, ed. J. Crook (1993), 13–20.
138. M. Biddle, 'Archaeology, architecture and the cults of saints in Anglo-Saxon England', in *The Anglo-Saxon Church*, ed. L. Butler and R. Morris, CBA report, *60* (1986), 1–31, at 19–25.
139. R.N. Quirk, 'Winchester cathedral in the tenth century', *Arch J, 114* (1957), 26–68.
140. Biddle, *'Felix Urbs Winthonia'*, espec. 138.
141. R. Deshman, *'Christus rex et magi reges*: kingship and Christology in Ottonian and Anglo-Saxon art', *Frühmittelalterliche Studien, 10* (1976), 367–405.

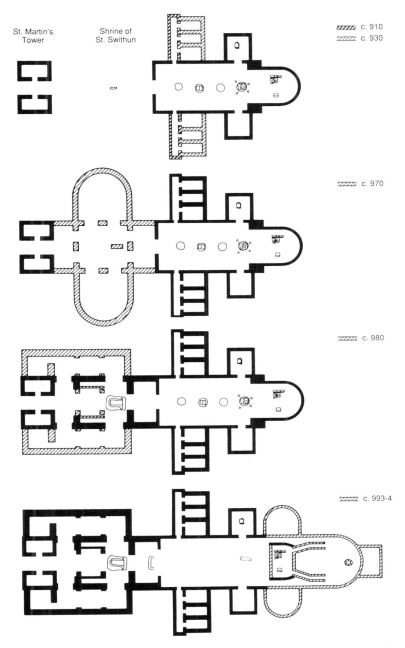

54. The later Saxon phases of Old Minster, Winchester [M. Biddle, 'Archaeology, architecture and the cult of the saints in Anglo-Saxon England', in *The Anglo-Saxon Church*, ed. L. Butler and R. Morris (1986), 1–31]

In such ways did the reformers repay the royal house for the support they gave.

The activities of Æthelwold and the histories of his foundations dominate the written records for the period of monastic reform, and it is particularly unfortunate that Dunstan's biographer 'B' knew little of his subject's activities after he became archbishop of Canterbury in 959.[142] Later *Lives* of Dunstan associated him with reform of other south-western houses, but the basis for these traditions is not known.[143] However, Wulfsige, who was appointed bishop of Sherborne in c. 993, had enjoyed Dunstan's patronage and been appointed by him as abbot of Westminster. He was authorized by King Æthelred to convert Sherborne into a Benedictine monastery and, like Æthelwold at Winchester, divided the foundation's estates to make separate provision for the monks and the bishopric.[144] Like Æthelwold, Wulfsige was promoted as a saint after his death and his body was translated in 1012. The minsters of Bath, Muchelney and Athelney also seem to have been reformed as monastic communities by the end of the tenth century, but little is known of them during this period.[145]

The West Saxon nunneries too were affected by the reform movement. They were included in the provisions of the *Regularis concordia* and placed under the particular protection of Queen Ælfthryth who founded two new nunneries at Wherwell (Hants) and Amesbury (Wilts) (fig. 53).[146] At Ælfthryth's request, Æthelwold produced an Old English translation of the *Rule of St Benedict* for use in female communities.[147] Nunnaminster was included in the reorganization of the estates of the three minsters in Winchester, and as a result was more strictly enclosed than previously; its church was rebuilt and the cult of St Eadburga was promoted.[148] Attempts were also made to safeguard the estates of the nunneries, for, as an addition to Æthelwold's account of the reforms of Edgar's reign acknowledged, they were more likely to be pressurized by kinsmen and 'secular grand persons'.[149] Queen Ælfthryth and Abbess Wulfthryth of Wilton both obtained charters from King Æthelred confirming that land

---

142. Brooks, *Church of Canterbury*, 244–6.
143. D. Knowles, *The Monastic Order in England* (2nd edn., 1963), 49–50.
144. S 895/O'Donovan, *Charters of Sherborne*, no. 11, 39–44; F. Barlow, *The English Church 1000–1066* (2nd edn., 1979), 222–4.
145. S 729 and 884 (Muchelney); for others see n. 143.
146. Symons, *Regularis concordia*, 2; Meyer, 'Women and tenth-century monastic reform', 51–61; D. Hinton, 'Amesbury and the early history of its abbey', in *The Amesbury Millennium Lectures*, ed. J. Chandler (1979), 20–31.
147. M. Gretsch, 'Æthelwold's translation of the *Regula Sancti Benedicti* and its Latin exemplar', *ASE*, 3 (1974), 125–51.
148. Biddle, *'Felix Urbs Winthonia'*, 132–9; Ridyard, *Royal Saints*, 105–14; G. Scobie and K. Qualmann, *Nunnaminster. A Saxon and Medieval Community of Nuns* (1993).
149. *EHD*, I, 922–3.

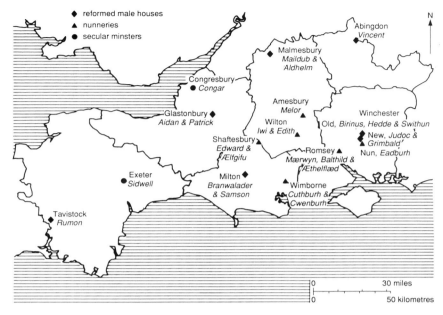

◆ reformed male houses
▲ nunneries
● secular minsters

N

Abingdon
Vincent ◆

Malmesbury
Maildub &
Aldhelm ◆

Congresbury
● *Congar*

Amesbury
Melor ▲

Winchester
Old, *Birinus, Hedde & Swithun*

Glastonbury ◆
Aidan & Patrick

Wilton
Iwi & Edith ▲

New, *Judoc &*
Grimbald ▲
Nun, *Eadburh*

Shaftesbury ▲
Edward &
Ælfgifu

Romsey ▲
Mærwyn, Balthild &
Æthelflæd

Exeter
● *Sidwell*

Milton ◆
Branwalader
& Samson

▲ Wimborne
Cuthburh &
Cwenburh

Tavistock
◆ *Rumon*

0   30 miles
0   50 kilometres

55. The West Saxon entries in the late Saxon lists of saints' resting-
places [after D. Hill, *Atlas of Anglo-Saxon England* (1981), fig. 245]

they wished to give to their foundations was their own and to be
granted in perpetuity.[150]

Because nunneries in the later Anglo-Saxon period seem to have
had limited influence on the general running of the Church, they
have often only appeared as a footnote to the resurgence of
Benedictine monasticism in England. However, in Wessex the
nunneries represent a significant proportion of the monastic
provision, even after its reintroduction to various male minsters. In
the 'list of saints' resting-places', which can be presumed to show
the major cult centres of the late Anglo-Saxon period, there are
fifteen foundations listed for the six West Saxon shires, of which six
are nunneries and seven reformed monasteries (fig. 55).[151] The
nunneries were particularly important for their saints with royal
associations and to the list of royal princess saints can be added
Edith of Wilton, the daughter of King Edgar, whose cult was
assiduously promoted by her half-brother King Æthelred and by
King Cnut, who was so devoted that, as her biographer remarked,
he might almost have been her kinsman.[152] The only male royal

150. S 904 and S 766; see Meyer, 'Women and tenth-century reform', 57–8, and
     Meyer, 'Patronage of West Saxon nunneries, 353–4.
151. Rollason, 'Lists of saints' resting-places'.
152. Ridyard, *Royal Saints*, 140–54, 168, though for a different view on Cnut's
     attitude to Edith see M.K. Lawson, *Cnut: The Danes in England in the Early*
     Eleventh Century (1993), 157–8.

saint produced in the tenth century, the murdered Edward the Martyr, was interred in the nunnery of Shaftesbury. It was a cult which needed particularly sensitive handling if it was to be used to the advantage of the reigning king, Edward's half-brother Æthelred, for there were those who were prepared to interpret it differently.[153] The continuing royal interest in nunneries meant continuing wealth so that great rebuilding projects could take place as at Nunnaminster or Wilton in the time of Edith,[154] but close links with the royal family also made it more difficult for nunneries to establish their independence as ecclesiastical foundations. At the end of the Anglo-Saxon period nunneries were still seen as places intimately associated with the royal house. King Edward the Confessor exiled his wife to Wilton nunnery when he sought to reduce the power of her family in 1051, and one of his sisters was abbess of Wherwell which had been founded by her grandmother Queen Ælfthryth.[155]

What has already been said makes it clear that monasteries continued to receive royal support after the reign of Edgar, and the royal enthusiasm came to be shared by the higher aristocracy though there were interludes when it appeared to waver. Some took advantage of the disturbed political situation on the death of Edgar to try to take back lands and rights which had been given to the reformed communities, but the West Saxon foundations do not seem to have been seriously affected.[156] Another danger point came with the death of Æthelwold in 984 when King Æthelred obtained his majority. Æthelred at first seems to have tried to reverse some of his father's actions in favour of monasteries, perhaps to curry favour with the dissatisfied among the aristocracy or to proclaim his independence. Abingdon, Old Minster and Glastonbury all seem to have had lands confiscated by the king or royal officials. Æthelred is said to have sold the position of abbot of Abingdon to the brother of Ealdorman Ælfric of eastern Wessex, who is himself accused of trying to dispossess Glastonbury of some of its estates.[157] However, after 993 the king had one of the sudden changes of direction for which he is noted. Confiscated estates were restored and a new monastery founded by the king at Cholsey (Berks) for the soul of his murdered half-brother Edward.[158] He credited his change of heart in part to the influence of his kinsmen Ordulf (his maternal uncle)

153. C. Fell, *Edward King and Martyr* (1971); S. Keynes, *The Diplomas of King Æthelred 'The Unready', 978–1016* (1980), 163–76; Ridyard, *Royal Saints*, 154–71.
154. Scobie and Qualmann, *Nunnaminster*; C. Dodwell, *Anglo-Saxon Art: A New Perspective* (1982), 33–5.
155. Yorke, '"Sisters under the skin?"', 109–10.
156. D. Fisher, 'The anti-monastic reaction in the reign of Edward the Martyr', *Cambridge Historical Journal*, 10 (1950–2), 254–70.
157. Keynes, *Diplomas of Æthelred*, 176–86.
158. Keynes, *Diplomas of Æthelred*, 186–93.

and Æthelmær. Both men were themselves patrons of reform and responsible for building monasteries at Tavistock[159] and Cerne Abbas (Dorset) respectively.[160] These places seem to have been former minsters, perhaps originally founded before the Anglo-Saxons conquered the south-west, which seem at some point to have come under the control of the families of Ordulf and Æthelmær. It may be appropriate to see the two foundations as further examples of former ecclesiastical lands being returned to their original use. However, Ordulf and Æthelmær also had some pretensions to learning and a more general interest in theological matters. Ordulf was left a martyrology and a work of Hrabanus in the will of Bishop Ælfwold of Crediton;[161] Æthelmær and his father Æthelweard, the translator of the *Anglo-Saxon Chronicle*, were patrons of Ælfric the homilist, whose translations into English of the Books of Genesis and Joshua were commissioned by Æthelweard.[162] Ælfric was master of the novices at Cerne Abbas and subsequently became abbot of a second foundation made by Æthelmær at Eynsham (Oxon) in 1005, when he seems to have had to retire from his position as ealdorman.[163] New monasteries continued to be founded in the eleventh century including Buckfast (Devon), Horton and Abbotsbury (Dorset).[164]

The wealth of the new foundations was reflected in their buildings and furnishings, and it is unfortunate not more of these have survived. Most of the Anglo-Saxon monasteries remained important ecclesiastical sites and so were rebuilt in subsequent centuries. Their treasures were subject to various depredations or changes of taste in the course of the Middle Ages. For instance, many of Æthelwold's gifts to Abingdon were taken to Normandy after the Norman Conquest, while Edgar's reliquary for St Swithun, constructed from 'three hundred pound of silver, ruby gems and gold, all measured out on a level balance', was probably melted down in the fifteenth century to make a new shrine.[165] Excavations

---

159. H.P.R. Finberg, 'The house of Ordgar and the foundation of Tavistock Abbey', *EHR, 58* (1943), 190–201.
160. G.D. Squibb, 'The foundation of Cerne Abbey', *Notes and Queries for Somerset and Dorset, 31* (1984), 373–6; B.A.E. Yorke, 'Æthelmær: the foundation of the abbey at Cerne and the politics of the tenth century', in *The Cerne Abbey Millennium Lectures*, ed. K. Barker (1988), 15–26 (the paper by George Squibb is reprinted in the same volume, 11–14).
161. *EHD*, I, 580–1.
162. A. Campbell (ed.), *The Chronicle of Æthelweard* (1962), xii–xvi.
163. S 911; H.E. Salter (ed.), *The Cartulary of the Abbey of Eynsham*, vol, 1, Oxford Historical Society, *49* (1907), 19–28; see also Ch. 3, 135.
164. Abbotsbury: S. Keynes, 'The lost cartulary of Abbotsbury', *ASE, 18* (1989), 207–43. Buckfast: H.P.R. Finberg, 'Supplement to the early charters of Devon and Cornwall', in W.G. Hoskins, *The Westward Expansion of Wessex* (1960), 23–33, at 23, 29–30. Horton: O'Donovan, *Charters of Sherborne*, lviii–lxii, 61–80.
165. Stevenson, *Chronicon Abingdon*, I, 343–4; II, 278; Thacker, 'Æthelwold and Abingdon', 57–8; J. Crook, 'King Edgar's reliquary of St Swithun', *ASE, 21* (1992), 177–202.

56. The late Saxon church of Bradford-on-Avon (Wilts) [photograph: author]

have been carried out on a number of sites, but only the church of Old Minster, Winchester, has been more or less completely un-covered under modern conditions (figs. 52 and 54).[166] Excavations have tended to focus on churches rather than monastic buildings, but work at Glastonbury and at Æthelmær's foundation of Eynsham (Oxon)[167] confirm indications in written sources that the formal arrangement of monastic buildings around a cloister was introduced at this time.[168] No monastic buildings still stand, but parts of the walls of the late Saxon churches survive at Wimborne and Sherborne.[169] However, the best surviving monastic church is the church of St Laurence, Bradford-on-Avon (fig. 56), which is thought to have been built after Æthelred gave an estate at Bradford to the

166. However, not yet fully published; M. Biddle and B. Kjølbye-Biddle (forthcoming), *The Anglo-Saxon Minsters of Winchester*, Winchester Studies, *4.1*. Interim reports are in *Antiquaries Journal*, 1962–72, and for the most recent discussions of Old Minster's later Saxon architecture see n. 137 and 138.
167. C.A.R. Radford, 'Glastonbury abbey before 1184: interim report of the excavations 1908–64', in *Medieval Art and Architecture at Wells Cathedral*, British Archaeological Society Conference Transactions, *4* (1981), 110–34; B. Nenk, S. Margeson and M. Hurley, 'Medieval Britain and Ireland in 1990', *Med Arch, 35* (1991), 180–3.
168. M. Spurrell, 'The architectural interest of the *Regularis Concordia*', *ASE, 21* (1993), 161–76.
169. RCHM, 'Wimborne' in *Dorset V: East* (1975), 78–80; J. Gibb, 'The Anglo-Saxon cathedral at Sherborne', *Arch J, 132* (1975), 71–110.

57. Late Saxon rood from the nunnery at Romsey (Hants)
[photograph: P. Stonell]

nuns of Shaftesbury to provide an alternative resting-place for the
bones of Edward the Martyr in case of Viking attack.[170] The church
is small and simple in plan compared to the Old Minster, consisting
originally of a nave, chancel and two porches or side chapels, but is
notable for the fine quality of its stonework and in particular the
blind arcading and decorative pilaster strips and quoins. High up
on the wall at the east end of the nave are two flying angels,
probably all that remains of a Crucifixion scene. A life-size sculpture of the crucified Christ at Romsey was probably from a similar
scene (fig. 57),[171] and recalls the large statue of Christ which hung
on the walls of the refectory at Abingdon and which reputedly came
to life and pelted Viking raiders with stones pulled from the walls
on which it stood.[172]

The monumental sculptures in churches were important prayer
stations for the more elaborate liturgy required in the *Regularis
concordia* which was one of the reasons why monastic churches had

---

170. S 899; H.M. Taylor, 'The Anglo-Saxon church at Bradford-on-Avon', *Arch J*,
    130 (1973), 141–71.
171. E. Coatsworth, 'Late pre-Conquest sculptures with the crucifixion south of the
    Humber', in *Bishop Æthelwold: His Career and Influence*, ed. B.A.E. Yorke
    (1988), 161–93, espec. 167–9.
172. Stevenson, *Chronicon Abingdon*, I, 47–9; Thacker, 'Æthelwold and Abingdon',
    60.

to be enlarged or rebuilt at this time.[173] A large church like Old Minster would have had numerous side altars at which individual monks could say their own devotions and also room for processions by different choirs of monks. In a smaller church like that at Breamore the choir probably stood under the central tower with the high altar in the easternmost *porticus*. Walls would have been decorated with wall-paintings like the sequence that Benna from Trier was employed to provide at Wilton.[174] Only the church of Nether Wallop (Hants) is known to have fragments of Anglo-Saxon wall-painting *in situ*,[175] and to get some idea of the original schemes one has to turn to illuminated manuscripts like the magnificent *Benedictional of St Æthelwold* produced by Godeman of Old Minster for the bishop.[176] Excavations, primarily those at Winchester, have produced evidence of some internal fittings such as window glass, tiles and bells, but in spite of some finds in metalwork and ivory we have nothing to match the written accounts of the ecclesiastical treasures once owned by the foundations.[177] Æthelwold, for instance, gave to Abingdon a golden-plated wheel which supported lamps and numerous little bells, a gold and silver altar table costing £300 decorated with figures of the twelve apostles and three crosses of gold and silver which were each four feet in length.[178]

What have survived in greater profusion are the manuscripts.[179] Some of these like the *Benedictional of St Æthelwold* are major works of art which drew their inspiration from continental works, especially those of the Carolingian Renaissance. They have their own distinctive style with large acanthus-leaved borders enclosing lively figures in 'frenzied' draperies which ultimately derive from late Antique prototypes. The style is often referred to as that of the 'Winchester School' which is misleading, because although Winchester was a leading centre, it was not the only one. The so-called 'Salisbury Psalter', which has unusual zoomorphic initials, may have been produced at Shaftesbury. Glastonbury was another significant centre and may have specialized in the production of line

---

173. H.M. Taylor, 'Tenth-century church building in England and on the Continent', in *Tenth-Century Studies*, ed. D. Parsons (1975), 141–68; R. Gem, 'Anglo-Saxon architecture of the tenth and eleventh centuries', in *The Golden Age of Anglo-Saxon Art*, ed. J. Backhouse, D. Turner and L. Webster (1984), 139–42.
174. Dodwell, *Anglo-Saxon Art*, 33–5.
175. R. Gem and P. Tudor-Craig, 'A "Winchester School" wall-painting at Nether Wallop, Hampshire', *ASE*, 9 (1981), 115–36.
176. G.F. Warner and H.A. Wilson, *The Benedictional of St Æthelwold*, Roxburghe Club (1910).
177. J. Backhouse, D. Turner and L. Webster (eds), *The Golden Age of Anglo-Saxon Art* (1984), *passim*; M. Biddle (ed.), *Object and Economy in Medieval Winchester* (2 vols), Winchester Studies, 7.ii (1990), *passim*.
178. Stevenson, *Chronicon Abingdon*, I, 343–7; Thacker, 'Æthelwold and Abingdon', 57–8.
179. E. Temple, *Anglo-Saxon Manuscripts 900–1066* (1976).

drawings.[180] However, not all the works have elaborate illustrations; some were intended for humbler use during services or periods of study. The reform period not only saw a liturgical revival, but an intellectual revival as well with works in both Latin and Old English being copied and studied. Not that many original works were produced in the West Saxon monasteries, but pride of place must go to Old Minster, Winchester, where Æthelwold, himself an accomplished writer in both Latin and Old English, established a notable school whose star pupils were Wulfstan and Ælfric.[181]

MINSTER AND LOCAL CHURCHES

There were limits to the spread of monasticism in late Anglo-Saxon Wessex. Winchester and Sherborne were reformed as monastic cathedrals, but Ramsbury, Wells and Crediton never were, even though some of those appointed to them as bishops in the late tenth and early eleventh centuries were monks. Wells, for instance, had a series of bishops from 974–1033 who had previously been abbots of reformed Benedictine communities, but there is no evidence of any attempt to introduce monasticism into the cathedral community.[182] The promotion of monks as bishops in non-monasticized sees must often have been less than ideal; Brihtwold, who was a monk of Glastonbury appointed as bishop of Ramsbury (1005–45), seems to have been more interested in his former monastery than in his bishopric and may have plundered episcopal estates to benefit Glastonbury.[183] As in the monasticized cathedrals, it is likely that the bishops' households were distinct from those of the cathedral clergy who would be supported from their own estates; such at least seems to have been the case at Crediton as reflected in the will of Bishop Ælfwold III (997–1012) and by Leofric's decision to leave the clergy there when he moved his episcopal household to Exeter.[184] The cathedral clergy at the three sees were not necessarily unaffected by the changes in the Church in the late tenth century which led to a greater emphasis on the importance of learning and the liturgy. Bishop Ælfwold, for instance, left three service books, a missal, a benedictional, an epistle-book and a set of Mass vestments to Crediton. Nevertheless bishops appointed to these sees in the eleventh century found them unsatisfactory and inadequately supported.

In the reigns of Cnut and Edward the Confessor there was a move away from the appointment of monks as bishops and instead

---

180. Higgitt, 'Glastonbury'.
181. Lapidge, 'Æthelwold as scholar'; Lapidge, *Wulfstan, Æthelwold* lxxxvi–xcviii.
182. Robinson, 'Saxon bishops of Wells'; Barlow, *English Church*, 224.
183. Barlow, *English Church*, 220–1.
184. S 1492; *EHD*, I, 580–1; Orme, 'The church in Crediton', 98–100.

secular priests from the royal household were favoured. Duduc, an Old Saxon (1033–60), and Giso, a Lotharingian (1060–88), were appointed to Wells, Herman, another Lotharingian, was created bishop of Ramsbury (1058–78), and Leofric, who was probably of Anglo-Saxon birth but trained in Lotharingia, became bishop of Crediton (and of St Germans, Cornwall) (1046–72).[185] Their expectations from their continental training would have included a regular and communal life for canons according to the *Rule of Chrodegang*, but the Rule does not seem to have been known at these episcopal minsters. The bishops' reforms included the recovery of estates which had passed out of episcopal control, but even so Herman and Leofric found their endowments inadequate and sought amalgamation with better endowed minsters located in more urbanized centres. Herman tried to move his see to Malmesbury Abbey, but was resisted by the monks. In 1058 he was allowed to combine Ramsbury with Sherborne and then initiated the process by which the sees were eventually to move to Old Sarum.[186] In 1050 Leofric was granted permission by King Edward to move the sees of Devon and Cornwall to the monastery of St Peter's in Exeter.[187] St Peter's was the monastery in which Boniface had been entered in the late seventh century. As a minster it had received patronage from King Athelstan and was reformed as a monastery in the reign of Edgar, but its exact status in 1050 remains unclear.[188] Leofric is reputed to have found Exeter poorly equipped, but Patrick Connor has shown recently that records have been misunderstood and that Leofric's famous library must have benefited from manuscripts acquired or written under his predecessors, including the notable anthology of Old English poetry the 'Exeter Book', for which Leofric himself has often received the credit.[189] Leofric reconstituted Exeter as a cathedral chapter observing the *Rule of Chrodegang*, with a common refectory and dormitory.[190] Giso also seems to have established a regular life for his canons at Wells, and part of their cloister and domestic buildings are thought to have been located in recent excavations. Giso was probably also responsible for extending the cathedral church so that it adjoined the previously free-standing chapel of

---

185. Barlow, *English Church*, 75, 81–4.
186. *GP*, 182–3; Barlow, *English Church*, 220–1.
187. S 1021; P. Chaplais, 'The authenticity of the royal Anglo-Saxon diplomas of Exeter', *Bulletin of the Institute of Historical Research, 39* (1966), 1–34, at 28–31.
188. Robertson, *Anglo-Saxon Charters*, 98–9, 343–4; see also S 954; Barlow, *English Church*, 213–4; C. Henderson and P. Bidwell, 'The Saxon minster at Exeter', in *The Early Church in Western Britain and Ireland*, ed. S. Pearce, BAR, *102* (1982), 145–75; P. Connor, *Anglo-Saxon Exeter: A Tenth-Century Cultural History* (1993), 21–32.
189. Connor, *Anglo-Saxon Exeter*, *passim*; for older views see F. Barlow, K. Dexter, A. Erskine and L. Lloyd, *Leofric of Exeter* (1972).
190. Barlow, *English Church*, 212–4.

St Mary on the site of the early Christian mausoleum (see figs. 38 and 58).[191]

The majority of minsters were not refounded as monasteries in the later Saxon period, but continued to be served by communities of secular priests. These institutions were not neglected in the late Saxon revival of the Church, for one of its aims, as in the Carolingian Renaissance, was a regeneration of the whole Christian people and that could only be achieved through the parochial work of the priests. The renewal of Viking attacks in Æthelred's reign was widely interpreted as divine judgement on a sinful nation and gave further impetus to the campaign for a broader moral and spiritual reform. Such movements were not of course restricted to Wessex, but one of the most important authors of works for the education of priests was Ælfric, monk of Winchester and Cerne and abbot of Eynsham.[192] His books directed at priests were in the vernacular and included two volumes of *Catholic Homilies, Lives of the Saints* and a grammar. He also composed letters of advice to the bishops who were responsible for the training of the parochial clergy and established within them a virtual Rule for priests based on Carolingian precedents. The first of these was written for his own diocesan Wulfsige III of Sherborne, and the second and third sent to the archbishop of Canterbury.[193]

Many of the clergy who provided for the religious needs of local populations were based in the minster churches which could trace their origins back to the period before the ninth century. It is however likely that the system had been modified since its introduction; some minsters had disappeared and the reorganization of local government into hundreds may have been accompanied by some subdivision of minster parishes into subminsters or hundredal minsters.[194] The importance of these often long established ecclesiastical centres in the religious life of localities should not be underestimated nor their ability to continue to attract patronage. Some of the wills of the later West Saxon nobility include grants to local minsters as well as to Benedictine communities. Wynflæd, for instance, left gifts to the minsters of Milborne Port (Som), Yeovil

191. W. Rodwell, 'The Anglo-Saxon and Norman churches at Wells', in *Wells Cathedral. A History*, ed. L.S. Colchester (1982), 1–23, at 6–10.

192. Barlow, *English Church*, 277–88; M. McGatch, *Preaching and Theology in Anglo-Saxon England; Ælfric and Wulfstan* (Toronto, 1977); E. John, 'The world of Abbot Ælfric', in *Ideal and Reality in Frankish and Anglo-Saxon Society*, ed. P. Wormald *et al.* (1983), 300–16.

193. Whitelock *et al.*, *Councils and Synods*, 191–231; J. Hill, 'Monastic reform and the secular church: Ælfric's pastoral letters in context', in *England in the Eleventh Century. Proceedings of the 1990 Harlaxton Symposium*, ed. C. Hicks (1992), 103–17.

194. See Chapter 4, 185; W. Page, 'Some remarks on the churches of the Domesday Survey', *Archaeologia*, 2nd ser., *16* (1915), 61–102; J. Blair, 'Introduction', in *Minsters and Parish Churches. The Local Church in Transition 950–1200*, ed. J. Blair, OUCA, *17* (1988), 1–19, at 7 and 18, n. 40.

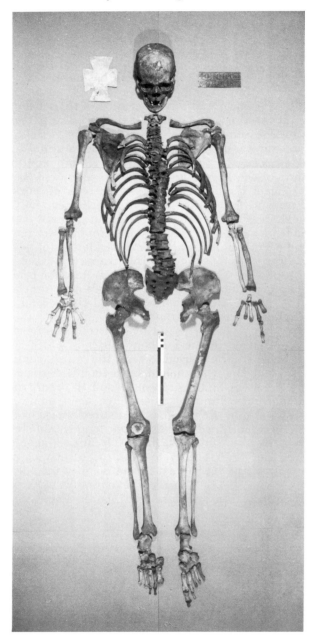

58. Skeleton and mortuary cross of Bishop Giso of
Wells [photograph: W. Rodwell]

(Dorset), Wantage, Coleshill, Shrivenham and Childrey (Berks).[195] Minsters might be endowed with their own estates and be served by a community of priests; Kintbury (Berks) was left an estate at Inkpen by Ealdorman Wulfgar (d. 949) whose father and grandfather were buried there, [196] while Stoke St Nectan (Devon) was served by twelve canons in 1066, each apparently supported by his own endowment.[197] Only two non-monastic minsters appear in the entries for Wessex in the 'list of saints' resting-places', Congresbury where St Congar was buried and St Sidwell's, Exeter (fig. 55).[198] However, later medieval records suggest that there was a widespread survival of saints' cults, in western Wessex at least, which were likely to have had their origins in the early Middle Ages and to have been based in minsters.[199] Many of these cults are difficult to evaluate, such as that of St Hwite or Candida at the minster of Whitchurch Canonicorum where her later medieval shrine still stands within the church. Several examples of the place-name 'Whitchurch', literally 'white church', are known and are thought to derive from the original appearance of a church which was either built of stone or lime-washed.[200] It therefore seems possible that Hwite's name derives from the place-name rather than the other way around, but nevertheless her cult was evidently a potent one in the medieval period and such local cults must have contributed to the income and popularity of many surviving minsters.

The evangelization of the people of Wessex would have been aided in the later Anglo-Saxon period by the building of more local churches, the ancestors of our modern parish churches, within the large minster *parochiae*. The foundation dates of these local churches are hard to establish as they are not recorded in such documents as charters. Frequently Domesday Book contains the earliest indications of a settlement's church, but many churches in existence by 1086 were not included in the survey.[201] Local churches could in theory have been founded at any point after the introduction of Christianity, but there is reason to believe that a considerable proportion of them were founded in the tenth or eleventh centuries.[202] They appear to be part of broader processes

---

195. Whitelock, *Anglo-Saxon Wills*, 10–15, 108–14; Blair, *Minsters and Parish Churches*, 4–6.

196. S 1533/Robertson, *Anglo-Saxon Charters*, 52–3, 307–9.

197. S. Pearce, 'The early church in the landscape: the evidence from north Devon', *Arch J, 142* (1985), 263–9; C. and F. Thorn (ed.), *Domesday Book: Devon* (2 vols. 1985), I, 117a.

198. Rollason, 'Lists of saints' resting-places'.

199. See Chapter 4, 156–7.

200. R. Morris, *Churches in the Landscape* (1989), 158–9; G.V. Syer, *The Church of St Candida (St Wite) and Holy Cross, Whitchurch Canonicorum* (1984).

201. J. Blair, 'Secular minster churches in Domesday Book', in *Domesday Book: A Reassessment*, ed. P.H. Sawyer (1985), 104–42; J. Blair, 'The local church in Domesday Book and before', in *Domesday Studies*, ed. J. Holt (1987), 265–78.

202. Morris, *Churches in the Landscape*, 140–67.

at work in the later Anglo-Saxon period which included the dismemberment of large estates and increasing manorialization.[203] The smaller churches in Domesday Book are recorded among the money-making appurtenances of the estate alongside such items as mills and woodland, and in some cases their priests are listed among the peasantry. The foundation of these churches therefore seems to be part of the increasing power of local lordship in the later Anglo-Saxon period, and the bounds of the parishes served by these churches, which in many cases are identical with modern parish boundaries, preserve those of the estates on which they were founded. It therefore seems appropriate to refer to these churches in their late Anglo-Saxon context as 'estate churches'.

Such churches were found on both lay and ecclesiastical estates by the end of the Anglo-Saxon period. Those on ecclesiastical estates may well be the oldest. There is evidence to suggest that when the bishops of Winchester began to acquire former minster churches and their *parochiae* from the late eighth century they absorbed the minster functions and founded local churches served by individual priests.[204] A lease of land at Easton (Hants) provided by Bishop Ealhferth of Winchester ($862 \times 7 - 871 \times 7$) refers to the priest's dues which were payable by the lessees which presumably implies the existence of a church.[205] The lessees also had to pay eightfold church dues and burial fees to the bishopric, thus firmly underlining that Easton Church was a daughter church of the Old Minster. In Domesday Book a large number of the Winchester episcopal estates had their own churches, many supported by one hide of land. In contrast the bishopric of Wells seems to have preferred not to found local churches on its dependent estates, and the same seems to have been true of most of the monastic estates in Somerset, at least as depicted in the Domesday survey.[206] Nobles were acquiring their own estates from the eighth century, but there was increasing subdivision of estates to provide for them during the tenth century. By the end of the Anglo-Saxon period possession of an estate church was a hallmark of nobility and one of the requirements if an individual was to be raised from ceorl to noble status.[207] That plus profits from church dues help to explain the phenomenon of estate church foundation, but the climate created by the church reformers should perhaps be allowed some credit. Lesser nobles could not afford to build monasteries as Ordulf and Æthelmær had done, but they could endow a small church on their estates.

Bishop Herman of Ramsbury when he visited Pope Leo IX in

---

203. See Chapter 6, 269–74.
204. P. Hase, 'The mother churches of Hampshire', in *Minsters and Parish Churches. The Local Church in Transition*, ed. J. Blair, OUCA, *17* (1988), 45–66, at 48–9.
205. S 1275/Robertson, *Anglo-Saxon Charters*, 26–7, 286–8.
206. Page, 'Churches of the Domesday Survey', 70; Barlow, *English Church*, 202–4.
207. *EHD*, I, 468, n. 7.

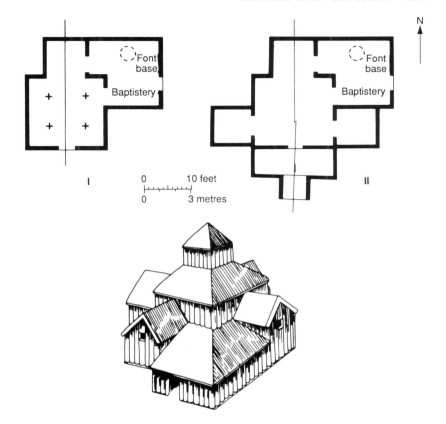

59. Two phases of the late Saxon timber church with baptistery at Potterne (Wilts), with a conjectural reconstruction of phase II [after N. Davies, 'A pre-Conquest church and baptistery at Potterne', and 'Medieval timber buildings at Potterne', in *WAM 59* (1964), 116–23 and *83* (1990), 57–69]

1050 is reputed to have told him of 'England being filled everywhere with churches, which daily were being added anew in new places',[208] and it would appear that the late Anglo-Saxon period was a time of much new church building in Wessex as elsewhere. Many of the churches built at this time would probably have been of timber, like the church which has been excavated at Potterne (Wilts), an estate church of the bishop of Ramsbury.[209] The church, which was probably constructed in the tenth century, consisted of a

---

208. R. Gem, 'The English parish church in the eleventh and early twelfth centuries: a Great Rebuilding?', in *Minsters and Parish Churches. The Local Church in Transition*, ed. J. Blair, OUCA, *17* (1988), 21–30, at 21.
209. N. Davey, 'A pre-Conquest church and baptistery at Potterne', *WAM, 59* (1964), 116–23; N. Davey, 'Medieval timber buildings in Potterne', *WAM, 83* (1990), 57–69.

small square-towered nave with an adjoining chancel and baptistery (fig. 59). The excavation uncovered the indentations of timber pads which would have formed a base on which timber sills could be placed into which the vertical timbers of the walls could be slotted. In appearance the Potterne church may have resembled the stave-built nave of Greensted church in Essex. The small square baptistery contained a recess cut into the floor which was of the right dimensions to take the simple stone tub font in the present parish church at Potterne. A timber stable and a house constructed in a similar way to the church have been excavated nearby and were probably the dwelling place of the priest at Potterne referred to in the Domesday Book survey. In the twelfth century the site of the parish church was moved thus allowing the remains of the timber church to survive below ground; traces of many similar churches must have been obliterated by later rebuilding on the same site.

Some late Saxon estate churches were built in stone and were typically of a simple one or two-cell plan. The excavated chapel of St Columbanus associated with the royal palace at Cheddar (Som) is a good example of the type, although perhaps more elaborately finished than many manorial churches (fig. 66). In the early tenth century it consisted of a single cell built of limestone rubble, but with ashlar door and window-frames; a small rectangular chancel was added in the late tenth or early eleventh century.[210] The nave of a small church of similar proportions has been recently identified in the market area of Malmesbury; like the chapel at Bradford-on-Avon its true nature had been obscured when it was turned into a cottage.[211] However, the dating of many surviving simple stone churches with some Anglo-Saxon features, such as Little Somborne (Hants) or Burcombe (Wilts), is at present controversial, and Richard Gem has challenged the view that many of them were actually built within the Anglo-Saxon period as they often include some Romanesque features as well.[212] He argues for a 'great rebuilding' in stone of churches beginning during the reign of Edward the Confessor, but continuing into the twelfth century.

The provision of local churches was the result of the patronage of the nobility, perhaps following the example of the royal court and reflecting the high profile of ecclesiastical matters in the late Saxon period. But the intention seems to have been that the churches should also be used by local communities and they represent a considerable advance in provision of ecclesiastical structures for humbler people. The circumstances of foundation are reflected in the two commonest topographical locations for estate churches; either standing adjacent to a manor house (see fig. 64), often isolated from other dwellings, or in a central position in a nucleated settlement.[213]

210.   P. Rahtz, *The Saxon and Medieval Palaces at Cheddar*, BAR, 65 (1979), 53–5.
211.   J. Bowen, *Malmesbury Town Trail* (1993); Graham Soffe (RCHM) pers. comm..
212.   Gem, 'Great Rebuilding'.
213.   Morris, *Churches in the Landscape*, 227–74.

However, pre-existing religious foci may also have influenced the siting of churches. Stone crosses may have been a focus for local religious gatherings before the foundation of churches. Willibald's parents dedicated their son to the service of God at the foot of a cross on an estate in the vicinity of Bishop's Waltham (Hants). His biographer Huneburc goes on to explain:

> On the estates of the nobles and good men of the Saxon race it is a custom to have a cross, which is dedicated to our Lord and held in great reverence, erected on some prominent spot for the convenience of those who wish to pray daily before it.[214]

The remains of stone crosses are known from throughout Wessex; many of them are dated to between the late eighth and early tenth centuries and are now located within churches or churchyards. It is difficult to know whether the church was founded where a cross already stood or if, as antiquarian accounts sometimes record, crosses were moved to churchyards from other locations. In other cases churches may have been founded within pre-existing burial grounds, and the sequence of enclosed cemetery which subsequently acquired a church has been proposed for a number of sites in western Wessex including Lustleigh and Lydford (Devon).[215] Few early Christian graveyards have yet been recognized in eastern Wessex, but excavations in eighth-century Hamwic produced evidence of several small graveyards, one of which seems likely to have had a church, and the church of St Mary, Tanner Street, in Winchester was built on top of a small cemetery.[216]

These developments were not restricted to the countryside. Another feature of the later Saxon period in Wessex was the growth of towns and in them we also find a provision of small churches on the various 'estates' into which late Saxon towns were divided.[217] There were fifty-seven parish churches in Winchester by the early thirteenth century, most of which were likely to have been founded by the end of the Anglo-Saxon period; Exeter may have had about twenty-five.[218] Excavations at Lower Brook Street in Winchester uncovered two small churches in close proximity; St Mary's was fitted into a small building plot amidst houses lining the Saxon

---

214. C. Talbot (trans.), *Anglo-Saxon Missionaries in Germany* (1954), 154–5.
215. Pearce, 'Early church in the landscape' and see Ch. 4, 159–60.
216. A. Morton, 'Burial in Middle Saxon Southampton', in *Death in Towns*, ed. S. Bassett (1993), 68–77; M. Biddle, 'Excavations at Winchester: tenth and final interim report, part II', *Ant J, 55* (1975), 295–337, at 303–12, and D. Keene, *Survey of Medieval Winchester*, Winchester Studies, 2 (2 vols, 1985), 761–3.
217. J. Campbell, 'The church in Anglo-Saxon towns', in *The Church in Town and Countryside*, ed. D. Baker, Studies in Church History, *16* (1979), 119–35; Morris, *Churches in the Landscape*, 168–226.
218. Biddle, *Winchester in the Early Middle Ages*, 329–35; J. Allan, C. Henderson and R. Higham, 'Saxon Exeter', in *Anglo-Saxon Towns in Southern England*, ed. J. Haslam (1984), 385–414, at 397–400.

60. The late Saxon church of St Mary's, Tanner Street (Lower Brook Street), Winchester in the course of excavation [photograph: M. Biddle, Winchester Research Unit]

predecessor of Lower Brook Street (Tanner Street) (fig. 60), while St Pancras was only a few yards distant, but away from the main street, behind the yards of the houses and approached by a small path (see fig. 52).[219] Urban churches had their own characteristic locations such as beside gateways (St Martin's, Wareham) or adjacent to a market (Malmesbury). Like their rural counterparts,

219.   Keene, *Survey of Medieval Winchester*, 761–3.

minsters whose sites were developed as burhs and towns frequently experienced subdivision of their original parishes; for instance, when Wareham was enlarged by the building of burghal defences, the nunnery of St Mary's seems to have lost much of its large *parochia* to the new foundations of St Martin's and Holy Trinity.[220] The desire to found new churches inevitably impinged upon the rights of minster churches, and royal legislation in the reigns of Edgar and Æthelred Unræd sought to protect the rights of the minsters.[221] Minsters were to receive all the tithe from estates which had a church, but no graveyard, and where there was a graveyard they still received tithe from the land of the dependent peasants and two-thirds of that from the lord's demesne. The main annual payment for the support of churches, church-scot, was also to go to the minsters and they could claim the burial payment of soul-scot even if the body was buried elsewhere. Many minsters were successful in retaining their rights. Mottisfont minster (Hants) is recorded in Domesday Book as possessing six dependent chapels and the rights to claim all customs from them.[222] When King Edward the Confessor granted the church of Mottisfont to the archbishop of York the rights over its dependent chapels were transferred as well. Possibly the chapels would not have had their own priests but would have been served by priests from the minster. An agreement drawn up just after our period in the 1090s between the Anglo-Saxon lord of Milford (Hants) and the 'elder' of the minster of Christchurch (now Dorset) made just such a provision.[223] One of the minster's priests was to say mass as required in the chapel in return for half a virgate and a guarantee of the minster's parochial rights.

Some minsters had powerful patrons in the eleventh century who protected their rights and endowed their foundations, such as Gytha, the widow of Earl Godwine, who was patroness of St Nectan's Hartland (Devon) and Nether Wallop (Hants).[224] Part of the late Saxon minster church at Nether Wallop with remains of its wall-paintings still stands.[225] But the church at Breamore (Hants), which was probably erected in the early eleventh century, gives the fullest impression of a prosperous late Saxon minster.[226] It has the

220. D. Hinton and C.J. Webster, 'Excavations at the church of St Martin, Wareham, 1985–6, and "minsters" in south-east Dorset', *PDNHAS, 109* (1987), 47–54.
221. Barlow, *English Church*, 183–208.
222. J. Munby (ed.), *Domesday Book: Hampshire* (1982), 42a.
223. Hase, 'Mother churches of Hampshire', 51–7.
224. Pearce, 'Early church in the landscape', 263–9; Barlow, *English Church*, 195; Munby, *Domesday Book: Hants*, 38c.
225. Gem and Tudor-Craig, 'Nether Wallop'.
226. Taylor and Taylor, *Anglo-Saxon Architecture*, 94–6; W. Rodwell and C. Rouse, 'The Anglo-Saxon rood and other features in the south porch of St Mary's church, Breamore, Hants', *Ant J, 64* (1984), part 2, 298–325. For minster status of church see Hase, 'Mother churches of Hampshire', 63, n. 27.

same plan as some of the smaller monastic churches already discussed, with a central tower at the east end of the nave with flanking transeptal chapels and chancel (fig. 61). There are remains of decorative pilaster strips and of round-headed double-splayed windows in the nave. In the south porch is the remains of a carved rood, unfortunately severely mutilated at the Reformation, which probably originally stood in a western porch above the main entrance to the nave. The arch over the entrance to the southern *porticus* from the main body of the church bears an inscription 'HER SÞUTELAÐ SEO GECÞYDRÆDNES ÐE', 'Here is made manifest the covenant to you' (fig. 61). A recent study has proposed that this is an allusion to the covenant established between God and Noah with the arch on which the words are inscribed recalling the rainbow which was to be a sign to mankind and a reminder of God's first judgement of mankind and of the Last Judgement to come.[227] Presumably the allusion was intended to benefit the priests rather than their less literate congregations and the arch from Breamore may be rare evidence for standards of literacy and comprehension among minster clergy which second-generation reformers like Ælfric had strived to achieve.

However, it is also the case that many minsters continued to fall prey to circumstances which had threatened them since the eighth century. Unlike reformed monasteries, minsters seem to have failed to achieve an independent corporate status, even if they possessed their own landed endowments, and they do not appear among the ecclesiastical landholders in the Domesday survey. Put another way, they remained the possessions of their 'lords' who could make appointments as they wished or grant away control of the minster to another foundation. Many bishoprics and monasteries received grants of minster churches in the tenth and eleventh centuries; the nunnery of Amesbury was endowed with the church at Letcombe (Berks), but not with the rest of the estate which remained in royal hands.[228] When bishoprics and monasteries obtained control of minsters they might absorb the 'mother' church functions into their own foundations, particularly if the minsters were in their vicinity. Thus Winchester Cathedral acted as the minster church of all its surrounding estates,[229] but in its major hundred of Taunton (Som) the 'mother' church rights remained vested in its minster church there.[230] Kings had always found the granting of control of minster churches an appropriate way of rewarding churchmen in royal

227. F. and R. Gameson, 'The Anglo-Saxon inscription at St Mary's church, Breamore, Hampshire', *ASSAH, 6* (1993), 1–11, but for reservations about their interpretation see E. Okasha, 'The English language in the eleventh century: the evidence from inscriptions', *England in the Eleventh Century. Proceedings of the 1990 Harlaton Symposium*, ed. C. Hicks (1992), 333–45.
228. P. Morgan (ed.), *Domesday Book: Berkshire* (1979), 57c and d.
229. Hase, 'Mother churches of Hampshire', 48–9.
230. Robertson, *Anglo-Saxon Charters*, appendix 1, n. 4, 236–9.

61. The inscribed archway to the southern *porticus* of Breamore
church (Hants) [photograph: author]

service, as when Alfred had granted Banwell and Congresbury to Asser. But in the reigns of Cnut and Edward the Confessor the instances of granting minsters to royal clerks sharply increased and many alienations became permanent; Edward's chancellor Regenbald built up a formidable endowment of minster churches which included Wellington, Milborne Port and Frome (Som), Avebury and Pewsey (Wilts) and Shrivenham, Cookham and Bray (Berks).[231] Such clerks might squander the resources and neglect church buildings: at Netheravon (Wilts) held by Nigel the Physician in 1086 it was recorded that the church was 'ruinous and the roof so out of repair that it is almost tumbling down', while at Collingbourne Ducis held by Gerald the priest the church was derelict and had been dismantled.[232] Worse was to come for many minster churches after the Norman Conquest when those who became 'lords' of minsters often granted them to monasteries in Normandy and elsewhere abroad, which contributed substantially to the decline of the minster church network.[233]

In the Church, as in many areas of English life, features which are often seen as characteristic of the Norman period had their origins before the Norman Conquest. The Normans were scathing about many facets of Anglo-Saxon church provision and there are some aspects, such as the pluralism of Stigand who was both archbishop of Canterbury and bishop of Winchester in 1066, which cannot be defended. Other matters on which the Anglo-Saxon Church was attacked, such as the existence of married or cohabiting clergy, were characteristic of the early medieval Church as a whole. But there is no sign that the Church in Wessex was moribund in 1066. Although the peak period of monastic foundation or refoundation had passed, the great centres of manuscript art such as Winchester continued to practise and to develop their distinctive styles.[234] In the reign of Edward the Confessor the secular Church was actively extending itself and several of the bishops he appointed had begun a critical reassessment of existing episcopal provision. Laymen were continuing to found local churches on their estates and a fashion for rebuilding these in stone may have begun during Edward's reign. Although evidence of popular piety is rare, to say the least, one sign that tenth-century church reform had had an effect further down the social scale are the guild statutes from Exeter, Bedwyn and Abbotsbury with their concern for provision of communal church services, funerals and masses for dead brothers.[235] Throughout its

231. Barlow, *English Church*, 134–5; S. Keynes, 'Regenbald the Chancellor [sic]', *Anglo-Norman Studies, 10* (1987), 185–222, at 196.
232. C. and F. Thorn (ed.), *Domesday Book: Wiltshire* (1979), 65b and c.
233. Page, 'Churches of the Domesday Survey'.
234. R. Gameson, 'English manuscript art in the mid-eleventh century: the decorative tradition', *Ant J, 71* (1991), 64–122.
235. G. Rosser, 'The cure of souls in English towns before 1000', in *Pastoral Care Before the Parish*, ed. J. Blair and R. Sharpe (1992), 267–84; *EHD*, I, 605–7.

history the West Saxon Church had followed cycles of renewal and decay and had been stimulated by developments and ideas from abroad, though often these were adapted by local custom and taste. There is no reason to doubt that such cycles would have continued whether or not the Norman Conquest had occurred.

6 Social Structure and Rural Life

The written sources for Anglo-Saxon Wessex are dominated by the king and the Church; references to other members of the population tend to be haphazard and there is the problem of knowing whether what is being briefly illuminated is typical or atypical. However, Domesday Book does provide a survey of some facets of the different classes of society and their relationship to one another at the end of the Anglo-Saxon period. By relating other sources for society, such as references in charters or the no doubt idealized depictions in the lawcodes, to the Domesday survey we may be able to get some idea of changes and continuities within the Anglo-Saxon era.

DOMESDAY BOOK AND THE STUDY OF ANGLO-SAXON WESSEX

The Domesday Book survey was commissioned by King William I at his Christmas court at Gloucester in 1085 and, it is generally believed, was speedily carried out in the course of the following year.[1] The range of functions which Domesday Book may have been designed to serve need not concern us here, but amongst them was a desire to know how various matters stood in 1086 compared to during the reign of Edward the Confessor. The whole scope of the survey is conveniently summarized in a record of the questions which the king's commissioners put to the local communities and authorities which has survived among the records of Ely Abbey. They had to enquire in respect of each manor (1) what is its name? (2) who held it in the time of King Edward? (3) who holds it now? (4) how many hides does it contain? (5) how many ploughs are there in demesne? (6) how many ploughs among the villeins? (7) how many villeins, cottagers, slaves and freemen are there? (8) how much woodland? (9) how much meadowland? (10) how many mills? (11) how much has been added or taken away? (12) how much was

---

1. *ASC* E *s.a.* 1085; for studies too numerous to mention see D. Bates, *Bibliography of Domesday Book* (1986).

the whole manor worth and how much now? (13) how much did each freeman have, and how much now? (14) could more be had from it than is now obtained?[2] From the list we can see how the survey could be of value to those wishing to study late Anglo-Saxon England as well as to scholars of the Norman period. Indeed, the implication is that the Domesday Book manors are institutions which had also existed during the reign of Edward the Confessor and the commissioners are specifically instructed to note changes which had occurred in their ownership, composition and profitability since that time.

To ease the composition of the survey the country was divided into circuits for each of which a small group of commissioners gathered and co-ordinated the required information.[3] Hampshire and Berkshire were in what is generally known as Circuit 1, together with Kent, Sussex and Surrey; Wiltshire, Dorset, Somerset and Devon plus Cornwall constituted Circuit 2. The commissioners seem to have received their information from two main sources which could be cross-checked against one another. Firstly, there were returns made by royal officials and tenants-in-chief concerning the manors under their control; a survey of seven manors belonging to the abbey of St Peter's, Bath, which was probably submitted at this stage, has survived separately.[4] Secondly, there were submissions from juries of local men to whom the questions listed in the Ely memoranda were put, and sometimes it is noted in Domesday Book where their testimony differed from that of a manor's owner. An entry for Charford (Hants) contains a rare example of the testimony of the senior men of the hundred being challenged by the men of a township:

> William of Chernet claims this land stating that it belongs to Charford manor, Hugh of Port's holding, through the inheritance of his predecessor. He adduced his testimony for this from the better and the old men of the whole county and hundred. Picot brought his opposing testimony from the villeins, the common folk (*vili plebe*) and the reeves who wish to defend by oath or by a judgement day that the landholder was a free man and could go with his land whither he would. But William's witnesses refuse to accept any law but King Edward's until it is defined by the King.[5]

The gathering of material was made possible because it drew upon existing Anglo-Saxon practices and traditions of record-

---

2. Adapted from citation in F. Barlow, 'Domesday Book: an introduction', in *Domesday Essays*, ed. C. Holdsworth (1986), 16–28, at 19.
3. V.H. Galbraith, *The Making of Domesday Book* (1961).
4. H.B. Clarke, 'The Domesday Satellites', in *Domesday Book: A Reassessment*, ed. P. Sawyer (1985), 50–70.
5. *DB: Hants*, 23.3; fo. 44d.

keeping by royal officials and estate holders.[6] The submission of evidence from local jurors was a regular part of the Anglo-Saxon judicial system in which the senior men of a district might be called upon to ratify local transactions or testify to local customs through the medium of the hundred court.[7] Lists of estates arranged under the hundreds in which they lay, drawn up in the reign of Edward the Confessor, survive from the abbeys of Abingdon and Bath, while from outside our region there is evidence for pre-Conquest taxation (geld) lists which were probably utilized by the local shire reeves.[8] Winchester was not included in the Domesday Book entries (though a blank space was left for it) perhaps because it already possessed a survey of property owners and their tenants drawn up in *c.* 1057, though it only survives in part through incorporation in the so-called 'Winton Domesday' made in the reign of Henry I.[9]

The returns were probably first co-ordinated at county level before the production of regional returns for each circuit. The provincial draft for Circuit 2 has survived in part and is known as the *Exon* or Exeter Domesday.[10] Unfortunately, by the time the various booklets of which it was composed came to be bound together in the fourteenth century, entries for almost the whole of Wiltshire, a large part of Dorset and some of Devon had been lost. *Exon* shows every sign of having been a rough draft rather hastily put together and presumably a fairer copy was sent to the appointed centre, probably either Winchester or Salisbury, for incorporation, with the other provincial surveys, into the document known as Great Domesday. We can see by comparing entries in *Exon* and Great Domesday that some further rearrangement and compression of material was made in the final stages. A major difference between *Exon* and Great Domesday is that the former includes totals of animals for each manor.

The Domesday survey therefore has great potential for revealing the structure of society at the end of the Anglo-Saxon period and for allowing comparisons to be drawn between different areas of our region. But there are also many problems involved in utilizing its evidence. The commissioners for the different circuits did not necessarily present their material in the same way, and sometimes there were variations between the shires of different circuits. For instance, in Circuit 1 the amount of woodland possessed by each manor is expressed in terms of annual renders for the right of

---

6. S. Harvey, 'Domesday Book and its predecessors', *EHR, 86* (1971), 753–73.
7. See Chapter 3, 124–9.
8. Clarke, 'Domesday Satellites'.
9. F. Barlow (ed.), 'The Winton Domesday', in *Winchester in the Early Middle Ages*, ed. M. Biddle, Winchester Studies, *1* (1976), 1–142, especially 9–10.
10. Galbraith, *The Making of Domesday Book*; R. Welldon Finn, *Domesday Studies: The Liber Exoniensis* (1964); A. Rumble, 'The palaeography of the Domesday manuscripts', in *Domesday Book: A Reassessment*, ed. P. Sawyer (1985), 28–49; Barlow, 'Domesday Book: an introduction'.

pannage, that is how many pigs would be due to the manorial owner from pannage renders. In Circuit 2, however, woodland is usually measured in terms of its length and breadth, though in Devon (and in some entries for other shires in Circuit 2) measurement is more frequently given in acres. Such variations, of course, make it difficult to compare the distribution and utilization of woodland across the region, let alone convert it into modern measurements. Omissions in the data gathered must also be allowed for; there are no entries of woodland for eight hundreds in north-western Berkshire although charters, not to mention modern observation of the landscape, indicate that there were major tracts of woodland in the area.[11] Examples of this type could be multiplied and will feature in subsequent discussions. There are also significant problems in identifying place-names and personal names which have been distorted through having been written down by Norman scribes unused to Old English pronunciation.[12]

LORDSHIP, NOBILITY AND THE OWNERSHIP OF LAND

One thing which emerges very clearly from the pages of Domesday Book is the importance of land tenure in eleventh-century society, and the entries indicate that this was not a new concern imported from Normandy, but something which was inherent in late West Saxon society as well. The entries for each shire are first subdivided under the holdings of each landowner in 1086, beginning with royal lands and proceeding through those who held land of the crown, that is ecclesiastical tenants-in-chief, secular tenants-in-chief and minor secular tenants. The estates of each landowner are listed under the hundreds in which they were situated. As in most cases the pre-Conquest holder of the land is given, we can reconstruct part of the land-owning pattern during the reign of Edward the Confessor and by relating it to the charter evidence trace something of the evolution of estate holding during the pre-Conquest period.

The royal estates in Wessex included several large manors which had no assessment in hides, indicating that they did not pay geld, and instead contributed to the 'farm of one night'. This payment is presumed to be a relic of the system by which West Saxon kings were originally supported by renders in kind from their subjects,[13] the kingdom being organized into large 'multiple estates' for this purpose. By the eleventh century the payments in kind had been commuted for money; in Hampshire the normal payment by 1066

---

11. H.C. Darby, *Domesday England* (1977), 172–94, and Darby, 'Domesday Book and the geographer', in *Domesday Studies*, ed. J.C. Holt (1987), 101–19.
12. J. McN. Dodgson, 'Domesday Book: place-names and personal names', in *Domesday Studies*, ed. J.C. Holt (1987), 121–38.
13. See Chapter 2, 72–9.

seems to have been £76 16s 8d, but in Somerset and Wiltshire it may have been £104 12s 2d, which was the amount collected in 1086.[14] The system is also likely to have been modified in other respects since the days of the early West Saxon kings and reorganization can in particular be detected where large estates had been split up into smaller units. Thus when the large Worthy estate near Winchester was split into four, the parts which were retained in royal hands, King's Worthy and Headbourne Worthy, were combined with the nearest royal holding at Barton Stacey to make up half a day's revenue.[15] King Edward and King William also held estates gelded in the normal way, and King William had evidently taken advantage of the circumstances of conquest to claim back various estates for the crown; a subsection of the royal entries for Dorset is devoted to lands formerly held by Earl Harold. Anglo-Saxon kings also received back estates as well as granting them out. We can see that this occurred because of charters in which the same estates are recorded as having been granted by different kings to different individuals.[16] The laws indicate that estates might be forfeited to the king for various crimes, including treason and failure to carry out public services,[17] and sometimes such confiscations are referred to in charters; Old Minster, for instance, was able to (temporarily) reclaim an estate at Alresford (Hants) in the reign of Edward the Elder because the nobleman Alfred, who had acquired it, had forfeited it to the crown for a sexual crime.[18]

The major churches between them held a considerable amount of land including individual estates of 100 hides or more. It would appear that kings initially handed over for support of the Church some of the large estates from which they had drawn the 'farm of one night'. Cædwalla is said to have given a quarter of the Isle of Wight, some 300 hides, to Bishop Wilfrid.[19] Some of the large estates recorded in Domesday Book may represent such early, generous grants, and, as we have seen, that is what was claimed by some religious houses during the tenth century.[20] However, genuine charters recording such large foundation grants do not survive and religious houses evidently had considerable trouble in retaining land that was granted at an early date. Thus the Old Minster's 40-hide estate at Alresford was claimed to be an original grant from

---

14. P. Stafford, '"The farm of one night" and the organization of King Edward's estates in Domesday', *Economic History Review*, 33 (1980), 491–502.
15. *DB: Hants*, I, 17; fo. 38c.
16. See, for instance, the history of the estate at Bedwyn discussed in D.N. Dumville, *Wessex and England from Alfred to Edgar* (1992), 107–12.
17. M.K. Lawson, 'The collection of Danegeld and Heregeld in the reigns of Æthelred II and Cnut', *EHR*, 99 (1984), 721–38.
18. S 375/B 623.
19. *HE*, IV, 16.
20. See Chapter 5, 213–15.

King Cenwalh (642–72), but was in lay hands by the ninth century, if not earlier. It was reclaimed in the reign of Edward the Elder (as mentioned above), but was in lay hands again after his death and not securely part of the Old Minster's land until Æthelwold's episcopate.[21] The early bishops of Wessex who came from Europe, Birinus, Agilbert and Leuthere, would have been used to the concepts of permanent grants of land to the Church made in accordance with late Roman law and recorded by charter,[22] but it seems likely that, as Bede seems to indicate for Northumbria, Anglo-Saxon kings were accustomed to reward their followers with temporary grants of the profits from land which were made only for the lifetime of the individual, or perhaps only lasted as long as the king who made them did.[23] The earliest grants to the Church in Wessex may never have been recorded by charter and may not have been made originally on the same terms.[24]

Permanent grants of land with rights of free alienation were known in Wessex by the third quarter of the seventh century; the earliest surviving West Saxon grant whose validity is not in question is a grant from Cenred (probably King Cenred, father of Ine) of land in Dorset to Bectun, abbot of an unknown monastery, made probably between 670 and 676, though it has only been preserved because it was incorporated in a later transaction.[25] In addition to the foreign ecclesiastics, important influences on the development of the charter in Wessex are likely to have been Aldhelm, who may have introduced forms he encountered while studying at Canterbury, Bishop Earconwald of London and Bishop Wilfrid of Northumbria; both of the latter seem to have been significant figures in the history of the charter who were in the ambit of West Saxon kings in the late seventh century.[26] It is possible that British leaders were granting charters before the Saxon conquest, like their contemporaries in southern Wales, but no Celtic influences have been definitely detected in West Saxon charters.[27] West Saxon laymen eventually wanted the same advantages of holding bookland, that is land whose grant was

---

21. As recounted in S 814/B 1150.
22. E. Levy, *West-Roman Vulgar Law: The Law of Property* (Philadelphia, 1954).
23. Bede, 'Letter to Egbert', in *Baedae Opera Historica*, ed. C. Plummer (2 vols, 1896), I, 405–23; *EHD*, I, 804–6. For discussion see E. John, *Land Tenure in Early England* (1960), 44–6, 73–4; R. Abels, *Lordship and Military Obligation in Anglo-Saxon England* (1988), 28–31.
24. M.A. O'Donovan (ed.), *Charters of Sherborne* (1988), lii.
25. S 1164/B 107; P. Chaplais, 'The origin and authenticity of the royal Anglo-Saxon diploma', *Journal of the Society of Archivists, 3* (1965), 48–61, at 55–6.
26. P. Wormald, *Bede and the Conversion of England: The Charter Evidence*, Jarrow lecture (1984); H. Edwards, 'Two documents from Aldhelm's Malmesbury', *Bulletin of the Institute of Historical Research, 59* (1986), 1–19; P. Sims-Williams, 'St Wilfrid and two charters dated AD 676 and 680', *Journal of Ecclesiastical History, 39* (1988), 163–83.
27. W. Davies, *The Llandaff Charters* (1979).

supported by the issue of a *boc* (charter) and the earliest surviving grant for a West Saxon layman is probably the grant of land at Little Bedwyn (Wilts) made by King Cynewulf to *comes* Bica in 778.[28]

The more widespread granting of land by charters had potentially serious implications for kings as there was a danger that their power would be diminished if too much land was permanently alienated. By granting land by charter the king was allowing the beneficiaries the right to exact services and payments from those who lived on the land which he had enjoyed previously. It was therefore very important from the Crown's point of view that kings established that they retained residual rights in lands that they granted by charter, and that ownership of land carried public obligations which had to be met or the land was forfeited to the king. The ninth century was the crucial period here and the circumstances of the Viking wars helped Alfred and his brothers enforce the three common burdens which had to be borne by all landowners; military service, building of roads and bridges and fortress-work.[29] There is an important shift of emphasis in the ninth century; previously, it would appear from Ine's lawcode among other sources, military service in Wessex had been due from those of free status.[30] But an ambiguity would have come in with the spread of bookland; would freemen living on an estate granted into the hands of others continue to owe services directly to the king or to their new lords? It would appear that, probably during the ninth century, while military service was still expected from the nobility as a matter of course, the extent of a landowner's military obligations depended on the size of the estate. The Domesday Book's entry for Wallingford (Berks) states that when the king raised an army, one man-at-arms (*miles*) was required from every five hides, and it is likely that such requirements were general from West Saxon estates.[31] Domesday Book entries for Glastonbury estates record numerous 'thanes' (*taini*) who were supported by small subtenancies, and these are probably the men retained by the abbey to meet its military obligations to the king. Landowners also had to make 'voluntary' contributions if the king had to make extraordinary payments such as the tributes Alfred and Æthelred made to the Vikings, and in 1012 Æthelred instigated a new tax, the *heregeld*, to pay for the Scandinavian troops he had recruited; failure to meet such demands could also lead to confiscation of land.[32]

---

28. S 264/B 225.
29. See Chapter 3, 121–2.
30. 'Laws of Ine', Ch. 51, in F.L. Attenborough (ed.), *The Laws of the Earliest English Kings* (1922), 36–61, at 52–3; *EHD*, I, 398–407; for problems in interpretation see Abels, *Lordship and Military Obligation*, 11–25.
31. *DB: Berks*, fo. 56.
32. Lawson, 'Danegeld and heregeld'.

An important movement therefore during the later Saxon period was the closer association of nobility with the ownership of land. This is not to say that nobles had not lived off estates previously, as the laws of King Ine seem to envisage noblemen who were in possession of estates: a nobleman who was evicted, for instance, could be expelled from his house, but not from the cultivated land.[33] But presumably these were, as discussed before, fixed-term grants and perhaps a specific reward for services rendered. In contrast, land held by book could be bequeathed or alienated as the owner wished even though the king retained certain inalienable rights over all land.

The increase in estates held by hereditary tenure among the nobility did not, though, lead to a decline in a more personal lordship between king and noble. Young nobles, such as Æthelwold before he began his monkish and episcopal career, entered the entourage of the king and, as well as taking a solemn oath of allegiance, would be invested by the king with arms and armour appropriate to their rank which would be returned to the king as heriot on their deaths.[34] They might eventually hope for a grant of bookland (Æthelwold appears to have received an estate of 60 hides from his 'lord' King Athelstan),[35] which was not returned on death, but was acknowledged by a monetary payment which ensured inheritance by the heir. Heriot payments are mentioned in the wills of leading West Saxons in later Anglo-Saxon England; that of Ealdorman Æthelmær of eastern Wessex (d. 982) records a heriot payment of '300 mancuses of gold, 4 swords, 8 horses, 4 with trappings and 4 without, 4 helmets, 4 byrnies (mail-armour), and 8 spears and shields'.[36] In contrast, Æthelwold, a king's thegn in the reign of Æthelred, paid only 'an armlet of 30 mancuses, 2 scabbards (?), 2 horses, 2 swords and 2 shields and 2 spears'.[37] These West Saxon examples correspond well with the definitions of heriot payments in a lawcode of Cnut,[38] and with the customs of Berkshire recorded under the entry for Wallingford in Domesday Book: 'at his death a thane or a king's household *miles* [i.e. a man-at-arms of free, but non-noble status] sent to the king as death duty all his arms and horse, one with a saddle, another without a saddle; but if he had dogs or hawks they were presented to the king to accept if he wished'.[39] The lesser or median thegns, that is those who had an intermediary lord between themselves and the

---

33. Attenborough, 'The laws of Ine', Ch. 68, see also 50, 51 and 63.
34. For Æthelwold see M. Lapidge (ed.), *Wulfstan of Winchester, Life of St Æthelwold* (1991), Ch. 7, 10–11; N. Brooks, 'Arms, status and warfare in late-Saxon England', in *Ethelred the Unready*, ed. D. Hill, BAR, *59* (1978), 81–104.
35. E.O. Blake (ed.), *Liber Eliensis*, Camden Society 3rd series, *92* (1962), 75–6.
36. D. Whitelock (ed.), *Anglo-Saxon Wills* (1930), no. 10, 24–7.
37. Whitelock, *Anglo-Saxon Wills*, no. 12, 30–1.
38. Brooks, 'Arms, status and warfare'.
39. *DB: Berks*, fo. 56.

king like Glastonbury Abbey's *taini*, paid either £2½ or a single horse and tack together with weapons to their lord.[40]

Royal service could bring both profit and status and so remained highly desirable. It was the most powerful families whose members filled the offices of ealdorman and earl who also became the wealthiest. The rise in power of the kings of Wessex when they became kings of England in the tenth century was accompanied by that of the families of West Saxon origin who provided their chief ealdormen, such as those of Athelstan Half-King, Ælfhere of Mercia and Æthelweard the Chronicler, who possessed substantial estates in Wessex even if their ealdormanries were based elsewhere. However, these families fell from power after the conquest of Cnut when members either died in the fighting or were executed for treason, which presumably allowed Cnut to confiscate their estates. Cnut promoted new families, including that of Earl Godwine of Wessex, and, at a lesser level, housecarls like Urk of Abbotsbury, and many of these suffered a fate similar to that of the lords they had succeeded after William won at Hastings.[41] Domesday Book shows how William absorbed some of Harold Godwineson's estates into the royal holdings as well as granting out others to new lords.

The Domesday Book entries for the family of Earl Godwine and indications from charter donations of the families of Athelstan Half-King and Ælfhere of Mercia show that they held large holdings of estates, but with a tendency for these to be more widely dispersed and less concentrated within Wessex than those of the Crown and major churches.[42] The bulk of the nobility had much smaller holdings which would be more likely to be concentrated in a single shire; the king's thegns were of vital importance in carrying out duties on behalf of the Crown at a local level and were a key element in the functioning of local courts. The holdings of lesser thegns tended to be limited to a single estate and there cannot have been much to choose in terms of wealth between some of them and the non-noble free who held similar estates in return for military or other services rendered. The entries for king's servants at the end of the Domesday Book entries for each shire indicate that land might be granted for other services besides the military, and even some female grantees are recorded; Leofgeat of Wiltshire, for instance, did gold embroidery for the king while the wife of Godric fed the king's dogs.[43]

---

40. Brooks, 'Arms, status and warfare'.
41. R. Fleming, *Kings and Lords in Conquest England* (1991).
42. C. Hart, 'Athelstan "Half King" and his family', *ASE, 2* (1973), 115–44; A. Williams, 'Land and power in the eleventh century: the estates of Harold Godwineson', *Anglo-Norman Studies, 3* (1980), 171–88; A. Williams, '*Princeps Merciorum gentis*: the family, career and connections of Ælfhere, ealdorman of Mercia, 956–83', *ASE, 10* (1982), 143–72.
43. P. Stafford, 'Women in Domesday Book', in *Medieval Women in Southern England, Reading Medieval Studies, 15* (1989), 75–94.

The need of the nobility to be supported by grants of bookland led to a number of significant developments. The large West Saxon estates which had formed the earliest fiscal units and grants to the Church had to be broken up into smaller units for the kings to be able to afford to grant bookland to their nobles, and for the Church to be able to provide for the military contingents demanded from it. The subdivisions made at this time had a lasting impact on the landscape and on the civil and ecclesiastical boundaries within it. For instance, Edward Roberts and Gary Allam have demonstrated that the bounds of the Old Minster's 40-hide estate at Alresford (Hants), as defined in its Anglo-Saxon charters, are identical to those of the manor of Alresford in a detailed survey of 1550 and to the parish of Alresford in the nineteenth-century tithe awards.[44] However, as the map clearly indicates, the Alresford estate had once been larger, and a smaller 10-hide estate of Bighton had been carved out by 957 when King Eadwig granted the reversion of it to New Minster, Winchester (fig. 62).[45] The original grant separating Bighton from Alresford may have been to a nobleman called Bica who gave his name to the estate (*Bicincgtun*).[46] Once separated from Alresford, Bighton followed a different estate history and eventually became a parish in its own right.

There are many examples of subdivided estates in Wessex being called after men or women to whom they had been granted. At one time it was believed that such names were those of pioneer settlers who had colonized the land in the days of the Anglo-Saxon settlements, but it is now appreciated that they belong to this later stage when individual estates or manors were being created.[47] In the process the original name of the large estate, which is usually a topographical name, either became restricted to one part of the estate, as may have happened with Alresford, 'the alder ford', or was lost altogether. The last point is particularly well illustrated by the example of the estate at *Æscesbyrig* (Berks) studied by Margaret Gelling.[48] The estate was first subdivided when its most westerly 20 hides were granted to a nobleman called Aldred in 856;[49] in 944 the estate was acquired by the thegn Wulfric, who in 958 was granted an adjoining 20 hides (also originally part of *Æscesbyrig*).[50] The two subdivisions of *Æscesbyrig* became one called 'Wulfric's *tun*', modern Woolstone. The eastern part continued for a while to be called *Æscesbyrig* and appears with that name in a charter of 953 in which the estate was granted to Ælfsige and his wife Eadgifu.[51] By the

44. E. Roberts and G. Allam, 'Saxon Alresford and Bighton', *Hampshire Field Club Newsletter, 20* (1993), 9–13.
45. S 660/B 1045.
46. R. Coates, *The Place-Names of Hampshire* (1989), 33.
47. M. Gelling, *The Place-Names of Berkshire, Part III*, EPNS, *51* (1976), 822–9.
48. Gelling, *Place-Names of Berkshire, III*, 675, 823–5.
49. S 317/B 491.
50. S 575/B 902.
51. S 561/B 899.

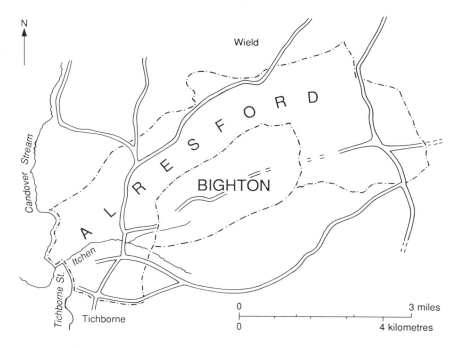

62. The bounds of Alresford and Bighton (Hants) [after E. Roberts and G. Allam, 'Saxon Alresford and Bighton', *Hampshire Field Club Newsletter 20* (1993), 9–13]

end of the Anglo-Saxon period the estate had come into the possession of Abingdon Abbey and was known as 'Uffa's *tun*', modern Uffington, perhaps the name of the last secular owner before it passed to Abingdon. The hill-fort of *Æscesbyrig* which had given its name to the original multiple estate was on Uffa's land and is today known as Uffington Castle. Estates might also be named from female owners; Tolpuddle (Dorset) takes its name from Tola, the widow of the housecarl Urk, the founder of Abbotsbury, and Afflington (Dorset) from Ælfrun who held the estate in 1066.[52]

It is by no means clear why estates, which as the examples show often had a complex tenurial history, became known by the name of one owner rather than another, but they do seem to demonstrate an increasing tendency in the later Anglo-Saxon period for the West Saxon nobility to identify themselves through the estates they possessed. A tract known as *Geþyncþo*, or the 'promotion law', from

52. F.M. Stenton, 'The historical bearing of place-name studies: the place of women in Anglo-Saxon society', in *Preparatory to Anglo-Saxon England*, ed. D.M. Stenton (1970), 314–24.

the end of the Anglo-Saxon period gives a (no doubt idealized) definition of how a ceorl might be promoted to the rank of thegn:

And if a ceorl prospered so that he had fully five hides of his own land, [church and kitchen], bell [house] and *burh-geat*, seat and special office in the king's hall, then was he thenceforward entitled to the rank of thegn.[53]

A king's thegn is being described here with the emphasis on royal service and possession of five hides of bookland; according to the Domesday customs for Berkshire anyone in possession of five hides would have had to perform military service in any case. *Gebyncþo*, however, shows that it was not enough to possess the estate; it must also be equipped with buildings appropriate to its status as a manorial centre.[54] The building requirements can to a certain extent be confirmed by excavations within Wessex, though the sites examined to date are not numerous. From Portchester (Hants) we may have an example of the residence of a ceorl with aspirations.[55] Domesday Book records that the royal manor of Portchester was held by three freemen as three manors, and one of these may have been based within the Roman shore fort which had been utilized as a burh in the early tenth century. Excavation on a site within the walls, adjacent to the site of the twelfth-century priory, showed that it was occupied in the late Saxon period by a series of substantial rectangular timber buildings, including an aisled hall, arranged around a courtyard. By the end of the tenth century or early in the eleventh century a rectangular tower, some 20 feet square in its second phase and built of flints and mortar, was added to the complex and became the focus of a small cemetery (fig. 63). It is possible that this would fit the requirement of a bell-house or belfry in *Gebyncþo*, and it recalls the prominent church towers of Barton upon Humber (Lincs) and Earl's Barton (Northants) which seem to have been associated with residences of late Saxon noblemen.[56] The walls of Portchester would provide more substantial defences than was normal for Anglo-Saxon noble residences, but the Watergate, which seems to have been rebuilt in the later Anglo-Saxon period, could have served as an impressive *burhgeat* as the treatise envisaged.[57] It is possible that the manorial complex of buildings

---

53. F. Liebermann, *Die Gesetze der Angelsachsen* (3 vols, Halle, 1903–16), I, 456; *EHD*, I, 468–70. The words in square brackets are found only in the *Textus Roffensis* version.
54. A. Williams, 'A bell-house and a burh-geat: lordly residences in England before the Norman Conquest', *The Ideals and Practice of Medieval Knighthood, 4* (1992), 221–40.
55. B. Cunliffe, *Excavations at Portchester Castle. Volume II: Saxon* (1976), especially 1–3, 44–61 and 300–4.
56. Williams, 'Bell-house and burh-geat', 233–5.
57. Cunliffe, *Portchester*, 9–14.

63. The late Saxon tower at Portchester (Hants) under excavation, with walls of Saxon shore-fort and medieval castle behind; note burials in foreground, probably also of late Saxon date [photograph: B. Cunliffe]

was separately delineated within the walls, but that the evidence lay outside the area of Professor Cunliffe's excavations.

The results of the excavation of a noble's residence in the deserted village of Faccombe Netherton (Hants), on the north-east edge of Salisbury Plain, have been published recently.[58] The estate is one of those mentioned in the will (c. 950) of the wealthy noblewoman Wynflæd, who was probably the mother-in-law of King Edmund. At that time the residence consisted of an aisled hall, a building of private apartments with a latrine, and a detached kitchen (fig. 64). The site was remodelled early in the eleventh century and enclosed with a substantial bank and ditch (fig. 65). By this time a church had been constructed adjoining the manorial complex, and a ditch surrounding the churchyard joined with that of the residence. The arrangements at Faccombe Netherton recall those of the ideal thegnly residence of *Geþyncþo* and of the royal residence at Cheddar (Som), the only palace in late Anglo-Saxon Wessex to have been excavated.[59] The second phase of occupation at

58. J.R. Fairbrother, *Faccombe Netherton. Excavations of a Saxon and Medieval Manorial Complex* (2 vols), British Museum Occasional Paper, 74 (1990).
59. P. Rahtz, *The Saxon and Medieval Palaces at Cheddar*, BAR, 65 (1979).

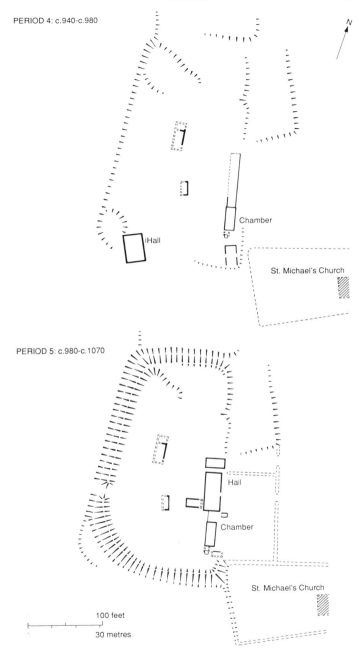

PERIOD 4: c.940-c.980

N

Chamber

Hall

St. Michael's Church

PERIOD 5: c.980-c.1070

Hall

Chamber

St. Michael's Church

100 feet

30 metres

64. Two phases of the late Saxon manorial complex at Faccombe
Netherton (Hants) [after J. Fairbrother, *Faccombe Netherton.
Excavations of a Saxon and Medieval Manorial Complex*, 2 vols
(1990), 60 and 63]

65. Reconstruction of second late Saxon phase at Faccombe Netherton (Hants) [after J. Fairbrother, *Faccombe Netherton. Excavations of a Saxon and Medieval Manorial Complex*, 2 vols (1990), 64]

Cheddar was probably completed by 941 when King Edmund held a major court assembly there. Buildings inside a ditched enclosure included a substantial aisled hall, another timber building which could have been private apartments, a stone chapel and a possible detached latrine (fig. 66). The method of construction of the phase II hall at Cheddar and that of the final Saxon phase at Faccombe were very similar, namely large squared timber posts set in a trench which would probably have had vertical boards (staves) set between.

It is not surprising to find noble residences echoing those of the kings, for nobles, like the owners of Faccombe, had been granted certain regalian rights over the inhabitants of their estates with the granting of bookland. The rights of *sac* and *soc, toll* and *team*, and *infangthief*, listed in late Anglo-Saxon writs, gave the landowner the obligations and profits from holding courts (*hallmoots*) for their tenants with limited law and order responsibilities.[60] Public halls were as necessary for the nobles as for their monarchs for transacting such business and for receiving and entertaining tenants and followers. The Domesday Book commissioners seem to have seen the existence of a hall as one of the criteria for identifying a manor.[61] Thus when we read for Warnford (Hants) that Wulfric and

---

60. F. Harmer (ed.), *Anglo-Saxon Writs* (1952), 73–8; W.L. Warren, *The Governance of Norman and Angevin England 1086–1272* (1987), 44–52.
61. R. Welldon Finn, *An Introduction to Domesday Book* (1963), 50–1; Williams, 'Bell-house and burh-geat', 228–9.

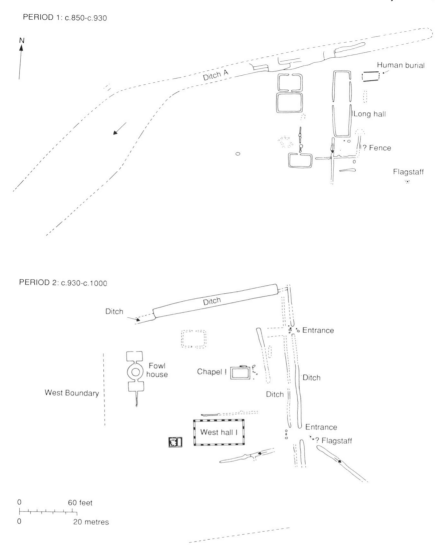

PERIOD 1: c.850-c.930

N

Ditch A

Human burial

Long hall

? Fence

Flagstaff

PERIOD 2: c.930-c.1000

Ditch

Ditch

Entrance

Fowl house

Chapel I

Ditch

West Boundary

Ditch

West hall I

Entrance

? Flagstaff

| 0 | | 60 feet |
| 0 | | 20 metres |

66. Two phases of late Saxon occupation of the royal palace at Cheddar (Som) [after P. Rahtz, *The Saxon and Medieval Palaces at Cheddar* (1979), figs. 12 and 13]

Wulfward held it jointly from King Edward, but that it had two halls, the commissioners are recording that they had divided the estate into two manors.[62]

---

62. *DB: Hants*, 23, 18; fo. 45b.

THE PEASANTRY

The laws of later Anglo-Saxon England envisaged that every man would have a lord and that included the non-noble inhabitants of the estates we have been discussing, who generally had to accept the lordship of their estate holder. The Domesday Book entries for each manor enumerate the number of inhabitants on the estate, though the figures given are usually interpreted as representing the male heads of households, so that a multiplier (often five is favoured) must be used to reach any estimation of the real size of the population.[63] The two categories of dependent peasant to be found on most West Saxon manors are those of *villanus* and *bordarius*, though instead, or sometimes in addition, to the latter might be that of the *cotarius* or *coscet* (the last term being particularly favoured in Wiltshire). The distinction to be drawn between the *bordarius* and the other lesser dependent peasants is no longer clear,[64] but, with the exception of Devon, the West Saxon shires are credited with an above average proportion of all these groups of lesser peasants in Domesday Book.[65] On the other hand, entries for freemen are relatively few in Wessex, compared to some other areas of the country.[66] Freehold tenures are sometimes noted with the subtenancies of estates with particular interest shown in whether the freeman can withdraw from the manor or not, that is, choose his own lord. Slaves were also to be found on a very large number of West Saxon estates, with freed slaves (*coliberti*) identified in some instances, particularly on royal estates in Wiltshire and Somerset.[67] Occasionally specialist workmen may be specified. Swineherds are often listed on the western circuit, especially for Devon, and shepherds, bee-keepers, millers, smiths and foresters occasionally appear.[68]

The *villani* and *bordarii* of Domesday Book seem to correspond to the *gebures* and *kotsetlas* in the *Rectitudines Singularum Personarum*, a late Saxon document specifying the services and payments a lord could expect from the different inhabitants of his estate.[69] The complex history of the transmission of this document and its likely date and provenance have been greatly clarified in a recent article by Paul Harvey.[70] Professor Harvey would see the document, as originally composed, as a practical guide for reeves based on conditions on an actual estate or group of estates, though in the

---

63. Darby, *Domesday England*, 57–94.
64. R. Welldon Finn, *Domesday Book; A Guide* (1973), 33–9.
65. Darby, *Domesday England*, figs. 22–3.
66. Darby, *Domesday England*, fig. 20.
67. Darby, *Domesday England*, 72–4, 76–8.
68. Darby, *Domesday England*, 81–7.
69. Liebermann, *Gesetze*, I, 444–53; *EHD* II, 875–9.
70. P.D.A. Harvey, '*Rectitudines Singularum Personarum* and *Gerefa*', *EHR, 108* (1993), 1–22.

form we now have it *Rectitudines* has been adapted, probably by Archbishop Wulfstan, in order to have a more general import. He argues that *Rectitudines* may have been written originally in the mid-tenth century within the Wessex region. Features of the vocabulary are consistent with composition in east Somerset or western Wiltshire, and similarities with an estate survey for Tidenham (Gloucs),[71] which belonged to St Peter's, Bath, could mean that *Rectitudines* was written for that abbey's estates. The document makes it clear that many of the features associated with the post-Conquest manorial system were present in late Saxon Wessex. Both *kotsetlas* and *gebures* owed labour services to their manorial lord in respect of the land they held. The *kotsetla* was only a smallholder whose typical holding is envisaged as five acres; he did not pay rent and therefore owed substantial work services. The *gebur*, the equivalent to the Domesday villein, could be a person of greater substance who might have his own ploughteam, horses and hunting dogs. He paid rent to his lord, but also had to render heavy labour services which are carefully defined; for instance, 'from the time when ploughing is first done until Martinmas he must each week plough 1 acre (i.e. for the lord), and himself present the seed in the lord's barn'. He is envisaged as having been provided with land, stock and house by his lord, essential features of post-Conquest villein tenure, and in consequence 'when death befalls him let the lord take charge of what he leaves'. However, as Wulfstan adds in his additions to the document, 'the estate-law is fixed on each estate: at some places ... it is heavier, at some places, also, lighter, because not all customs about estates are alike'.

The agricultural nature of the work demanded of the *gebur* distinguishes him from the superior peasant or *geneat*, the freeman of the Domesday Book survey. The *geneat* was clearly a person of some standing who possessed horses and a residence suitable for entertaining a lord. He paid rent, performed carrying and riding services, and helped organize the hunt. The only agricultural services were boonworks at harvest-time. It was probably from this class of peasant that the ceorls who performed military service came,[72] and acting as guard to the lord is one of the services of the *geneat* specified in *Rectitudines*. The unsaddled horses and spare spears and shields which appear in heriots of ealdormen and king's thegns may have been for the use of such ceorls.[73] *Rectitudines* also discusses various specialists on the manorial estate who are either rarely mentioned or do not feature at all in Domesday Book. Specialist workers included the bee-keeper and swineherd, who

---

71. A.J. Robertson (ed.), *Anglo-Saxon Charters* (2nd edn., 1956), 205, 451; *EHD*, II, 879–80.
72. Abels, *Lordship and Military Obligation*, 142–5.
73. Brooks, 'Arms, status and warfare', 81–104.

might work away from the estate centre and lease the livestock in return for specified renders, the *folgere* (probably the ploughman), the sower, oxherd, cowherd, shepherd, goatherd and – the only person in the document specifically said to be female – the cheesemaker. All had special entitlements connected with their work, and the range of jobs and even the order in which they are listed corresponds to what can be found in later manorial documents. Some of these positions could be filled by slaves; the possibility of slave bee-keepers, swineherds and herdsmen is specifically mentioned, and other sources indicate the likelihood of ploughmen being slaves. Four manorial officers are described, though the survey is mainly concerned with the customary payments to which they were entitled: the *bere brytta* (in charge of the granary), beadle, hayward and woodward; possibly these workers were chosen from among the *gebures*. Above them all would be the reeve for whom presumably the *Rectitudines* was produced; a text associated with it in some manuscripts known as *Gerefa* describes the functions of the reeve, but is interpreted by Professor Harvey as a literary exercise rather than a practical document of instruction like the *Rectitudines*.[74]

The *Rectitudines* shows that the lord of at least one set of tenth-century manors in Wessex was able to claim the type of work services and customary payments which are familiar from later manorial records and the implication of the entries in Domesday Book is that such manorial organization was widespread in Wessex. How far can it be traced back into earlier Anglo-Saxon periods? We do not have earlier documents with the wealth of detail in *Rectitudines*, but facets of manorial organization can be seen. A charter from King Edward the Elder for Old Minster, Winchester, dated to 900 specifies the dues which the ceorls of Stoke are to render to the manorial centre at Hurstbourne.[75] Earlier historians were unwilling to believe that the arrangements at Hurstbourne could date to as early as 900,[76] but Professor Finberg produced compelling arguments for seeing them as contemporary with the rest of the charter and demonstrated how the recent history of the Hurstbourne estate might have made Old Minster anxious to make clear the dependency of the peasants of Stoke on Hurstbourne.[77] There are distinct echoes of the arrangements for the *gebures* described in *Rectitudines*. Like the *gebures* the Hurstbourne ceorls owed a variety of payments in money and kind, as well as substantial labour service. For instance, they must 'plough three

74. Harvey, '*Rectitudines*'.
75. S 359/B 594/Robertson, *Anglo-Saxon Charters*, 206.
76. F.W. Maitland, *Domesday Book and Beyond* (1897), 330–2; F.M. Stenton, *Anglo-Saxon England* (3rd edn., 1971), 476; *EHD*, II, 879.
77. H.P.R. Finberg, 'The churls of Hurstbourne', *Lucerna: Studies of Some Problems in the Early History of England* (1964), 131–43.

acres in their own time and sow them with their own seed and bring it to the barn in their own time' as well as working as directed on the demesne. The payment they must make at the autumn equinox of 'forty pence from each hide' is the equivalent of '10 pence per yardland' which the *gebures* of *Rectitudines* gave at Michaelmas. When Old Minster leased their estate at Alresford to the nobleman Alfred at about the same time, they were anxious not to lose all the work services they had customarily enjoyed from the men of the estate: 'when the need arises, his men shall be ready both for harvesting and hunting'.[78]

Evidence for earlier periods is even scarcer, but there are some important indicators in the laws of King Ine (composed 688×694).[79] Chapter 67 describes lords providing men with land and a house and being able to exact rent and labour services in return; there is also an implication that the lord provided the seed for the crops in such circumstances. Another chapter (6.3) distinguishes between the *gafolgelda* (rent payer) and *gebur*, perhaps indicating a distinction between the free tenant and the dependent peasant owing labour services as defined in Chapter 67. Chapter 50 states that:

> If a nobleman comes to terms with the king, or with the king's ealdorman or with his lord, on behalf of his dependants, free or unfree, he, the nobleman, shall not have any portion of the fines, because he has not previously taken care at home to restrain them from evil doing.

The implication is that the lord normally was responsible for law and order on his estate and consequently could claim a share in the fines paid by his tenants like manorial lords in later Anglo-Saxon Wessex. Written sources cannot take us back any further. Archaeological evidence in the form of grave-goods from the fifth and sixth centuries suggest major variations in status were always a feature of West Saxon society, but it would be hazardous to try to relate such evidence to the relations of dependence depicted in Ine's laws.[80]

Ine's lawcodes also show that varieties of peasant were to be found amongst his British subjects.[81] Categories mentioned in the laws include, on a rising scale according to wergeld tariffs allotted to them, landless Briton (60s), landed Briton with half a hide (80s), a British *gafolgelda* and a landed Briton with one hide (the last two have the same wergeld of 120s and so may be different definitions

---

78. S 1287/B 617/Robertson, *Anglo-Saxon Charters*, 28–9.
79. Attenborough, *Laws*, 36–61; H.P.R. Finberg, *The Agrarian History of England and Wales, vol. I.ii, AD 43–1042* (1972), 438–42.
80. H. Härke, 'Changing symbols in a changing society: the Anglo-Saxon weapon burial rite in the seventh century', in *The Age of Sutton Hoo*, ed. M. Carver (1992), 149–66.
81. Attenborough, 'Laws of Ine', Ch. 23.3, 24.2, 32 and 33.

of the same category, as the terms appear in different chapters). There is also what appears to be a superior British freeman described as a 'British horseman in the king's service' whose wergeld was 200s, apparently the same as that of a West Saxon ceorl.[82] The gradations among the British peasantry need occasion no surprise as a dependent peasantry was also to be found in the Welsh kingdoms,[83] and it is highly likely that villa owners in the late Roman period exercised seigneurial rights over some at least of their peasant tenants.[84] When attempting to reconstruct the position of the peasantry in early Anglo-Saxon Wessex it is important to bear in mind that, irrespective of what traditions Germanic settlers brought from their homelands, they came to a country where lords had been exercising rights over men subject to them for many generations, if not centuries.

We need not doubt that the origins of the manor in Wessex can be traced back at least as far as the relationships between lords and dependent peasants depicted in Ine's lawcodes, and that by 1066 many of the diagnostic features of the medieval manor were clearly in place.[85] But in emphasizing continuities in the control lords had over peasants, there is a danger in missing the changes which undoubtedly must have taken place during the Anglo-Saxon period. Shortage of sources means that changes may be masked from us. But one possibly significant pointer is the small number of references to freemen compared to *villani* and *bordarii*, in the Domesday Book entries for Wessex. There is a significant contrast here between Wessex and other areas of the country covered by the Domesday survey, particularly eastern England. Now it could be that the commissioners for the two circuits which included Wessex did not make a point of including freemen except where they owned land in their own right or there was a dispute over whether they were dependants of a manor; freemen tied to an estate could have been included with the villeins. But it is also possible that manorialism was more advanced in Wessex by 1066 than in some other areas of the country with a concomitant decline in the number of free peasants, men with the status of the *geneat* of the *Rectitudines*. The Domesday entries record many instances in which land held in 1066 by a freeman or group of freemen had subsequently been allocated to a nobleman, and this tendency for ceorls holding bookland to lose status could have been a trend

82. Attenborough, 'Laws of Ine', Ch. 33 and 70.
83. G.R.J. Jones, 'Post-Roman Wales', in *The Agrarian History of England and Wales, vol. I.ii, AD 43–1042*, ed. H.P.R. Finberg (1972), 281–382; W. Davies, *Wales in the Early Middle Ages* (1982), 41–7; 64–8.
84. J. Percival, 'Seigneurial aspects of late Roman estate management', *EHR, 84* (1969), 449–73; A.H.M. Jones, *The Later Roman Empire AD 284–602: A Social, Economic and Administrative Survey* (2nd edn., 1973), 761–808; M. Millett, *The Romanization of Britain* (1990), 181–211.
85. T.H. Aston, 'The origins of the manor in England', *TRHS, 8* (1956), 59–83.

occurring before the Conquest as well.[86] To understand more of the fate of the peasant community in late Saxon Wessex we need to look at what was happening to slavery and to the internal organization of estates.

SLAVERY

Slaves are recorded on the majority of Domesday Book manors in Wessex and constituted about ten per cent of the recorded population, though there is some uncertainty about whether the recorded slaves are heads of households, like the dependent peasantry, or if all slaves are listed.[87] Slaves were very much a feature of early Wessex as well and there are several references to their ownership in the laws of Ine;[88] from the laws of Alfred it is apparent that even ceorls might own slaves.[89] Slaves were in a worse position than the dependent peasants as they possessed no wergeld in their own right. If they were killed their masters received compensation, not themselves or their families, if they had one. They could be bought and sold as desired and might be disposed of in wills with other chattels of the estate. Punishment for crimes might be severe as they could not pay compensation; a slave who raped another slave could be castrated according to the laws of Alfred.[90] However, some other factors meant that the humanity of slaves had to be acknowledged. The Church recognized them as people with souls who could be converted to Christianity. Because slaves were Christians their lords were forbidden to make them work on Sundays.[91] Slaves did not have the same holidays as ceorls, but the laws of Alfred allowed them the four Wednesdays of Ember weeks in which to sell goods.[92] For slaves might have the opportunity to get more than a basic allowance. In the *Rectitudines* a slave swineherd was allowed a pig in a sty and every male slave was allowed a strip of land for ploughing.

One source of slaves that must have been particularly important in early Wessex was warfare. Gildas describes enslavement as one of the fates that awaited the British at the hands of the Anglo-Saxons,[93] and no doubt that was the fate of many, though the

---

86. M. Aston, 'Rural settlement in Somerset: some preliminary thoughts', in *Medieval Villages*, ed. D. Hooke, OUCA, 5 (1985), 80–100.
87. Darby, *Domesday England*, 72–4; J.S. Moore, 'Domesday slavery', *Anglo-Norman Studies, 11* (1989), 191–220.
88. Attenborough, 'Laws of Ine', 3.2, 7.1, 11, 23.3, 24, 47, 53, 62; Finberg, *Agrarian History*, 437–8.
89. Attenborough, *Laws*, 62–93, Ch. 25.
90. Attenborough, *Laws*.
91. Attenborough, 'Laws of Ine', Ch. 3.
92. Attenborough, 'Laws of Alfred', Ch. 43.
93. M. Winterbottom (ed.), *Gildas, The Ruin of Britain and Other Documents* (1978), Ch. 25.

British slaves in the laws of Ine may have included slaves owned by his British subjects.[94] The heavy concentration of slaves in west Devon in Domesday Book may indicate that the enslavement of some Britons continued as the West Saxons advanced westwards. However, although the word *walh*, which was used in the laws of Ine with the primary meaning of someone of British nationality, had come to have the more general meaning of 'slave' in later Saxon Wessex, in the process it seems to have lost its racial connotations.[95] Anglo-Saxons from rival kingdoms might also be enslaved and seized as war-booty during raids. A letter from Archbishop Brihtwold of Canterbury to Bishop Forthhere of Sherborne requests that he help persuade the abbot of Glastonbury to release a Kentish girl he has as a slave; the ransom her kinsmen are prepared to pay would suggest she was of noble birth. The letter cannot be dated closely, but must be after 709. The most likely occasion for the girl to have been taken would have been Ine's raid on Kent in 694 to avenge the death of Mul.[96]

However, the girl could have been acquired through the slave-trade which was also a feature of life throughout the Anglo-Saxon period.[97] The Church did not object to slavery as such, as is apparent from Brihtwold's letter and the large-scale ownership of slaves on church lands revealed in Domesday Book. But the Church was concerned that Christian slaves might be sold to non-Christians as then they might have no opportunity to practise their religion. The laws of Ine contain the first recorded attempt from Wessex to prohibit the sale of slaves overseas,[98] but it was still an issue at the end of the Anglo-Saxon period when Bishop Wulfstan II of Worcester sought to end the slave-trade from Bristol.[99] Bristol had emerged as a major market for slaves because of its convenience for Ireland – the Viking colonists were great users and traders of slaves.[100] During the Viking raids some West Saxons would have been carried off as slaves and that was probably the fate of some of the citizens of Southampton captured in a raid in 980.[101]

Warfare and trade were not the only sources of new slaves. Throughout the Anglo-Saxon period enslavement was the punishment for certain crimes; for instance, in the laws of Ine it is recorded as the punishment for a freeman who worked of his own

94.   Attenborough, 'Laws of Ine', Ch. 23.3, though see also Ch. 74.
95.   M. Faull, 'The semantic development of Old English *walh*', *Leeds Studies in English, 8* (1976), 20–44.
96.   *EHD*, I, no. 166, 794–5.
97.   D. Pelteret, 'Slave raiding and slave trading in early England', *ASE, 9* (1981), 99–114.
98.   Attenborough, 'Laws of Ine', Ch. 11.
99.   *The Vita Wulfstani of William of Malmesbury*, ed. R. Darlington, Camden soc. 3rd ser., *40* (1928), 43–4.
100.   Pelteret, 'Slave raiding', 112–13.
101.   *Anglo-Saxon Chronicle* C *s.a.* 980.

free will on a Sunday and in some circumstances for theft.[102] Wynflæd in her will of about 950 names several penal slaves on her estates whom she says she has enslaved herself;[103] possibly these would have been people who had not been able to pay their rent or other dues as debt seems to have been another cause of enslavement.[104] Men who could not afford to support themselves or their families might sell them into slavery, one of the misfortunes that befell the people of the country during the military and agricultural disasters of King Æthelred's reign according to Wulfstan in his *Sermon of the Wolf to the English.*[105] But there were also ways out of slavery. Wynflæd mentions her penal slaves because she was freeing them, and references to freeing of slaves in wills is particularly common as it was believed that the act of manumission benefited the soul. Manumissions at other times might be specially recorded and a gospel book from Exeter records that:

> King Eadwig ordered Ælfnoth the sacrist to free Abunet at Exeter, free and with the right to depart, in the witness of Ealdorman Æthelwold and Bishop Daniel and Brihtric the prior and Wulfric the sacrist. And King Eadwig ordered Brihtric to put it here in Christ's book.[106]

The decline in the type of warfare which allowed the taking of slaves as booty might have been expected to lead to a gradual downturn in the number of slaves in later Anglo-Saxon England as fresh entrants are usually considered necessary to sustain a steady slave population. Although penal enslavement did bring in new slaves, this seems likely to have been balanced by acts of manumission. After the Norman Conquest slavery quickly died out, not so much because the Normans had finer feelings than the Anglo-Saxons, but because slavery had outlived its usefulness for the exploitation of estates.[107] Slaves were not so much set free as set up as dependent peasants owing substantial labour services, but with enough land to support themselves – the *coliberti* of the Domesday survey. It is likely that the process had begun well before 1066 and there are references to freedmen living on the land in late West Saxon documents such as the will of Wynflæd. It will be apparent that there might be little to choose between the freed slave set up

---

102. Attenborough, 'Laws of Ine', 3.2, 7.1; for other sources of evidence see Pelteret, 'Slave raiding'.
103. Whitelock, *Anglo-Saxon Wills*, no. 3, 10–15.
104. Attenborough, 'Laws of Ine', Ch. 62.
105. *EHD*, I, 928–34.
106. *EHD*, I, no. 149, 610.
107. A. Verhulst, 'The decline of slavery and the economic expansion of the early middle ages', *Past and Present, 133* (1991), 195–203; H. Goetz, 'Serfdom and the beginnings of a "seigneurial system" in the Carolingian period: a survey of the evidence', *Early Medieval Europe, 1* (1993), 29–51.

by his lord with land, stock and house and the *gebur* who is represented in a very similar way in the *Rectitudines*. Indeed, there is confusion in some Domesday Book entries about whether *'bures'* and *coliberti* (freedmen) were the same; the entry for Nether Wallop (Hants) reads *coliberti vel bures*.[108] One receives the impression that in the earlier Anglo-Saxon period, when ceorls in Wessex might own slaves, that there was a marked difference between the rights lords enjoyed over slaves and over their dependent peasants as a whole. By the end of the Anglo-Saxon period the lot of the dependent peasantry of Wessex may have come closer to that of slaves earlier, particularly with regard to the amount of labour on the lord's lands which might be expected from them. The decline of slavery seems to argue also for a decline in personal freedom for many ceorls; for slavery became obsolete when the work of slaves was replaced by labour services from a dependent peasantry also responsible for providing for themselves.

SETTLEMENTS AND FIELDS

The Domesday Book entries give no indication of the topography of the manors beyond indicating something of the extent of arable, woodland, meadow and, sometimes, other varieties of pasture. Totals of the population are given, but not how they were distributed within the manor and it should not be assumed that they all lived at their estate centres. Only where subtenancies are recorded are indications given of significant subdivisions within an estate. Further understanding can only be reached through relating Domesday entries to topography and subsequent land use, as in the important studies of Domesday geography by Professor Darby.[109] To understand the dynamics of change which may have occurred during the Anglo-Saxon period programmes of intensive field-walking within estate boundaries are needed. Unfortunately, relatively few surveys of this type have been undertaken, but an important pioneering study was made by Professor Cunliffe in the 1960s within the downland parishes of Chalton and Catherington (Hants).[110] Pottery evidence from field-walking suggested that settlement in the immediate post-Roman period continued on sites occupied during the late Roman period, but that by the beginning of the seventh century it had coalesced at the ridge-top sites of Catherington and Church Down, both of them centrally placed

108.   Darby, *Domesday England*, 76–8; D. Pelteret, 'The *coliberti* of Domesday Book', *Medieval Culture*, 12 (1978), 43–54.
109.   Darby, *Domesday England*; H.C. Darby and E.M. Campbell, *The Domesday Geography of South-East England* (1962); H.C. Darby and R. Welldon Finn, *The Domesday Geography of South-West England* (1967).
110.   B. Cunliffe, 'Saxon and Medieval settlement-pattern in the region of Chalton, Hampshire', *Med Arch*, 16 (1972), 1–12; B. Cunliffe, 'Chalton, Hants: the evolution of a landscape', *Ant J*, 53 (1973), 173–90.

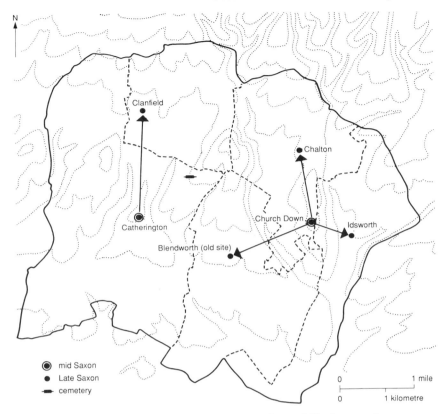

67. Saxon settlement sites in the parishes of Chalton and
Catherington (Hants) [after B. Cunliffe, 'Saxon and medieval
settlement-pattern in the region of Chalton, Hampshire', *Med. Arch.*
16 (1972), 1–12, at 6]

within their dependent blocks of land. By the late Saxon period the
settlement pattern had shifted again (fig. 67). Church Down was
abandoned altogether and replaced by three settlement foci on
lower land at Chalton, Blendworth and Idsworth, all of which
eventually became parishes. The settlement of Catherington, on the
other hand, continued to be occupied throughout the Anglo-Saxon
period, though with at least one subsidiary settlement at Clanfield
('cleared land') appearing in a lightly wooded area to the north.

The site at Church Down has been excavated, though only
interim reports are available, so that the complicated sequence of
occupation has yet to be fully elucidated.[111] 61 structures,

---

111. P.V. Addyman and D. Leigh, 'The Anglo-Saxon village at Chalton, Hampshire:
first interim report', *Med Arch, 16* (1972), 13–31; Addyman and Leigh, 'The
Anglo-Saxon village at Chalton, Hampshire: second interim report', *Med Arch,*
17 (1973), 1–25; B. Cunliffe, *Wessex to AD 1000* (1993), 290–1.

representing several phases of occupation, were recovered and it is thought that the greater part of the settlement area was excavated (fig. 68). The majority of the structures were rectangular timber 'halls' of individual post-hole or post-in-trench construction, and there were only four sunken-floored buildings, a building form thought to have been introduced to Britain by the Germanic settlers. Probably only some of the buildings were dwelling-houses and others would have been used for a variety of agricultural functions. There were indications of buildings grouped inside fenced enclosures perhaps indicating individual 'farms'. The arrangement of one of these units, with a clearly delineated enclosure joined to a substantial timber hall which lay outside it, recalls a similar structure at the probably high status settlement of Cowdery's Down, near Basingstoke (Hants) (fig. 20).[112] However, not all early Saxon settlements in Hampshire may have been dominated by halls of the Church Down and Cowdery's Down type. At Abbots Worthy, Winchester and Old Down Farm, Andover, only small groups of sunken-floored huts were recovered.[113] Field-walking at Abbots Worthy and adjacent sites in the Itchen valley showed a similar pattern of shifting settlement to that suggested for Chalton. In the early Anglo-Saxon period there was a move away from the settlement sites on the valley slopes utilized in the Iron Age and Roman periods in favour of riverside sites. By the late Saxon period there was a shift again to the medieval village sites on the 50-foot contour.

This survey of the development of West Saxon settlement patterns has concentrated on sites in Hampshire because the published sites happen to have been concentrated there; however, preliminary findings from the Thames Valley suggest comparable patterns and settlement-forms.[114] The evidence, sparse though it is, must be viewed against the also rather limited documentary record in laws and charters. The laws of Ine, as we have seen, suggest that peasant communities at the turn of the seventh century could be controlled by lords. Church Down has the appearance of a planned settlement and the apparent disappearance of the sites which were in use in the immediate post-Roman period and their replacement by new sites in central locations suggests an organizing power (perhaps represented by the superior residence) and settlement control. The large planned settlement of Hamwic, which by the middle of the eighth century must have contained several hundred

112. M. Millett and S. James, 'Excavations at Cowdery's Down, Basingstoke, Hampshire, 1978–81', *Arch J, 140* (1983), 151–279.
113. P. Fasham and R. Whinney (eds), *Archaeology and the M3*, Hampshire Field Club monograph, 7 (1991); S. Davies, 'Excavations at Old Down Farm, Andover. Part I: Saxon', *PHFCAS, 36* (1980), 161–80.
114. D. Benson and D. Miles, *The Upper Thames Valley: An Archaeological Survey of the River Gravels* (1974); J. Blair, *Anglo-Saxon Oxfordshire* (1994), 14–29, 124–45.

68. High level photograph of Saxon 'halls' under excavation at
Church Down, Chalton (Hants) [photograph: Department of
Archaeology, University of Southampton]

people brought in from the surrounding countryside, and the similarly centrally planned burhs also suggest the ability of West Saxon authorities to move the rural population at will.[115] Early charters suggest the existence of large 'multiple' estates as economic units and within these specialization of agricultural activities at different centres would have been possible.[116] Place-names may indicate these; for instance, Shepton (Mallett), Shapwick (Som), Shipton (Gorge) (Dors) and Shipton (Bellinger) (Hants) were probably places specializing in the rearing of sheep. The sites at Old Down Farm and Abbots Worthy possibly need to be viewed within a broader estate structure and may have been specialist work-places perhaps for temporary or seasonal use.

The laws of Ine provide some indications of how the land was cultivated by the peasants. One type of land unit that could be associated with ceorls is the *worpig* which, according to the laws, should be fenced both winter and summer.[117] It is just possible that the 'worthy' could mean one of the fenced enclosures of farm buildings of the type excavated at Chalton, but that something more extensive was meant is suggested by its appearance in field and place-names. A 'worthy' may have been a small, enclosed farm or 'a piece of land farmed severally, not necessarily with a dwelling place'.[118] 'Worths' or 'worthys' occur throughout the region, but particularly in the three western shires. Only to be found in the west is the place-name element 'huish' which, like the term 'hide', seems to have been derived from a root-word meaning 'a family', and seems to have designated, on the basis of fieldwork in Somerset by Michael Costen, a self-contained agricultural unit of 80–90 hectares in size.[119] The huish of one hide at Uddens (Dorset) granted by King Eadwig to his *optimas* Alfred was still being run as a single farm in the eighteenth century.[120] The 'huish' and 'worth' names could indicate the small, self-contained farms of West Saxon ceorls who settled in the three western shires after the Anglo-Saxon take-over and established themselves in a landscape already being worked by British peasants on established estates or smaller farmsteads. New land may have been taken into cultivation at this

115. This is not to say that medieval peasants might not collude with such developments nor find them to their advantage: H.S.A. Fox, 'Approaches to the adoption of the Midland system', in *The Origins of Open-Field Agriculture*, ed. T. Rowley (1981), 64–111; C. Dyer, 'The retreat from marginal land: the growth and decline of medieval rural settlements', in *The Rural Settlements of Medieval England*, ed. M. Aston, D. Austin and C. Dyer (1989), 45–58.

116. G.R.J. Jones, 'Multiple estates and early settlements', in *Medieval Settlement*, ed. P. Sawyer (1976), 11–40; M. Costen, *The Origins of Somerset* (1992), 87–93.

117. Attenborough, 'Laws of Ine', Ch. 40.

118. Gelling, *Place-Names of Berkshire, Part III*, 943–4; see also Fox, 'Approaches to the adoption of the Midland system', 86–8.

119. M. Costen, 'Huish and worth: Old English survivals in a later landscape', *ASSAH*, 5 (1992), 65–83.

time as Michael Costen has shown that the 'huish' names in Somerset tend to be on underdeveloped or newly cultivated land. Ine's laws also speak of ceorls who:

> have a common meadow or other land divided in shares to fence, and some have fenced their portion and some have not, and [if cattle] eat up their common crops or grass, those who are responsible for the gap are to go and pay to the others, who have fenced their part, compensation for the damage that has been done there.[121]

This suggests a different system of farming where ceorls were joining together to work the land, and might have their own blocks of land within larger arable fields which were sometimes used for common pasture.[122] Evidence from western Germany suggests that Germanic settlers would have been familiar both with individual farmsteads and with this simple type of open-field system which one could envisage being practised from a settlement such as Church Down, Chalton.[123] However, the latter may also have been a mode of farming practised in late Roman Britain on the large rectangular fields that have been observed in various parts of lowland Britain.[124] Abandoned fields of this type are visible on the higher land of the Vale of the White Horse (Berks, now Oxon).[125] Similar fields on lower ground may have continued in use during the early Anglo-Saxon period and may be responsible for the stepped profile observable in some of the parish boundaries in this area (fig. 69).[126] Elsewhere, especially on the higher ground in the south-west, the small rectangular 'Celtic' fields may have remained in use.

A variety of written, place-name and archaeological evidence, including the Hampshire field surveys discussed above, can be combined to suggest that there were major changes in land use in the later Anglo-Saxon period and that it was at this time that the patterns of settlement, including nucleated villages, to be found in the later Middle Ages came into being. A parallel development was the system of open-field agriculture in which the arable land was

---

120. S 609/B 958; C. Taylor, *Dorset* (1970), 61–3.
121. Attenborough, 'Laws of Ine', Ch. 42.
122. Fox, 'Adoption of the Midland system', 86–8.
123. Fox, 'Adoption of the Midland system', 85–6; M. Welch, 'Rural settlement patterns in the early and middle Anglo-Saxon periods', *Landscape History, 7* (1985), 13–26.
124. S. Applebaum, 'Roman Britain', in *The Agrarian History of England and Wales, vol. I.ii, AD 43–1042*, ed. H.P.R. Finberg (1972), 83–107.
125. D. Hooke, 'Regional variation in southern and central England in the Anglo-Saxon period and its relationship to land units and settlement', in *Anglo-Saxon Settlements*, ed. D. Hooke (1988), 123–52, espec. 126–8.
126. Hooke, 'Regional variation'; Gelling, *Place-Names of Berkshire, Part III*, 626–7, 845–6.

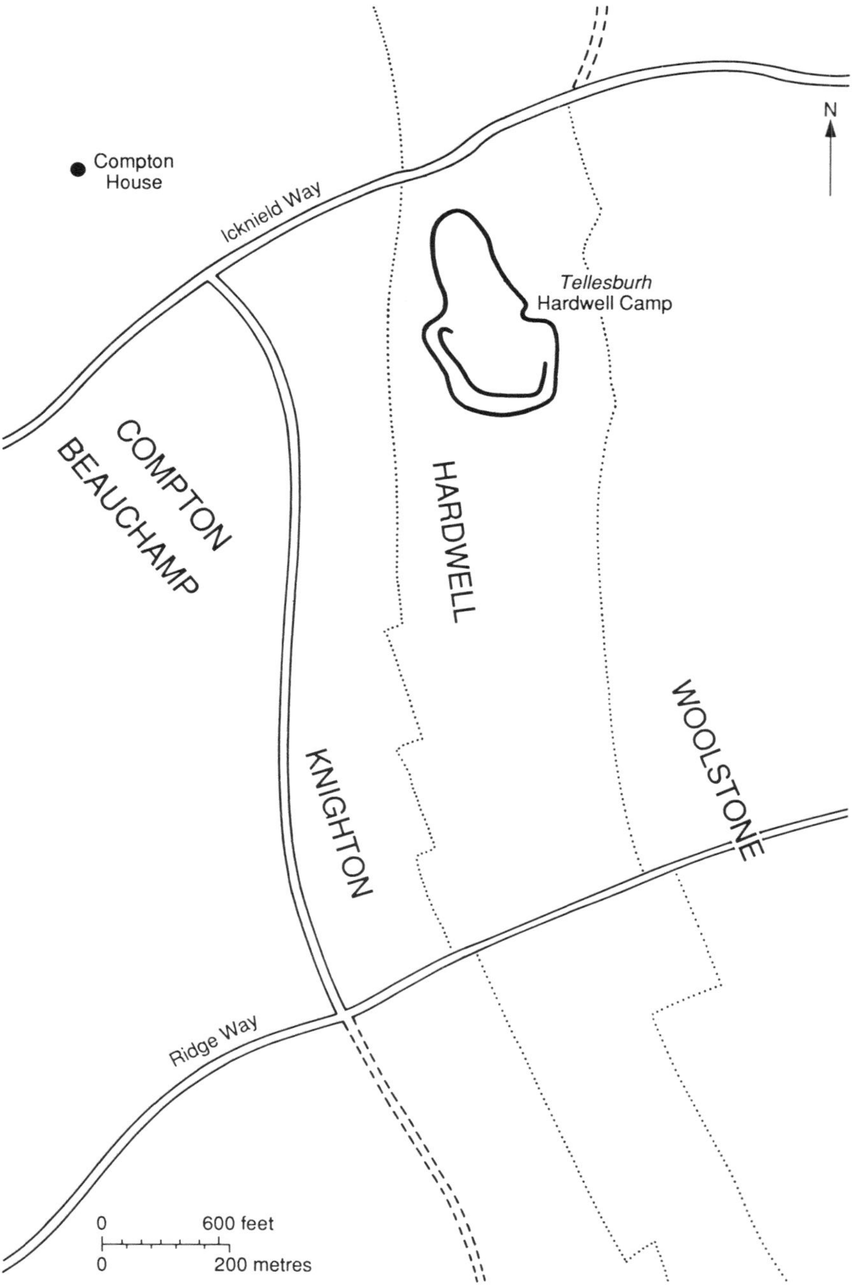

Compton
House

N

Icknield Way

Tellesburh
Hardwell Camp

COMPTON
BEAUCHAMP

HARDWELL

WOOLSTONE

KNIGHTON

Ridge Way

0   600 feet

0   200 metres

69. Estate of Hardwell (Berks) [after D. Hooke, 'Regional variation in
southern and central England in the Anglo-Saxon period', *Anglo-
Saxon Settlements* (1988), 133]

divided into two or three large fields which were worked in furlongs that were subdivided into unfenced strips allocated to individual cultivators.[127] There are many references from tenth-century charters, especially from the chalklands of Berkshire and Wiltshire, to indicate that areas of Wessex were being worked in this way in the later Saxon period. Three hides at Avon (Wilts) are specifically said to consist of 'single strips (*jugera*) dispersed in a mixture here and there in common land', while five hides at Charlton (Berks) are said to lie in common land and 'are not demarcated on all sides by clear bounds because to left and right lie *jugera* in combination with one another'.[128] Boundary clauses of Berkshire charters refer to features of open-field farming familiar from later in the Middle Ages such as the furlong, the *heafod* or *heafodland*, 'headland', where the oxen were turned at the end of the furlong and the *gara* or gore, a triangular piece of land that might be left at the edge of a field when the furlongs were laid out and had to be ploughed separately.[129] It might not be only the arable land that was farmed in common; a charter for Ardington (Berks) says that 'the open pasture is common and the meadow is common and the arable is common'.[130]

The implementation of these more complex systems of open-field agriculture implies a major reorganization of estates. Furlongs with names in *worth, hiwisc* and *ton* suggest that earlier settlements, perhaps individual farmsteads, had been supplanted and cleared to make open fields.[131] Such reorganization should be viewed in the context of the major changes to estate organization which were occurring from the eighth century onwards whereby large estates were split up into smaller units. In 729 Glastonbury Abbey was granted an estate of 60 hides at *Pouholt* on the Polden hills (Som).[132] Subsequently the estate was subdivided into a number of smaller units and this is likely to have occurred by 1066, for according to Domesday Book the estate supported, in addition to Glastonbury's own manor at Shapwick, 14 thegns who 'could not be separated from the church' and may have been part of Glastonbury's military quota (fig. 70). In the Middle Ages Shapwick had two open fields of almost equal size separated by a north-south road on which the village stood. Adjoining settlements which were also carved out of the *Pouholt* estate have similar planned villages and field systems, and the names of some of them – Woolavington (formerly *Hunlavington*), Cossington and Edington – would appear

127. Fox, 'Adoption of the Midland system'.
128. Finberg, *Agrarian History*, 487–91.
129. Gelling, *Place-Names of Berkshire. Part III*, 625–8.
130. S 691/B 1079; Fox, 'Adoption of the Midland system', 84.
131. Gelling, *Place-Names of Berkshire. Part III*, 629–30, 939–42; Costen, 'Huish and worth'.
132. S 253/B 147; N. Corcos, 'Early estates on the Poldens and the origin of settlement at Shapwick', *PSANHS, 127* (1982), 47–54.

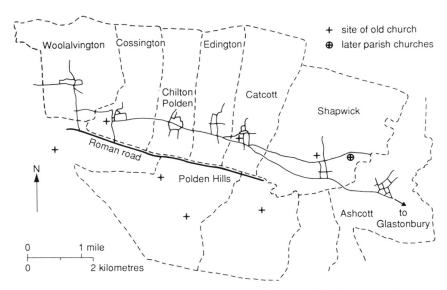

70. Shapwick and adjoining estates which constituted the estate of
Pouholt in the late seventh century [after M. Costen *The Origins of
Somerset* (1992), 120]

to derive from those of Old English estate owners. Another
example from Somerset is the estate at Chinnock which was a
single unit in the will of Wynflæd (*c.* 950), but had been divided
into three estates by the time of Domesday Book (East, West and
Middle Chinnock) (fig. 71).[133] The boundary between West and
Middle Chinnock is a straight line and the open fields are laid out
in relation to the boundary and must post-date it; it is particularly
likely that the fields were established when the estate was divided
up because the east field of West Chinnock is separated from the
rest of West Chinnock by the estate of Middle Chinnock. In
Berkshire, the village and fields of Woolstone must have been
established after Wulfric acquired the two western estates of
Æscesbyrig, for the village straddles the former boundary between
his two estates.[134]

    Although more confirmation is needed from fieldwork and
excavation, it seems a reasonable working hypothesis to place the
origins of many West Saxon medieval nucleated villages in the later
Anglo-Saxon period and relate their foundation to other developments in the countryside including the subdivision of estates and
the laying out of large open fields. Financial pressures may have
been an important factor in encouraging more effective use of the
land. Many small landowners must have been severely stretched

133.   Costen, *Origins of Somerset*, 126–8.
134.   Gelling, *Place-Names of Berkshire. Part III*, 675.

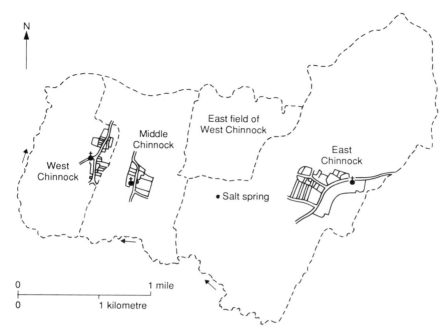

N

0   1 mile

0   1 kilometre

71. The estates of East, West and Middle Chinnock (Som) [M. Costen, *The Origins of Somerset* (1992), 128]

during the periods of Viking attacks, and in the reigns of Cnut and his sons, when large gelds were levied which had to be met if land was to be retained. Population pressure may have been another stimulus and may be implied also by the bringing of new lands into cultivation; settlement names in *feld*, like Clanfield (Hants) (fig. 67), may indicate light woodland which has been cleared.[135] There were also new incentives for producing an agricultural surplus through the growth of towns, as well as the need to have products to trade for coin with which to make payments to the Crown.[136]

Changes in farming practice may have been a necessity for both lord and peasant, but it also seems likely that the changes would have added to the burdens of dependent peasants and perhaps may have led to a decline in the number of freeholders and an increase in those with villein/*gebur* and cottager status. For when new settlements were laid out the lord may have been responsible for building the new houses and peasants who received them from him may have been obliged to acknowledge dependent status in return; the laws of Ine and *Rectitudines* present the acceptance of a house, crops and stock from a lord as a hallmark of the dependent peasant.

---

135. Gelling, *Place-Names of Berkshire. Part III*, 926–7; Cunliffe, 'Chalton', 6–7.
136. See below in this chapter.

However, pressure on the land was not as great as it was to be in the twelfth and thirteenth centuries and, as Wulfstan reminds us in his additions to *Rectitudines*, there are likely to have been considerable variations in the demands made on peasant tenants. Those who were tenants of the Crown or larger ecclesiastical institutions may have had fewer demands made of them than the tenants of a lord who had to make ends meet on a relatively small estate, especially as it would appear that when estates were divided those granted out to nobles might contain the poorer agricultural land.[137] Michael Costen's analysis of the estates of Glastonbury Abbey led him to conclude that the monastery was not exploiting its estates to full capacity and got a relatively poor return from them; in contrast the Crown and the bishops of Winchester appeared to have been more effective exploiters of their lands.[138]

However, it would be wrong to imply uniformity of development throughout Wessex for there were a great variety of land types within the six shires and consequently different forms of utilization of the land. On the higher ground it would have been impossible and inappropriate to lay out an open-field system of agriculture and a pattern of scattered rather than nucleated settlement has always been the norm. W.G. Hoskins was able to demonstrate that for a number of Devon manors the number of villeins listed in Domesday Book could be equated with the number of farms in the same area which could be identified from later records and maps or from current use.[139] Heavily wooded estates, like some in the forest of Windsor or Savernake Forest (Wilts), would also be more likely to have scattered settlements and individual peasant farms, especially where there was the potential to clear land for cultivation.[140] In areas where there were open fields variations in farming practice might still be found; in east Devon, for instance, although fields were divided into furlongs and strips in the Middle Ages and worked in common there might be several fields rather than the two or three of the classic open-field systems, including outfield which might be cultivated only occasionally.[141]

Relatively few areas of Wessex ever conformed to the classic 'Midland system' of open-field agriculture, as defined by Joan Thirsk, largely because on many estates there was land that could not be used for crop production and so was available for pasturage, with the result that control of the arable for this purpose was less

137. Fairbrother, *Faccombe Netherton*, 22–7.
138. M. Costen, 'Dunstan, Glastonbury and the economy of Somerset in the tenth century', in *St Dunstan. His Life, Times and Cult*, ed. N. Ramsay, M. Sparks and T. Tatton-Brown (1992), 25–44.
139. W.G. Hoskins, 'The Highland Zone in Domesday Book', in *Provincial England. Essays in Social and Economic History* (1965), 15–52.
140. Hooke, 'Regional variation', 141–50.
141. H.S.A. Fox, 'Field systems of East and South Devon, Part I: East Devon', *Dev Assoc, 104* (1972), 81–135.

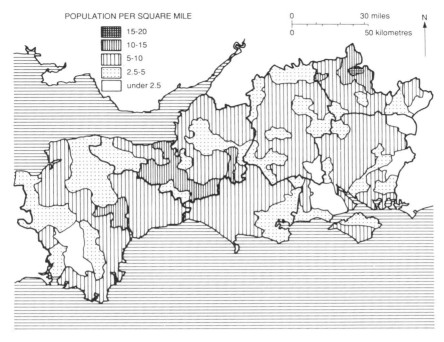

POPULATION PER SQUARE MILE

▦	15-20
▥	10-15
▥	5-10
⬚	2.5-5
☐	under 2.5

0   30 miles   N

0   50 kilometres

72. Distribution of population in 1086, from Domesday Book entries for Wessex [after H.C. Darby, *Domesday England* (1977), fig. 35 and D. Hill, *Atlas of Anglo-Saxon England* (1981), fig. 26]

crucial.[142] The large downland and other hill estates which were a feature of many areas of Wessex may have been ancient units of exploitation and consisted of blocks of land running from hilltop to valley bottom which therefore included a cross-section of locally available soils and types of land. When these were subdivided in the later Saxon period, characteristic long, thin estates were produced which each had a share of these varied resources.[143] The land beside the river could be used as meadow, the adjoining relatively flat but drier land provided the arable, and the hill slopes and hilltops could be used for sheep pasturage. The indifferent nature of a significant portion of the land probably accounts for why, in spite of the changes towards more intensive agriculture in some parts of the region, Wessex was not one of the most densely settled areas of England according to Domesday Book (fig. 72). However, distribution of the population was about average for England south of the Humber, except for areas with land with limited possibilities for exploitation, notably the high ground of

---

142. J. Thirsk, 'The origin of the common fields', *Past and Present, 133* (1966), 142–7; Fox, 'Adoption of the Midland system', 98–102.
143. C. Taylor, *Dorset* (1970), 51–78; Hooke, 'Regional variation', 176–91.

Devon and Somerset, the heathlands of Hampshire and Dorset, the Somerset levels, the poorly drained soils of the north of the Isle of Wight and the heavily forested areas of Wiltshire.[144] Inhabitants of these areas often had their own distinctive means of land exploitation, such as transhumance and a heavier reliance on animal husbandry.

THE FAMILY

In addition to the rights and obligations of lordship, the lives of individuals in Anglo-Saxon Wessex were affected by ties of kinship. The laws of Ine and Alfred, the only lawcodes that we can be certain were directed to a predominantly West Saxon audience, reveal various ways in which kinsmen had to take responsibility for their relatives. Kinsmen might have to ensure that compensation was paid for crimes committed by other members of the family, though, on the other hand they would pursue claims or vendettas on behalf of injured or dead kin and might themselves receive compensation in the latter case; Alfred's code records a judgement which must surely be based on an actual incident whereby, if one man killed another accidentally by allowing a tree to fall on him, the dead man's kindred were to be allowed the tree, providing they carried it away.[145] Occasional glimpses are provided of other services kindred were expected to perform, such as providing for orphaned relatives and bringing food for an imprisoned kinsman.[146] Individuals without kin were clearly in a vulnerable position as they might be robbed or killed with impunity if there was no one to safeguard their interests. But special categories, like foreign visitors, might look to the king for protection and the promise of vengeance for any crimes against their person,[147] while the man detained at his majesty's pleasure without kindred to hand would be fed by the royal reeve.

The laws do not indicate the degree of kindred who might be obliged to intervene on a kinsman's behalf, but there is no evidence to suggest the existence of large 'clans' at any stage in the development of Wessex.[148] At first sight the royal house, as it was constituted in the seventh and eighth centuries, might seem to contradict this point for it apparently consisted of many different branches claiming common ancestors in the sixth century. But although distant cousins might succeed one another to the throne,

144. Darby, *Domesday England*, 87–94, figs. 35 and 36.
145. Attenborough, 'Laws of Alfred', Ch. 13; H.R. Loyn, 'Kinship in Anglo-Saxon England', *ASE, 3* (1974), 197–209.
146. Attenborough, 'Laws of Ine', Ch. 38; 'Laws of Alfred', Ch. 2.
147. Attenborough, 'Laws of Ine', Ch. 23.
148. L. Lancaster, 'Kinship in Anglo-Saxon society', *British Journal of Sociology, 9* (1958), 230–48, 359–77.

there is no evidence that they identified with or supported each other's interests; on the contrary, they seem to have been in competition with one another and formed several rival families rather than an undivided 'royal house'.[149] Old English had no vocabulary to cover a complicated range of family relationships and no specialist words for kindred beyond descendants of a common grandfather. In the lawcodes the household seems to have been typically seen as consisting of husband, wife and children – though richer households might contain other individuals such as slaves and servants who were not usually kinsmen; a nobleman moving his residence was allowed in the laws of Ine to take his reeve, smith and children's nurse with him. When wills appear, which in Wessex only survive for leading members of the aristocracy, we can see that the main beneficiaries were close family members.[150] The testatrixes Wynflæd and Wulfwaru are mostly concerned with leaving lands and goods to their children or grandchildren; the will of Ealdorman Ælfheah (d. 970) includes only a slightly broader range of relatives, with gifts to siblings, a nephew and his more distant kinsman Æthelweard (subsequently ealdorman of the western shires) as well as his immediate family.[151]

The kinsmen who might be regarded as being responsible for an individual consisted of both paternal and maternal kin; the former were the more important and in some matters at least responsibilities and payments in Wessex were divided on the basis of two-thirds to the paternal and one-third to the maternal kin.[152] Presumably, as today, factors such as proximity and compatibility decided which relatives played the greatest roles in the lives of individuals. Where relatives were few relatively distant kin could assume greater importance; the nun Leoba sought the protection and friendship of her kinsman Boniface who was related to her mother as she had no closer kin.[153] No doubt those who were wealthy and powerful found themselves with many kinsmen who wished to press their relationship; Ælfheah's kinsman Æthelweard (the exact relationship is uncertain) who subsequently became an ealdorman was presumably a significant person in his own right whose goodwill Ælfheah was pleased to cultivate.[154] Many different sources of evidence testify to the strength of the bond between kin and the obligation that relatives felt to assist one another. Boniface did become, as Leoba wished, like a brother to her and arranged for her burial beside him at Fulda, although it was contrary to the law and spirit of the reforming church he encountered in Francia and by

---

149. See Chapter 2, 79–84.
150. Attenborough, 'Laws of Ine', Ch. 63; see also Ch. 38.
151. Whitelock, *Wills*, nos. 3, 8 and 9.
152. Attenborough, 'Laws of Alfred', Ch. 30.
153. Tangl, no. 29.
154. Williams, *'Princeps Merciorum gentis'*, 143–72.

which he had been influenced in many respects.[155] The letters of the West Saxons involved in the missions at home and abroad reveal that many were related to one another and that whole families were joined in missionary endeavour.[156] Family relationships were just as important in the later Anglo-Saxon Church; Bishop Ælfwold of Crediton was clearly from the local aristocracy and left bequests to four kinsmen and his brother-in-law Godric of Crediton.[157] A subsequent bishop of Crediton, Lyfing, combined the see with that of Cornwall which had previously been held by his own uncle; Bishop Herman of Ramsbury, a Lotharingian, complained he could not live on the revenues of Ramsbury because he had no relatives to hand to help support him.[158] The promotion of kin by churchmen could easily lead to accusations of corruption by later ages, especially if lay kin were granted church estates – an accusation made by church reformers in tenth-century Winchester against Bishop Denewulf (878×9–908), for instance.[159] Such behaviour should be seen as reflecting the pressure and obligation which kinsmen felt to support one another.

Church lands were particularly vulnerable to counter-claims from kindred. The anathemas of charters promise dire punishments for the kin of any donors who tried to reclaim lands, but these were clearly not sufficient to deter claimants, including kings. The history of Winchester's estate at Alresford documents a long-running battle between the bishopric and a noble family for control of the land. Bishop Tunbeorht (871×7–878×9) is recorded as having leased the land to the parents of the thegn Alfred; his reasons are not given, but such leases often seem to have been given for a lifetime to buy off claims to an estate.[160] Alfred succeeded in getting a renewal of the lease with reversion to Winchester, but Winchester's claim to the estate may have been seriously weakened, for when Alfred was found guilty of a crime the estate reverted to the Crown and the bishop of Winchester had to buy it back.[161] The claims of Alfred's family had not been defeated for Alfred's son Ælfric, also a king's thegn, persuaded King Eadwig to allow him the estate, though the decision was subsequently reversed by Eadwig's brother Edgar who returned the estate to Winchester.[162]

West Saxon nobles seem to have been ever alert to the possibility of pressing a hereditary claim to an estate as is brought out by the history of an estate at Fonthill (Wilts) in the late ninth and early

155. S. Hollis, *Anglo-Saxon Women and the Church* (1992), 113–50, 271–97.
156. See Chapter 4, 187.
157. S 1492; *EHD*, I, no. 122, 580–1.
158. F. Barlow, *The English Church 1000–1066* (2nd edn., 1979), 212–14, 220–1.
159. S 814/B 1150.
160. S 1287/B 617.
161. S 375/B 623.
162. S 589/B 938; S 814/B 1150.

tenth centuries.[163] A kinswoman of Æthelhelm Higa had sold the estate to Oswulf from whom it had passed to a certain Helmstan. Æthelhelm's first attempt to reclaim the estate was made after Helmstan was found guilty of theft, which would have seriously weakened his ability to defend himself on oath in the shire court. However, Helmstan had influential connections and the charters which proved his case. When Helmstan was subsequently found guilty of cattle rustling, Æthelhelm Higa seems to have tried again, but the estate had by then passed through the hands of Ealdorman Ordlaf to the bishopric of Winchester and the memoranda from which we learn the history of the estate seem to have been made by Ordlaf to counter Æthelhelm's claims. Æthelhelm was obliged to withdraw his suit.

The numerous attempts by West Saxon families to reclaim lands alienated by one of their members has helped form the hypothesis that before the advent of bookland much land would have been held as family land which (unlike land held by charter) could not be alienated from the family.[164] No specific reference to such a system of landholding is known, unless it is the folkland for which only a few references exist, none of which are clearly associated with Wessex.[165] However, Alfred did allow in his lawcode that bookland could not be alienated from a kindred if there was a specific injunction against it.[166] One reason why Alfred may have included the provision in his lawcode was that it was one of which he wished to make use. In his will Alfred decrees:

> I desire that the person to whom I have bequeathed my bookland should not dispose of it outside my kindred after their lifetime, but I desire that after their lifetime it should pass to my nearest of kin, unless any of them have children; then I prefer that it should pass to the child in the male line as long as any is worthy of it. My grandfather [King Egbert] had bequeathed his land on the spear side and not on the spindle side. If, then, I have given to any one on the female side what he acquired, my kinsmen are to pay for it, if they wish to have it during the lifetime [of the holders]; otherwise, it should go after their lifetime as we have previously stated. For this reason I say that they are to pay for it, because they are receiving my property, which I may give on the female side as well as on the male side, whichever I please.[167]

---

163. S 1445/B 591; S. Keynes, 'The Fonthill letter', in *Words, Texts and Manuscripts. Studies in Anglo-Saxon Culture Presented to Helmut Gneuss*, ed. M. Korhammer (1992), 53–97.
164. Wormald, *Bede and the Conversion of England*, 22–3.
165. Keynes and Lapidge, *Alfred the Great*, 308 and 325, but for a different interpretation E. John, *Orbis Britanniae and Other Studies* (1966), 64–127.
166. Attenborough, 'Laws of Alfred', Ch. 41.
167. Keynes and Lapidge, *Alfred the Great*, 173–8, 313–26.

Alfred is bequeathing booklands which he had acquired and could dispose of as he pleased and which he wishes should not be granted outside the family. He has inherited other booklands acquired by his grandfather Egbert who placed an injunction on them to the effect they should be granted to the male line only. It is likely that there were other royal lands over which Alfred had no rights of disposition and which perhaps would pass with the Crown.

The success of Alfred's family depended on the acquisition of substantial amounts of new land (some of which had once been granted to churches) and its careful husbanding by Alfred's grandfather Egbert, the founder of the branch's success, and his father Æthelwulf, whose testamentary provisions are alluded to by Alfred in his own will and in Asser's biography.[168] Alfred's brothers had agreed to keep the patrimony intact for whichever of them held the crown and Alfred had, as it were, won the jackpot as he was the last of the four brothers who survived Æthelwulf to rule. It is likely that the noble families which rose with the house of Egbert, like those of Athelstan Half-King or Ordlaf of the Fonthill case, tried to cultivate similar patrimonies for themselves and that these helped to sustain some of them in power until the old order was overturned in the reigns of Æthelred and Cnut. From the ninth and tenth centuries, when we have sufficient documents for the first time, we can see a desire by males of the royal house and aristocracy to establish their own lines with agnatic descent of land as an important element of this.

THE STATUS OF WOMEN

We have seen that the provisions in the wills of Alfred's family did not give female members of the royal house the same opportunities to own family land as men and the implication is that women had less standing in the family nexus. To a certain extent that was true; women were judged differently from men in West Saxon lawcodes and generally not to their advantage.[169] We can see, for example, the type of double standards operating in sexual matters which are common in many patriarchal societies. In Alfred's laws a man guilty of adultery had to pay compensation to the aggrieved husband, but there is no provision for payment to an aggrieved wife in a parallel situation. A nun abducted from a nunnery was presumed to have acquiesced in the act; the lord of the nunnery was compensated for the actions, but the nun was allowed no claim on her abductor's

---

168. Asser, Ch. 16, and see Ch. 3, 94–6.
169. A. Klinck, 'Anglo-Saxon women and the law', *Journal of Medieval History, 8* (1982), 107–22; M. Richards and J. Stanfield, 'Concepts of Anglo-Saxon women in the laws', in *New Readings on Women in Old English Literature*, ed. H. Damico and A.H. Olsen (Indiana, 1990), 89–99.

estate, though his kindred could claim their normal share of the wergeld if her child was slain![170] However, such legislation can be contrasted with the very real affection between kinsmen and kinswomen of which several instances have already been given. Although Alfred was anxious that women of the royal house should not dispose of land outside the family, he nevertheless made provision for a number of female relatives and insisted that male kinsmen should not take land away from them (evidently a very real possibility) without providing financial compensation.

In his *Life of Alfred* Asser devotes his first chapter to Alfred's descent in the male line, but his second chapter to Alfred's maternal ancestors who were clearly also of importance in enhancing his position. Alfred's mother Osburh was descended from the royal house of the Jutes of Wight, whose supposed founders Stuf and Wihtgar featured prominently in the annals describing the origins of Wessex in the *Anglo-Saxon Chronicle*, produced, of course, in Alfred's reign.[171] Osburh's Jutish blood also enabled Alfred to claim Scandinavian descent, which may have been important when Alfred wished to have his lordship recognized by Vikings and may be linked with the inclusion of Scandinavian ancestors in the West Saxon royal genealogy.[172] Alfred's position was enhanced through the connections he could claim through his mother, but Osburh's family must also have benefited from her marriage to King Æthelwulf because through her they became kinsmen of the royal house. Her father Oslac held the important position of *pincerna* ('butler') at the court of Æthelwulf, though we do not know whether he had received this position before or after the marriage. A number of prominent individuals with names whose first element was *Os* are known from the reigns of Alfred and his son Edward who could conceivably be members of Osburh's family.[173] They include Osferth, who received eight estates in Alfred's will and is called his kinsman. Another woman whose marriage to a king seems to have enhanced the position of her own family is that of Ælfthryth, the second wife of Edgar. Her father and brother probably owed their elevation to the office of ealdorman to the kinship with the royal house with which she provided them.[174] Kings like other individuals drew their closest relations from both their maternal and paternal kin and also felt the same obligations to aid their kindred.

170. Attenborough, 'Laws of Alfred', Ch. 10 and 8.
171. See Ch. 1, 36–9.
172. A.C. Murray, '*Beowulf*, the Danish invasions and royal genealogy', in *The Dating of Beowulf*, ed. C. Chase (Toronto, 1981), 101–12; J. Nelson, 'Reconstructing a royal family: reflections on Alfred', in *People and Places in Northern Europe 500–1600. Essays in Honour of Peter Hayes Sawyer*, ed. I. Wood and N. Lund (1991), 47–60.
173. Nelson, 'Reconstructing a royal family'.
174. H.P.R. Finberg, 'The house of Ordgar and the foundation of Tavistock Abbey', *EHR*, 58 (1943), 190–201.

73. Roundel of copper alloy with gold and silver repoussé foils from satchel in rich female barrow-burial on Swallowcliffe Down (Wilts) [photograph: Salisbury and South Wiltshire Museum]

West Saxon women might not generally be the equals of the men in their families, either the one they were born into or that they married into, but as members of a family group they shared in its status and would be superior to men of lesser birth. Rich male burials of the seventh century are matched, if not surpassed, by those of rich female burials, like those of Swallowcliffe (fig. 73) and Roundway Down (fig. 44) (Wilts).[175] Through marriage, as we have seen, women could even become the highest ranked members of their own kin-group; Queen Ælfthryth was the most influential person of her kin to whom relatives – and many others – turned for assistance.[176] Although daughters might not be as generously endowed as sons, many West Saxon women did inherit bookland or enjoyed it for their lifetimes. Women of high status would expect to have land settled on them when they married.[177] In addition to the

175. G. Speake, *A Saxon Bed Burial on Swallowcliffe Down*, English Heritage arch. rep., *10* (1989) – for Roundway Down see G. Speake, *Saxon Bed Burial*, 58, 80, 107, 110 and 126.

176. See, in particular, Robertson, *Charters*, nos. 45, 92–5; B.A.E. Yorke, 'Æthelwold and the politics of the tenth century', in *Bishop Æthelwold: His Career and Influence*, ed. B.A.E. Yorke (1988), 80–4.

177. M.A. Meyer, 'Land charters and the position of women in Anglo-Saxon England', in *The Women of England*, ed. B. Kanner (Hamden CT, 1982), 53–84; Klinck, 'Anglo-Saxon women and the law'.

arrangements for support during widowhood, which in Wessex seems to have consisted of a life interest in a third of the husband's property, women received on marriage a 'morning-gift' from their husbands over which they had rights of free disposal. Fonthill had been Æthelthryth's morning-gift which she had chosen to sell and Æthelhelm Higa, presumably a kinsman of her husband's, was unsuccessful in his attempts to reclaim the land.[178] The testatrix Wynflæd left the manor of Faccombe, her morning-gift, to her son, then to her daughter with reversion to her grandson (her son's son).[179] As landowners women had control of one of the main sources of power in Anglo-Saxon Wessex and might have to perform the public duties which came with landownership. A certain Wynflæd, who may be the same person as the testatrix, defended her right to two estates in Berkshire in public court, and of the twenty-four oath-helpers she produced to support her claim, thirteen were women, including two abbesses; she also had the support of Queen Ælfthryth, who was apparently a witness to the transaction by which Wynflæd had acquired the land.[180] Wynflæd was probably a widow at the time of the court case, as all the West Saxon women who have left wills seem to have been, and it would appear that widows enjoyed more independence of action than wives.

There was no absolute bar on women achieving positions usually held by men. The West Saxon regnal list is the only one from Anglo-Saxon England to include the rule of a queen, namely that of Seaxburh, widow of Cenwalh, though she only ruled for a year.[181] Whether Seaxburh ruled by virtue of being Cenwalh's widow, mother to his heirs or in her own right is not known. In the later Anglo-Saxon period the restriction of the throne to the sons of kings might provide opportunities for their mothers to exercise power during the reigns of young sons.[182] Eadgifu was an important influence on her sons Edmund and Eadred, and Ælfthryth probably even more powerful during the minority of her son Æthelred Unræd. However, women were not generally expected to take on the same roles as men and, in particular, to have a public role. A verse from the *Exeter Book* warns:

> It is fitting for a woman to be busy with her needle. A roving woman spreads rumour: often people defame her with shameful deeds; men speak of her insultingly; her beauty often fades.[183]

178. S 1445/B 591.
179. Whitelock, *Wills*, no. 3, 10–15.
180. Robertson, *Charters*, no. 66, 136–9.
181. See Ch. 2, 82.
182. P. Stafford, 'The king's wife in Wessex 800–1066', *Past and Present, 91* (1981), 3–27.
183. As cited by M. Clunies Ross, 'Concubinage in Anglo-Saxon England', *Past and Present, 108* (1985), 3–34, at 9.

Ælfthryth, perhaps the most powerful of all West Saxon queens, was a victim of such rumours. Tales about her involvement in the death of her first husband and murder of her stepson Edward the Martyr circulated and were gleefully written down by Anglo-Norman historians such as William of Malmesbury and the Worcester chronicler ('Florence') who paint her as the worst type of termagant.[184] Women needed the backing of powerful relatives or other men if they were to survive in a man's world and were vulnerable to challenges to their position. This was acknowledged in an addition to Æthelwold's account of the reforms of Edgar's reign which urged abbesses in particular not 'to give God's estates either to kinsmen or secular grand persons, neither for money or flattery',[185] a statement which seems to leave much unsaid about the type of pressures which might be put upon them.

As part of their kin-group women might receive a share in the family's power and wealth and so some of the wealthiest women in the country would have been in Wessex, but it was more difficult for them to achieve the type of public roles that might be filled by their male kinsmen or to escape the supervision of male relatives. There were assumptions about the roles and behaviour appropriate to women which we might describe as misogynistic, and these had been enhanced rather than diluted by the adoption of Christianity.[186] It is true that the Church did provide new roles for women and that abbesses like Bugga and Cuthburh could be powerful individuals within it, but their power really stemmed from the fact that they were princesses, though seventh and eighth-century Wessex was characterized by fewer foundations for royal women than some of the other Anglo-Saxon kingdoms. To a churchman like Lul it would be quite normal to accept Abbess Cynethryth as his lord, for she was of royal descent and so of higher birth than himself.[187] However, the greater knowledge of church teachings acquired as a result of the Carolingian Renaissance was antithetical to women playing an active role in the Church, and royal nuns of the tenth century like Eadburga and Edith did not have the same opportunities as some of their predecessors, even though they were apparently more likely to become saints. There were more nunneries in tenth and eleventh-century Wessex than there had been earlier, and they remained more subject to the wishes of their founding kin-group (i.e. in most cases the royal house) than did the minsters and monasteries.[188] Although much of

---

184. C.E. Wright, *The Cultivation of Saga in Anglo-Saxon England* (1939), 146–71.
185. *EHD*, I, 992–3.
186. Ross, 'Concubinage'; Hollis, *Anglo-Saxon Women and the Church*.
187. See Chapter 4, 186–7.
188. S. Ridyard, *The Royal Saints of Anglo-Saxon England* (1988), 96–154; B.A.E. Yorke, '"Sisters under the skin?" Anglo-Saxon nuns and nunneries in southern England', *Medieval Women in Southern England, Reading Medieval Studies, 15* (1989), 95–118.

the discussion on women has of necessity had to draw on material about royal or noble women there is no reason why *mutatis mutandis* much of it should not also apply to women of lower birth and it is likely too that they experienced both circumscription and support from their roles within their kin-groups.

CLASS AND SOCIAL MOBILITY

There were certain factors about West Saxon society which would have promoted social stability and pre-eminent among these was its class system. The early lawcodes of Ine and Alfred recognized four main classes, those of noble, *geneat*, ceorl and slave, each distinguished by the wergeld payment to which they were entitled, that is the compensation payable if they were killed and from which other compensatory payments were calculated on a *pro rata* basis; however, in the case of the slave generally payments were made to their owners rather than themselves. The payments for the three other groups were 1,200, 600 and 200 shillings respectively.[189] The 600-shilling group is perhaps the most difficult to define, but may be that elusive group of freemen (the *geneat* of *Rectitudines*) who were generally the thegns of other lords besides the king and might form part of their lord's military entourage. A Briton with five hides was allotted a 600s wergild in Ine's laws which seem to recognize a greater number of class divisions among the British peasantry than are formally acknowledged among the Anglo-Saxons. However, a close reading of the codes suggests that there were similar distinctions between rent-paying peasants (*gafolgelda*) and those who had less land, and such subdivisions were, as we have seen, recognized in late Saxon documents like the *Rectitudines*. At a simple level it might appear that the social structure of Wessex remained unchanged during the period covered by written records.

To project further back beyond the lawcodes to a time before written records is a risky business and those who have tried to equate variations in the provision of grave-goods with the class divisions of the lawcodes have come in for criticism.[190] Nevertheless, the grave-goods from cemeteries in eastern Wessex do seem to indicate that there were considerable variations in wealth and in social status. One important distinction appears to have been between men buried with weapons and those without them, and a further distinction can be drawn between those buried only with a

---

189. Attenborough, 'Laws of Ine', 70; Attenborough, 'Laws of Alfred', 10, 25–8, 39–40; Finberg, *Agrarian History*, 438–41, 450–1.
190. C.J. Arnold, 'Wealth and social structure: a matter of life and death', in *Anglo-Saxon Cemeteries, 1979*, ed. P. Rahtz, T. Dickinson and L. Watts, BAR, *81* (1980), 81–142.

spear or spear and shield and an elite with a greater range or number of weapons, such as a sword, seax or axe, and often other prestige items as well.[191] Weapons are not just found with men who could have had actual careers as warriors, but could be buried with boys and those suffering from physical defects which would have precluded a life as a warrior, such as an individual believed to have had spina bifida from the cemetery at Berinsfield near Dorchester-on-Thames (Oxon).[192] Such burials suggest that weapon burials signalled rank which could be inherited – an assumption basic to the West Saxon lawcodes – though Heinrich Härke has also suggested that they may be a statement of ethnicity, that is of Germanic descent. Burial practices appear to have changed in the seventh century, but before the absorption of Christianity, with the proportion of adult males buried with weapons declining significantly, but with the elite apparently signalling their status even more ostentatiously than before.[193] Possibly what can be seen here are the results of the spread of West Saxon kingship with the elites who had controlled smaller independent/quasi-independent groups now becoming (or being replaced by) king's thegns. That would not necessarily be a decline in status, for a king's thegn of an expanding kingdom might have greater opportunities to acquire wealth than the leader of a smaller concern.[194] The change in status though might subtly alter his relations with his followers. However, if Heinrich Härke is correct in seeing weapon-burial in Wessex as a statement of ethnicity, it may be that by the seventh century the distinction between those of British and those of Germanic descent in eastern Wessex had become meaningless; something else which might also be connected with the formation of new kingdoms.

It may be that in the fifth and sixth centuries the kindred as a sort of self-help group was of vital importance in providing the individual with protection. However, the message of the lawcodes, and the view which kings presumably wished to promote, was that although the kin-group had its role, the ties of lordship were more important. Thus a man might fight on behalf of a relative who was attacked unjustly without incurring a vendetta providing it did not involve him fighting against his lord.[195] The relative strengths of the ties of lordship and kinship are stressed in the account of the ætheling Cyneheard's attack on King Cynewulf recorded in the *Anglo-Saxon Chronicle*, which may possibly have been composed to

---

191. H. Härke, 'The Anglo-Saxon weapon burial rite', *Past and Present, 126* (1990), 22–43.
192. Härke, 'Anglo-Saxon weapon burial rite', 36.
193. H. Geake, 'Burial practice in seventh and eighth-century England', in *The Age of Sutton Hoo*, ed. M. Carver (1992), 83–94; Härke, 'Changing symbols in a changing society', 149–66.
194. See below, 288–9.
195. Attenborough, 'Laws of Alfred', 42.

make this very point.[196] When after the attack Cynewulf's men ride up the ætheling tries to deflect their vengeance:

> And then the ætheling offered them money and land on their own terms, if they would allow him the kingdom, and told them that kinsmen of theirs, who would not desert him, were with him. Then they replied that no kinsman was dearer to them than their lord, and they would never serve his slayer; and they offered their kinsmen that they might go away unharmed. Their kinsmen said that the same offer had been made to their comrades who had been with the king. Moreover they said that they would pay no regard to it, any more than did your comrades who were slain along with the king.

Lordship, as we have seen, was one of the transforming facets of West Saxon society. Every man must have a lord according to the Anglo-Saxon lawcodes, and a law of Athelstan regarded it as the responsibility of kinsmen to ensure that a 'lordless man from whom no legal satisfaction could be obtained' should be provided with a lord.[197] For, as this code makes clear, it was the lord who was responsible for the public standing of his men in relationship to royal officialdom. The role of the kindred came to be seen as looking after the social welfare of their relatives, though they might also be called upon to enforce judgements of royal officials and lords.

Although social position was dependent to a certain extent on inherited caste, from an early period West Saxon kings seem to have been successful in ensuring that royal service was also an essential element, and that could be one factor ensuring a certain social mobility.[198] Being born into the right family would get a young man entrée to the royal court, but only royal favour and service could ensure that he became a king's thegn. Land and position could be forfeited to the king for serious crimes. In practice kings did tend to favour the same families and the sons of an ealdorman had a good chance of becoming ealdormen themselves: Æthelweard was followed in the position of ealdorman of western Wessex by a son, grandson and husband of a granddaughter. The problem for kings came if a family became so entrenched in power that it came to threaten royal interests. King Æthelred Unræd dealt harshly with men he suspected of disloyalty, in Wessex as elsewhere, but it could be argued that his actions were counter-

---

196. *Chronicle s.a.* 757; S.D. White, 'Kinship and lordship in early medieval England: the story of Sigeberht, Cynewulf and Cyneheard', *Viator*, 20 (1989), 1–18; and see Ch. 2.
197. Attenborough, 'II Athelstan', Ch. 2; Abels, *Lordship and Military Obligation*, 79–96.
198. W. Runciman, 'Accelerating social mobility: the case of Anglo-Saxon England', *Past and Present*, 104 (1984), 3–30.

productive and weakened the country's resistance to Viking attack. His son Edward the Confessor found that he was ultimately unable to enforce exile on Earl Godwine and his sons.[199] In spite of their obligations to the king as their lord, powerful men of the later Anglo-Saxon period might be swayed by their own obligations to kinsmen and commended men, even in Wessex where arguably royal power was strongest. The Fonthill letter, which is one of the few surviving documents to give a real feel of how power structures worked in Anglo-Saxon Wessex, shows how Ealdorman Ordlaf twice intervened to save the disreputable Helmstan from the full force of the law.[200] He was encouraged to do so partly by the fact that Helmstan recognized Ordlaf as his lord by surrendering his estate at Fonthill to him and receiving it back for his lifetime and because he was obligated by ties of spiritual kinship, which were as binding – or perhaps more binding – than familial ties, for Ordlaf had been sponsor at Helmstan's confirmation.[201]

The possibility of rising through service was not just one which affected the upper end of society. In the *Geþyncþo* we are presented with a ceorl who might aspire to thegnhood and one of his characteristics was the possession of a 'special office in the king's hall', that is he was in the king's service,[202] and there were a multitude of lesser administrative positions which a king could bestow as well as the great offices.[203] Nobles too needed administrators and men to fill their military quotas. The *Rectitudines*, in addition to presenting a survey of peasantry heavily burdened with labour services, lists manorial officials who were presumably drawn from the peasantry as well and might have various opportunities to further their own interests.[204] In fact, situations which might be disastrous for some would furnish opportunities for others and as the Anglo-Saxon era was one which was subject to periodic disasters, both natural ones such as famine, pestilence and bad weather and man-made ones such as war, it experienced greater social mobility than its apparently rigid class system might at first suggest.[205] At the two extremes of our period Gildas and Archbishop Wulfstan (who knew *De Excidio*) wrote vividly of the disruption to their societies caused primarily by the attacks of, in Gildas's case, Anglo-Saxons and, in Wulfstan's, Vikings.[206] Wulfstan, who believed in a God-given social order and was horrified by what he considered to be a 'world turned

199. S. Keynes, *The Diplomas of King Æthelred 'the Unready' 978–1016* (1980), 176–231; and see Ch. 3, 146–7.
200. S 1445/B 591; Keynes, 'The Fonthill letter'.
201. Attenborough, 'Laws of Ine', Ch. 76; J.H. Lynch, *Godparents and Kinship in Early Medieval Europe* (Princeton, 1986).
202. *EHD*, I, 468–9; Williams, 'A bell-house and a burh-geat', 225–6.
203. J. Campbell, 'Some agents and agencies of the late Anglo-Saxon state', in *Domesday Studies*, ed. J.C. Holt (1987), 201–18.
204. *EHD*, II. 875–9; see above.
205. Runciman, 'Social mobility'.
206. Winterbottom, *Gildas*, Ch. 23–6; *EHD*, I, 928–34.

upside down' during the reign of Æthelred, gave an extreme example whereby a slave running away to join the Vikings might be in a position to enslave his former master and take his position. Certainly Cnut's accession did bring a dramatic reversal of fortune for some aristocratic families as some leading nobles were executed (and family lands may have been confiscated) while others such as Earl Godwine were promoted.[207]

Birth and royal service were not the only routes to social enhancement; wealth was an important element as well. The socially-upward ceorl not only needed a position in royal service, but the wealth with which to purchase the accoutrements of thegnhood. At the other social extreme, inability to be able to pay debts or royal dues could lead to a loss of status and even reduction to slavery. An increase in royal demands may have led to more economic hardship for many in the later Anglo-Saxon period, but there were probably also more opportunities in the later period for West Saxons to amass personal wealth. It would appear that even *gebures* were sometimes able to better themselves, and two at Bedwyn (Wilts) were able to purchase their release 'out of *geburland*' for 300 pence during the tenth century.[208] Agricultural exploitation and royal service were not the only routes to wealth and social advancement. The *Geþyncþo*, in the version in the *Textus Roffensis*, records that:

> If a trader prospered, that he crossed thrice the open sea at his own expense, he was then afterwards entitled to the rights of a thegn.[209]

The growth in towns and trade, to be examined in greater detail in the final chapter, is another important example of developments in society and economy which occurred during the Anglo-Saxon period.

We have a clearer picture of society in Wessex at the end of the Anglo-Saxon period than we do at the beginning which, of course, makes it difficult to recognize exactly where changes have occurred. The simplified classifications in the lawcodes can give an impression of relative stability within Anglo-Saxon society and at a certain level it could be said that within a pre-industrial Christian society one will find, as Alfred defined in his translation of Boethius, the three main classes of 'praying men, fighting men and working men'.[210] As

207. K. Mack, 'Changing thegns: Cnut's conquest and the English aristocracy', *Albion*, 16 (1984), 375–87.
208. H.P.R. Finberg, *The Formation of England* (1974), 66; Runciman, 'Social mobility', 20–1.
209. *EHD*, I, 468–9.
210. Keynes and Lapidge, *Alfred the Great*, 132. This is one of the earliest written appearances of the concept of the 'three orders' in medieval society: see G. Duby, *The Three Orders: Feudal Society Imagined* (1980), especially 99–109.

the last group had to support through their labours the first two groups as well as themselves, it is not surprising to find that the lives of many of the peasantry were circumscribed throughout the period for which we have written sources. On the other hand, there are definite signs of change occurring within the Anglo-Saxon period. Archaeological studies, for instance, have shown a shift in many parts of Wessex away from the individual farmstead or hamlet towards the nucleated village as the characteristic form of rural settlement. Although there were no doubt many factors involved, one that must be counted significant is the growth of lordship in its many different manifestations. Rights and obligations were probably more vigorously defined at the end of the Anglo-Saxon period than they had been earlier, with kings leading the way in exploiting those subject to them. At the same time later Anglo-Saxon Wessex had a more diverse society than that of the earlier period. There were career opportunities in the Church, in trade and in royal administration, in addition to those of warrior and agricultural labourer, even if the options of certain groups such as women and slaves were limited.

7 Trade and the growth of towns

TRADE AND THE TRANSFER OF COMMODITIES C. 400–650

It is likely that most settlement units in early Wessex were characterized by a high degree of self-sufficiency. Chalton (Hants), for instance, had a mixed farming economy, with sheep the most important of the animals kept, but could also draw on resources of surrounding countryside, especially woodland – the most obvious surviving sign of this in the excavations was deer bones.[1] Loom-weights, spindle-whorls and thread-pickers testified to the sheep's wool being processed to make textiles on the site, and small-scale smithing and bronze-casting were carried out, probably recycling metalwork rather than working from raw materials. Nevertheless some items needed to be acquired from outside. Oyster shells presumably indicate the acquisition of shellfish from south coast communities, and an essential item they may also have provided would have been salt. Non-essential, luxury items were represented by sherds of north French pottery and a hanging-bowl escutcheon. The range of goods from cemeteries also suggests that most early Anglo-Saxon communities possessed a variety of goods that could not have been made on their estates. Some items would have been made within England including specialist metalwork such as weapons and brooches which seem to have been important indicators of status in early Saxon Wessex as well as being of practical use. Some of the objects would have been made locally but presumably by specialist craftsmen. The varieties of disc and cast saucer brooches which are most frequently found with female burials in the upper Thames were probably manufactured in the region,[2] and so would have been a

---

1. P. Addyman and D. Leigh, 'The Anglo-Saxon village at Chalton, Hampshire: second interim report', *Med Arch, 17* (1973), 1–25; B. Cunliffe, *Wessex to AD 1000* (1993), 290–1.
2. T.M. Dickinson, 'The Anglo-Saxon burial sites of the Upper Thames region and their bearing upon the History of Wessex' (D. Phil. thesis, Oxford University, 1979); T.M. Dickinson, 'On the origin and chronology of the early Anglo-Saxon disc brooch', *ASSAH, 1*, BAR, *72* (1979), 39–80.

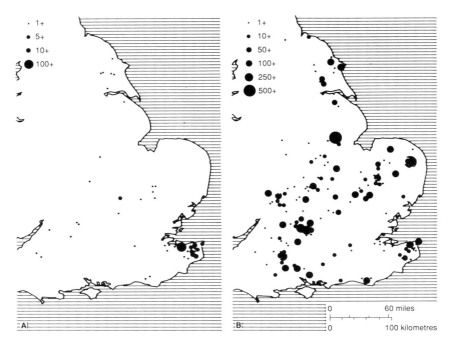

74. Distribution of (a) amethyst beads and (b) amber beads in early
Anglo-Saxon cemeteries [after J.W. Huggett, ' Imported grave-goods
and the early Anglo-Saxon economy', *Med. Arch. 32* (1988), 63–96]

distinctive form of shield boss (Dickinson and Härke group 4) more
commonly found there than anywhere else in the Germanic
settlement area.[3] Upper Thames brooches were also more widely
circulated, occurring in cemeteries in Hampshire and Wiltshire, for
example. Most of the West Saxon cemeteries also have a few
examples of brooches apparently made outside the Wessex region,
with Kent one of the commonest sources of supply. Objects from
overseas are rarer, but amber beads, which were probably imported,
are relatively widely dispersed (fig. 74).[4]

The richer graves of the late sixth and seventh centuries, which
were characteristically under barrows or burial mounds, contain a
larger selection of items imported from elsewhere in Britain and
from overseas, and it may be presumed that these were prestigious
objects to which access was restricted. The limited number of
findspots in Wessex of amethyst beads, which probably came from
the Mediterranean, can be contrasted with the relatively prolific

3. T.M. Dickinson and H. Härke, *Early Anglo-Saxon Shields (Archaeologia, 110)*
    (1992), 17–19, 24.
4. J.W. Huggett, 'Imported grave goods and the early Anglo-Saxon economy', *Med
    Arch, 32* (1988), 63–96, at 64–6.

distribution of amber beads (fig. 74).[5] Prestige items whose origins can be ascertained include silver-gilt, inlaid brooches and buckles from Kent; pails and cauldrons from Byzantium; metalwork, glass and crystal balls from Francia. The importation of luxury goods from overseas was not limited to eastern Wessex. The British communities of western Wessex were also able to acquire foreign items of which the most visible is pottery, fine table wares and amphorae which may have contained wine or oil, from the Mediterranean.[6] Some glassware may have come from the same source,[7] and it is tempting to see a Byzantine censor, discovered just outside the monastic precinct at Glastonbury, as another example of the trade, but it must remain uncertain whether it arrived in Glastonbury before the Anglo-Saxon conquest.[8]

There may also have been some transfer of commodities between British and Saxon Wessex. Excavations at South Cadbury (Som) produced two pieces of Germanic metalwork: a gilt bronze button brooch of a type probably manufactured somewhere in central southern England (perhaps on the Isle of Wight) and a silver ring with style I zoomorphic decoration;[9] and three Saxon brooches have been found in Ilchester (Som).[10] Glass vessels, beads and some metalwork items found at Cadbury Congresbury (Som) may have been imported from eastern Wessex,[11] as may have been a pail and a blue-glass jar carefully deposited in a shaft at Pagan's Hill (Som).[12] Christopher Loveluck has suggested that tin, used in the production of copper alloy objects in the upper Thames, may have been one commodity that went eastwards in exchange.[13] In the seventh century objects of Celtic origin were among the prestige goods included in rich burials in western Wessex, though it is not always certain where they were manufactured. Such objects include hanging-bowls; two of similar form and decoration came from male burials at Oliver's Battery (Winchester), and Lowbury Hill (Berks), and others were included in burials at Chessell Down (I of W), Ford

5. Huggett, 'Imported grave goods', 64–8, 90–4.
6. M. Fulford, 'Byzantium and Britain: a Mediterranean perspective on post-Roman Mediterranean imports in Western Britain and Ireland', *Med Arch*, *33* (1989), 1–6; C. Thomas, '"*Gallici nautae de Galliarum provinciis*" – a sixth/seventh century-trade with Gaul reconsidered', *Med Arch*, *34* (1990), 1–26.
7. J. Price, 'The glass', in *Cadbury Congresbury 1968–73. A Late/Post Roman Hilltop Settlement in Somerset*, ed. P. Rahtz, BAR, *223* (1992), 131–43.
8. L. Webster and J. Backhouse (eds), *The Making of England, Anglo-Saxon Art and Culture AD 600–900* (1991), 94.
9. L. Alcock, 'Cadbury-Camelot: a fifteen-year perspective', *PBA*, *68* (1982), 355–88, at 378–9; and for the button brooches see C. Arnold, *The Anglo-Saxon Cemeteries of the Isle of Wight* (1982), 104–5.
10. P. Leach, *Ilchester. Vol. I: Excavations 1974–5* (1982), 12.
11. Rahtz (ed.), *Cadbury Congresbury*, 237–8.
12. P. Rahtz and L. Watts, 'Pagan's Hill revisited', *Arch J*, *146* (1989), 330–71.
13. Paper at conference on 'The Anglo-Saxons in the Thames valley', Oxford 1993.

and Wilton (Wilts).[14] The rich female burial at Swallowcliffe Down (Wilts) contained the very rare find of a bronze sprinkler which is likely to have been of Celtic manufacture, while some of the foils included in a satchel mount may be of 'British' origin (fig. 73).[15] Another rich female burial from Wiltshire, at Roundway Down, contained a pin-set which incorporated a blue-glass stud whose closest parallels are from Ireland (fig. 44).[16]

It is likely that different types of transaction lay behind the varying distribution of commodities.[17] Items with a widespread distribution, such as the brooches manufactured in the upper Thames and the amber beads, are most likely to have been acquired through trade. Exactly how such trade was carried on we do not know, but itinerant merchants are indicated in the earliest lawcodes.[18] It has also been envisaged that people would gather together for certain occasions such as religious festivals or district meetings when trading could have taken place, but there is no hard evidence for such activities in Wessex for the period before the advent of written records.[19] Huggett in his analysis of early trading patterns has suggested that local peaks, represented in the distribution map of amber beads by graves with particularly large concentrations of beads at Long Wittenham/Abingdon (Berks) and Collingbourne Ducis (Wilts), may be a guide to local centres of 'redistribution' (fig. 74).[20] Of course, trade is likely also to have involved many substances which have not survived for archaeologists to discover, but whose desirability and restricted availability may be indicated in later written sources, items such as salt or honey, for instance.[21]

Some objects may have been acquired through trade, that is an exchange of commodities, but have a distribution that was governed by other factors such as gift-exchange. The exchange of gifts between peers to seal alliances, peace treaties and marriages and the giving of gifts between lords and clients to secure services are practices well evidenced in the written sources of early medieval Europe and an essential part of the exercise of power and social relationships during the period.[22] It has been proposed, for instance, that the imported pottery in western Wessex may have been part of what was

---

14. S. Youngs (ed.), *'The Work of Angels', Masterpieces of Celtic Metalwork, 6th–9th Centuries* (1989), 48–9; J. Brennan, *Hanging Bowls and their Contexts*, BAR, *220* (1991).
15. G. Speake, *A Saxon Bed Burial on Swallowcliffe Down*, English Heritage arch. rep., *10* (1989), 30–43, 58–80.
16. Youngs (ed.), *'Work of Angels'*, 53–4.
17. Huggett, 'Imported grave goods', 94–6.
18. See below, 299–300.
19. P. Sawyer, 'Kings and merchants', in *Early Medieval Kingship*, ed. P. Sawyer and I.N. Wood (1977), 139–58, at 145–6.
20. Huggett, 'Imported grave goods', 90–1.
21. Sawyer, 'Kings and merchants', 146–9.
22. See n. 6; Rahtz, *Cadbury Congresbury*, 238–42.

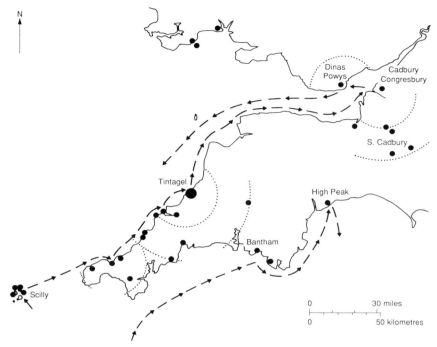

75. Distribution of imported pottery finds of fifth and sixth centuries
in south-west Britain, with conjectural reconstructions of trade-routes
and landfalls [after C. Thomas, '"Gallici nautae de Galliarum
provinciis" – a sixth/seventh century trade with Gaul reconsidered',
Med. Arch. 34 (1990), 1–26]

exchanged by merchants from the Mediterranean for metal ores of
the West Country. One of the grounds for the hypothesis is the *Life
of St John the Almsgiver* who is reported to have made such a voyage
and returned with a cargo of half tin and half *nomisma*, possibly
bronze Roman coins – a small group of them were found at Cadbury
Congresbury.[23] One route may have travelled up the west coast of
Cornwall and into the Bristol Channel calling at Tintagel (where the
largest concentration of imported pottery has been found) for tin and
along the north Somerset coast for lead and silver from the Mendips.
Devon tin could have been collected from landfalls in south Devon,
and the site of Bantham, which has produced imported pottery, but
only appears to have been seasonally occupied, could have been one
of these (fig. 75).[24] However, the cargoes of luxury items such as

---

23. P. Grierson, 'Commerce in the Dark Ages: a critique of the evidence', *TRHS, 9*
    (1959), 123–40.
24. A. Fox, 'Some evidence for a Dark Age trading site at Bantham, near
    Thurlestone, South Devon', *Ant J. 35* (1955), 55–67; F.M. Griffith, 'Salvage
    observations at the Dark Age site at Bantham Ham, Thurlestone, in 1982',
    PDAS, 44 (1986), 39–57.

wine, glass and fine tableware may not have gone on the open market in the West Country, but stayed in the hands of local potentates who may have overseen the transactions and would pass some of the contents on to their own clients. Finds of the imported items are generally restricted to what appear to have been high status sites such as Cadbury Congresbury (the second largest findspot in south-west England), Glastonbury Tor and South Cadbury.

Gift-exchange may also account for the limited circulation of some luxury commodities in eastern Wessex as well. Many such items were either made in Kent or are of Frankish or Byzantine origin (the latter probably transported via Francia) and more commonly found in Kent than in eastern Wessex. It is therefore likely that many of these luxury goods came to eastern Wessex through Kent and may reflect, or even be one of the means of underpinning, the overlordship Kent seems to have enjoyed in south-east England at the turn of the sixth century.[25] One such item is the early seventh-century silver-gilt buckle with applied gold plates and filigree from the cemetery at Alton (Hants) (fig. 76).[26] The buckle was probably made in Kent where eight similar ones are known and the only findspots of such buckles outside Kent, in addition to Alton, are the 'princely burials' at Taplow (Bucks) and Broomfield (Essex). The buckle is an exceptional object within the Alton cemetery and Professor Evison has suggested its owner was likely to have been the 'leading man in the district' and its presence a sign that he was under Kentish overlordship.[27] The 'Kentish orientation' of eastern Hampshire in the early seventh century is also suggested by the hoard of thrymsas and tremisses found at Crondall in 1828, for most of the coins were of Kentish or Merovingian origin.[28] The Isle of Wight, and especially the cemetery at Chessell Down, has also produced a significant number of Kentish and Frankish objects, apparently of sixth-century date.[29] The Isle of Wight's links with Kent are symbolized by their rulers' claims for a common Jutish origin;[30] the exceptionally rich female burial at Chessell Down (grave 45) has so much material which is otherwise typical of a rich Kentish woman's grave that it has been proposed that she may

---

25. S. Chadwick Hawkes, 'Anglo-Saxon Kent c. 425–725', in *Archaeology in Kent to AD 1500*, ed. P.E. Leach, CBA rep., *48* (1982), 64–78; R. Hodges, *Dark Age Economics: The Origins of Towns and Trade AD 600–1000* (1982), 29–46.
26. V. Evison, *An Anglo-Saxon Cemetery at Alton, Hants*, Hampshire Field Club monograph, *4* (1988), 18–20.
27. Evison, *Anglo-Saxon Cemetery*, 45.
28. C.H.V. Sutherland, *Anglo-Saxon Gold Coinage in the Light of the Crondall Hoard* (1948); I. Stewart, 'Anglo-Saxon gold coins', in *Scripta Nummaria Romana. Essays Presented to Humphrey Sutherland*, ed. R. Carson and C.M. Kraay (1978), 143–72; D.M. Metcalf, *Thrymsas and Sceattas in the Ashmolean Museum Oxford*, I (1993), 29–62.
29. Arnold, *Cemeteries of the Isle of Wight*.
30. B.A.E. Yorke, 'The Jutes of Hampshire and Wight and the origins of Wessex', in *The Origins of Anglo-Saxon Kingdoms*, ed. S. Bassett (1989), 84–96.

76. Silver-gilt buckle from cemetery at Alton (Hants), probably of early seventh-century date. Decoration includes gold filigree, garnets, shell, stylised bird-heads and interlaced animals [photograph: D. Allen]

actually have been a high status Kentishwoman married into the ruling dynasty of Wight to strengthen the relationship between the two kingdoms (fig. 12).[31] However, we should not rule out the

---

31. Arnold, *Cemeteries of the Isle of Wight*, 26–8, 50–72, 106–7.

possibility that Wight had its own links to Francia, as by the eighth century there seem to have been a number of landfalls in the Solent used by Frankish and other merchants.

Kentish and Frankish material has also been found in the cemeteries of the upper Thames and while some of it may indicate the results of Kentish - or, indeed, Frankish[32] – overlordship or diplomacy, the Thames could have provided the Germanic settlers with their own route to the sea, while its tributaries could have connected the region, on the one hand, with trade routes from the Wash (see distribution of amber beads in fig. 74) and, on the other, with western Wessex. The upper Thames area's involvment in trade in the late sixth and early seventh centuries is also suggested by finds of scales and weights from burials in the region for, as Chris Scull has shown, Kent and the upper Thames are the only areas in southern England where they have been found.[33] Particularly notable was a male burial at Watchfield (Oxon, originally Berks) which was equipped with a balance and set of weights (including Iron Age and Roman coins) in a leather case.[34] The upper Thames is also a likely candidate for the place of minting of the issue of thrymsas coinage which has a runic inscription beginning *BENU*.[35] There were no *BENU* coins in the Crondall hoard, possibly because they were not in circulation when it was put together, but the absence might also indicate different patterns of monetary circulation. The possibility of coins with a runic inscription being produced in the upper Thames is particularly interesting, as the case containing the scales and weights at Watchfield had a copper alloy fitting with a runic inscription and use of runes seems to have been very rare in early Saxon Wessex; the only other place in the region from which they are known is the Isle of Wight.[36]

However, the interpretation of much of this material is controversial. It is disputed, for instance, whether coins were used in this period for commercial transactions (as opposed to social or symbolic ones) and whether the issues should be seen as royally controlled or not.[37] It is uncertain whether the individual buried at Watchfield with the balance, and other material commoner in Kent or Merovingian Francia than in the upper Thames, was a native of the area or an itinerant trader or other traveller.[38] The weighing of bullion implied by the scales and weights may not have been exclusively for trading purposes, but rather connected with other

32. I. Wood, *The Merovingian North Sea* (Alingsås, 1983).
33. C. Scull, 'Scales and weights in early Anglo-Saxon England', *Arch J, 147* (1990), 183–215.
34. C. Scull, 'Excavations and survey at Watchfield, Oxfordshire, 1983–92', *Arch J, 149* (1992), 124–281.
35. Metcalf, *Thrymsas and Sceattas*, 31–2.
36. Two examples are known; Arnold, *Cemeteries of the Isle of Wight*, 60, 107 and fig. 76.
37. For example, see Metcalf, *Thrymsas and Sceattas*, 10–25, compared to P. Grierson and M. Blackburn, *Medieval European Coinage*, I (1986), 158–9.
38. Scull, 'Watchfield', 261–2.

payments, for instance, of the type of fines recorded in the earliest lawcodes.[39] The interpretation of the runic inscription on his case is also disputed, including whether the runes are of Anglo-Saxon or Continental type. One suggested reading is *hæriboki: wusæ* which Bengt Odenstedt translates as '(These are) army (account) "books". Wusa (kept them)', raising the exciting possibility that its owner may have had some official position in the emergent Gewissan kingdom.[40] It would appear that objects which could be interpreted as being indicative of trade (coins, scales and weights) might alternatively, or additionally, be linked with the exercise of kingship. The two areas of eastern Wessex with the greatest concentrations of imported materials, that is the upper Thames and the Isle of Wight, are the two areas which written sources suggest were the centres of Germanic kingdoms by the early seventh century. Some further encouragement for making a connection in the early Anglo-Saxon period between the control of trade and the development of kingship is provided by the interest in trade shown by the West Saxon kings in the eighth and ninth centuries.

TRADE AND TRADING-PLACES IN MID-SAXON WESSEX

The laws of Ine reveal the king supervising the activities of traders and foreigners – some of the latter might presumably fall into the first category as well. Traders at work in the interior of the country should do so before witnesses, presumably royal officials.[41] Strangers travelling off the highway were instructed to shout or blow a horn in order not to be mistaken for thieves as they might be slain or captured.[42] An almost identical clause in the near contemporary laws of King Wihtred of Kent suggests that there was agreement between the two kingdoms on the matter.[43] In order not to fall a victim to aggressive West Saxons, a foreigner needed royal protection and in exchange the king would receive two-thirds of the wergeld if he were killed.[44] Ine's laws do not spell out the procedures that should take place when a trader from outside Wessex arrived in the kingdom, but the laws of Alfred record that traders should bring before a king's reeve at a public meeting the

---

39. Scull, 'Scales and weights'; M. Gaimster, 'Scandinavian gold bracteates in Britain; money and media in the Dark Ages', *Med Arch, 36* (1992), 1–28.
40. However, the validity of this interpretation has been challenged by R.I. Page; see B. Odenstedt and R.I. Page, 'The runic inscription from Grave 67', in Scull, 'Watchfield', 246–51.
41. 'Laws of Ine', Ch. 25, in *The Laws of the Earliest English Kings*, ed. F.L. Attenborough (1922), 36–61.
42. Attenborough, 'Laws of Ine', Ch. 20.
43. 'Laws of Wihtred', Ch. 28, in *Laws*, ed. Attenborough, 24–31; Sawyer, 'Kings and merchants', 150–1.
44. Attenborough, 'Laws of Ine', Ch. 23.

men whom they wished to take with them into the country.[45] We are also given an insight into procedures involving traders in Æthelweard's account of the arrival of three Norwegian ships off the coast of Dorset during the reign of King Beorhtric (786–802).[46] The king's reeve came to conduct them to the king's vill in Dorchester 'thinking they were merchants rather than marauders'. The combined evidence of these sources suggests that those coming from outside to trade in Wessex in the eighth and ninth centuries were closely supervised by royal officials from the time of their arrival. These were not necessarily arrangements which had been recently introduced for some of the relevant clauses in the laws read like additions to existing practices which were well known. Although the sources do not say so one would imagine, from later analogies, that payments of some kind had to be made by foreign traders for the privilege of working in Wessex.

By the time Ine concerned himself with the activities of traders, Mercian expansion had obliged West Saxon interests to move away from the Thames Valley.[47] Although the history of the wars between the Mercians and West Saxons suggest the latter made determined efforts to recover land in the upper Thames, they were not to do so for any length of time until the ninth century and even then the north bank remained Mercian territory. Desire to find alternative access to overseas trading routes may have been an important factor in concentrating West Saxon objectives on the conquest of the Jutish provinces in Hampshire and the Isle of Wight.[48] By the time of Cædwalla's death in 688 they were securely in possession of the safe harbourage of the Solent from which (then as now) a direct crossing could be made to the part of north Francia later known as Normandy. There may have been a number of places, at river mouths in particular, at which a ship could hove to. When Willibald from Bishop's Waltham and his companions set out on a pilgrimage to Rome in *c.* 721 they travelled to the mouth of the River Hamble nearby:

> Shortly afterwards they embarked on a ship. When the captain of the swift-sailing ship had taken their fares, they sailed with the [north]-west wind blowing and a high sea running, amidst the shouting of sailors and the creaking of oars. When they had braved the dangers at sea and the perils of the mountainous waves, a swift course brought them with full sails and following winds, safely to dry land. At once they gave thanks and pitching their tents on the banks of the River Seine, they encamped near the city which is called Rouen, where there is a market.[49]

---

45. 'Laws of Alfred', Ch. 34, in *Laws*, ed. Attenborough, 62–93.
46. Æthelweard III, 1, 26–7; see also Chapter 3, 107.
47. See Chapter 2, 57–60.
48. Yorke, 'Jutes of Hampshire and Wight'.
49. C.H. Talbot (trans.), *Anglo-Saxon Missionaries in Germany* (1954), 157.

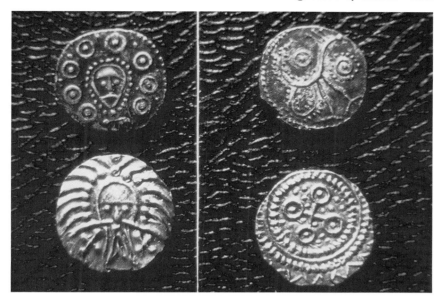

77. Two sceatta finds from Hamwic (Hants) (top) type 49, series H
sceat, probably minted in Hamwic (bottom) type 81, series X sceat,
possibly of insular manufacture but with obverse resembling 'Wodan'
head from type 31 coins, probably minted in Ribe (Denmark)
[photograph: Southampton City Council]

The journey seemingly remained fresh in Willibald's mind when he
recounted it to his biographer Huneburc, who recorded it some fifty
years later. Dorset also offered some safe landings for sailors from
overseas. According to the annals of St Neots the three Norwegian
ships put in at Portland,[50] and it would not appear from any of the
accounts that unannounced arrivals by merchantmen were that
unusual. Wareham was another obvious Dorset port, but has
produced little evidence for foreign trade to date.[51]

Frisians may have been among the foreign nationals who put in
at various places along the coast of Wessex. The main signs of their
presence are 'porcupine' sceattas (series E) which were probably
minted at Dorestad in the early eighth century and have been
found at various south coast locations and inland to Wiltshire.[52]
The rarer and slightly later Wodan/monster sceattas (series X) may

50. D.N. Dumville and M. Lapidge (eds), *The Annals of St Neots with Vita Prima
Sancti Neoti* (1984).
51. D. Hinton and R. Hodges, 'Excavations in Wareham, 1974–5', *PDNHAS, 99*
(1977), 42–83.
52. D.M. Metcalf, 'A note on sceattas as a measure of international trade, and on
the earliest Danish coinage', in *Sceattas in England and on the Continent*, ed. D.
Hill and D.M. Metcalf, BAR, *128* (1984), 159–64; D.M. Metcalf, 'A "porcupine"
sceat from Market Lavington, with a list of other sceattas from Wiltshire', *WAM
83* (1990), 205–8.

have come from Ribe in Denmark (fig. 77),[53] and imply that the Norwegian marauders may not have been the first Scandinavian ships to land in Wessex. A West Saxon primary sceatta coinage (series W) may have been minted somewhere in southern Wessex during the reign of Ine. Only a few specimens are known, but they are widely distributed in England, though with a concentration in southern Wessex, and four, or possibly five, are known from France, perhaps serving to underline the importance of cross-Channel traffic, both of goods and people, from south coast ports.[54]

It may have been a desire to concentrate dispersed activity in one place where it could more easily be supervised that led to the development of Hamwic. Practically all we know about Hamwic comes from excavation and it is not surprising that there are still major problems in its interpretation. Although it has been the scene of much rescue archaeology since 1960, only about five per cent of the settlement was examined during these campaigns and final analysis and publication is still taking place. Any conclusions presented so far must be seen as tentative and the history of Hamwic's study has already seen several reversals of hypotheses.[55] The latest publication by Alan Morton argues for the settlement having its origins, as a place of any size, in the early eighth century; the small number of primary series sceattas and other artefacts which could date before 700 argue against any earlier date.[56] It is possible that settlement may have begun in an area between St Mary's Church and the waterfront and spread steadily northwards, but if so growth must have been rapid as the settlement was at its peak in the second half of the eighth century. At its height occupation was spread over an area of between 42 and 52 hectares, and although there was settlement over the whole of that area, it was not as densely built up as in a later medieval town (fig. 78). The latest population estimate is between 2,000–3,000 people, considerably less than some earlier estimations, but still substantial when viewed alongside the apparently small-sized contemporary rural settlements.

Three major components of a street system can be recognized; two north-south streets which would have connected with Roman roads to the north; a number of east and west streets linking the north-south roads; and a southern component of three east-west streets

53. Metcalf, 'Sceattas as a measure of international trade'.
54. Metcalf, *Thrymsas and Sceattas*, 152–7.
55. Major analyses include L.A. Burgess, *Origins of Southampton* (1964); P. Addyman and D. Hill, 'Saxon Southampton: a review of the evidence, parts 1 and 2', *PHFCAS, 25* and *26* (1968 and 1969), 61–93, and 61–96; P. Holdsworth, 'Saxon Southampton', in *Anglo-Saxon Towns in Southern England*, ed. J. Haslam (1984), 331–43; M. Brisbane, 'Hamwic (Saxon Southampton): an eighth-century port and production centre', in *The Rebirth of Towns in the West AD 700–1050*, ed. R. Hodges and B. Hobley, CBA res. rep., *68* (1988), 101–8.
56. A Morton, 'A synthesis of the evidence', in *Excavations in Hamwic: Volume I*, ed. A, Morton, CBA res. rep., *84* (1992), 20–77.

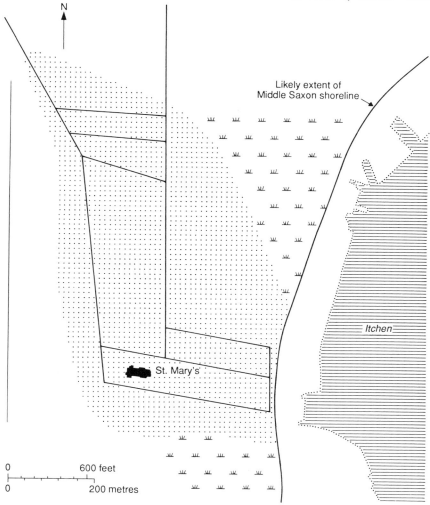

N

Likely extent of
Middle Saxon shoreline

Itchen

St. Mary's

0   600 feet
0   200 metres

78. Conjectural plan of mid-Saxon Hamwic, showing extent of roads
and occupation implied by excavations in the St Mary's area of
Southampton [source: A. Morton, *Excavations at Hamwic: Volume 1*
(1992), 33]

running down to the river frontage. Timber houses fronted these
streets, together with some less substantial rectangular buildings
which are likely to have been workshops; a series of irregular alleys
supplemented the main streets. A variety of crafts were carried on in
these buildings of which the ones which have left most substantial
traces were bone-working (fig. 79), metalworking and textile
manufacture. There is little sign of zoning of particular industries or
of variations in the wealth of the inhabitants; nor is there any
evidence that they were involved in agricultural activities. Some

79. Fragments for the assemblage of a bone comb from excavations at Six Dials, Southampton (Hamwic) [photograph: Southampton City Council]

retraction of population seems to have occurred in the early ninth century and by the end of the century occupation at Hamwic appears to have virtually ceased except in one area of the site where some settlement may have continued throughout the Anglo-Saxon period.

Hamwic, as its name implies, was a *wic* or trading place; Willebald's biographer Huneburc calls it a *mercimonium*.[57] It should be viewed alongside other such sites of the same date such as, in England, Ipswich and London's *wic* on the Strand and, in Europe, Quentovic, Dorestad and Ribe.[58] One function of these settlements was to allow foreign trade to take place and at Hamwic such trade is represented by finds of pottery from northern France, the Low Countries and the Rhineland, glass, probably also from France, quern-stones from the Eifel region of Germany and hone stones from Brittany or Normandy.[59] There was some concentration of imported pottery closer to the waterfront, and as the pottery was being used (and broken) by people living in the settlement, it may be that some foreign traders were actually resident there.[60] Coin finds also indicate the areas from which traders came. Some were from other areas of England, predominantly Kent and the upper Thames

57. See n. 49.
58. H. Clarke and B. Ambrosiani, *Towns in the Viking Age* (1991), 5–45.
59. Morton, *Excavations at Hamwic*, 59–68.
60. J. Timby, 'The Middle Saxon pottery', in *Southampton Finds I: The Coins and Pottery from Hamwic*, ed. P. Andrews, Southampton archaeology monographs, *4* (1988), 73–123.

Valley. 'Porcupine' and 'Wodan/monster' sceattas suggest traders from Frisia and Jutland (fig. 77), and there is even a coin from Arab Spain. But there is a surprising lack of coinage from Merovingian Francia even though the bulk of the imported pottery and glass came from there, and the discrepancy has yet to be fully explained.[61]

Many transactions in the town were presumably carried out using sceattas which are believed to have been minted in the settlement as they are rarely found elsewhere (series H).[62] The earliest Hamwic coins are classified as type 39 and, on the basis of their silver content, minting is likely to have begun around 720. More prolific are the coins of type 49 which make up about a third of the entire sceatta coinage, and it is possible that several million were originally minted (fig. 77). Its dating is more controversial; if it is seen, like type 39, as one of the secondary series of sceattas, the likely date range might be expected to be *c.* 735–50. Phil Andrews and Michael Metcalf have argued for it being a 'tertiary' series which they have tentatively dated to the third quarter of the eighth century or possibly to the reign of King Cynewulf (757–86), which would mean Wessex continued to use a sceatta coinage when the 'penny' coinage had come into use in Francia and Kent.[63] Neither solution seems entirely satisfactory, as the earlier dating would leave Hamwic without a coinage in its heyday in the second half of the eighth century (as the number of pennies is small and there is no evidence of a West Saxon penny coinage before the latter part of Beorhtric's reign [d. 802]).[64] On the other hand, the later dating seems to leave a gap in minting between type 39 and the appearance of type 49; a possible intermediary issue type 48 may not actually have been minted in Hamwic as it has a wider distribution than the other issues. Whatever the solution, the volume of coins finds from Hamwic is impressive: some 230 coins in all of which 150 are sceattas (fig. 80).[65] In 1988 the total of sceattas found at other *wic* sites in England was 23 from York and 8 from Ipswich and the other most prolific sites are Reculver with 57 and Flixborough with 53 to date.[66] Michael Metcalf has estimated that the 250 coins from the five per cent of the site excavated could stand for 3,500–5,000 coins lost in the settlement as a whole and for every transaction which took place during which

61. D.M. Metcalf, 'The coins', in *Southampton Finds I: The Coins and Pottery from Hamwic*, ed. P. Andrews, Southampton archaeology monographs, *4* (1988) 17–57.
62. Metcalf, 'The coins', 27–33.
63. P. Andrews and D.M. Metcalf, 'A coinage for King Cynewulf', in *Sceattas in England and on the Continent*, ed. D. Hill and D.M. Metcalf, BAR, *128* (1984), 175–80, and for a contrary view, Grierson and Blackburn, *Medieval European Coinage*, 169–71.
64. R.H.M. Dolley, 'The location of the pre-Ælfredian mint(s) of Wessex', PHFCAS, 27 (1970), 57–61; Grierson and Blackburn, *Medieval European Coinage*, 294–5.
65. Metcalf, 'The coins', 17–23.
66. M. Blackburn, 'Coin finds and coin circulation in Lindsey, *c.* 600–900', in *Pre-Viking Lindsey*, ed. A. Vince, Lincoln arch. rep., *1* (1993), 80–90.

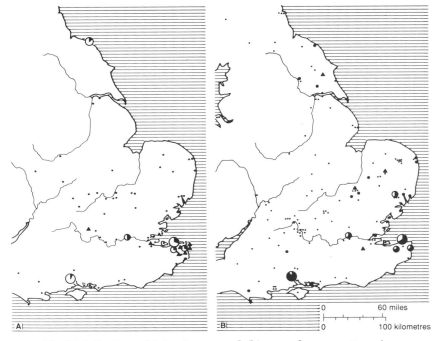

80. Distribution of (a) primary and (b) secondary sceatta coinages within England [after D. Metcalf and D. Hill, *Sceattas in England and on the Continent*, BAR *128* (1984), 33–35]

a coin was lost, there would have been a substantial number during which no losses occurred.[67]

However, although we can see the results of various activities which took place in the settlement, it is still not entirely clear what the main purpose of Hamwic was. There must have been some central organization behind it; for instance, not only was the settlement laid out regularly along streets, but these streets were regularly regravelled throughout – in contrast, the alleys presumably provided by the inhabitants themselves were irregularly paved, if provided with any sort of surfaces at all, and did not run in a straight line.[68] Hamwic was undoubtedly a planned settlement and its inhabitants must have been deliberately moved in from the countryside. It is hard to see who in the Middle Saxon period could have done that except the king. What is more the *hamm*, the 'peninsula' between the Itchen and Test rivers, on which the *wic* was situated also contained a royal *tun*.[69] Hamtun gave its name to

---

67. Metcalf, 'The coins', 17–23.
68. Morton, *Excavations in Hamwic*, 32–8.
69. A. Rumble, 'Hamtun alias Hamwic (Saxon Southampton): the place-name traditions and their significance', in *Excavations at Melbourne Street, Southampton, 1971–6*, ed. P. Holdsworth, CBA res. rep., *33* (1980), 7–20.

the shire which is first recorded in the *Chronicle* entry for 757, when the *wic* was at its height; King Æthelwulf of Wessex issued a charter from there in 840.[70] Presumably a reeve based there included among his duties supervision of activities in the *wic*, though we cannot tell which came first, the *tun* or the *wic*. The *tun* site was not necessarily situated in the same part of the peninsula as the *wic*, though a site which is of potential interest within the trading settlement is SOU 47 which was dug out in the nineteenth century and apparently produced high status items of a type not found elsewhere in the settlement and where occupation may have continued for longer.[71]

So any assessment of Hamwic's functions should take into account why a West Saxon king should want to establish a settlement of this type. Of course, to a certain extent the West Saxons were following the example of other *wic* sites which had already been established when Hamwic was founded. A *wic* would have been one way of acquiring objects of foreign manufacture which were regarded as essential for the dignity and operation of kingship. As the objects would not stay in the settlement little trace of them would remain unless (like the pottery) they were broken. A *wic* would also be a convenient place to supervise merchants and to collect tolls. But what would the merchants have taken away from Hamwic? The large amount of local sceattas could suggest that the West Saxons were doing more buying than selling, but it would be unlikely that foreign merchants would have gone away completely empty-handed. West Saxon kings may have found Hamwic a convenient place for exploiting the agricultural and other surpluses from their estates. For instance, iron smelting does not seem to have taken place in Hamwic, only smithing. But large-scale iron-working did take place while Hamwic was in operation at Gillingham (Dorset), Ramsbury (Wilts) and Romsey (Hants), all of which were probably sites in royal hands.[72] Sheep and cattle could have been provided from surrounding royal estates and have been turned into profitable by-products by the industrious inhabitants who also seem to have eaten the meat of the rather elderly animals which were presumably taken to the settlement when past their prime for ordinary agricultural functions.[73] In spite of the amount of coinage in circulation, there is little sign of personal wealth amongst the inhabitants of Hamwic which could suggest that much of the profits was going into other (royal) coffers.

---

70. S 288/B 431; see also S 273/B 389, and Chapter 2, 88–9.
71. Morton, *Excavations in Hamwic*, 28–9.
72. M. Heaton, 'Two mid-Saxon grain-driers and later medieval features at Chantry Field, Gillingham, Dorset', *PDNHAS*, 114 (1992), 97–126; J. Haslam, 'A Middle Saxon smelting site at Ramsbury, Wiltshire', *Med Arch*, 24 (1980), 1–68; A. Russel, 'Romsey: market place', in *Archaeology and Historic Buildings in Hampshire: Annual Report for 1986*, ed. M. Hughes (1987), 18.
73. J. Bourdillon, 'Countryside and town: the animal resources of Saxon Southampton', in *Anglo-Saxon Settlements*, ed. D. Hooke (1988), 176–96.

However, even if Hamwic fulfilled particular functions for the king, that need not preclude its use as a marketing centre by others. Inhabitants of the surrounding countryside may have brought in their own agricultural surpluses and they are more likely customers than foreign traders for the bone combs and metal trinkets produced in the settlement. Of course, not all of Wessex would have wanted to come to Hamwic and, as before, there must have been other local centres where the larger buying and selling transactions would have taken place. Royal *tuns* are the obvious places for such activities where the necessary supervision by royal officials could have occurred as envisaged by the laws. Jeremy Haslam has argued that many such sites should be considered as 'proto-urban' and that a market-place was part of the basic topography of many of them.[74] Such theories have yet to be proved by excavation. Another type of site where it has been proposed there would be opportunities for buying and selling are the sites of significant churches where substantial numbers of people could be expected to gather, such as Malmesbury where Aldhelm allegedly preached to people coming into the 'town' from the countryside, having first attracted their attention with Old English poems.[75]

Ecclesiastical foundations were another facet of Middle Saxon society which had a need for items manufactured abroad and they were also likely to have surpluses to dispose of from their large holdings of land though we have little information about how church estates were exploited at this time. Churchmen were among those who travelled abroad and 'imported' goods into the country; the letters of Boniface record several exchanges of 'gifts' between Anglo-Saxons at home and in Francia.[76] Aldhelm is reputed to have brought back a marble altar from Rome; according to William of Malmesbury a flaw visible in it in his day marked where it had been split in two in an accident on the journey home over the Alps, but had been miraculously joined together again by the saint.[77] Willibald successfully smuggled balsam through the customs at Tyre, concealed in the false bottom of a gourd.[78] These are scattered references, but do serve to illustrate the points that the growth in trade in the Middle Saxon period took place at a time when both kings and churches were extending their hold on West Saxon society and that both had needs which would have stimulated trade abroad and exploitation of tradeable commodities at home. Kings,

74. J. Haslam, 'Introduction' and 'The towns of Wiltshire', in *Anglo-Saxon Towns in Southern England*, ed. J. Haslam (1984), xi–xviii, 87–147.
75. *GP*, 336; G. Rosser, 'The cure of souls in English towns before 1000', in *Pastoral Care Before the Parish*, ed. J. Blair and R. Sharpe (1992), 267–84.
76. For example, Talbot (trans.), *Anglo-Saxon Missionaries*, nos. 4, 21, 27, 30, 33, 34, 38 and 44.
77. *GP*, 371–3.
78. Talbot (trans.), *Anglo-Saxon Missionaries*, 170; M.L. Cameron, 'Bald's *Leechbook* and cultural interactions in Anglo-Saxon England', *ASE, 19* (1990), 5–12.

in particular, seem to have been very aware of how they might utilize resources available from their land and it is not impossible that commerce was one of the spurs for the expansion of West Saxon territory, into the Jutish province for control of the Solent, for example, or into Devon for its tin and other mineral resources.[79] That West Saxon kings were known to have quantities of metals at their disposal is suggested by a letter from Lupus, abbot of Ferrières to King Æthelwulf of Wessex seeking lead to reroof his church.[80] Of course, more ordinary inhabitants also had surpluses to dispose of and items they wished to acquire, and a major expansion of trade and visible trading-places occurred when kings made use of these needs to increase their own revenues and the controls they exercised over their subjects.

THE GROWTH OF TOWNS IN LATER ANGLO-SAXON WESSEX

The study of the growth of towns in the later Saxon period in Wessex is complicated by the campaign of fortress-building in the face of the Viking threat in the ninth century. Did the construction of the burhs mark the beginning of urbanization, or would towns have emerged anyway? Should burhs be seen in any case not so much as fortresses or trading centres, but as places for the control and supervision of the surrounding population? The complications of unravelling the trend towards urbanization can be exemplified by the rise of Winchester and the decline of Hamwic. For by the middle of the ninth century the scale and nature of occupation in Winchester seems to have begun to change, with evidence, for instance, of iron smithing being carried out on the site later to be occupied by Nunnaminster, and from later accounts of St Swithun (852×3–862×865) connecting him with the building of a stone bridge at East Gate and provision of new churches.[81] It is tempting to see the population of Hamwic moving to Winchester in the aftermath of the Viking raids on the settlement recorded for 840 and 842.[82] The exposed low-lying position of Hamwic on the banks of the River Itchen can be contrasted with that of Winchester protected by its Roman walls which by the end of the ninth century had been reinforced with a substantial double ditch. By the beginning of the tenth century a system of gridded streets had been

---

79. J.R. Maddicott, 'Trade, industry and the wealth of King Alfred', *Past and Present, 123* (1989), 3–51.
80. Haddan and Stubbs, III, 648–9; *EHD*, I, no. 217.
81. M. Biddle, 'The study of Winchester: archaeology and history in a British town', *PBA, 69* (1983), 119–26; B.A.E. Yorke, 'The bishops of Winchester, the kings of Wessex and the development of Winchester in the ninth and early tenth centuries', *PHFCAS, 40* (1984), 61–70.
82. Differing interpretations are reviewed in Morton, *Excavations in Hamwic*, 70–7.

laid down which could have housed the substantial garrison provided for the town in the Burghal Hidage and given it easy access to the defences.[83] Nevertheless, fear of the Vikings was not so great that all Winchester's citizens chose to huddle within its walls, for a settlement at Sussex Street lay outside the defences.[84] Nor was the danger of Viking attack so great that Hamtun was abandoned; it too is listed as having defences in the Burghal Hidage.[85]

There is a danger that concentration on Winchester as a burh may mask other reasons for its redevelopment in the ninth century. Following Egbert's successes in south-eastern England, Winchester occupied a central position within the enlarged West Saxon kingdom and had excellent communications with other regions through the network of Roman roads. For a short period at the end of the reign of Alfred and the beginning of that of Edward the Elder it was the premier minting place in southern England from which dies were supplied for other mints.[86] The choice of Winchester as the burial place of Egbert, Æthelwulf, Alfred and Edward and the foundation there of New Minster and Nunnaminster could imply that it was seen by the royal house as a prestige site. In the aftermath of the Carolingian Renaissance, its walls may have been valued as much for their demonstration of *Romanitas* as for their defensive capabilities.

Further discussion of the relationship between burghal defences and the emergence of towns is best kept until the late Saxon towns of Wessex have been identified. One sign of urban status in late Anglo-Saxon England was the presence of a mint. According to the laws issued by Athelstan at Grately (Hants) money was only to be minted in a town (*port*).[87] The number of minting places rose steadily throughout the late Saxon period. Alfred is only certainly known to have had coins minted, within the six shires of Wessex, at Winchester, Exeter and Bath. By the end of the reign of Athelstan 11 minting places in Wessex have been identified,[88] and the number rose steadily from then on to reach a total of 30 minting places by 1066 (fig. 81), though not all of these were in use at the same time.[89]

83. M. Biddle and D. Hill, 'Late Saxon planned towns', *Ant J, 51* (1971), 70–85; see also Ch. 3, 115–21.

84. D. Hinton, S. Keene and K. Qualmann, 'The Winchester reliquary', *Med Arch, 25* (1981), 45–77.

85. It is not clear exactly where Hamtun (as opposed to Hamwic) and its defences were. For the case for the former reusing the Roman fort at Bitterne see D. Hill, 'The Burghal Hidage – Southampton', *PHFCAS, 24* (1967), 59–61.

86. C. Blunt, I. Stewart and C.S. Lyon, *Coinage in Tenth-Century England: From Edward the Elder to Edgar's Reform* (1989), 25–34.

87. 'II Athelstan', in *Laws of Kings*, ed. Attenborough, 134–5; H.R. Loyn, 'Boroughs and mints, AD 900–1066', in *Anglo-Saxon Coins*, ed. R.H.M. Dolley (1961), 122–35.

88. Blunt *et al.*, *Coinage in Tenth-Century England*, 108–11, 255–63.

89. D. Hill, *An Atlas of Anglo-Saxon England* (1981), 126–32.

Mints by 939	Mints 957–1066	Burghal Hidage	Domesday Book Boroughs
	Axbridge	Yes	Yes
Barnstaple	Barnstaple	(Pilton)	Yes
Bath	Bath	Yes	Yes
	Bedwyn	(Chisbury)	Yes
Bridport	Bridport	(Bredy)	Yes
	Bruton	No	Yes
	S. Cadbury	No	No
	Crewkerne	No	No
	Cricklade	Yes	Yes
Darent	(Totnes?)	(Halwell)	No
	Dorchester	No	Yes
Exeter	Exeter	Yes	Yes
	Frome	No	Yes
	Ilchester	No	Yes
Langport	Langport	Yes	Yes
	Lydford	Yes	Yes
	Malmesbury	Yes	Yes
	Milborne	No	Yes
	Old Sarum	No	Yes
	Petherton	No	No
	Reading	No	Yes
Shaftesbury	Shaftesbury	Yes	Yes
Southampton	Southampton	Yes	Yes
	Taunton	No	Yes
	Totnes	(Halwell)	Yes
Wallingford	Wallingford	Yes	Yes
Wareham	Wareham	Yes	Yes
	Warminster	No	Yes
	Watchet	Yes	No
	Wilton	Yes	Yes
Winchester	Winchester	Yes	Yes

81. Mints, burhs and Domesday boroughs in Wessex

However, the place of minting was only included as a matter of course on the coins from the reign of Edgar, and intermittent use of mint signatures before then causes problems in identification.

A second means of identifying the towns of late Anglo-Saxon Wessex is through entries in Domesday Book. The compilation of such a list is not entirely straightforward as a variety of terms and modes of description are used in the survey, but, following Professor Darby, we may accept that a place was defined as a town if it was called *civitas* or *burgus*, possessed burgesses or burgage plots or made the payment known as 'third penny' (that is, a third of the borough's public revenue went to the earl, two-thirds to the king).[90]

---

90. H.C. Darby, *Domesday England* (1977), 289–320, 364–8; classic studies include A. Ballard, *The Domesday Boroughs* (1904) and J. Tait, *The Medieval English Borough* (1936).

Shire	Burghal Hidage only	Domesday Book borough only	Domesday Book market
Berks	Sashes	Windsor	Abingdon Cookham
Devon		Okehampton	Otterton
Dorset		Wimborne	
Hants	Twynham Portchester	Twynham	Basingstoke Neatham Titchfield
Somerset	Lyng	Milverton	Crewkerne Ilminster
Wilts		Bradford Calne Marlborough Tilshead	

82. Marginal towns in late Saxon Wessex which appear in the Burghal Hidage or in Domesday Book as a borough or market, but which never possessed a mint

Places described simply as possessing a market are marginal cases and are listed separately in fig. 82.[91] On the basis of possession of at least one of the borough qualifications, 35 places can be identified as Domesday towns from the six shires of Wessex. They too are listed in fig. 81, which reveals that there was a very close correspondence between them and the late Saxon mint sites. Only four places which minted coins in the late Saxon period are not among the Domesday boroughs, and of these (South) Cadbury was an 'emergency' burh brought in during the reign of Æthelred II,[92] and Crewkerne is recorded in Domesday Book as possessing a market. On the other hand, there are nine places which meet the criteria of Domesday boroughs, but which are not known to have minted Anglo-Saxon coins (fig. 82), though some of these (e.g. Okehampton, Devon) may have come to greater prominence following the Norman Conquest.

It is also the case that a considerable number of the places listed in the Burghal Hidage became the sites of mints and Domesday boroughs (fig. 81).[93] The coincidence becomes stronger when it is appreciated that some entries in the Burghal Hidage were defended sites (in several cases reused Iron Age forts) in the vicinity of places

---

91. Darby, *Domesday England*, 369–70.
92. D. Hill, 'Trends in the development of towns during the reign of Æthelred II', in *Ethelred the Unready*, ed. D. Hill, BAR, *59* (1978), 223–5.
93. D. Hill, 'The Burghal Hidage: the establishment of a text', *Med Arch, 13* (1969), 84–92; see also Chapter 3, 115–21.

which became mints. Thus Pilton could be seen as a defensive site for Barnstaple (Devon), Chisbury for Bedwyn (Wilts), Bredy for Bridport (if it was not Bridport itself) (Dorset) and Halwell for what may have been successive mints at 'Darent' (possibly Dartmouth or Dartington) and Totnes (Devon). Four Burghal Hidage entries did not become the sites of Anglo-Saxon mints as far as is known (fig. 82), but of these Twynham/Christchurch (Hants, now Dorset) was a Domesday borough and Sashes could be seen as the defensive site for Cookham (Berks), which is described as possessing a market in Domesday Book. In all there were 22 Burghal Hidage sites in Wessex, which seems to have been roughly the maximum number of mint sites in operation at any one time when the system was at its height in the eleventh century.[94]

Many of the sites which became burhs and/or mints in the later Saxon period had filled what can loosely be described as some central place functions in the Middle Saxon period, that is they can be identified either as royal *tuns* or minster sites.[95] In Somerset some apparently new Burghal Hidage sites which became commercial centres were in fact closely linked with a nearby *tun* from which, as their Domesday Book entries make clear, they were administered; Axbridge, for instance, was the 'port' for the estate based on Cheddar, Langport (fig. 83) that for Somerton and Watchet (which seems to have failed by 1066) probably had a similar role for Williton.[96] Although the scope of their commercial functions increased considerably, it seems likely that places which emerged as towns in the later Saxon period were building on foundations laid in the Middle Saxon period when they were already serving a dependent region. They had been, in many instances, places where people came to pay royal dues and one can see them as candidates for the sites where buying and selling took place under the supervision of royal officials, as envisaged in the laws of Ine and Alfred. The building of the burhs can be seen not so much as bringing forward new sites as providing protection for a network of existing royal administrative sites, many of which were provided with their own defences, or had existing defences strengthened. Others were protected by reuse of a defensive site in their vicinity; possibly in these cases one should envisage functions of royal *tuns* being temporarily moved within the defensive enclosure, as seems to have happened with King Æthelred II's emergency burh at South Cadbury.

The desirability of royal *tuns* to the Vikings is shown by the

---

94. See Hill, *Atlas of Anglo-Saxon England*, 31–2.
95. Unfortunately there is not sufficient space to discuss the evidence here; see P. Sawyer, 'The royal *tun* in pre-Conquest England', in *Ideal and Reality in Frankish and Anglo-Saxon Society*, ed. P. Wormald *et al.* (1983), 273–99, and relevant chapters in J. Haslam (ed.), *Anglo-Saxon Towns in Southern England* (1984).
96. M. Aston, 'The towns of Somerset', in *Anglo-Saxon Towns in Southern England*, ed. J. Haslam (1984), 167–202.

83. Aerial photograph of Langport (Som); existing roads and property boundaries preserve the form of the late Saxon burh and small town [photograph: M. Aston]

attacks of the 'great heathen army' on Reading, Basing, Wilton, Wareham and Exeter;[97] presumably one of the attractions was the likelihood of finding supplies, bullion and other worthwhile loot in such places. Exeter, for instance, may already have been an important administrative centre for the local production of tin, and so on a smaller scale may have been Lydford and Darent/Totnes.[98] Of course, many of the *tuns* also occupied important strategic sites on the coast, at the heads of rivers or river-crossings which might in any case be a priority for defence. Wallingford, for instance, was not only an important crossing-point of the Thames, but somewhere from which traffic up and down the Thames could be controlled.[99] The needs of defence no doubt helped to decide which sites became burhs and may have caused some modifications to local administration, but such modifications may only have been temporary and behind the mint sites and burhs we can see an older pattern of local central places emerging.

However, the late Saxon distribution pattern of towns was not the same throughout the six shires. There is a striking contrast, for instance, between Somerset with its numerous small towns and Hampshire and Berkshire where one town dominated. Winchester and Wallingford are both burhs to which 2,400 hides were allotted in the Burghal Hidage and, as discussed at an earlier point, may have emerged as dominant centres for northern Hampshire and Berkshire as a result of a major administrative reorganization that may initially have been unconnected with the burghal campaign.[100] Late Saxon Somerset can be seen as fossilizing an older pattern whereby lesser *tuns* serviced the needs of dependent estates. The Axbridge Chronicle, a compilation of the fourteenth or fifteenth century, which seems to have had access to some material stemming from the pre-Conquest period, acknowledges this arrangement when it records that burhs were established on royal estates in the tenth century so that if the king did not come to stay on his estate the supplies which would have fed him could be sold in the market by royal reeves.[101] However, the contrast between Somerset and Hampshire and Berkshire is not as great as it might first appear, for the two eastern shires had a second rank of lesser burhs and Domesday markets which preserve an older pattern. Places like Abingdon, Cookham, Reading and Windsor (Berks) and Basingstoke, Neatham, Titchfied and Twynham/Christchurch (Hants) can be seen as comparable to the small towns of Somerset and like

---

97. See Chapter 3, 109–11.
98. Maddicott, 'Trade, industry and wealth'.
99. P. Morgan (ed.), *Domesday Book: Berkshire* (1979), 56 b–c; G. Astill, 'The towns of Berkshire', in *Anglo-Saxon Towns in Southern England*, ed. J. Haslam (1984), 53–86.
100. See Chapter 2, 88–90.
101. P. Rahtz, *The Saxon and Medieval Palaces at Cheddar*, BAR, *65* (1979), 5–19; D. Hill, 'Trends in towns'.

them had been estate and/or minster centres in the Middle Saxon period.

The lawcodes of late Saxon kings tried to restrict buying and selling of goods of any value (over twenty pence according to the Grately code) to towns.[102] One of the reasons for their interest was the profit from rents, tolls, the witnessing of transactions and the borough courts which, according to a decree of Edgar, were to meet three times a year. By the end of the Saxon period the revenue from the towns was split, with two-thirds going to the king and one-third to the earl, but it is not known when this arrangement came into force.[103] It is likely that in the late Saxon period most royal dues were payable in coin thus stimulating trade to raise money and necessitating the increase in mints. Kings also made a profit when a new issue of coinage was produced as moneyers had to purchase the new dies from a central die-cutting centre; in Wessex in the early eleventh century these were at Winchester and Exeter.[104] According to Domesday Book the two moneyers based in Dorchester paid the king 1 silver mark and 20 shillings whenever the coinage was changed.[105] Under reforms to the coinage in the reign of Edgar, which led to standardization of designs throughout the country (fig. 84), the changes of coin types were to take place every six years, but in the reign of Edward the Confessor the coinage was being changed every three years.[106] Only the current coinage was presumably acceptable for royal payments and hoards suggest that old issues did not long remain in circulation.

Coinage seems to have been in general use in later Anglo-Saxon Wessex and the rapid dissemination of coins from their places of issue suggests the existence of active markets. A hoard of 92 coins deposited on the outskirts of Shaftesbury in 1002/3 contained only one coin from Shaftesbury; 21 mints were represented in the hoard with over half the coins coming from York, Chester and Lincoln.[107] It is not always clear what was being bought or sold, but the split-up of large estates may have occasioned more demand for specialist items and agricultural by-products which smaller estates could not obtain from their own resources. One area where considerable expansion can be seen is the pottery trade. In earlier Anglo-Saxon Wessex local wares had been crude and handmade and the only wheel-turned pottery was that imported from Europe; large areas of

---

102. Loyn, 'Boroughs and mints'.
103. F.M. Stenton, *Anglo-Saxon England* (3rd edn., 1971), 534–5.
104. R.H.M. Dolley, 'The reform of the English coinage under Eadgar', in *Anglo-Saxon Coins*, ed. R.H.M. Dolley (1961), 136–68.
105. C. and F. Thorn (eds), *Domesday Book: Dorset* (1983), 75a.
106. Dolley, 'Reform of the English coinage'.
107. R.H.M. Dolley, 'The Shaftesbury hoard of pence of Æthelred II', *Numismatic Chronicle*, *18* (1958), 267–80; D.M. Metcalf, 'The ranking of boroughs: numismatic evidence from the reign of Æthelred II', in *Ethelred the Unready*, ed. D. Hill, BAR, *59* (1978), 168–73.

a

b

84. Pennies from the reign of Edgar minted at (a) Lydford and (b) Totnes (Devon) [photograph: Exeter City Museums and Art Gallery]

western Wessex seem not to have used pottery at all. In contrast in late Saxon Wessex, locally-made, wheel-turned pottery seems to have been readily available in a variety of forms including cooking pots, bowls, storage jars, spouted pitchers and lamps, though some handmade pottery might also be found particularly for cruder kitchen wares.[108] The best pottery such as 'Winchester ware' might be glazed.[109] Some of the pottery was made in towns – a kiln and wasters have been excavated in Exeter (fig. 85)[110] – but much of it

---

108. M.R. McCarthy and C.M. Brooks, *Medieval Pottery in Britain AD 900–1600* (1988), 62–8.

109. M. Biddle and K. Barclay, 'Winchester ware', in *Medieval Pottery from Excavations. Studies presented to Gerald Clough Dunning*, ed. V. Evison, H. Hodges and J.G. Hurst (1974), 137–65.

110. J.P. Allan, *Medieval and Post-Medieval Finds from Exeter 1971–1980* (1984), 27–30.

a

b

85. (a) Saxo-Norman pottery made in a kiln on the site of the Bedford Garage, Exeter (b) Saxo-Norman pottery imported from northern France found in Exeter [photograph: Exeter City Museums and Art Gallery]

was rurally based like the kiln site excavated at Michelmersh (Hants),[111] though the place of production of some wares, such as Winchester ware or the pottery found at the royal palace of

111. P. Addyman, B. Hopkins and G. Norton, 'A Saxon-Norman pottery-kiln producing stamped wares at Michelmersh, Hampshire', *Med Arch, 16* (1972), 127–30.

Cheddar, is not known.[112] Presumably pottery was also brought into towns to be traded; for instance, the pottery from the Beer/Salcombe area which has been found in Exeter.[113] Pottery might also be imported into Wessex from other regions of England; Stamford ware, for instance, has been found at sites throughout the region.[114]

Presumably the trade in pottery is likely to reflect a much more widespread trade in less durable substances. However, important though trade in towns may have been, there was still a role for itinerant workmen. Excavations at Cheddar and Faccombe Netherton (Hants) showed that substantial metalworking took place at the sites on a number of occasions.[115] Kings and major noble families no doubt employed their own craftsmen who might move between their estates and it is likely to have been lesser people who made their purchases in towns and were catered for by metalworking sites like that at Lower Brook Street in Winchester.[116] Nor should overseas trade be overlooked. By the middle of the tenth century at the latest a new trading enclave, enclosed by a bank and ditch, had been founded at Southampton, this time on the Test side of the peninsula, on the site of the later medieval town. Finds of red-painted Beauvais ware show a continuation of the north French links seen at Hamwic, but late Saxon Southampton was on a smaller scale than its Middle Saxon predecessor.[117] The most significant late Saxon port in Wessex was at Exeter. Pottery finds suggest links with Normandy, Brittany and the Loire valley (fig. 85).[118] According to Orderic Vitalis, Exeter was on a major route between Ireland and Brittany, and its links with Ireland may have been particularly significant in the reign of Æthelred II when Chester was in temporary eclipse and for a short time Exeter provided almost ten per cent of the coinage minted in England.[119] The export of tin is also likely to have been a major reason for the importance of Exeter's mint and overseas trade.

Some idea of the relative size of the Wessex towns can be reached by looking at their scale of minting and the number of burgage tenements recorded in Domesday Book. Whether measured in terms of the number of moneyers or the output of the mints Winchester

---

112. Rahtz, *Saxon Palaces at Cheddar*, 308–18.
113. J. Allan, C. Henderson and R. Higham, 'Saxon Exeter', in *Anglo-Saxon Towns in Southern England*, ed. J. Haslam (1984), 404–6.
114. McCarthy and Brooks, *Medieval Pottery*, 62–8.
115. Rahtz, *Saxon Palaces at Cheddar*, 263–87, 381–2; J.R. Fairbrother, *Faccombe Netherton. Excavations of a Saxon and Medieval Manorial Complex*, BM occ. paper, *74*, (2 vols, 1990), 403–35, 512–15.
116. D. Hinton, 'The medieval gold, silver and copper-alloy objects', and I. Goodall, 'The medieval iron objects', in *Object and Economy in Medieval Winchester*, ed. M. Biddle, Winchester Studies, *7.ii* (2 vols, 1990), I, 29–41.
117. Holdsworth, 'Saxon Southampton', 337–42, and A. Russel pers. comm.
118. Allan, *Medieval and Post-Medieval Finds*, 13–18; Allan et al., 'Saxon Exeter', 404–6.
119. M. Chibnall (ed.), *The Ecclesiastical History of Orderic Vitalis* (6 vols, 1969–81), ii, 211; Maddicott, 'Trade, industry and wealth', 23–32.

emerges as easily the most significant of the West Saxon towns, and on average it was the fourth most prolific mint in England (fig. 86).[120] Its closest rival in Wessex was Exeter, but, as discussed above, the output of its mint was more variable. The other minting-centres in Wessex are led by Wallingford, followed by Ilchester, Wilton, Bath, Shaftesbury, Old Sarum, Cricklade, Lydford and Totnes. The output of the smaller mints, such as those of the Somerset royal estates, was slight. On the whole the ranking by mints is commensurate with the population sizes implied by the number of tenements in Domesday Book.[121] Winchester was not included in Domesday Book, but a survey of the royal holdings in the town made in c. 1057 was incorporated in a survey made in the reign of Henry I. Calculations based on these figures have suggested a possible total of 1,130 tenements in late Saxon Winchester which could imply a population of between 5,000–6,000 and confirm its ranking as approximately the fourth largest town in the country.[122] Exeter is recorded as having 399 tenements with an additional 51 destroyed, suggesting a late Saxon population more in the region of 2,000 (fig. 87); Wallingford with 491 tenements was marginally larger. Other towns were considerably smaller though the entries do not seem to be complete in all cases; no indications are given of the size of Old Sarum or Marlborough, for instance. Only Bath, Dorchester, Ilchester, Shaftesbury, Totnes and Wareham have over 100 tenements recorded; the majority of others fall somewhere between 30 and 60 tenements, but some were even smaller.

Winchester was not only the largest town in Wessex, it is also the one we know most about from written records and excavation. However, when looking at the picture we get of the late Saxon town we must remember that it was neither typical of other towns in the region nor, it would appear, of other large towns in England. Its close links with the royal house and the reform movement in the Church seem to have placed it in a unique position.[123] The south-eastern quarter of Winchester was filled by the three minsters, the episcopal palace at Wolvesey and a royal palace (fig. 52). The rest of the town retained the street system that had begun to be laid out in the late ninth century. The land between the streets was divided into tenements (*hagae*) and at Lower Brook Street, where a series of these were excavated, the wooden houses fronted the street with outhouses and industrial structures behind.[124] Settlement continued into suburbs outside the four main gates of the city. The king owned a substantial number of tenements, but in 1148 most of

---

120. Metcalf, 'Ranking of boroughs', 159–212; Hill, 'Trends in towns', 213–17.
121. Darby, *Domesday England*, 364–8.
122. M. Biddle and D. Keene, 'The late Saxon "burh"', in *Winchester in the Early Middle Ages*, ed. M. Biddle, Winchester Studies, *1* (1976), 467–9.
123. Biddle and Keene, 'The late Saxon "burh"', 449–69.
124. M. Biddle, 'Excavations at Winchester, 1971: tenth and final interim report, part II', *Ant J, 55* (1975), 295–321.

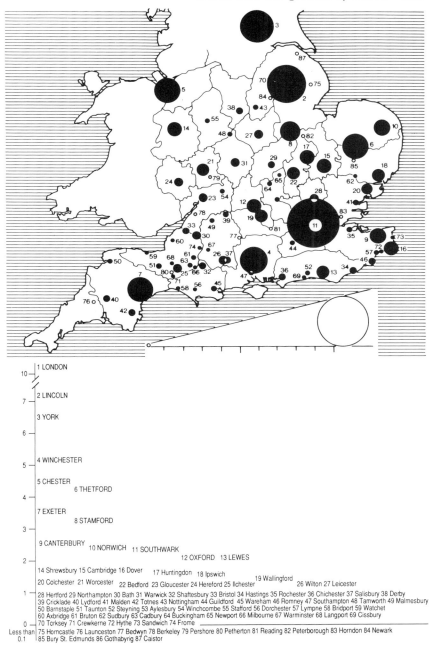

86. The ranking of mints in late Anglo-Saxon England based on a percentage of total known moneyers [D. Hill, *Atlas of Anglo-Saxon England* (1981), figs. 222–23]

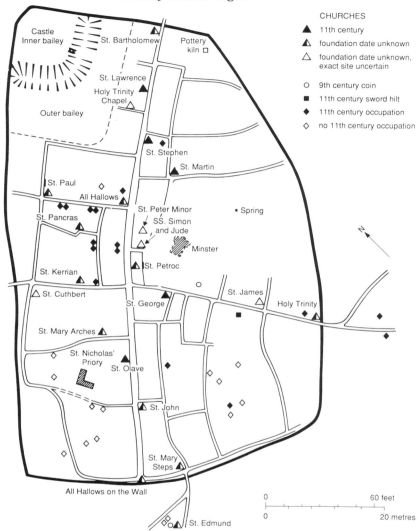

CHURCHES

▲ 11th century

◣ foundation date unknown

△ foundation date unknown, exact site uncertain

○ 9th century coin

■ 11th century sword hilt

◆ 11th century occupation

◇ no 11th century occupation

Castle Inner bailey

St. Bartholomew

Pottery kiln □

St. Lawrence

Holy Trinity Chapel

Outer bailey

St. Stephen

St. Martin

St. Paul

All Hallows

St. Peter Minor

• Spring

St. Pancras

SS. Simon and Jude

Minster

St. Kerrian

St. Petroc

St. Cuthbert

St. George

St. James

Holy Trinity

St. Mary Arches

St. Nicholas' Priory

St. Olave

St. John

St. Mary Steps

All Hallows on the Wall

St. Edmund

0 ———— 60 feet

0 ———— 20 metres

87. Eleventh-century Exeter [after J. Allan, C. Henderson and R. Higham, 'Saxon Exeter', in *Anglo-Saxon Towns in Southern England*, ed. J. Haslam (1984), 385–414, fig. 128]

the rest of the town was divided between the bishop of Winchester, the prior of the cathedral, the abbot of Hyde (formerly New Minster), the abbess of St Mary's (Nunnaminster), the abbess of Wherwell and the abbess of Romsey, and it is thought likely that these fiefs were established in the pre-Conquest period.[125] Shared

---

125. Biddle and Keene, 'Land ownership', in *Winchester in the Early Middle Ages*, 349–86.

ownership between king and Church is known from some other West Saxon towns as well, though on a lesser scale. For instance, Shaftesbury is said in Domesday Book to be divided between the king and the abbess.[126] The minsters and other strong ecclesiastical elements account for some of the finest objects and most advanced technologies practised in the late Saxon city.

Late Saxon charters name some of the streets in Winchester and a more comprehensive list is given in the surveys.[127] Some of them apparently indicate where specialist trades were being carried out. These include *Flesmangerestret* ('street of the butchers'), *Goldestret* (perhaps 'street of the goldsmiths'), *Scowrtenestret* ('street of the shoemakers') and *Sildwortenestret* ('street of the shield-makers'). Excavation of one of the streets has shown that the industry which gave it its name was practised within it in the late Saxon period; *Tannerestret* ('street of the tanners') has produced evidence of tanning pits, water channels, specialist tools and offcuts and hair from the hides (fig. 88).[128] Occupational bynames from the incorporated Edwardian survey provide some other occupations some of which would be hard to detect archaeologically, including a money-changer, a sword-maker, a herring-monger, a ladder-maker and a glover. Other bynames indicate places from which their owners came; recruitment from other parts of Hampshire is only to be expected as many rural manors are recorded as having attached burgesses in Winchester (like many other late Saxon towns), but pre-Conquest inhabitants are also indicated as coming from Keynsham (Som), Chitterley (Dorset) and Cricklade (Wilts), while the personal names include French, Continental Germanic and Scandinavian forms.[129] Although there are some broad similarities to be drawn between late Saxon Winchester and Middle Saxon Hamwic, there are differences as well, and later Saxon Winchester with its diversified economy and population drawn from a wide range of social classes with varying standards of living was a fully medieval town.

By the end of the Anglo-Saxon period towns were a well-established feature of Wessex and, on a conservative estimate, around eight per cent of the population might be said to live within them.[130] The impetus for their foundation may have come through a royal desire to supervise the population and maximize revenue, but by 1066 they were also an integral part of the rural economy and those that did not have a sufficiently thriving rural hinterland, such

---

126. Thorn and Thorn (eds), *Domesday Book: Dorset*, 75a.
127. Biddle and Keene, 'The early place-names of Winchester', in *Winchester in the Early Middle Ages*, 231–35.
128. Now Lower Brook Street, see n. 124 and D. Keene, 'Tanning', in *Object and Economy*, I, 243–5.
129. O. von Feilitzen, 'The personal names and bynames of the Winton Domesday', in *Winchester in the Early Middle Ages*, 143–230.
130. C. Dyer, 'Towns and cottages in eleventh-century England', in *Studies in Medieval History Presented to R.H.C. Davis*, ed. H. Mayr-Harting and R.I. Moore (1985), 91–106, at 91–2.

88. Tanning pit, Tanner Street (Lower Brook Street), Winchester
[photograph: M. Biddle, Winchester Research Unit]

as Watchet (Som), did not survive. Late Saxon Wessex was not characterized by the small seigneurial towns to be found after the Norman Conquest, though some of the major ecclesiastical foundations, such as Abingdon and Glastonbury, may have begun to anticipate such developments by encouraging local markets.[131] Christopher Dyer has suggested that local lords may have sought to exploit the revenue-making opportunities provided by towns by establishing nearby communities of dependent peasants who might be chiefly employed within them, such as the 18 cottars who were the sole residents of an estate at Ditchampton near Wilton.[132] But, as he also argues, it is likely that many landless peasants were drawn of their own accord to the vicinity of towns where there would have been opportunities to support themselves as craftsmen, labourers and servants. As in other periods, towns would only flourish if there was a continual recruitment of new populace from the countryside. There may have been a measure of forced settlement of population when the burhs were established, but settlements with a future would soon have become self-sustaining. The history of towns in Anglo-Saxon Wessex cannot be written apart from that of the countryside, for they were part of the developments which changed the nature of settlement in much of late Saxon Wessex, as discussed in the previous chapter. The local towns provided the markets for the new villages and absorbed some of their surplus populations; they were both stimulated by and stimulators of the developing market economy of the later Saxon period.

131. Astill, 'Towns of Berkshire', 73, and Aston, 'Towns of Somerset', 178.
132. Dyer, 'Towns and cottages', 91–106.

Epilogue

1066 is probably the most famous date in English history and one that commonly has been used to mark the end of one significant era and the beginning of another. However, things are rarely this simple and like other 'decisive' dates 1066 no longer carries all the connotations that it was once held to possess. Undoubtedly the Norman Conquest did inaugurate some major changes in the province of Wessex as elsewhere in England. One can point in particular to the impact caused by the introduction of a new aristocracy with different expectations of their rights as landowners and different priorities in the bestowal of patronage. But arguably the similarities between late Saxon society in Wessex and that of Normandy were greater than their differences. Many of the significant features of Wessex of the twelfth and thirteenth centuries were already in place, or in the process of formation, by the time of the fateful battle of Hastings; features such as the shires and hundreds, towns, nucleated villages and open fields, the nobleman's estate with manorial residence and church. It would also be true to say that Wessex had begun to lose some of its distinctive features as an Anglo-Saxon province before 1066, following the upheavals at the end of the reign of Æthelred Unræd which culminated in the accession of the Danish king Cnut. The accession of Cnut began the replacement of native aristocracy with those of foreign birth and many leading families which would have identified themselves as 'West Saxon' disappeared at that time. The division of the six shires of Wessex into two provinces east and west of Selwood, which had been a distinctive administrative feature for centuries, ceased to be recognized in the eleventh century. In spite of Cnut's patronage of Winchester, kings of England in the eleventh century no longer spent so much time in the province of Wessex. Other areas of the country were equally favoured and London became increasingly important as a royal residence, as a place of royal burial and as an administrative centre. 'Foreign' churchmen were appointed to West Saxon bishoprics and began to cast a critical eye over arrangements in their dioceses. Edward the Confessor may have been a descendant of the West Saxon royal house, but his years in exile meant that he did not have the same ties with the province of Wessex as his predecessors.

Changes which occurred during the earlier part of the period 400 to 1066 were arguably more radical than what happened at the end. Until the seventh century what became the six shires of Wessex had no territorial or political coherence and probably nobody within that area would have described themselves as 'West Saxon'. The future West Saxon kings seem to have been based in the upper Thames; other areas of eastern Wessex were controlled by different Germanic groups some of which were connected with other Germanic provinces further east. In the west, in the former *civitates* of the Dumnonii and the Durotriges, were British kingdoms or other polities. The process by which those who claimed descent from Cerdic made themselves masters of this disparate territory and created the kingdom of Wessex must have been traumatic for many. Even though it is no longer necessary to believe that the British population was wiped out, many previously dominant people in the Germanic and British provinces which fell to the Gewissan kings must have lost their lives or at least their lands; the West Saxon conquest must have seen a transfer of landownership at least as substantial as that after the Norman Conquest and was probably accompanied by a greater movement of peasantry. Germanic language and culture became dominant throughout Wessex, though our surviving written sources may not do justice to the survival of many facets of British society.

Another transforming influence within the Anglo-Saxon period was the establishment of Christianity. It had, of course, been introduced into Wessex during the Roman period, but, even in areas where there may have been continuity of Christian worship from the fourth century, it was in the early Middle Ages that Christianity became the dominant and eventually the only official religion. Christianity introduced new rituals and beliefs, and firmly linked religion with personal morality, but how the inner lives of the people of Wessex were affected by the new religion is an impossible question for the historian to answer. However, there can be no doubt of the impact of the Christian Church as an institution or of the large amounts of land and other forms of wealth it controlled and to which everyone had to contribute annually through tithes and other payments. It was also instrumental in the establishment of ideas beyond the purely religious, such as the concept of 'bookland' which became the dominant aristocratic tenure, and of new technologies and skills. Not the least among the latter was the ability to read and write, which has also transformed the way we can study the West Saxon area, for the introduction of classical and Christian authors led ultimately to the production of local written records.

On the other hand, one aspect of the history of the period which has often been claimed as having a major impact perhaps should receive less emphasis. The reference is to the Viking attacks of the ninth century which have, for instance, been blamed for causing widespread decline and destruction in the West Saxon Church. The Vikings undoubtedly did have some impact on Wessex, not least in helping to depose or eradicate other Anglo-Saxon ruling houses so that the kings of Wessex were able to become kings of England. But in the ninth century the six central shires of Wessex suffered relatively few attacks compared to other areas of the country and to the ravages they endured during the reign of Æthelred Unræd. Any problems in the West Saxon Church are more likely to have been the result of internal changes within Wessex. King Alfred's complaints about falling standards in the Church of his day, from which the claims of Viking devastation have been developed, should be seen alongside his family's annexation of church lands; they provided a justification for his interference in church affairs. The need to provide an effective defence against the Vikings may have aided the rulers in making demands on their subjects, but their rights to public services already existed. Many burhs established to combat the Vikings became towns in later Anglo-Saxon England, but the desire to control trade and concentrate it in centres which could be supervised by royal officials is already manifest in the Middle Saxon period. Many places which became burhs and towns already had a history as central places (royal vills and/or minsters) to which people of the locality would have had to resort regularly.

But however radical some of the changes which occurred in Wessex during the Anglo-Saxon period may have been, one must also acknowledge other inherited factors which link the Anglo-Saxon to earlier periods. The landscape of Wessex, for instance, helped to dictate what could or could not be done within it. The needs of farmers did not vary drastically from period to period in the pre-industrial era and in many places the local geography provided its own constraints, so it is not surprising to find a certain continuity of basic units of exploitation in many parts of Wessex. The shifting patterns of settlements discerned in some parts of the province can be viewed as part of a longer pattern of dispersal and agglomeration of settlements in response to different economic and social pressures. Under the Roman Empire the best places for the location of towns had already been utilized and roads to link important centres had been built. Naturally the Anglo-Saxons made use of these aspects of their Roman inheritance, and when the need for defences or regional centres surfaced many Roman towns came into their own again. However, the particular circumstances of the period might influence whether places did or did not have a medieval future. Although Winchester, for instance, became an episcopal, administrative and trading centre, Silchester, although apparently with a very similar Roman heritage, was all but abandoned. Silchester lay within territory disputed between Wessex and Mercia in the late seventh and eighth centuries, and ended up marginalized on the borders of Hampshire and Berkshire.

Visible signs of Wessex's Anglo-Saxon past are still all around us; not just in museum collections and on archaeological excavations, but in such features as buildings still used for Christian worship and the street-plans of many towns and villages. The names of our settlements are in the majority of cases those which were bestowed during the Anglo-Saxon period and reflect the local geography, land use or landownership of the time they were formed; some include Celtic or Latin elements which acknowledge that there was not a complete break with earlier patterns of nomenclature and settlement. Other influences still felt today may not all be very visible in the landscape, but can be seen more easily on maps and plans. County, parish and estate boundaries in many places still follow the lines of their Anglo-Saxon predecessors, or did so until the fairly recent past. They too may have a visible presence in the landscape in the form of field boundaries or occasionally rather more impressive features such as Bokerley Dyke. They remind us of how much the pattern of secular and ecclesiastical administration of subsequent centuries owed to origins or consolidation within the Anglo-Saxon period. The Anglo-Saxons of Wessex do belong to a remote period when many aspects of life were quite different from our own and cannot now be reconstructed fully, but there are also many facets which link their time to ours, and decisions they made, for instance on how the land was to be divided up and administered, or where centres of religion and trade should be, still dictate aspects of life in Wessex today.

Abbreviations

Æthelweard	*The Chronicle of Æthelweard*, ed. A. Campbell (1962)
Ant J	*Antiquaries Journal*
Arch J	*Archaeological Journal*
ASC	*Anglo-Saxon Chronicle*
ASE	*Anglo-Saxon England*
ASSAH	*Anglo-Saxon Studies in Archaeology and History*
Asser	*Asser's Life of King Alfred*, ed. W.H. Stevenson (1904)
B	*Cartularium Saxonicum*, ed. W. de G. Birch (3 vols, 1885–99)
BAR	British Archaeological Reports (British series unless otherwise stated)
BNJ	*British Numismatic Journal*
CBA	Council for British Archaeology
Chronicle	*Two of the Saxon Chronicles Parallel*, ed. J. Earle and C. Plummer (2 vols, 1892 and 1899)
DB	Domesday Book
Dev Assoc	*Devonshire Association Report and Transactions*
DNHAS	*Dorset Natural History and Archaeology Society*
EETS o.s.	Early English Text Society original series
EHD, I	*English Historical Documents volume I, c. 500–1042*, ed. D. Whitelock (2nd edn., 1979)
EHD, II	*English Historical Documents volume II, 1042–1189*, ed. D.C. Douglas and G. Greenaway (1981)
EHR	*English Historical Review*
EPNS	English Place-Name Society
GP	*Willelmi Malmesbiriensis De Gestis Pontificum Anglorum libri quinque*, ed. N. Hamilton, Rolls series (1870)
Haddan and Stubbs	*Councils and Ecclesiastical Documents relating to Great Britain and Ireland*, ed. A.W. Haddan and W. Stubbs (3 vols, 1869–71)
HE	Bede, *Historia Ecclesiastica Gentis Anglorum*

	[Bede's Ecclesiastical History of the English People], ed. B. Colgrave and R.A.B. Mynors (1969)
Med Arch	*Journal of the Society of Medieval Archaeology*
MGH	*Monumenta Germaniae Historica*
OUCA	Oxford University Committee for Archaeology
PBA	*Proceedings of the British Academy*
PDAS	*Proceedings of the Devonshire Archaeological Society*
PHFCAS	*Proceedings of the Hampshire Field Club and Archaeological Society*
PDNHAS	*Proceedings of the Dorset Natural History and Archaeological Society*
PSANHS	*Proceedings of the Somerset Archaeology and Natural History Society*
RCHM	Royal Commission for Historical Monuments
S	P. Sawyer, *Anglo-Saxon Charters: An Annotated List and Bibliography* (1968)
s.a.	*sub anno*
Tangl	M. Tangl (ed.), *S. Bonifatii et Lulli Epistolae, MGH Epistolae Selectae 1* (Berlin, 1916)
TRHS	*Transactions of the Royal Historical Society* (5th series unless otherwise stated)
VCH	Victoria County History
WAM	*Wiltshire Archaeological and Natural History Magazine*

Bibliography

R. Abels, *Lordship and Military Obligation in Anglo-Saxon England* (1988)

L. Abrams, 'St Patrick and Glastonbury abbey: *nihil ex nihilo fit?*', in *Saint Patrick AD 493–1993*, ed. D.N. Dumville (1993), 233–44

P. Addyman and D. Hill, 'Saxon Southampton: a review of the evidence, part 1', *PHFCAS, 25* (1968), 61–93

P. Addyman and D. Hill, 'Saxon Southampton: a review of the evidence, part 2', *PHFCAS, 26* (1969), 61–96

P. Addyman, B. Hopkins and G. Norton, 'A Saxon-Norman pottery-kiln producing stamped wares at Michelmersh, Hampshire', *Med Arch, 16* (1972), 127–30

P. Addyman and D. Leigh, 'The Anglo-Saxon village at Chalton, Hampshire: first interim report', *Med Arch, 16* (1972), 13–31

P. Addyman and D. Leigh, 'The Anglo-Saxon village at Chalton, Hampshire: second interim report', *Med Arch, 17* (1973), 1–25

L. Alcock, *'By South Cadbury is that Camelot . . .' Excavations of Cadbury Castle 1966–70* (1972)

L. Alcock, 'Cadbury-Camelot: a fifteen-year perspective', *PBA, 68* (1982), 355–88

L. Alcock, 'New perspectives on post-Roman forts', in *Economy, Society and Warfare Among the Britons and the Saxons* (1987), 153–67

F. Aldsworth, 'Droxford Anglo-Saxon cemetery, Soberton, Hampshire', *PHFCAS, 35* (1979), 93–182

J. Allan, *Medieval and Post-Medieval Finds from Exeter 1971–1980* (1984)

J. Allan, C. Henderson and R. Higham, 'Saxon Exeter', in *Anglo-Saxon Towns in Southern England*, ed. J. Haslam (1984), 385–414

O.S. Anderson, *English Hundred Names* (Lund, 1939)

T. Andersson, 'The Viking policy of Ethelred the Unready', *Scandinavian Studies, 59* (1987), 284–98

P. Andrews and D.M. Metcalf, 'A coinage for King Cynewulf', in *Sceattas in England and on the Continent*, ed. D. Hill and D.M. Metcalf, BAR, *128* (1984), 175–80

A. Angenendt, 'The conversion of the Anglo-Saxons considered against the background of the early medieval mission', *Angli e Sassoni al di qua e al di la del Mare, Spoleto Settimane di Studio, 32* (2 vols, 1986), II, 747–81

S. Applebaum, 'Roman Britain', in *The Agrarian History of England and Wales, vol. I.ii, AD 43–1042*, ed. H.P.R. Finberg (1972)

C. Arnold, 'Wealth and social structure: a matter of life and death', in *Anglo-Saxon Cemeteries, 1979*, ed. P. Rahtz, T. Dickinson and L. Watts, BAR, *81* (1980), 81–142

C. Arnold, *The Anglo-Saxon Cemeteries of the Isle of Wight* (1982)

C. Arnold, *Roman Britain to Saxon England* (1984)

C. Arnold, *An Archaeology of the Early Anglo-Saxon Kingdoms* (1988)

G. Astill, 'The towns of Berkshire', in *Anglo-Saxon Towns in Southern England*, ed. J. Haslam (1984), 53–86

M. Aston, 'The towns of Somerset', in *Anglo-Saxon Towns in Southern England*, ed. J. Haslam (1984), 167–202

M. Aston, 'Rural settlement in Somerset: some preliminary thoughts', in *Medieval Villages*, ed. D. Hooke, OUCA, 5 (1985), 80–100

T.H. Aston, 'The origins of the manor in England', *TRHS, 8* (1956), 59–83

F.L. Attenborough, (ed.), *The Laws of the Earliest English Kings* (1922)

J. Backhouse, D.H. Turner and L. Webster, *The Golden Age of Anglo-Saxon Art* (1984)

BAFU (Birmingham University Field Archaeology Unit), *Romans in Shepton Mallett: Excavations at Fosse Lane 1990* (1990)

K. Bailey, 'The Middle Saxons', in *The Origins of Anglo-Saxon Kingdoms*, ed. S. Bassett (1989), 84–96

R. Baldwin, 'Intrusive burial groups in the late Roman cemetery at Lankhills, Winchester – a reassessment of the evidence', *Oxford Journal of Archaeology, 4:1* (1985), 93–104

A. Ballard, *The Domesday Boroughs* (1904)

N. Banton, 'Ealdormen and earls in England from the reign of King Alfred to the reign of King Æthelred II' (D. Phil. thesis, University of Oxford, 1981)

E.E. Barker, 'The Anglo-Saxon Chronicle used by Æthelweard', *Bulletin of the Institute of Historical Research, 40* (1967), 74–91

K. Barker, 'The early Christian topography of Sherborne', *Antiquity, 54* (1980), 229–31

K. Barker, 'The early history of Sherborne', in *The Early Church in Western Britain and Ireland*, ed. S. Pearce, BAR, *102* (1982), 77–116

K. Barker, 'Pen, Ilchester and Yeovil: a study in the landscape history and archaeology of south-east Somerset', *PSANHS, 30* (1986), 11–45

F. Barlow, (ed.), 'The Winton Domesday', in *Winchester in the Early Middle Ages*, ed. M. Biddle, Winchester Studies, *1* (1976), 1–142

F. Barlow, *The English Church 1000–1066* (2nd edn., 1979)

F. Barlow, 'Domesday Book: an introduction', in *Domesday Essays*, ed. C. Holdsworth (1986), 16–28

F. Barlow, K. Dexter, A. Erskine and L. Lloyd, *Leofric of Exeter* (1972)

P. Bartholemew, 'Fifth-century facts', *Britannia, 13* (1982), 261–70

P. Bartholemew, 'Fourth-century Saxons', *Britannia, 15* (1984), 169–85

P.C. Bartrum, (ed.), *Early Welsh Genealogical Tracts* (1966)

S. Bassett, 'Churches in Worcester before and after the conversion of the Anglo-Saxons', *Ant J, 69* (1989), 225–56

S. Bassett, 'In search of the origins of Anglo-Saxon kingdoms', in *The Origins of Anglo-Saxon Kingdoms*, ed. S. Bassett (1989), 3–27

J. Bately, 'The compilation of the Anglo-Saxon Chronicle, 60BC to AD890: vocabulary as evidence', *PBA, 64* (1978), 93–129

D. Bates, *Bibliography of Domesday Book* (1986)

D. Benson and D. Miles, *The Upper Thames Valley: An Archaeological Survey of the River Gravels* (1974)

M. Biddle, 'A late Saxon frieze sculpture from the Old Minster', *Ant J, 66* (1966), 329–32

M. Biddle, 'Excavations at Winchester 1966: fifth interim report', *Ant J, 67* (1967), 251–79

M. Biddle, 'Hampshire and the origins of Wessex', in *Problems in Economic and Social Archaeology*, ed. G. de G. Sieveking *et al.* (1968), 323–41

M. Biddle, 'Excavations at Winchester, 1971: tenth and final interim report, part II', *Ant J, 55* (1975), 295–337

M. Biddle, *'Felix Urbs Winthonia*: Winchester in the age of monastic reform', in *Tenth-Century Studies*, ed. D. Parsons (1975), 123–40

M. Biddle, 'Towns', in *The Archaeology of Anglo-Saxon England*, ed. D. Wilson (1976), 99–150

M. Biddle, (ed.), *Winchester in the Early Middle Ages*, Winchester Studies, *1* (1976)

M. Biddle, 'The study of Winchester: archaeology and history in a British town', *PBA, 69* (1983), 93–135

M. Biddle, 'Seasonal festivals and residence: Winchester, Westminster and Gloucester in the tenth to twelfth centuries', *Anglo-Norman Studies, 8* (1985), 51–72

M. Biddle, 'Archaeology, architecture and the cults of saints in Anglo-Saxon England', in *The Anglo-Saxon Church*, ed. L. Butler and R. Morris, CBA report, *60* (1986), 1–31

M. Biddle, (ed.), *Object and Economy in Medieval Winchester* (2 vols), Winchester Studies, *7.ii* (1990)

M. Biddle and K. Barclay, 'Winchester ware', in *Medieval Pottery from Excavations. Studies presented to Gerald Clough Dunning*, ed. V. Evison, H. Hodges and J.G. Hurst (1974), 137–65

M. Biddle and J. Blair, 'The Hook Norton hoard of 1848: a Viking burial from Oxfordshire?', *Oxoniensia, 57* (1987), 186–95

M. Biddle and D. Hill, 'Late Saxon planned towns', *Ant J, 51* (1971), 70–85

M. Biddle and D. Keene, 'Winchester in the eleventh and twelfth centuries', in *Winchester in the Early Middle Ages*, ed. M. Biddle, Winchester Studies, *1* (1976), 241–448

M. Biddle, M.T. Lambrick and J.N.L. Myres, 'The early history of Abingdon and its abbey', *Med Arch, 12* (1968), 26–69

P.G. Bidwell, *The Legionary Bath-House and Basilica and Forum at Exeter*, Exeter Archaeological Reports, *1* (1979)

W. de Gray Birch, (ed.), *Cartularium Saxonicum* (3 vols, 1885–99)

W. de Gray Birch, (ed.), *Liber Vitae: Register and Martyrology of New Minster and Hyde Abbey, Winchester* (1892)

E.W. Black, 'Romano-British burial customs and religious beliefs in south-east England', *Arch J, 143* (1986), 201–39

M. Blackburn, 'Æthelred's coinage and the payment of tribute', in *The Battle of Maldon in AD 991*, ed. D. Scragg (1991), 156–69

M. Blackburn, 'Coin finds and coin circulation in Lindsey *c.* 600–900', in *Pre-Viking Lindsey*, ed. A. Vince, Lincoln arch. rep., *1* (1993), 80–90

M. Blackburn and H. Pagan, 'A revised check-list of coin hoards from the British Isles *c.* 500–1100', in *Anglo-Saxon Monetary History*, ed. M. Blackburn (1986), 291–313

J. Blair, 'Secular minster churches in Domesday Book', in *Domesday Book: A Reassessment*, ed. P.H. Sawyer (1985), 104–42

J. Blair, 'The local church in Domesday Book and before', in *Domesday Studies*, ed. J.C. Holt (1987), 265–78

J. Blair, 'Minster churches in the landscape', in *Anglo-Saxon Settlements*, ed. D. Hooke (1988), 35–58

J. Blair, (ed.), *Minsters and Parish Churches. The Local Church in Transition 950–1200*, OUCA, *17* (1988)

J. Blair, 'Frithuwold's kingdom and the origins of Surrey', in *The Origins of Anglo-Saxon Kingdoms*, ed. S. Bassett (1989), 97–107

J. Blair, *Early Medieval Surrey. Landholding, Church and Settlement* (1991)

J. Blair, 'Anglo-Saxon minsters: a topographical review', in *Pastoral Care Before the Parish*, ed. J. Blair and R. Sharpe (1992), 226–66

J. Blair, *Anglo-Saxon Oxfordshire* (1994)

E.O. Blake, (ed.), *Liber Eliensis*, Camden Society 3rd series, *92* (1962)

E.O. Blake, (ed.), *The Cartulary of the Priory of St Denys near Southampton* (2 vols, 1981)

C. Blunt, I. Stewart and C.S. Lyon, *Coinage in Tenth-Century England: From Edward the Elder to Edgar's Reform* (1989)

A. Boddington, 'Models of burial, settlement and worship: the final phase reviewed', in *Anglo-Saxon Cemeteries: A Reappraisal*, ed. E. Southworth (1990), 177–99

H.W. Böhme, 'Das Ende der Römerherrschaft in Britannien und die angelsächsische Besiedlung Englands im 5. Jahrhundert', *Jahrbuch des Römisch-Germanischen Zentralmuseums, 33* (1986), 469–574

D. Bonney, 'Early boundaries in Wessex', in *Archaeology and the Landscape*, ed. P. Fowler (1972), 168–86

G.C. Boon, 'The latest objects from Silchester, Hants', *Med Arch, 3* (1959), 79–88

G.C. Boon, *Silchester: The Roman Town of Calleva* (2nd edn., 1974)

J. and C. Bord, *Sacred Waters* (1985)

J. Bourdillon, 'Countryside and town: the animal resources of Saxon Southampton', in *Anglo-Saxon Settlements*, ed. D. Hooke (1988), 176–96

E.G. Bowen, *Saints, Seaways and Settlements in the Celtic Lands* (1969)

H.C. Bowen, *The Archaeology of Bokerley Dyke* ed. B.N. Eagles (1990)

J. Bowen, *Malmesbury Town Trail* (1993)

K. Branigan, 'Villa settlement in the West Country', in *The Roman West Country*, ed. K. Branigan and P.J. Fowler (1976), 120–41

J. Brennan, *Hanging Bowls and their Contexts*, BAR, *220* (1991)

M. Brisbane, 'Hamwic (Saxon Southampton): an eighth-century port and production centre', in *The Rebirth of Towns in the West AD 700–1050*, ed. R. Hodges and B. Hobley, CBA res. rep., *68* (1988), 101–8

R. Bromwich, 'The character of early Welsh tradition', in *Studies in Early British History*, ed. N.K. Chadwick (1954), 83–136

R. Bromwich, (ed.), *Trioedd Ynys Prydein. The Welsh Triads* (2nd edn., 1978)

L.J. Bronnekant, 'Place-names and Anglo-Saxon paganism', *Nomina, 8* (1984), 72

D.A. Brooks, 'A review of the evidence for continuity in British towns in the 5th and 6th centuries', *Oxford Journal of Archaeology, 5:1* (1986), 77–102

N. Brooks, 'The unidentified forts of the Burghal Hidage', *Med Arch, 8* (1964), 74–90

N. Brooks, 'The development of military obligations in eighth and ninth-century England', in *England Before the Conquest: Studies in Primary Sources Presented to Dorothy Whitelock*, ed. P. Clemoes and K. Hughes (1971), 69–84

N. Brooks, 'Anglo-Saxon charters: the work of the last twenty years', *ASE, 3* (1974), 211–31

N. Brooks, 'Arms, status and warfare in late-Saxon England', in *Ethelred the Unready*, ed. D. Hill, BAR, *59* (1978), 81–104

N. Brooks, 'England in the ninth century: the crucible of defeat', *TRHS, 29* (1979), 1–20

N. Brooks, 'The oldest document in the college archives? The Micheldever forgery', in *Winchester College: Sixth-Centenary Essays*, ed. R. Custance (1982), 189–228

N. Brooks, *The Early History of the Church of Canterbury* (1984)

N. Brooks, 'The creation and early structure of the kingdom of Kent', in *The Origins of Anglo-Saxon Kingdoms*, ed. S. Bassett (1989), 55–74

N. Brooks, 'The career of St Dunstan', in *St Dunstan: His Life, Times and Cult*, ed. N. Ramsay and M. Sparkes (1992), 1–23

N. Brooks, 'The administrative background of the Burghal Hidage', in *The Burghal Hidage*, ed. D. Hill and A. Rumble (forthcoming)

N. Brooks and J.A. Graham-Campbell, 'Reflections on the Viking-Age silver hoard from Croydon, Surrey', in *Anglo-Saxon Monetary History*, ed. M. Blackburn (1986), 91–110

P. Brown, *The Cult of the Saints: Its Rise and Function in Latin Christianity* (Chicago, 1981)

J.D. Bu'lock, 'Early Christian memorial formulae', *Archaeologia Cambrensis, 105* (1956), 133–41

L.A. Burgess, *Origins of Southampton* (1964)

A. and T. Burkitt, 'The frontier zone and the siege of Mount Badon: a review of the evidence for their location', *PSANHS, 134* (1990), 81–93

I.C.G. Burrow, 'Roman material from hillforts', in *The End of Roman Britain*, ed. P.J. Casey, BAR, *71* (1979), 212–29

I.C.G. Burrow *Hillfort and Hill-Top Settlement in Somerset in the First to Eighth Centuries AD*, BAR, *91* (1981)

H. Cam, *Liberties and Communities in Medieval England* (1944)

H. Cam, *Law-Finders and Law-Makers in Medieval England* (1962)

K. Cameron, *English Place-Names* (1961)

M.L. Cameron, 'Bald's *Leechbook* and cultural interactions in Anglo-Saxon England', *ASE, 19* (1990), 5–12

A. Campbell, (ed.), *The Chronicle of Æthelweard* (1962)

J. Campbell, 'Observations on English government from the tenth to the twelfth centuries', *TRHS, 25* (1975), 39–54

J. Campbell, *Bede's Reges and Principes* (Jarrow lecture, 1979)

J. Campbell, 'The church in Anglo-Saxon towns', in *The Church in Town and Countryside*, ed. D. Baker, Studies in Church History, *16* (1979), 119–35

J. Campbell, 'Asser's Life of Alfred', in *The Inheritance of Historiography 350–900*, ed. C. Holdsworth and T.P. Wiseman (1986), 115–35

J. Campbell, *Essays in Anglo-Saxon History* (1986)

J. Campbell, 'Some agents and agencies of the late Anglo-Saxon state', in *Domesday Studies*, ed. J.C. Holt (1987), 201–18

M. Carver, 'Ideology and allegiance in early East Anglia', in *Sutton Hoo: Fifty Years After*, ed. R. Farrell and C. Neuman de Vegvar (Kalamazoo, 1989), 173–82

H.M. Chadwick, *Studies on Anglo-Saxon Institutions* (1905)

R.A. Chambers, 'The late and sub-Roman cemetery at Queenford Farm, Dorchester-on-Thames, Oxon.', *Oxoniensia, 52* (1987), 35–69

T.M. Charles-Edwards, 'Kinship, status and the origins of the hide', *Past and Present, 56* (1972), 3–33

T.M. Charles-Edwards, 'Early medieval kingships in the British Isles', in *The Origins of Anglo-Saxon Kingdoms*, ed. S. Bassett (1989), 28–39

P. Chaplais, 'The origin and authenticity of the royal Anglo-Saxon diploma', *Journal of the Society of Archivists, 3* (1965), 48–61

P. Chaplais, 'The authenticity of the royal Anglo-Saxon diplomas of Exeter', *Bulletin of the Institute of Historical Research, 39* (1966), 1–34

M. Chibnall, (ed.), *The Ecclesiastical History of Orderic Vitalis* (6 vols, 1969–81)

C. Clark, 'The narrative mode of the *Anglo-Saxon Chronicle* before the Conquest', in *England Before the Conquest*, ed. P. Clemoes and K. Hughes (1971), 224–30

G.N. Clarke, *Pre-Roman and Roman Winchester: Part II, The Roman Cemetery at Lankhills*, Winchester Studies, 3 (1979)

H. Clarke and B. Ambrosiani, *Towns in the Viking Age* (1991)

H.B. Clarke, 'The Domesday Satellites', in *Domesday Book: A Reassessment*, ed. P. Sawyer (1985), 50–70

J. Clarke and D. Hinton, *The Alfred and Minster Lovell Jewels* (3rd edn., 1971)

A.S. Esmonde Cleary, *The Ending of Roman Britain* (1989)

R. Coates, *The Place-Names of Hampshire* (1989)

R. Coates, 'On some controversy surrounding *Gewissae/Gewissei, Cerdic* and *Ceawlin'*, *Nomina, 13* (1989/90), 1–11

E. Coatsworth, 'Late pre-Conquest sculptures with the crucifixion south of the Humber', in *Bishop Æthelwold: His Career and Influence*, ed. B.A.E. Yorke (1988), 161–93

B. Colgrave, (ed.), *The Life of Bishop Wilfrid by Eddius Stephanus* (1927)

B. Colgrave and R.A.B. Mynors, (eds), *Bede's Ecclesiastical History of the English People* (1969)

P. Connor, *Anglo-Saxon Exeter: A Tenth-Century Cultural History* (1993)

A, Cook and M. Dacre, *Excavations at Portway Andover, 1973–1975*, OUCA monograph, *4* (1985)

G.J. Copley, *The Conquest of Wessex in the Sixth Century* (1954)

N. Corcos, 'Early estates on the Poldens and the origin of settlement at Shapwick', *PSANHS, 127* (1982), 47–54

M. Costen, 'Dunstan, Glastonbury and the economy of Somerset in the tenth century', in *St Dunstan. His Life, Times and Cult*, ed. N. Ramsay, M. Sparks and T. Tatton-Brown (1992), 25–44

M. Costen, 'Huish and worth: Old English survivals in a later landscape', *ASSAH, 5* (1992), 65–83

M. Costen, *The Origins of Somerset* (1992)

J. Cotterill, 'Saxon raiding and the role of the late Roman coastal forts of Britain', *Britannia, 24* (1993), 227–40

M.A. Cotton and P.W. Gathercole, *Excavations at Clausentum, South-ampton 1951–54* (1958)

B. Cox, 'The place-names of the earliest English records', *English Place-Name Society Journal, 8* (1976), 12–66

J. Crook, 'King Edgar's reliquary of St Swithun', *ASE, 21* (1992), 177–202

P. Crummy, 'The system of measurement used in town planning from the ninth to the thirteenth centuries', *ASSAH, 1*, BAR, *72*, 149–64

C. Cubitt, 'Pastoral care and conciliar canons: the provisions of the 747 Council of *Clofesho'*, in *Pastoral Care Before the Parish*, ed. J. Blair and R. Sharpe (1992), 193–211

B. Cunliffe, 'Saxon and Medieval settlement-pattern in the region of Chalton, Hampshire', *Med Arch, 16* (1972), 1–12

B. Cunliffe, 'Chalton, Hants: the evolution of a landscape', *Ant J, 53* (1973), 173–90

B. Cunliffe, *The Regni* (1973)

B. Cunliffe, *Iron Age Communities in Britain* (1974)

B. Cunliffe, *Excavations at Portchester Castle. Vol. I: Roman* (1975)

B. Cunliffe, *Excavations at Portchester Castle. Volume II: Saxon* (1976)

B. Cunliffe, 'Saxon Bath', in *The Anglo-Saxon Towns of Southern England*, ed. J. Haslam (1984), 345–58

B. Cunliffe, *The Temple of Sulis Minerva at Bath, vol. 2 The Finds from the Sacred Spring* (1988)

B. Cunliffe, *Wessex to AD 1000* (1993)

H.C. Darby, *Domesday England* (1977)

H.C. Darby, 'Domesday Book and the geographer', in *Domesday Studies*, ed. J.C. Holt (1987), 101–19

H.C. Darby and E.M. Campbell, *The Domesday Geography of South-East England* (1962)

H.C. Darby and R. Welldon Finn, *The Domesday Geography of South-West England* (1967)

R. Darlington, (ed.), *The Vita Wulfstani of William of Malmesbury*, Camden society 3rd ser., *40* (1928)

R. Darlington, 'Anglo-Saxon Wiltshire' in *VCH Wiltshire, 2*, ed. R.B. Pugh (1955), 1–34

N. Davey, 'A pre-Conquest church and baptistery at Potterne', *WAM, 59* (1964), 116–23

N. Davey, 'Medieval timber buildings in Potterne', *WAM, 83* (1990), 57–69

H.E. Davidson, *Myths and Symbols in Pagan Europe* (1988)

S. Davies, 'Excavations at Old Down Farm, Andover. Part I: Saxon', *PHFCAS, 36* (1980), 161–80

S. Davies, 'The excavation of an Anglo-Saxon cemetery (and some prehistoric pits) at Charlton Plantation, near Downton', *WAM, 79* (1985), 109–54

W. Davies, *The Llandaff Charters* (1979)

W. Davies, 'The Latin charter-tradition in western Britain, Brittany and Ireland in the early medieval period', in *Ireland in Early Medieval Europe*, ed. D. Whitelock, R. McKitterick and D.N. Dumville (1982), 258–80

W. Davies, *Wales in the Early Middle Ages* (1982)

W. Davies, *Patterns of Power in Early Wales* (1990)

W. Davies, 'The myth of the Celtic church', in *The Early Church in Wales and the West*, ed. N. Edwards and A. Lane, Oxbow monographs, *16* (1992), 12–21

W. Davies and H. Vierck, 'The contexts of Tribal Hidage: social aggregates and settlement patterns', *Frühmittelalterliche Studien, 8* (1974), 223–93

R.H.C. Davis, 'Alfred the Great: propaganda and truth', *History, 56* (1971), 169–82

R.H.C. Davis, 'Alfred and Guthrum's frontier', *EHR*, 97 (1982), 803–10

B.K. Davison, 'The Burghal Hidage fort of Eorþeburnan: a suggested identification', *Med Arch, 16* (1972), 123–7

R. Deshman, '*Christus rex et magi reges*: kingship and Christology in Ottonian and Anglo-Saxon art', *Frühmittelalterliche Studien, 10* (1976), 367–405

T.M. Dickinson, *Cuddesdon and Dorchester-on-Thames*, BAR, *1* (1974)

T.M. Dickinson, 'The Anglo-Saxon burial sites of the Upper Thames region and their bearing upon the history of Wessex' (D. Phil. thesis, Oxford University, 1979)

T.M. Dickinson, 'On the origin and chronology of the early Anglo-Saxon disc brooch', *ASSAH, 1*, BAR, 72 (1979), 39–80

T.M. Dickinson, 'The present state of Anglo-Saxon cemetery studies', in *Anglo-Saxon Cemeteries 1979*, ed. P. Rahtz, T.M. Dickinson and L. Watts, BAR, *82* (1980), 11–33

T.M. Dickinson and H. Härke, *Early Anglo-Saxon Shields (Archaeologia, 110)* (1992)

J. McN. Dodgson, 'Domesday Book: place-names and personal names', in *Domesday Studies*, ed. J.C. Holt (1987), 121–38

C. Dodwell, *Anglo-Saxon Art: A New Perspective* (1982)

N. Doggett, 'The Anglo-Saxon see and cathedral of Dorchester-on-Thames: the evidence reconsidered', *Oxoniensia, 51* (1986), 49–61

R.H.M. Dolley, 'The sack of Wilton in 1003 and the chronology of the "Long Cross" and "Helmet" types of Æthelred II', *Nordisk Numismatisk Unions Medlensbled* (1954), 152–6

R.H.M. Dolley, 'The emergency mint of Cadbury', *BNJ, 28* (1955–7), 99–105

R.H.M. Dolley, 'The Shaftesbury hoard of pence of Æthelred II', *Numismatic Chronicle, 18* (1958), 267–80

R.H.M. Dolley, 'The reform of the English coinage under Eadgar', in *Anglo-Saxon Coins*, ed. R.H.M. Dolley (1961), 136–68

R.H.M. Dolley, *The Hiberno-Norse Coins in the British Museum* (1966)

R.H.M. Dolley, 'The location of the pre-Ælfredian mint(s) of Wessex', *PHFCAS, 27* (1970), 57–61

D.C. Douglas and G. Greenaway, (eds), *English Historical Documents volume II, 1042–1189* (1981)

A. Down and M. Welch, *Chichester Excavations 7: Apple Down and the Mardens* (1990)

G. Duby, *The Three Orders: Feudal Society Imagined* (1980)

D.N. Dumville, 'The Anglian collection of royal genealogies and regnal lists', *ASE, 5* (1976), 23–50

D.N. Dumville, 'The ætheling: a study in Anglo-Saxon constitutional history', *ASE, 8* (1979), 1–33

D.N. Dumville, 'The chronology of *De Excidio Britanniae*, Book 1', in *Gildas: New Approaches*, ed. M. Lapidge and D.N. Dumville (1984), 61–84

D.N. Dumville, 'The West Saxon Genealogical Regnal List and the chronology of early Wessex', *Peritia, 4* (1985), 21–66

D.N. Dumville, 'The West Saxon Genealogical Regnal List: manuscripts and texts', *Anglia, 104* (1986), 1–32

D.N. Dumville, 'English square minuscule script: the background and earliest phases', *ASE*, 16 (1987), 147–79

D.N. Dumville, 'The Tribal Hidage: an introduction to its texts and their history', in *The Origins of Anglo-Saxon Kingdoms*, ed. S. Bassett (1989), 225–30

D.N. Dumville, *Wessex and England from Alfred to Edgar* (1992)

D.N. Dumville and M. Lapidge, (eds), *The Annals of St Neots with Vita Prima Sancti Neoti* (1984)

R.W. Dunning, 'Ilchester', in *Victoria History of Somerset*, III, ed. R.W. Dunning (1974), 179–203

R.W. Dunning, 'Ilchester: a study in continuity', *PSANHS, 119* (1975), 44–50

C. Dyer, 'Towns and cottages in eleventh-century England', in *Studies in Medieval History presented to R.H.C. Davis*, ed. H. Mayr-Harting and R.I. Moore (1985), 91–106

C. Dyer, 'The retreat from marginal land: the growth and decline of medieval rural settlements', in *The Rural Settlements of Medieval England*, ed. M. Aston, D. Austin and C. Dyer (1989), 45–58

B. Eagles, 'Pagan Anglo-Saxon burials at West Overton', *WAM, 80* (1986), 103–20

B. Eagles, 'The archaeological evidence for settlement in the fifth to seventh centuries AD', in *Medieval Settlement in Wessex* ed. M. Aston and C. Lewis (forthcoming)

B. Eagles and C. Mortimer, 'Early Anglo-Saxon artefacts from Hod Hill, Dorset', *Ant J, 73* (1993), 132–40

J. Earle, and C. Plummer, (eds), *Two of the Saxon Chronicles Parallel* (2 vols, 1892 and 1899)

E.A. Edmonds, M.C. Mckeown and M. Williams, *British Regional Geology. South-West England* (1975)

H. Edwards, 'Two documents from Aldhelm's Malmesbury', *Bulletin of the Institute of Historical Research, 59* (1986), 1–19

H. Edwards, *The Charters of the Early West Saxon Kingdom*, BAR, *198* (1988)

A. Ellison, 'Natives, Romans and Christians on West Hill, Uley: an interim report on the excavation of a ritual complex of the first millennium AD', in *Temples, Churches and Religion: Recent Research in Roman Britain*, ed. W. Rodwell, BAR, *77(i)* (1980), 303–28

A. Ellison and P. Rahtz, 'Excavations at Whitsbury Castle Ditches, Hampshire, 1960', *PHFCAS, 43* (1987), 63–81

M.J. Enright, 'Charles the Bald and Æthelwulf of Wessex: the alliance of 856 and the strategies of royal succession', *Journal of Medieval History, 5* (1979), 291–302

V.I. Evison, *The Fifth-Century Invasions South of the Thames* (1965)

V.I. Evison, 'A Viking grave at Sonning, Berkshire', *Ant J, 49* (1969), 330–45

V.I. Evison, *An Anglo-Saxon Cemetery at Alton, Hampshire*, Hampshire Field Club monograph, *4* (1988)

J.R. Fairbrother, *Faccombe Netherton. Excavations of a Saxon and Medieval Manorial Complex* (2 vols), British Museum Occasional Paper, *74* (1990)

D.E. Farwell and T.L. Molleson, (eds), *Excavations at Poundbury 1966–80. Volume II: The Cemeteries*, DNHAS monograph, *11* (1993)

P. Fasham and R. Whinney, (eds), *Archaeology and the M3*, Hampshire Field Club monograph, *7* (1991)

M. Faull, 'The semantic development of Old English *walh*', *Leeds Studies in English, 8* (1976), 20–44

G. Fehring, *The Archaeology of Medieval Germany*, trans. R. Samson (1991)

Olof von Feilitzen, 'The personal names and bynames of the Winton Domesday', in *Winchester in the Early Middle Ages*, ed. M. Biddle, Winchester Studies, *1* (1976), 143–229

C. Fell, *Edward King and Martyr* (1971)

H.P.R. Finberg, 'The house of Ordgar and the foundation of Tavistock Abbey', *EHR, 58* (1943), 190–201

H.P.R. Finberg, *Tavistock Abbey* (1953)

H.P.R. Finberg, 'Supplement to the early charters of Devon and Cornwall', in W.G. Hoskins, *The Westward Expansion of Wessex* (1960), 23–33

H.P.R. Finberg, *The Early Charters of Wessex* (1964)

H.P.R. Finberg, *Lucerna. Studies of Some Problems in the Early History of England* (1964)

H.P.R. Finberg, *The Agrarian History of England and Wales, vol. I.ii, AD 43–1042* (1972)

H.P.R. Finberg, *The Formation of England* (1974)

R. Welldon Finn, *An Introduction to Domesday Book* (1963)

R. Welldon Finn, *Domesday Studies: The Liber Exoniensis* (1964)

R. Welldon Finn, *Domesday Book; A Guide* (1973)

D. Fisher, 'The anti-monastic reaction in the reign of Edward the Martyr', *Cambridge Historical Journal, 10* (1950–2), 254–70

R. Fleming, 'Monastic lands and England's defence in the Viking age', *EHR, 100* (1985), 247–65

R. Fleming, *Kings and Lords in Conquest England* (1991)

R. Foot, 'An early Christian symbol from Winchester?', *Winchester Museums Service Newsletter, 13* (July 1992), 6–8

S. Foot, 'Anglo-Saxon minsters: a review of terminology', in *Pastoral Care Before the Parish*, ed. J. Blair and R. Sharpe (1992), 212–25

S. Foster, 'A gazetteer of the Anglo-Saxon sculpture in historic Somerset', *PSANHS, 131* (1987), 49–80

E. Fowler, 'The origins and development of the penannular brooch in Europe', *Proceedings of the Prehistoric Society, 26* (1960), 149–77

P.J. Fowler, 'Hill-forts, AD 400–700', in *The Iron Age and its Hill-Forts*, ed. D. Hill and M. Jesson (1971), 203–13

A. Fox, 'Some evidence for a Dark Age trading site at Bantham, near Thurlestone, South Devon', *Ant J, 35* (1955), 55–67

A. Fox, *South-West England* (2nd edn., 1973)

A. and C. Fox, 'Wansdyke reconsidered', *Arch J, 115* (1958), 1–48

H.S.A. Fox, 'Field systems of East and South Devon, Part I: East Devon', *Dev Assoc, 104* (1972), 81–135

H.S.A. Fox, 'Approaches to the adoption of the Midland system', in *The Origins of Open-Field Agriculture*, ed. T. Rowley (1981), 64–111

W.H.C. Frend, 'Romano-British Christianity in the west: comparison and contrast', in *The Early Church in Western Britain and Ireland*, ed. S. Pearce, BAR, *102* (1982), 5–16

S. Frere, 'The Silchester church: the excavation by Sir Ian Richmond in 1961', *Archaeologia, 105* (1975), 277–302

M. Fulford, 'Pottery production and trade at the end of Roman Britain: the case against continuity', in *The End of Roman Britain*, ed. P.J. Casey, BAR,*71* (1979), 120–32

M. Fulford, *Guide to the Silchester Excavations 1979–81: Amphitheatre and Forum Basilica* (1982)

M. Fulford, 'Byzantium and Britain: a Mediterranean perspective on post-Roman Mediterranean imports in Western Britain and Ireland', *Med Arch, 33* (1989), 1–6

M. Fulford and B. Sellwood, 'The Silchester ogham stone: a reconsideration', *Antiquity, 54* (1980), 95–9

M. Gaimster, 'Scandinavian gold bracteates in Britain; money and media in the Dark Ages', *Med Arch, 36* (1992), 1–28

V.H. Galbraith, *The Making of Domesday Book* (1961)

P. Gallious and M. Jones, *The Bretons* (1991)

F. and R. Gameson, 'The Anglo-Saxon inscription at St Mary's Church, Breamore, Hampshire', *ASSAH, 6* (1993), 1–11

R. Gameson, 'English manuscript art in the mid-eleventh century: the decorative tradition', *Ant J, 71* (1991), 64–122

R. Gameson, 'The decoration of the Tanner Bede', *ASE, 21* (1992), 115–59

F.L. Ganshof, *Frankish Institutions under Charlemagne* (New York, 1965, reprinted 1970)

H. Geake, 'Burial practice in seventh and eighth-century England', in *The Age of Sutton Hoo*, ed. M. Carver (1992), 83–94

M. Gelling, 'Place-names and Anglo-Saxon paganism', *University of Birmingham Historical Journal, 8* (1961–2), 7-25

M. Gelling, *The Place-Names of Berkshire. Part I*, EPNS, *49* (1973)

M. Gelling, *The Place-Names of Berkshire. Part II*, EPNS, *50* (1974)

M. Gelling, 'Further thoughts on pagan place-names', in *Place-Name Evidence for Anglo-Saxon Invasion and Scandinavian Settlement*, ed. K. Cameron (1975), 99–114

M. Gelling, *The Place-Names of Berkshire. Part III*, EPNS, *51* (1976)

M. Gelling, 'Latin loan-words in Old English place-names', *ASE, 6* (1977), 1–14

M. Gelling, *Signposts to the Past. Place-Names and the History of England* (1978)

M. Gelling, 'A chronology for English place-names', in *Anglo-Saxon Settlements*, ed. D. Hooke (1988), 59–76

R. Gem, 'The Romanesque rebuilding of Westminster abbey', *Anglo-Norman Studies, 3* (1980), 33–64

R. Gem, 'Anglo-Saxon architecture of the tenth and eleventh centuries', in *The Golden Age of Anglo-Saxon Art*, ed. J. Backhouse, D. Turner and L. Webster (1984), 139–42

R. Gem, 'The English parish church in the eleventh and early twelfth centuries: a Great Rebuilding?', in *Minsters and Parish Churches. The Local Church in Transition*, ed. J. Blair, OUCA, *17* (1988), 21–30

R. Gem, 'Church architecture', in *The Making of England*, ed. L. Webster and J. Backhouse (1991), 185–8

R. Gem and P. Tudor-Craig, 'A "Winchester School" wall-painting at Nether Wallop, Hampshire', *ASE, 9* (1981), 115–36

J. Gibb, 'The Anglo-Saxon cathedral at Sherborne', *Arch J, 132* (1975), 71–110

J. Gillingham, '"The most precious jewel in the English crown": levels of Danegeld and Heregeld in the early eleventh century', *EHR, 104* (1989), 373–84

J. Gillingham, 'Chronicles and coins as evidence for levels of tribute and taxation in late tenth and early eleventh century England', *EHR, 105* (1990), 939–50

C.J. Gingell, 'The excavation of an early Anglo-Saxon cemetery at Collingbourne Ducis', *WAM, 70/71* (1978), 61–98

H. Goetz, 'Serfdom and the beginnings of a "seigneurial system" in the Carolingian period: a survey of the evidence', *Early Medieval Europe, 1* (1993), 29–51

B.J. Golding, 'An introduction to the Hampshire Domesday', in *The Hampshire Domesday*, Alecto historical editions (1989), 1–27

I. Goodall, 'The medieval iron objects', in *Object and Economy in Medieval Winchester*, ed. M. Biddle, Winchester Studies, *7.ii* (2 vols, 1990), *I*, 36–41

J.E.B. Gover, A. Mawer and F.M. Stenton, *The Place-Names of Devon. Part I*, EPNS, *8* (1931)

A. Gransden, 'The growth of Glastonbury traditions and legends in the twelfth century', *Journal of Ecclesiastical History, 27* (1976), 337–58

R. Grant, 'Royal forests: Selwood', in *VCH Wiltshire, IV*, ed. E. Crittall (1959), 414–17

C.J.S. Green, 'The cemetery of a Romano-British Christian community at Poundbury, Dorchester, Dorset', in *The Early Church in Western Britain and Ireland*, ed. S.M. Pearce, BAR, *102* (1982), 61–76

C.J.S. Green, 'Early Anglo-Saxon burials at the "Trumpet Major" public house, Allington Avenue, Dorchester', *PDNHAS, 106* (1984), 148–52

C.J.S. Green, *Excavations at Poundbury, volume I: The Settlements*, DNHAS monograph, 7 (1988)

H.S. Green, 'Wansdyke, excavations 1966 to 1970', *WAM, 66* (1971), 129–46

G. Greenaway, 'Saint Boniface as a man of letters', in *The Greatest Englishman*. ed. T. Reuter (1980), 31–46

N. Gregson, 'The multiple estate model: some critical questions', *Journal of Historical Geography, 11* (1985), 339–51

M. Gretsch, 'Æthelwold's translation of the *Regula Sancti Benedicti* and its Latin exemplar', *ASE, 3* (1974), 125–51

P. Grierson, 'Grimbald of St Bertin's', *EHR, 55* (1940), 529–61

P. Grierson, 'Commerce in the Dark Ages: a critique of the evidence', *TRHS, 9* (1959), 123–40

P. Grierson and M. Blackburn, *Medieval European Coinage*, I (1986)

F.M. Griffith, 'Salvage observations at the Dark Age site at Bantham Ham, Thurlestone, in 1982', *PDAS, 44* (1986), 39–57

L.V. Grinsell, 'Barrows in Anglo-Saxon land charters', *Ant J*, 71 (1991), 46–63

A.W. Haddan and W. Stubbs, (eds), *Councils and Ecclesiastical Documents relating to Great Britain and Ireland* (3 vols, 1869–71)

N. Hamilton, (ed.), *Willelmi Malmesbiriensis De Gestis Pontificum Anglorum, libri quinque*, Rolls series (1870)

M.J. Hare, 'The Anglo-Saxon church of St Peter, Titchfield', *PHFCAS, 32* (1976), 5–48

M.J. Hare, 'Investigations at the Anglo-Saxon church of St Peter, Titchfield, 1982–9', *PHFCAS, 47* (1992), 117–44

H. Härke, 'The Anglo-Saxon weapon burial rite', *Past and Present, 126* (1990), 22–43

H. Härke, 'Changing symbols in a changing society: the Anglo-Saxon weapon burial rite in the seventh century', in *The Age of Sutton Hoo*, ed. M. Carver (1992), 149–66

F. Harmer, (ed.), *Anglo-Saxon Writs* (1952)

K. Harrison, 'Early Wessex annals in the Anglo-Saxon Chronicle', *EHR, 86* (1971), 527–33

K. Harrison, *The Framework of Anglo-Saxon History to AD 900* (1976)

C. Hart, 'The Tribal Hidage', *TRHS, 21* (1971), 133–57

C. Hart, 'Athelstan "Half King" and his family', *ASE, 2* (1973), 115–44

C. Hart, *The Early Charters of Northern England and the North Midlands* (1975)

P.D.A. Harvey, '*Rectitudines Singularum Personarum* and *Gerefa*', *EHR, 108* (1993), 1–22

S. Harvey, 'Domesday Book and its predecessors', *EHR, 86* (1971), 753–73

P.H. Hase, 'The development of the parish in Hampshire' (Ph. D. thesis, Cambridge University, 1975)

P.H. Hase, 'The mother churches of Hampshire', in *Minsters and Parish Churches*, ed. J. Blair, OUCA, *17* (1988), 45–66

J. Haslam, 'A Middle Saxon smelting site at Ramsbury, Wiltshire', *Med Arch, 24* (1980), 1–68

J. Haslam, 'Introduction', in *Anglo-Saxon Towns in Southern England*, ed. J. Haslam (1984), xi–xviii

J. Haslam, 'The towns of Devon', in *Anglo-Saxon Towns in Southern England*, ed. J. Haslam (1984), 249–83

J. Haslam, 'The towns of Wiltshire', in *Anglo-Saxon Towns in Southern England*, ed. J. Haslam (1984), 87–147

J. Haslam, 'The metrology of Anglo-Saxon Cricklade', *Med Arch, 30* (1986), 100–2

S. Chadwick Hawkes, 'Anglo-Saxon Kent *c.* 425–725', in *Archaeology in Kent to AD 1500*, ed. P.E. Leach, CBA rep., *48* (1982), 64–78

S. Chadwick Hawkes, 'The early Saxon period', in *The Archaeology of the Oxford Region*, ed. G. Briggs, J. Cook and T. Rowley (1986), 64–108

S. Chadwick Hawkes, 'The south-east after the Romans: the Saxon settlement', in *The Saxon Shore. A Handbook*, ed. V.A. Maxfield (1989), 78–95

S. Chadwick Hawkes and G.C. Dunning, 'Soldiers and settlers in Britain, fourth to fifth century', *Med Arch, 5* (1961), 1–71

T. Hearne, (ed.), *Johannis Glastoniensis Chronica sive Historia de rebus Glastoniensibus* (2 vols, 1727)

M. Heaton, 'Two mid-Saxon grain-driers and later medieval features at Chantry Field, Gillingham, Dorset', *PDNHAS, 114* (1992), 97–126

C. Heighway, *Anglo-Saxon Gloucestershire* (1987)

C.G. Henderson and P.T. Bidwell, 'The Saxon minster at Exeter', in *The Early Church in Western Britain and Ireland*, ed. S. Pearce, BAR, *102* (1982), 145–75

M.W. Herren, 'Gildas and early British monasticism', in *Britain 400–600: Language and History*, ed. A. Bammesberger and A. Wollmann (Heidelberg, 1990), 65–83

J. Higgitt, 'Glastonbury, Dunstan, monasticism and manuscripts', *Art History, 2* (1979), 275–90

N.J. Higham, 'Gildas, Roman walls and British dykes', *Cambridge Medieval Celtic Studies, 22* (1991), 1–14

N.J.Higham, 'Old light on the Dark Age landscape: the description of Britain in the *De Excidio Britanniae* of Gildas', *Journal of Historical Geography, 17* (1991), 363–72

N.J. Higham, *Rome, Britain and the Anglo-Saxons* (1992)

D. Hill, 'The Burghal Hidage – Southampton', *PHFCAS, 24* (1967), 59–61

D. Hill, 'The Burghal Hidage: the establishment of a text', *Med Arch, 13* (1969), 84–92

D. Hill, 'Continuity from Roman to Medieval: Britain', in *European Towns*, ed. M. Barley (1977), 293–302

D. Hill, 'Trends in the development of towns during the reign of Æthelred II', in *Ethelred the Unready*, ed. D. Hill, BAR, *59* (1978), 213–26

D. Hill, *An Atlas of Anglo-Saxon England* (1981)

J. Hill, 'Monastic reform and the secular church: Ælfric's pastoral letters in context', in *England in the Eleventh Century. Proceedings of the 1990 Harlaxton Symposium*, ed. C. Hicks (1992), 103–17

J. Hinchcliffe, 'An early medieval settlement at Cowage Farm, Foxley, near Malmesbury', *Arch J, 143* (1986), 240–59

R. Hingley, 'A Romano-British "religious complex" at Frilford', *Oxford Journal of Archaeology, 4* (1985), 201–14

D. Hinton, 'Amesbury and the early history of its abbey', in *The Amesbury Millennium Lectures*, ed. J. Chandler (1979), 20–31

D. Hinton, 'Hampshire's Anglo-Saxon origins', in *The Archaeology of Hampshire*, ed. S.J. Shennan and R.T. Schadla Hall, Hampshire Field Club monograph, *1* (1981), 56–65

D. Hinton, 'The topography of Sherborne – early Christian?', *Antiquity, 55* (1981), 222–3

D. Hinton, 'The place of Basing in mid-Saxon history', *PHFCAS, 42* (1986), 162–3

D. Hinton, *Archaeology, Economy and Society. England from the Fifth to the Fifteenth Century* (1990)

D. Hinton, 'The medieval gold, silver and copper alloy objects', in *Object and Economy in Medieval Winchester*, ed. M. Biddle, Winchester Studies 7.ii (2 vols, 1990), I, 29–35

D. Hinton, 'The inscribed stones in Lady St Mary Church, Wareham', *PDNHAS, 114* (1992), 260

D. Hinton, 'Is there anything hidden in the hidages?', in *The Burghal Hidage*, ed. D. Hill and A. Rumble (forthcoming)

D. Hinton and R. Hodges, 'Excavations in Wareham, 1974–5', *PDNHAS, 99* (1977), 42–83

D. Hinton, S. Keene and K. Qualmann, 'The Winchester reliquary', *Med Arch, 25* (1981), 45–77

D. Hinton and C.J. Webster, 'Excavations at the church of St Martin, Wareham, 1985–6, and "minsters" in south-east Dorset', *PDNHAS, 109* (1987), 47–54

R. Hodges, 'State formation and the role of trade in Middle Saxon England', in *Social Organisation and Settlement*, ed. D. Green, C. Haselgrove and M. Spriggs (2 vols), BAR International series, *47* (1978), II, 439–53

R. Hodges, *Dark Age Economics: The Origins of Towns and Trade, AD 600–1000* (1982)

O. Holder-Egger, (ed.), *Vitae Willibaldi et Wynnebaldi, MGH Scriptores*, 15.i (Hanover, 1887), 80–117

P. Holdsworth, 'Saxon Southampton', in *Anglo-Saxon Towns in Southern England*, ed. J. Haslam (1984), 331–43

S. Hollis, *Anglo-Saxon Women and the Church* (1992)

C. Warren Hollister, *Anglo-Saxon Military Institutions* (1962)

D. Hooke, *The Anglo-Saxon Landscape: The Kingdom of the Hwicce* (1985)

D. Hooke, 'Regional variation in southern and central England in the Anglo-Saxon period and its relationship to land units and development', in *Anglo-Saxon Settlements*, ed. D. Hooke (1988), 123–52

D. Hooke, 'Studies on Devon charter boundaries', *Dev Assoc, 122* (1990), 193–211

N. Hooper, 'The housecarls in England in the eleventh century', *Anglo-Norman Studies, 7* (1984), 161–76

N. Hooper, 'Some observations on the navy in late Anglo-Saxon England', in *Studies in Medieval History Presented to R. Allen Brown*, ed. C. Harper-Bill, C. Holdsworth and J. Nelson (1989), 203–13

B. Hope-Taylor, *Yeavering: An Anglo-British Centre of Early Northumbria* (1977)

E. Horne, 'The Anglo-Saxon cemetery at Camerton, Somerset, part I', *PSANHS, 74* (1928), 61–70

E. Horne, 'The Anglo-Saxon cemetery at Camerton, Somerset, part II', *PSANHS, 79* (1933), 39–63

W.G. Hoskins, 'The Highland Zone in Domesday Book', in *Provincial England. Essays in Social and Economic History* (1965), 15–52

W.G. Hoskins, *The Westward Expansion of Wessex* (1970)

N. Howe, *Migration and Mythmaking in Anglo-Saxon England* (Yale, 1989)

D. Howlett, 'Inscriptions and design of the Ruthwell Cross', in *The Ruthwell Cross*, ed. B. Cassidy (Princeton, 1992), 71–93

J.W. Huggett, 'Imported grave goods and the early Anglo-Saxon economy', *Med Arch, 32* (1988), 63–96

J.E. Jackson, 'Selwood Forest', *WAM, 23* (1887), 268–94

K. Jackson, *Language and History in Early Britain* (1953)

S.T. James, A. Marshall and M. Millett, 'An early medieval building tradition', *Arch J, 141* (1985), 182–215

K.S. Jarvis, *Excavations in Christchurch 1969–1980*, DNHAS monograph, *5* (1983)

E. John, *Land Tenure in Early England* (1960)

E. John, 'The church of Winchester and the tenth-century reformation', *Bulletin of the John Rylands Library, 74* (1964–5), 404–29

E. John, *Orbis Britanniae and Other Studies* (1966)

E. John, 'The world of Abbot Ælfric', in *Ideal and Reality in Frankish and Anglo-Saxon Society*, ed. P. Wormald (1983), 300–16

D.E. Johnson, (ed.), *The Saxon Shore*, CBA res. rep., *18* (1977)

S. Johnson, *The Roman Forts of the Saxon Shore* (1979)

J.E.A. Joliffe, *Pre-Feudal England: The Jutes* (1933)

A. Jones, 'The significance of the regal consecration of Edgar in 973', *Journal of Ecclesiastical History, 33* (1982), 375–90

A.H.M. Jones, *The Later Roman Empire AD 284–602: A Social, Economic and Administrative Survey* (2nd edn., 1973)

G.R.J. Jones, 'Post-Roman Wales', in *The Agrarian History of England and Wales, vol. I.ii, AD 43–1042*, ed. H.P.R. Finberg (1972), 281–382

G.R.J. Jones, 'Multiple estates and early settlements' in *Medieval Settlement*, ed. P. Sawyer (1976), 11–40

L. Keen, 'The towns of Dorset', in *Anglo-Saxon Towns in Southern England*, ed. J. Haslam (1984), 203–47

D. Keene, *Survey of Medieval Winchester*, Winchester Studies, *2* (2 vols, 1985)

D. Keene, 'Tanning', in *Object and Economy in Medieval Winchester*, ed. M. Biddle, Winchester Studies, *7.ii* (2 vols, 1990), I, 243–5

B.R. Kemp, 'The mother church of Thatcham', *Berkshire Archaeological Journal, 63* (1967–8), 15–22

A Kennedy, 'Cnut's law code of 1018', *ASE, 11* (1983), 57–81

J. Kent, 'The end of Roman Britain: the literary and numismatic evidence reviewed', in *The End of Roman Britain*, ed. P.J. Casey, BAR, *71* (1979), 15–27

S. Keynes, 'The declining reputation of King Æthelred the Unready', in *Ethelred the Unready*, ed. D. Hill, BAR, *59* (1978), 227–53

S. Keynes, *The Diplomas of King Æthelred 'The Unready' 978–1016* (1980)

S. Keynes, 'King Athelstan's books', in *Learning and Literature in Anglo-Saxon England*, ed. M. Lapidge and H. Gneuss (1985), 143–201

S. Keynes, 'A tale of two kings: Alfred the Great and Æthelred the Unready', *TRHS, 36* (1986), 195–217

S. Keynes, 'Regenbald the Chancellor' [*sic*], *Anglo-Norman Studies, 10* (1987), 185–222

S. Keynes, 'The lost cartulary of Abbotsbury', *ASE, 18* (1989), 207–43

S. Keynes, 'Crime and punishment in the reign of King Æthelred the Unready', in *People and Places in Northern Europe 500–1600. Essays in Honour of Peter Hayes Sawyer*, ed. I. Wood and N. Lund (1991), 67–81

S. Keynes, 'The historical context of the Battle of Maldon', in *The Battle of Maldon AD 991*, ed. D. Scragg (1991), 81–113

S. Keynes, 'The Fonthill letter', in *Words, Texts and Manuscripts. Studies in Anglo-Saxon Culture Presented to Helmut Gneuss*, ed. M. Korhammer (1992), 53–97

S. Keynes and M. Lapidge, (trans.), *Alfred the Great* (1983)

A. King, 'The Roman church at Silchester reconsidered', *Oxford Journal of Archaeology, 2* (1983), 225–38

A. King, 'Excavations at Meonstoke, Hampshire' (forthcoming)

D. Kirby, 'Problems of early West Saxon history', *EHR, 80* (1965), 10–29

D. Kirby, 'Bede's native sources for the *Historia Ecclesiastica*', *Bulletin of the John Rylands Libarary, 48* (1966), 341–71

D. Kirby, 'Asser and his Life of King Alfred', *Studia Celtica, 6* (1971), 12–35

D. Kirby, *The Earliest English Kings* (1991)

B. Kjølbye-Biddle, 'The 7th century minster at Winchester interpreted', in *The Anglo-Saxon Church*, ed. L. Butler and R. Morris, CBA res. rep., *60* (1986), 196–209

B. Kjølbye-Biddle, 'Dispersal or concentration: the disposal of the Winchester dead over 2000 years', in *Death in Towns*, ed. S. Bassett (1993), 210–47

B. Kjølbye-Biddle, 'Old Minster, St Swithun's Day 1093', in *Winchester Cathedral: Nine Hundred Years*, ed. J. Crook (1993), 13–20

B. Kjølbye-Biddle and R.I. Page, 'A Scandinavian rune-stone from Winchester', *Ant J, 55* (1975), 389–94

A. Klinck, 'Anglo-Saxon women and the law', *Journal of Medieval History, 8* (1982), 107–22

E. Klingelhöfer, 'Anglo-Saxon manors of the Upper Itchen valley: their origin and evolution', *PHFCAS, 46* (1991), 31–40

J. Knight, 'The early Christian Latin inscriptions of Britain and Gaul: chronology and context', in *The Early Church in Wales and the West*, ed. N. Edwards and A. Lane, Oxbow monographs, *16* (1992), 45–50

G.M. Knocker, 'Early burials and an Anglo-Saxon cemetery at Snell's Corner near Horndean, Hampshire', *PHFCAS, 19* (1955), 117–70

D. Knowles, *The Monastic Order in England* (2nd edn., 1963)

V. Lagorio, 'The evolving legend of St Joseph of Glastonbury', *Speculum, 46* (1971), 209–31

L. Lancaster, 'Kinship in Anglo-Saxon society', *British Journal of Sociology, 9* (1958), 230–48, 359–77

M. Lapidge, 'St Dunstan's Latin poetry', *Anglia, 98* (1980), 101–6

M. Lapidge, 'Some Latin poems as evidence for the reign of Athelstan', *ASE, 9* (1981), 61–98

M. Lapidge, 'The cult of St Indract at Glastonbury', in *Ireland in Early Medieval Europe*, ed. D. Whitelock, R. McKitterick and D.N. Dumville (1982), 179–212

M. Lapidge, 'Gildas's education and the Latin culture of sub-Roman Britain', in *Gildas: New Approaches*, ed. M. Lapidge and D.N. Dumville (1984), 27–50

M. Lapidge, 'Æthelwold as scholar and teacher', in *Bishop Æthelwold: His Career and Influence*, ed. B.A.E. Yorke (1988), 89–117

M. Lapidge, (ed.), *Wulfstan of Winchester. Life of St Æthelwold* (1991)

M. Lapidge and M. Herren, (trans.) *Aldhelm: The Prose Works* (1979)

M. Lapidge and J. Rosier, (trans.) *Aldhelm: The Poetic Works* (1985)

V. Law, 'The study of Latin grammar in eighth-century Southumbria', *ASE*, 12 (1983), 43–71

M.K. Lawson, 'The collection of Danegeld and Heregeld in the reigns of Æthelred II and Cnut', *EHR, 99* (1984), 721–38

M.K. Lawson, '"Those stories look true": levels of taxation in the reigns of Æthelred II and Cnut', *EHR, 104* (1989), 385–406

M.K. Lawson, 'Danegeld and Heregeld once more', *EHR, 105* (1990), 951–61

M.K. Lawson, *Cnut: The Danes in England in the Early Eleventh Century* (1993)

P. Leach, *Ilchester. Vol. I: Excavations 1974–5* (1982)

R. Leech, 'Religion and burials in South Somerset and North Dorset', in *Temples, Churches and Religion: Recent Research in Roman Britain*, ed. W. Rodwell, BAR, *77(i)* (1980), 329–66

R. Leech, 'The excavation of a Romano-British farmstead and cemetery on Bradley Hill, Somerset', *Britannia, 12* (1981), 177–252

R. Legg, *Cerne's Giant and Village Guide* (1986)

W. Levison, (ed.), *Vitae Sancti Bonifatii, MGH Scriptores Rerum Germanicarum* (Hanover, 1905)

W. Levison, *England and the Continent in the Eighth Century* (1946)

E. Levy, *West-Roman Vulgar Law: The Law of Property* (Philadelphia, 1954)

F. Liebermann, *Die Gesetze der Angelsachsen* (3 vols, Halle, 1903–16)

H.R. Loyn, 'Boroughs and mints, AD 900–1066', in *Anglo-Saxon Coins*, ed. R.H.M. Dolley (1961), 122–35

H.R. Loyn, 'The hundred in England in the tenth and early eleventh centuries', in *British Government and Administration: Studies Presented to S.B. Chrimes*, ed. H. Hearder and H.R. Loyn (1974), 1–15

H.R. Loyn, 'Kinship in Anglo-Saxon England', *ASE, 3* (1974), 197–209

H.R. Loyn, *The Governance of Anglo-Saxon England, 500–1087* (1984)

N. Lund, *Two Voyagers at the Court of King Alfred: Ohthere and Wulfstan* (1984)

J.H. Lynch, *Godparents and Kinship in Early Medieval Europe* (Princeton, 1986)

R.A.S. Macalister, *Corpus Inscriptionum Insularum Celticarum*, II (Dublin, 1949)

F. McAvoy, 'Excavations at Daw's Castle, Watchet, 1982', *PSANHS, 130* (1986)

M.R. McCarthy and C.M. Brooks, *Medieval Pottery in Britain AD 900–1600* (1988)

E. McClure, 'The Wareham inscriptions', *EHR, 22* (1907), 728–30

M. McGarvie, *The Bounds of Selwood*, Frome Historical Research Group occasional papers, *1* (1978)

M. McGatch, *Preaching and Theology in Anglo-Saxon England; Ælfric and Wulfstan* (Toronto, 1977)

K. Mack, 'Changing thegns: Cnut's conquest and the English aristocracy', *Albion, 16* (1984), 357–87

K. Mack, 'The stallers: administrative innovation in the reign of Edward the Confessor', *Journal of Medieval History, 12* (1986), 123–34

R. McKitterick, *The Frankish Church and the Carolingian Reforms 789–895* (1977)

J.R. Maddicott, 'Trade, industry and the wealth of King Alfred', *Past and Present, 123* (1989), 3–51

F.W. Maitland, *Domesday Book and Beyond* (1897)

V.A. Maxfield, (ed.), *The Saxon Shore. A Handbook* (1989)

A. Meaney, *A Gazetteer of Early Anglo-Saxon Burial Sites* (1964)

A. Meaney, *Anglo-Saxon Amulets and Curing Stones*, BAR, *96* (1981)

A. Meaney and S. Chadwick Hawkes, *Two Anglo-Saxon Cemeteries at Winnall, Winchester, Hampshire* (1970)

L. Mendelssohn, (ed.), *Zosimus: Historia Nova* (Leipzig, 1887)

D.M. Metcalf, 'The ranking of boroughs: numismatic evidence from the reign of Æthelred II', in *Ethelred the Unready*, ed. D. Hill, BAR, *59* (1978), 159–212

D.M. Metcalf, 'A note on sceattas as a measure of international trade, and on the earliest Danish coinage', in *Sceattas in England and on the Continent*, ed. D. Hill and D.M. Metcalf, BAR, *128* (1984), 159–64

D.M. Metcalf, 'The coins', in *Southampton Finds I: The Coins and Pottery from Hamwic*, ed. P. Andrews, Southampton archaeology monographs, *4* (1988), 17–57

D.M. Metcalf, 'Large Danegelds in relation to war and kingship; their implications for monetary history and some numismatic evidence', in *Weapons and Warfare in Anglo-Saxon England*, ed. S. Chadwick Hawkes (1989), 179–89

D.M. Metcalf, 'A "porcupine" sceat from Market Lavington, with a list of other sceattas from Wiltshire', *WAM, 83* (1990), 205–8

D.M. Metcalf, *Thrymsas and Sceattas in the Ashmolean Museum Oxford*, I (1993)

M.A. Meyer, 'Women and the tenth-century English monastic reform', *Revue Bénédictine, 87* (1977), 34–61

M.A. Meyer, 'Patronage of the West Saxon royal nunneries in late Anglo-Saxon England', *Revue Bénédictine, 91* (1981), 332–58

M.A. Meyer, 'Land charters and the position of women in Anglo-Saxon England', in *The Women of England*, ed. B. Kanner (Hamden CT, 1982), 53–84

D. Miles and S. Palmer, *Invested in Mother Earth: The Anglo-Saxon Cemetery at Lechlade* (1986)

M. Millett, *The Romanization of Britain* (1990)

M. Millett and D. Graham, *Excavations on the Romano-British Small Town at Neatham, Hampshire, 1969–1979* (1986)

M. Millett and S. James, 'Excavations at Cowdery's Down, Basingstoke, Hampshire, 1978–81', *Arch J, 140* (1983), 151–279

H. Moisl, 'Anglo-Saxon royal genealogies and Germanic oral tradition', *Journal of Medieval History, 7* (1981), 215–48

J.S. Moore, 'Domesday slavery', *Anglo-Norman Studies, 11* (1989), 191–220

P. Morgan, (ed.), *Domesday Book: Berkshire* (1979)

J. Morris, *The Age of Arthur; A History of the British Isles from 350 to 650* (1973)

R. Morris, *Churches in the Landscape* (1989)

R. Morris and J. Roxon, 'Churches on Roman buildings', in *Temples, Churches and Religion: Recent Research in Roman Britain*, ed. W. Rodwell, BAR, *77(i)* (1980), 175–209

W.A. Morris, *The Frankpledge System* (New York, 1910)

J. Morrish, 'King Alfred's letter as a source on learning in England', in *Studies in Earlier Old English Prose*, ed. P. Szarmach (Albany NY, 1986), 87–107

A. Morton, (ed.), *Excavations in Hamwic: Volume 1*, CBA res. rep., *84* (1992)

A. Morton, 'Burial in Middle Saxon Southampton', in *Death in Towns*, ed. S. Bassett (1993), 68–77

J. Munby, (ed.), *Domesday Book: Hampshire* (1982)

A.C. Murray, '*Beowulf*, the Danish invasions and royal genealogy', in *The Dating of Beowulf*, ed. C. Chase (Toronto, 1981), 101–12

J. Musty and J.E.D. Stratton, 'A Saxon cemetery at Winterbourne Gunner, near Salisbury', *WAM, 59* (1964), 86–109

J.N.L. Myres, 'Wansdyke and the origin of Wessex', in *Essays in British History Presented to Sir Keith Feiling*, ed. H. Trevor-Roper (1964), 1–28

J.N.L. Myres, *Anglo-Saxon Pottery and the Settlement of England* (1969)

J.N.L. Myres, *The English Settlements* (1986)

A.S. Napier and W.H. Stevenson, *The Crawford Collection of Early Charters and Documents* (1895)

J.L. Nelson, 'Inauguration rituals', in *Early Medieval Kingship*, ed. P. Sawyer and I. Wood (1977), 50–71

J. Nelson, 'Reconstructing a royal family: reflections on Alfred', in *People and Places in Northern Europe 500–1600. Essays in Honour of Peter Hayes Sawyer*, ed. I. Wood and N. Lund (1991), 47–60

B. Nenk, S. Margeson and M. Hurley, 'Medieval Britain and Ireland in 1990', *Med Arch, 35* (1991), 180–3

M. O'Donovan, (ed.), *Charters of Sherborne* (1988)

E. Okasha, 'The English language in the eleventh century: the evidence from inscriptions', *England in the Eleventh Century. Proceedings of the 1990 Harlaxton Symposium*, ed. C. Hicks (1992), 333–45

E. Okasha, *Corpus of Early Christian Inscribed Stones of South-West Britain* (1993)

L. Olson, *Early Monasteries in Cornwall* (1989)

B.H.St.J. O'Neil, 'Grim's Bank, Padworth, Berkshire', *Antiquity, 17* (1943), 188–98

B.H.St.J. O'Neil, 'The Silchester region in the 5th and 6th centuries AD', *Antiquity, 18* (1944), 113–22

N. Orme, 'The church in Crediton from Saint Boniface to the Reformation', in *The Greatest Englishman*, ed. T. Reuter (1980), 97–131

N. Orme, (ed.), *Nicholas Roscarrock's Lives of the Saints: Cornwall and Devon*, Devon and Cornwall Record Society, new series, *35* (1992)

W. Page, 'Some remarks on the churches of the Domesday Survey', *Archaeologia* 2nd ser., *16* (1915), 61–102

M.B. Parkes, 'The palaeography of the Parker manuscript of the Chronicle, Laws and Sedulius and historiography at Winchester in the late ninth and tenth centuries', *ASE, 5* (1976), 149–71

S. Pearce, 'The traditions of the royal king-list of Dumnonia', *The Transactions of the Honourable Society of Cymmrodorion* (1971), 128–39

S. Pearce, 'The dating of some Celtic dedications and the hagiographical traditions in South Western Britain', *Dev Assoc, 105* (1973), 95–120

S. Pearce, *The Kingdom of Dumnonia: Studies in History and Tradition in South-Western Britain AD 350–1100* (1978)

S. Pearce, *The Archaeology of South-West Britain* (1981)

S. Pearce, 'Estates and church sites in Dorset and Gloucestershire: the emergence of a Christian society', in *The Early Church in Western Britain and Ireland*, ed. S. Pearce, BAR, *102* (1982), 117–43

S. Pearce, 'The early church in the landscape: the evidence from north Devon', *Arch J, 142* (1985), 255–75

J. Peddie, *Alfred the Good Soldier* (1989)

D. Pelteret, 'The *coliberti* of Domesday Book', *Medieval Culture, 12* (1978), 43–54

D. Pelteret, 'Slave raiding and slave trading in early England', *ASE, 9* (1981), 99–114

J. Percival, 'Seigneurial aspects of late Roman estate management', *EHR, 84* (1969), 449–73

G.H. Pertz and E. Muller, (eds), *Nithardi Historiarum Libri III, MGH Scriptores Rerum Germanicarum, Separatim Editi* (Hanover, 1956)

E. Plenderleith, C. Hohler and R. Freyhan, 'The stole and maniples', in *The Relics of Saint Cuthbert: Studies by Various Authors*, ed. C.F. Battiscombe (1956), 375–432

C. Plummer, (ed.), *Baedae Opera Historica* (2 vols, 1896)

C. Plummer, (ed.), *Two of the Saxon Chronicles Parallel* (2 vols, 1899)

A. Preston-Jones, 'Decoding Cornish churchyards', in *The Early Church in Wales and the West*, ed. N. Edwards and A. Lane, Oxbow monographs, *16* (1992), 104–24

K. Pretty, 'Defining the Magonsæte', in *The Origins of Anglo-Saxon Kingdoms*, ed. S. Bassett (1989), 171–83

H. Pryce, 'Pastoral care in early medieval Wales' in *Pastoral Care Before the Parish*, ed. J. Blair and R. Sharpe (1992), 41–62

R.N. Quirk, 'Winchester cathedral in the tenth century', *Arch J, 114* (1957), 26–68

O. Rackham, *Trees and Woodland in the British Landscape* (1976)

C.A.R. Radford, 'The Celtic monastery in Britain', *Archaeologia Cambrensis, 111* (1962), 1–24

C.A.R. Radford, 'The church in Somerset down to 1100', *PSANHS, 106* (1962), 28–45

C.A.R. Radford, 'The pre-Conquest boroughs of England, ninth to eleventh centuries', *PBA, 64* (1978), 131–53

C.A.R. Radford, 'Glastonbury abbey before 1184: interim report of the excavations 1908–64', in *Medieval Art and Architecture at Wells Cathedral*, British Archaeological Society Conference Transactions, *4* (1981), 110–34

C.A.R. Radford and K. Jackson, 'Early Christian Inscriptions', in *An Inventory of Historical Monuments in the County of Dorset, II, South-East*, RCHM (1970), 304–12

P. Rahtz, 'An excavation on Bokerley Dyke', *Arch J, 118* (1958), 65–99

P. Rahtz, 'Excavations on Glastonbury Tor', *Arch J, 127* (1971), 1–81

P. Rahtz, *The Saxon and Medieval Palaces at Cheddar*, BAR, *65* (1979)

P. Rahtz, 'Celtic society in Somerset AD 400–700', *Bulletin of the Board of Celtic Studies, 30* (1982), 176–200

P. Rahtz, 'Pagan and Christian by the Severn Sea', in *The Archaeology and History of Glastonbury Abbey*, ed. L. Abrams and J.P. Carley (1991), 3–37

P. Rahtz and L. Watts, 'The end of Roman temples in the west of Britain', in *The End of Roman Britain*, ed. P.J. Casey, BAR, *71* (1979), 183–201

P. Rahtz and L. Watts, 'Pagan's Hill revisited', *Arch J, 146* (1989), 330–71

P. Rahtz *et al.*, *Cadbury Congresbury 1968–73. A Late/Post Roman Hilltop Settlement in Somerset*, BAR, *223* (1992)

J. Raine, (ed.), *The Historians of the Church of York and its Archbishops*, Rolls series (3 vols, 1879–94)

D. Raraty, 'Earl Godwine of Wessex: the origins of his power and his political loyalties', *History, 74* (1989), 3–19

RCHM, *Dorset II, West* (1970)

RCHM, 'Wareham west walls', *Medieval Archaeology, 3* (1959), 120–38

J. Richards, *Viking Age England* (1991)

M. Richards, 'The manuscript contexts of the Old English laws: tradition and innovation', in *Studies in Earlier Old English Prose*, ed. P. Szarmach (Albany NY, 1986), 171–92

M. Richards and J. Stanfield, 'Concepts of Anglo-Saxon women in the laws', in *New Readings on Women in Old English Literature*, ed. H. Damico and A.H. Olsen (Indiana, 1990), 89–99

S. Ridyard, *The Royal Saints of Anglo-Saxon England* (1988)

E. Roberts and G. Allam, 'Saxon Alresford and Bighton', *Hampshire Field Club Newsletter, 20* (1993), 9–13

A.J. Robertson, (ed.), *Laws of the Kings of England from Edmund to Henry I* (1925)

A.J. Robertson, (ed.), *Anglo-Saxon Charters* (2nd edn., 1956)

J. Armitage Robinson, *The Saxon Bishops of Wells; A Historical Study in the Tenth Century*, British Academy supplemental papers, *4* (1918)

J. Armitage Robinson, *St Oswald and the Church of Worcester* (1919)

J. Armitage Robinson, *The Times of St Dunstan* (1923)

W. Rodwell, 'From mausoleum to minster: the early development of Wells cathedral', in *The Early Church in Western Britain and Ireland*, ed. S. Pearce, BAR, *102* (1982), 49–59

W. Rodwell, 'The Anglo-Saxon and Norman churches at Wells', in *Wells Cathedral. A History*, ed. L.S. Colchester (1982), 1–23

W. Rodwell and G. Rouse, 'The Anglo-Saxon rood and other features in the south porch of St Mary's Church, Breamore, Hants', *Ant J, 64* (1984), part 2, 298–325

D. Rollason, 'Lists of saints' resting-places in Anglo-Saxon England', *ASE, 7* (1978), 61–93

D. Rollason, 'The shrines of saints in later Anglo-Saxon England: distribution and significance', in *The Anglo-Saxon Church*, ed. L. Butler and R. Morris (1986), 32–43

D. Rollason, *Saints and Relics in Anglo-Saxon England* (1989)

G. Rolleston, 'Researches and excavations carried on in an ancient cemetery at Frilford, near Abingdon, Berkshire, in the years 1867–1868', *Archaeologia, 42* (1869), 417–85

A. Ross, *Pagan Celtic Britain* (1967)

M. Clunies Ross, 'Concubinage in Anglo-Saxon England', *Past and Present, 108* (1985), 3–34

G. Rosser, 'The cure of souls in English towns before 1000', in *Pastoral Care Before the Parish*, ed. J. Blair and R. Sharpe (1992), 267–84

T. Rowley, 'Early Saxon settlements in Dorchester on Thames', in *Anglo-Saxon Settlement and Landscape*, ed. T. Rowley (1974), 42–50

A. Rumble, 'Hamtun alias Hamwic (Saxon Southampton): the place-name traditions and their significance', in *Excavations at Melbourne Street, Southampton, 1971–6*, ed. P. Holdsworth, CBA res. rep., *33* (1980), 7–20

A. Rumble, 'The purposes of *Codex Wintoniensis*', *Anglo-Norman Studies, 4* (1981), 153–66

A. Rumble, 'The palaeography of the Domesday manuscripts', in *Domesday Book: A Reassessment*, ed. P. Sawyer (1985), 28–49

W. Runciman, 'Accelerating social mobility: the case of Anglo-Saxon England', *Past and Present, 104* (1984), 3–30

A. Russel, 'Romsey: market place', in *Archaeology and Historic Buildings in Hampshire: Annual Report for 1986*, ed. M. Hughes (1987), 18

H.E. Salter, (ed.), *The Cartulary of the Abbey of Eynsham*, vol. 1, Oxford Historical Society, *49* (1907)

P. Salway, *Roman Britain* (1981)

A.D. Saunders, 'Lydford Castle, Devon', *Med Arch, 24* (1980), 123–86

E.P. Sauvage, (ed.), 'Goscelin, *Vita Sancti Swithuni*', *Analecta Bollandiana, 7* (1888), 373–80

P. Sawyer, *Anglo-Saxon Charters: An Annotated List and Bibliography* (1968)

P. Sawyer, 'Kings and merchants', in *Early Medieval Kingship*, ed. P. Sawyer and I. Wood (1977), 139–58

P. Sawyer, *From Roman Britain to Norman England* (1978)

P. Sawyer, 'The royal *tun* in pre-Conquest England', in *Ideal and Reality in Frankish and Anglo-Saxon Society*, ed. P. Wormald, D. Bullough and R. Collins (1983), 273–99

J. Scherr, 'Springs and wells in Somerset', *Nomina, 10* (1986), 79–91

M. Schütt, 'The literary form of Asser's *Vita Alfredi*', *EHR, 62* (1957), 209–20

G. Scobie and K. Qualmann, *Nunnaminster. A Saxon and Medieval Community of Nuns* (1993)

J. Scott, (ed.), *The Early History of Glastonbury: An Edition, Translation and Study of William of Malmesbury's De Antiquitate Glastonie Ecclesie* (1981)

C. Scull, 'Scales and weights in early Anglo-Saxon England', *Arch J, 147* (1990), 183–215

C. Scull, 'Excavations and survey at Watchfield, Oxfordshire, 1983–92'. *Arch J, 149* (1992), 124–281

D.J. Sheerin, 'The dedication of the Old Minster in Winchester in 980', *Revue Bénédictine, 88* (1978), 261–73

J. Shephard, 'The social identity of the individual in isolated barrows and barrow cemeteries in Anglo-Saxon England', in *Space, Hierarchy and Society, Interdisciplinary Studies in Social Area Analysis*, ed. B.C. Burnham and J. Kingsbury, BAR Int ser., *59*, 47–79

R.J. Sherlock, 'A nineteenth-century manuscript book on coins', *BNJ, 28* (1956), 394–6

T.A. Shippey, 'Wealth and wisdom in King Alfred's *Preface* to Old English *Pastoral Care*', *EHR, 94* (1979), 346–55

R.J. Silvester, 'An excavation on the post-Roman site at Bantham, South Devon', *PDAS, 39* (1981), 89–118

P. Sims-Williams, 'Continental influence at Bath monastery in the seventh century', *ASE, 4* (1975), 1–10

P. Sims-Williams, 'Gildas and the Anglo-Saxons', *Cambridge Medieval Celtic Studies, 6* (1983), 1–30

P. Sims-Williams, 'The settlement of England in Bede and the *Chronicle*', *ASE, 12* (1983), 1–41

P. Sims-Williams, 'St Wilfrid and two charters dated AD 676 and 680', *Journal of Ecclesiastical History, 39* (1988), 163–83

P. Sims-Williams, *Religion and Literature in Western England, 600–800* (1990)

K. Sisam, 'Anglo-Saxon royal genealogies', *PBA, 39* (1953), 287–346

T. Slater, 'Controlling the South Hams: the Anglo-Saxon *burh* at Halwell', *Dev Assoc, 123* (1991), 57–78

A.H. Smith, 'The Hwicce', in *Medieval and Linguistic Studies in Honor of Francis Peabody Magoun Jr*, ed. J.B. Bessinger and R.P. Creed (1965), 56–65

A.P. Smyth, *Scandinavian Kings in the British Isles 850–880* (1977)

G. Speake, *A Saxon Bed Burial on Swallowcliffe Down*, English Heritage arch. rep., *10* (1989)

M. Spurrell, 'The architectural interest of the *Regularis Concordia*', *ASE, 21* (1993), 161–76

G.D. Squibb, 'The foundation of Cerne Abbey', *Notes and Queries for Somerset and Dorset, 31* (1984), 373–6

P. Stafford, 'The "farm of one night" and the organization of King Edward's estates in Domesday', *Economic History Review, 33* (1980), 491–502

P. Stafford, 'Charles the Bald, Judith and England', in *Charles the Bald: Court and Kingdom*, ed. M. Gibson and J. Nelson, BAR International series, *101* (1981), 137–51

P. Stafford, 'The king's wife in Wessex 800–1066', *Past and Present, 91* (1981), 3–27

P. Stafford, 'The laws of Cnut and the history of Anglo-Saxon royal promises', *ASE, 10* (1982), 173–90

P. Stafford, *Queens, Concubines and Dowagers. The King's Wife in the Early Middle Ages* (1983)

P. Stafford, *Unification and Conquest: A Political and Social History of England in the Tenth and Eleventh Centuries* (1989)

P. Stafford, 'Women in Domesday Book', in *Medieval Women in Southern England, Reading Medieval Studies, 15* (1989), 75–94

F.M. Stenton, *The Early History of the Abbey of Abingdon* (1913)

F.M. Stenton, *The Latin Charters of the Anglo-Saxon Period* (1953)

F.M. Stenton, 'The foundations of English history', in *Preparatory to Anglo-Saxon England*, ed. D.M. Stenton (1970), 116–26

F.M. Stenton, 'The historical bearing of place-name studies: the place of women in Anglo-Saxon society', in *Preparatory to Anglo-Saxon England*, ed. D.M. Stenton (1970), 314–24

F.M. Stenton, 'The south-western element in the Old English Chronicle', in *Preparatory to Anglo-Saxon England*, ed. D.M. Stenton (1970), 106–15

F.M. Stenton, *Anglo-Saxon England* (3rd edn., 1971)

J. Stevenson, (ed.), *Chronicon Monasterii de Abingdon* (2 vols, 1858)

W.H. Stevenson, *Asser's Life of King Alfred* (1904; repr. 1959)

I. Stewart, 'Anglo-Saxon gold coins', in *Scripta Nummaria Romana. Essays Presented to Humphrey Sutherland*, ed. R. Carson and C.M. Kraay (1978), 143–72

W. Stubbs, (ed.), *Memorials of St Dunstan, Archbishop of Canterbury*, Rolls series (1874)

W. Stubbs, (ed.), *Willelmi Malmesbiriensis Monachi De Gestis Regum Anglorum* (2 vols, 1887–9)

C.H.V. Sutherland, *Anglo-Saxon Gold Coinage in the Light of the Crondall Hoard* (1948)

M. Swanton, 'The "dancer" on the Codford cross', *ASSAH, 1* (1979), BAR, 72, 139–48

M. Swanton and S. Pearce, 'Lustleigh, South Devon: its inscribed stone, its churchyard and its parish', in *The Early Church in Western Britain and Ireland*, ed. S. Pearce, BAR, *102* (1982), 139–44

H. Sweet, (ed.), *King Alfred's West Saxon Version of Gregory's Pastoral Care*, EETS o.s., 45 and 50 (2 vols, 1871–2)

G.V. Syer, *The Church of St Candida (St Wite) and Holy Cross, Whitchurch Canonicorum* (1984)

T. Symons, (ed.), *Regularis concordia Angliae nationis monachorum sanctimonialumque* (1953)

J. Tait, *The Medieval English Borough* (1936)

C.H. Talbot, (trans.), *The Anglo-Saxon Missionaries in Germany* (1954)

C. Taylor, *Dorset* (1970)

C.S. Taylor, 'Bath, Mercian and West Saxon', *Transactions of the Bristol and Gloucestershire Archaeological Society, 23* (1900), 129–61

H.M. Taylor, 'The Anglo-Saxon church at Bradford-on-Avon', *Arch J, 130* (1973), 141–71

H.M. Taylor, 'Tenth-century church building in England and on the Continent', in *Tenth-Century Studies*, ed. D. Parsons (1975), 141–68

H.M. and J. Taylor, *Anglo-Saxon Architecture* (2 vols, 1965)

E. Temple, *Anglo-Saxon Manuscripts 900–1066* (1976)

A.T. Thacker, 'Some terms for noblemen in Anglo-Saxon England, *c.* 650–900', *ASSAH, 2* (1981), 201–36

A.T. Thacker, 'Æthelwold and Abingdon', in *Bishop Æthelwold: His Career and Influence*, ed. B.A.E. Yorke (1988), 43–64

J. Thirsk, 'The origin of the common fields', *Past and Present, 133* (1966), 142–7

C. Thomas, *The Early Christian Archaeology of North Britain* (1971)

C. Thomas, *Christianity in Roman Britain to AD 500* (1981)

C. Thomas, '"Gallici nautae de Galliarum provinciis" – a sixth/seventh-century trade with Gaul reconsidered', *Med Arch, 34* (1990), 1–26

C. Thomas, *Tintagel* (1993)

C. Thomas, P. Fowler and K. Gardner, 'Lundy', *Current Archaeology, 16* (1969), 138–42

E.A. Thompson, 'Britain AD 406–410', *Britannia, 8* (1977), 303–18

E.A. Thompson, 'Gildas and the history of Britain', *Britannia, 10* (1979), 203–26

E.A. Thompson, 'Fifth-century facts?', *Britannia, 14* (1983), 272–4

C. and F. Thorn, (eds), *Domesday Book: Wiltshire* (1979)

C. and F. Thorn, (eds), *Domesday Book: Somerset* (1980)

C. and F. Thorn, (eds), *Domesday Book: Dorset* (1983)

C. and F. Thorn, (eds), *Domesday Book: Devon* (2 vols, 1985)

F. Thorn, 'The hundreds of Devonshire', in *The Devonshire Domesday*, ed. A. Williams and R. Erskine (1991), 26–42

B. Thorpe, (ed.), *Florentii Wigorniensis Chronicon ex Chronicis* (2 vols, 1849)

J. Timby, 'The Middle Saxon pottery', in *Southampton Finds I: The Coins and Pottery from Hamwic*, ed. P. Andrews, Southampton archaeology monographs, *4* (1988), 73–123

M. Todd, *Roman Britain 55 BC–AD 400* (1981)

M. Todd, *The South-West to AD 1000* (1987)

D. Tweddle, 'Anglo-Saxon sculpture in south-east England before *c.* 950', in *Studies in Medieval Sculpture*, ed. F.H. Thompson (1983), 18–40

D. Tweddle, 'Sculpture', in *The Making of England*, ed. L. Webster and J. Backhouse (1991), 239–44

A. Verhulst, 'The decline of slavery and the economic expansion of the early middle ages', *Past and Present, 133* (1991), 195–203

H. Vollrath-Reichelt, *Königsgedanke und Königtum bei den Angelsachsen* (Cologne, 1971)

F.T. Wainwright, 'Æthelflæd, Lady of the Mercians', in *Scandinavian England*, ed. H.P.R. Finberg (1975), 305–24

G. Waitz, (ed.), *Vita S. Leobae, MGH Scriptores*, 15.i (Hanover, 1887), 118–31

H.E. Walker, 'Bede and the Gewissae: the political evolution of the Heptarchy and its nomenclature', *Cambridge Historical Journal, 12* (1956), 174–86

J. Wallace-Hadrill, *Early Germanic Kingship in England and on the Continent* (1971)

G.F. Warner and H.A. Wilson, *The Benedictional of St Æthelwold*, Roxburghe Club (1910)

W.L. Warren, *The Governance of Norman and Angevin England 1086–1272* (1987)

R. Waterhouse, 'Tone in Alfred's version of Augustine's *Soliloquies*', in *Studies in Earlier Old English Prose*, ed. P. Szarmach (Albany NY, 1986), 47–85

D.J. Watts, 'Infant burials and Romano-British Christianity', *Arch J, 146* (1989), 372–83

D.J. Watts, *Christians and Pagans in Roman Britain* (1991)

L. Webster and J. Backhouse, (eds), *The Making of England: Anglo-Saxon Art and Culture AD 600–900* (1991)

W.J. Wedlake, *The Excavation of the Shrine of Apollo at Nettleton, Wiltshire, 156–1971*, Soc. of Antiquaries research report, *40* (1982)

M. Welch, 'Rural settlement patterns in the early and middle Anglo-Saxon periods', *Landscape History, 7* (1985), 13–26

M. Welch, *Anglo-Saxon England* (1992)

L. Whitbread, 'Æthelweard and the Anglo-Saxon Chronicle', *EHR, 74* (1959), 577–89

R.H. White, *Roman and Celtic Objects from Anglo-Saxon Graves*, BAR, *191* (1988)

R.H. White, 'Scrap or substitute: Roman material in Anglo-Saxon graves', in *Anglo-Saxon Cemeteries: A Reappraisal*, ed. E. Southworth (1990), 125–52

S.D. White, 'Kinship and lordship in early medieval England: the story of Sigeberht, Cynewulf and Cyneheard', *Viator, 20* (1989), 1–18

D. Whitelock, (ed.), *Anglo-Saxon Wills* (1930)

D. Whitelock, (ed.), *Sermo Lupi ad Anglos* (3rd edn., 1963)

D. Whitelock, *The Genuine Asser* (1968)

D. Whitelock, *The Importance of the Battle of Edington* (1978)

D. Whitelock, (trans.) *English Historical Documents volume I, c. 500–1042* (2nd edn., 1979)

D. Whitelock, M. Brett and C.N.L. Brooke, (eds), *Councils and Synods and other Documents relating to the English Church, I, 871–1204*, Part I, 871–1066 (1981)

D. Whitelock, D.C. Douglas and S.I. Tucker, (eds), *The Anglo-Saxon Chronicle* (1961)

A. Williams, 'Some notes and considerations on problems connected with the English royal succession, 860–1066', in *Anglo-Norman Studies, 1* (1978), 144–67

A. Williams, 'Land and power in the eleventh century: the estates of Harold Godwineson', *Anglo-Norman Studies, 3* (1980), 171–88

A. Williams, '*Princeps Merciorum gentis*: the family, career and connections of Ælfhere, ealdorman of Mercia, 956–983', *ASE, 10* (1982), 143–72

A. Williams, 'A bell-house and a burh-geat: lordly residences in England before the Norman Conquest', *The Ideals and Practice of Medieval Knighthood, 4* (1992), 221–40

D. Wilson, 'The Scandinavians in England' in *The Archaeology of Anglo-Saxon England*, ed. D. Wilson (1976), 393–403

D. Wilson and J. Hurst, (eds), 'Medieval Britain in 1957', *Med Arch, 2* (1958), 183–5

D.M. Wilson, *Anglo-Saxon Paganism* (1992)

M. Winterbottom, (ed.), *Gildas. The Ruin of Britain and Other Documents* (1978)

I. Wood, 'Kings, kingdoms and consent', in *Early Medieval Kingship*, ed. P. Sawyer and I. Wood (1977), 3–29

I. Wood, *The Merovingian North Sea* (Alingsås, 1983)

I. Wood, 'The fall of the western empire and the end of Roman Britain', *Britannia, 18* (1987), 251–62

M. Wood, 'The making of King Athelstan's empire', in *Ideal and Reality in Frankish and Anglo-Saxon Society*, ed. P. Wormald (1983), 250–72

A. Woodward, *Shrines and Sacrifice* (1992)

F. Wormald, 'The "Winchester School" before St Æthelwold', in *England Before the Conquest*, ed. P. Clemoes and K. Hughes (1971), 305–13

P. Wormald, 'Bede, *Bretwaldas* and the origins of the *Gens Anglorum*', in *Ideal and Reality in Frankish and Anglo-Saxon Society*, ed. P. Wormald, D. Bullough and R. Collins (1983), 99–129

P. Wormald, *Bede and the Conversion of England: The Charter Evidence* (Jarrow lecture, 1984)

P. Wormald, 'Æthelwold and his continental counterparts', in *Bishop Æthelwold: His Career and Influence*, ed. B.A.E. Yorke (1988), 13–42

C.E. Wright, *The Cultivation of Saga in Anglo-Saxon England* (1939)

B.A.E. Yorke, 'The foundation of the Old Minster and the status of Winchester in the seventh and eighth centuries', *PHFCAS, 38* (1982), 75–84

B.A.E. Yorke, 'The bishops of Winchester, the kings of Wessex and the development of Winchester in the ninth and early tenth centuries', *PHFCAS, 40* (1984), 61–70

B.A.E. Yorke, 'The kingdom of the East Saxons', *ASE, 14* (1985), 1–36

B.A.E. Yorke, 'Æthelmær: the foundation of the abbey at Cerne and the politics of the tenth century', in *The Cerne Abbey Millennium Lectures*, ed. K. Barker (1988), 15–26

B.A.E. Yorke, 'Æthelwold and the politics of the tenth century', in *Bishop Æthelwold: His Career and Influence*, ed. B.A.E. Yorke (1988), 65–88

B.A.E. Yorke, 'The Jutes of Hampshire and Wight and the origins of Wessex', in *The Origins of Anglo-Saxon Kingdoms*, ed. S. Bassett (1989), 84–96

B.A.E. Yorke, '"Sisters under the skin?" Anglo-Saxon nuns and nunneries in southern England', in *Medieval Women in Southern England, Reading Medieval Studies, 15* (1989), 95–117

B.A.E. Yorke, *Kings and Kingdoms of Early Anglo-Saxon England* (1990)

B.A.E. Yorke, 'Fact or fiction? The written evidence for the fifth and sixth centuries AD', *ASSAH, 6* (1993), 45–50

B.A.E. Yorke, 'The identification of Boniface's female correspondents and of "double monasteries" in early Wessex' (forthcoming)

S. Youngs, (ed.), *'The Work of Angels'. Masterpieces of Celtic Metalwork, 6th–9th Centuries* (1989)

C. Zangmeister, (ed.), *Orosius, Libri Historiarum Adversum Paganos* (Vienna, 1882)

Index